THE COLLECTED WORKS OF
BILLY GRAHAM

THE COLLECTED WORKS OF
BILLY GRAHAM

3 BESTSELLING WORKS COMPLETE IN ONE VOLUME

Angels

❖❖❖

How to be Born Again

❖❖❖

The Holy Spirit

230
GRA

Galahad Books • New York

Published in 1993 by

Inspirational Press
A division of Budget Book Service, Inc.
386 Park Avenue South
New York, NY 10016

Inspirational Press is a registered trademark of Budget Book Service, Inc.

Published by arrangement with Word Inc.

Library of Congress Catalog Card Number: 93-78589

ISBN: 0-88486-087-6

Text designed by Hannah Lerner

Printed in the United States of America.

Contents

SCRIPTURE QUOTATION SOURCES

ANGELS

Unless otherwise indicated, all biblical quotations are taken from the King James Version. Those marked RSV are from the Revised Standard Version of the Bible, copyrighted 1946, 1953, © 1971, 1973 by the Division of Christian Education of the National Council of Churches of Christ in the U.S.A. and are used by permission. Those marked NIV are from the New International Version, copyright © 1978 by the New York Bible Society, and are used by permission.

Those marked TLB are from *The Living Bible*, copyright © 1971 by Tyndale House Publishers and used by permission. Excerpt from *A Prisoner and Yet* . . . by Corrie ten Boom, copyright 1954 by Christian Literature Crusade, London. Christian Literature Crusade, London and Fort Washington. Used by permission.

Those marked NASB are from the New American Standard Bible, copyright © 1975 by The Lockman Foundation and are used by permission. Those marked AB are from the Amplified Bible, copyright © 1965 by the Zondervan Publishing House.

HOW TO BE BORN AGAIN

Unless otherwise noted, Scripture quotations are from *The New American Standard Bible* (copyright 1960, 1962, 1963, 1968, 1971 by the Lockman Foundation and used by permission). Scripture quotations marked *The Living Bible* are from *The Living Bible, Paraphrased* (Wheaton: Tyndale House Publishers, 1971) and are used by permission. Quotations marked NIV are from the New International Version of the Bible (copyright © 1973 by New York Bible Society International). The quotation marked Goodspeed is from The New Testament: An American Translation by Edgar J. Goodspeed (copyright © 1923, 1948 by the University of Chicago). The quotation marked TEV is from the Today's English Version of the Bible (copyright © American Bible Society 1976). The quotations marked Phillips are from *The New Testament in Modern English* (rev. ed.), copyright © 1958, 1960, 1972 by J. B. Phillips.

THE HOLY SPIRIT

Unless otherwise indicated, Scripture quotations are from *The New American Standard Bible* (copyright 1960, 1962, 1968, 1971 by the Lockman Foundation and used by permission). Scripture quotations marked LB are from *The Living Bible Paraphrased* (Wheaton: Tyndale House Publishers, 1971). Quotations marked NIV are from the New International Version of the Bible—New Testament (copyright © 1973 by the New York Bible Society International). Those marked RSV are from The Revised Standard Version of the Bible, copyright 1946, 1952, © 1971, 1973 by the Division of Christian Education of the National Council of the Churches of Christ in the United States of America, and are used by permission. Those marked *Phillips* are from *The New Testament in Modern English* (rev. ed.), copyright © 1958, 1960, 1972 by J. B. Phillips. Quotations marked NEB are from *The New English Bible*, © 1961, 1970 The Delegates of the Oxford University Press and The Syndics of the Cambridge University Press. Those marked KJV are from the King James Version of the Bible.

THE COLLECTED WORKS OF
BILLY GRAHAM

Angels: God's Secret Agents

The angels are the dispensers and administrators of the divine beneficence toward us; they regard our safety, undertake our defense, direct our ways, and exercise a constant solicitude that no evil befall us.

JOHN CALVIN

Institutes of the Christian Religion, I

CONTENTS

PREFACE

WHEN I DECIDED to preach a sermon on angels, I found practically nothing in my library. Upon investigation I soon discovered that little had been written on the subject in this century. This seemed a strange and ominous omission. Bookstores and libraries have shelves of books on demons, the occult and the devil. Why was the devil getting so much more attention from writers than angels? Some people seem to put the devil on a par with God. Actually, Satan is a fallen angel.

Even when people in our modern age have had their attention drawn to the subject of angels from time to time, those ideas have often been fanciful or unbiblical. As I write this preface to the second edition, a popular television program tells the story of an "angel" who has been sent to earth in the form of a man to help people who are facing problems. The popularity of the program suggests many people find it great entertainment—but I cannot help but feel it also reinforces the idea in many minds that angels are just a product of our imagination, like Santa Clause or magical elves. But the Bible stresses their reality, and underlines their constant—if unseen—ministry on behalf of God's people. In a materialistic world which nevertheless is riddled with evil and suffering, we need to discover afresh the Bible's teaching about angels.

The English painter, Sir Edward Coley Burne-Jones, wrote to Oscar Wilde that "the more materialistic science becomes, the more angels shall I paint: their wings are my protest in favor of the immortality of the soul."

Angels have a much more important place in the Bible than the devil and his demons. Therefore, I undertook a biblical study of the subject of angels. Not only has it been one of the most fascinating studies of my life, but I believe the subject is more relevant today than perhaps at any time in history.

The Bible teaches that angels intervene in the affairs of nations. God often uses them to execute judgment on nations. They guide, comfort and provide for the people of God in the midst of suffering and persecution. Martin Luther once said in *Table Talk*, "An angel is a spiritual creature without a body created by God for the service of christendom and the church."

As an evangelist, I have often felt too far spent to minister from the pulpit to men and women who have filled stadiums to hear a message from the Lord. Yet again and again my weakness has vanished, and my strength has been renewed. I have been filled with God's power not only in my soul but physically. On many occasions, God has become especially real, and has sent His unseen angelic visitors to touch my body to let me be His messenger for heaven, speaking as a dying man to dying men.

In the midst of a world which seems destined to live in a perpetual state of crisis, the subject of angels will be of great comfort and inspiration to believers in God—and a challenge to unbelievers to believe.

Blaise Pascal, the French philosopher and mathematician, once said, "Certain authors, when they speak of their work say, 'my book,' 'my commentary,' 'my history.' They would be better to say 'our book,' 'our commentary,' 'our history,' since their writings generally contain more of other peoples' good things than their own."

This is *our* book, and I wish to thank all who have helped me with this intriguing and sometimes complicated subject.

In its writing, editing and counseling, I am indebted to—Ralph Williams, who helped with research for my original writing of the manuscript; Dr. Harold Lindsell, former editor of *Christianity Today*, who went through the original manuscript with many helpful suggestions; Mr. Paul Fromer, professor at Wheaton College, who helped with content, style and organization.

To my faithful staff at Montreat who typed, retyped, read and called to my attention many areas of possible improvement— Karlene Aceto, Elsie Brookshire, Lucille Lytle, Stephanie Wills and Sally Wilson.

To Calvin Thielman, Pastor of Montreat Presbyterian Church; and Dr. John Akers for their suggestions.

To my wife, Ruth, who was an encouragement and a help from start to finish.

Especially, to our heavenly Father who helped me see this neglected and important subject.

Through the months I have gathered ideas and even quotations from sources long-since forgotten. To everyone whose books and articles I have read, to every man or woman with whom I have talked or prayed about the subject of angels, I express my gratitude. Each has contributed to this book. I regret it is not possible to list each one by name.

This new edition of the book is largely as it was written in 1975. I have added some new material and expanded certain points.

It is still my prayer that God will use this book to bring comfort to the sick and the dying; to bring encouragement to those who are under the pressures of everyday living; to bring guidance to those who are frustrated by the events of our generation.

BILLY GRAHAM

Montreat, North Carolina

1

Are Angels God's Secret Agents?

Mʏ WIFE, WHO was born and raised in China, recalls that in her childhood days tigers lived in the mountains. One day a poor woman went up to the foothills to cut grass. To her back was tied a baby, and a little child walked beside her. In her hand she carried a sharp sickle to cut grass. Just as she reached the top of a hill she heard a roar. Frightened almost speechless, she looked around to see a mother tigress springing at her, followed by two cubs.

This illiterate Chinese mother had never attended school or entered a church. She had never seen a Bible. But a year or two earlier a missionary had told her about Jesus, "who is able to help you when you are in trouble." As the claws of the tigress tore her arm and shoulder, the woman cried out in a frenzy, "O Jesus, help me!" The ferocious beast, instead of attacking again to get an easy meal, suddenly turned and ran away.

The Bible says, "He will give his angels charge of you, to guard you in all your ways" (Psalm 91:11, RSV). Had God sent an angel to help this poor ignorant Chinese woman? Are there supernatural beings today who are able to influence the affairs of men and nations?

In *A Slow and Certain Light*, Elizabeth Elliot told about her father's experiences with angelic helpers:

"My father, when he was a small boy, was climbing on an upper story of a house that was being built. He walked to the end of a board that was not nailed at the other end, and it slowly began to tip. He knew that he was doomed, but inexplicably the board began to tip the other way, as though a hand had pushed it down again. He always wondered if it was an angel's hand."

Help from Angels

A celebrated Philadelphia neurologist had gone to bed after an exceptionally tiring day. Suddenly he was awakened by someone knocking on his door. Opening it he found a little girl, poorly dressed and deeply upset. She told him her mother was very sick and asked him if he would please come with her. It was a bitterly cold, snowy night, but though he was bone tired, the doctor dressed and followed the girl.

As the *Reader's Digest* reports the story, he found the mother desperately ill with pneumonia. After arranging for medical care, he complimented the sick woman on the intelligence and persistence of her little daughter. The woman looked at him strangely and then said, "My daughter died a month ago." She added, "Her shoes and coat are in the clothes closet there." Amazed and perplexed, the doctor went to the closet and opened the door. There hung the very coat worn by the little girl who had brought him to tend to her mother. It was warm and dry and could not possibly have been out in the wintry night.

Could the doctor have been called in the hour of desperate need by an angel who appeared as this woman's young daughter? Was this the work of God's angels on behalf of the sick woman?

The Reverend John G. Paton, pioneer missionary in the New Hebrides Islands, told a thrilling story involving the protective care of angels. Hostile natives surrounded his mission headquarters one night, intent on burning the Patons out and killing them. John Paton and his wife prayed all during that terror-filled night that God would deliver them. When daylight came they were amazed to see that, unaccountably, the attackers had left. They thanked God for delivering them.

A year later, the chief of the tribe was converted to Jesus Christ, and Mr. Paton, remembering what had happened, asked the chief what had kept him and his men from burning down the house and killing them. The chief replied in surprise, "Who were all those men you had with you there?" The missionary answered, "There were no men there; just my wife and I." The chief argued that they had seen many men standing guard—hundreds of big men in shining garments with drawn swords in their hands. They seemed to circle the mission station so that the natives were afraid to attack. Only then did Mr. Paton realize that God had sent His angels to protect them. The chief agreed that there was no other explanation. Could it be that God had sent a legion of angels to protect His servants, whose lives were being endangered?

A Persian colporteur was accosted by a man who asked him if he had a right to sell Bibles. "Why, yes," he answered, "we are allowed to sell these books anywhere in the country!" The man looked puzzled, and asked, "How is it, then, that you are always surrounded by soldiers? I planned three times to attack you, and each time, seeing the soldiers, I left you alone. Now I no longer want to harm you." Were these soldiers heavenly beings?

During World War II, Captain Eddie Rickenbacker and the rest of the crew of the B-17 in which he was flying ran out of fuel and "ditched" in the Pacific Ocean. For weeks nothing was heard of him. The newspapers reported his disappearance and across the country thousands of people prayed. Mayor LaGuardia asked the whole city of New York to pray for him. Then he returned. The Sunday papers headlined the news, and in an article, Captain Rickenbacker himself told what had happened. "And this part I would hesitate to tell," he wrote, "except that there were six witnesses who saw it with me. A gull came out of nowhere, and lighted on my head—I reached up my hand very gently—I killed him and then we divided him equally among us. We ate every bit, even the little bones. Nothing ever tasted so good." This gull saved the lives of Rickenbacker and his companions. Years later I asked him to tell me the story personally, because it was through this experience that he came to know Christ. He said, "I have no explanation except that God sent one of His angels to rescue us."

During my ministry I have heard or read literally thousands of similar stories. Could it be that these were all hallucinations or accidents or fate or luck? Or were real angels sent from God to perform certain tasks?

The Current Cult of the Demonic

Just a few years ago such ideas would have been scorned by most educated people. Science was king, and science was tuned in to believe only what could be seen or measured. The idea of supernatural beings was thought to be nonsense, the ravings of the lunatic fringe.

All this has changed. Think, for example, of the morbid fascination modern society has for the occult.

Walk into a bookstore; visit any newsstand at a modern airport; go to a university library. You will be confronted by shelves and tables packed with books about the devil, Satan worship and demon possession. A number of Hollywood films, television programs and as many as one in four hard-rock pop songs are devoted to, or thematically make reference to, the devil. Years ago the Rolling Stones sang their "Sympathy for the Devil" to the top of the popularity chart; another group answered back with a symphony to the devil.

The Exorcist proved to be one of the biggest moneymakers of any film in history. Arthur Lyons gave his book a title that is frighteningly accurate: *The Second Coming: Satanism in America*. This theme, which intellectuals would have derided a generation ago, is now being dealt with seriously by such people as noted author John Updike and Harvard professor Harvey Cox. Some polls indicate that seventy percent of Americans believe in a personal devil. Some years ago Walter Cronkite announced a poll over his CBS network news showing that the number of Americans who believed in a personal devil has increased twelve percent. This was in the mid–1970s. What would the figure be today? It is ironic that a generation ago, scientists, psychologists, sociologists and even some theologians were predicting that by the late 1970s there would be a sharp decline in the belief in the supernatural. The reverse is true!

Some years ago, in a medium-sized metropolitan area, I turned out of curiosity to the entertainment pages of the local newspaper and studied them carefully. I was unprepared for the shock I received as I read the descriptions of the themes and content of the feature motion pictures being shown in the theaters in that area. They focused on sadism, murder, demon possession and demonism, devil worship and horror, not to mention those that depicted erotic sex. It seemed that each advertisement tried to outdo the others in the degree of shock, horror and mind-bending emotional devastation. The picture hasn't changed. If anything, the movies are even worse today!

Even in the Christian world the presses have turned out a rash of books on the devil by both Catholic and Protestant writers. I myself have thought about writing a book on the devil and his demons.

The Reality and Power of Satan

The Bible does teach that Satan is a real being who is at work in the world together with his emissaries, the demons. In the New Testament they intensified their activities and bent every effort to defeat the work of Jesus Christ, God's Son. The apparent increase in satanic activity against people on this planet today may indicate that the Second Coming of Jesus Christ is close at hand. Certainly, the activity of Satan is evident on every side. We can see it in the wars and other crises that affect all people daily. We can also see it in the attacks of Satan against individual members of the body of Christ.

Some years ago I had dinner with several senators and congressmen in a dining room in the Capitol building. We began discussing the rising interest in the occult with special reference to *The Exorcist*. One of the senators, who had recently passed through a deep religious experience, said that due to his past experience with the occult, whenever he knew of a theater that was showing *The Exorcist* he would drive a block around it. He was afraid even to go near it. He said, "I know that both angels and demons are for real."

Several years ago the late Pope Paul said he was sure that the evil forces attacking every level of society had behind them the work of a personal devil with a whole kingdom of demons at his command. The Roman Catholic Church has been rethinking its position on the reality of the spirit world; and interest in this sub-ject has revived among both theological liberals and evangelicals in Protestant churches everywhere.

Unidentified Flying Objects

The renewed interest in the occult and satanism is not the only evidence of the new openness to the supernatural. It also was revealed in the widespread revival of speculation about the so-called "unidentified flying objects"—UFOs—some years ago. Even some of today's popular movies, like *Cocoon*, center on visitors from outer space.

Some reputable scientists deny and others assert that UFOs do appear to people from time to time. Some scientists have reached the place where they think they can prove that these are possibly visitors from outer space. Some Christian writers have speculated that UFOs could very well be a part of God's angelic host who preside over the physical affairs of universal creation. While we cannot assert such a view with certainty, many people are now seeking some type of supernatural explanation for these phenom-ena. Nothing can hide the fact, however, that these unexplained events are occurring with greater frequency around the entire world and in unexpected places.

Some years ago, Japan witnessed a typical example of unex-plained objects that appeared in the night skies. On 15 January 1975, a squadron of UFO-like objects, resembling a celestial string of pearls, soared silently through the evening skies over half the length of Japan. As government officials, police and thousands of curious citizens stared at the sky in wonder, from fifteen to twenty glowing objects, cruising in straight formation, flew over Japan inside a strange misty cloud. Further, they were sighted and reported in cities seven hundred miles apart in less than an hour.

Hundreds of frantic telephone calls jammed switchboards of police stations and government installations as the spectacular formation sped south. "All the callers reported seeing a huge cloud passing over the city. They said they saw strange objects inside the cloud moving in a straight line," recalled Duty Officer Takeo Ohira. Were they planes? "No," said Hiroshi Mayazawa, "because no planes or natural phenomena appeared on my radar. It was an exceptionally clear night. To me the whole thing is a mystery."

Professor Masatoshi Kitamura watched the dazzling display in the night sky from the Control Room of Tokyo's Meteorological Bureau station near the airport. He said, "I was mystified. Nothing showed up on my radar. I reported my sighting to the airport control tower and they told me nothing showed on their radar either."

Other Explanations

Erich von Daniken's *Chariots of the Gods?*, published many years ago, was re-issued in paperback by Berkeley in 1984. It theorizes that in pre-history astronauts from distant stars visited earth in spaceships. From these visits grew man's idea of gods and many of his conceptions of them. Immanuel Velikovsky in his equally popular *Worlds in Collision* and *Ages in Chaos* put forward the notion that the turbulent history of the Middle East in the second millennium B.C. can be traced to a violent scattering of the solar system that caused ruin on earth. The knowledge of the intense suffering of those times was soon repressed, but lies buried in man's racial memory, explaining his modern self-destructive behavior.

Men would dismiss these grandiose cosmologies lightly if it were not that they, along with a number of other theories, have been put forward with such frequency and serious import that no one can shrug them off. They are being studied seriously at many of our universities. As a theme for talk shows, hardly anything or anyone can top concerns like this.

Some sincere Christians, whose views are anchored in a strong commitment to Scripture, contend that these UFOs are angels. But are they? These people point to certain passages in Isaiah, Ezekiel, Zechariah and the book of Revelation, and draw parallels to the reports of observers of alleged UFO appearances. They take the detailed descriptions, for example, of a highly credible airline crew and lay them alongside Ezekiel 10, and put forward a strong case. In Ezekiel 10 we read, "Each of the four cherubim had a wheel beside him—'The Whirl-Wheels,' as I heard them called, for each one had a second wheel crosswise within, sparkled like chrysolite, giving off a greenish-yellow glow. Because of the construction of these wheels, the cherubim could go straight forward in each of four directions; they did not turn when they changed direction but could go in any of the four ways their faces looked . . . and when they rose into the air the wheels rose with them, and stayed beside them as they flew. When the cherubim stood still, so did the wheels, for the spirit of the cherubim was in the wheels" (Ezekiel 10:9–13,16–17, TLB).

Any attempt to connect such passages with the visits of angels may, at best, be speculation. Nor should we become too preoccupied or overly fascinated with trying to identify contemporary theories and speculations about UFOs or similar phenomena with biblical passages. Secular speculations often, in fact, run counter to the Bible's teaching concerning the origin of life on this planet. What is interesting, however, is that such theories are now being given serious attention even by people who make no claim to believe in the God of the Bible.

A further evidence of the renewed interest in the supernatural is the widespread fascination with extrasensory perception—ESP. The subjective science of parapsychology is now one of the fastest growing fields of academic research in our universities today.

At Duke University, Dr. Joseph B. Rhine took up the study of extrasensory perception in the 1930s and championed it to the point where a department of parapsychology was established at the university. He became its pioneering professor. Today scientists are probing every conceivable frontier for ESP possibilities. Its line-up of protagonists reads like a *Who's Who*. Not only is serious intellectual and scientific study being carried on, but the subject is immensely popular because many of its aggressive proponents profess to be nonreligious. It has gained even more widespread respectability in communist societies (such as in the Soviet Union) than here in the United States. It plays a role of a "substitute religion" in some cases, although it has been used primarily as a technique to influence people.

Notice also the reaction on network talk shows. When a celebrity steps through the grand entrance and strolls to the guest chair, he is asked, "Do you believe in ESP?" To say, "No," in the middle 1980s would be as unfashionable as to have said, "Yes," a generation ago.

Why I Wrote This Book

But why write a book on angels? Isn't talking about angels merely adding to the speculation about supernatural phenomena? What possible value is there in such a discussion? Didn't the fascination with angels vanish with the Middle Ages?

Because all the powers of the evil world system seem to be preying on the minds of people already disturbed and frustrated in our generation, I believe the time has come to focus on the positives of the Christian faith. John the Apostle said, "greater is he that is in you, than he that is in the world" (1 John 4:4). Satan is indeed capable of doing supernatural things—but he acts only by the permissive will of God; he is on a leash. It is God who is all powerful. It is God who is omnipotent. God has provided Christians with both offensive and defensive weapons. We are not to be fearful; we are not to be distressed; we are not to be deceived; nor are we to be intimidated. Rather, we are to be on our guard, calm and alert "Lest Satan should get an advantage of us, for we are not ignorant of his devices" (2 Corinthians 2:11).

One of Satan's sly devices is to divert our minds from the help God offers us in our struggles against the forces of evil. However, the Bible testifies that God has provided assistance for us in our spiritual conflicts. We are not alone in this world! The Bible teaches us that God's Holy Spirit has been given to empower us and guide us. In addition, the Bible—in nearly three hundred different places—also teaches that God has countless angels at His command. Furthermore, God has commissioned these angels to aid His children in their struggles against Satan. The Bible does not give as much information about them as we might like, but what it does say should be a source of comfort and strength for us in every circumstance.

I am convinced that these heavenly beings exist and that they provide unseen aid on our behalf. I do not believe in angels because someone has told me about a dramatic visitation from an angel, impressive as such rare testimonies may be. I do not believe in angels because UFOs are astonishingly angel-like in some of their reported appearances. I do not believe in angels because ESP experts are making the realm of the spirit world seem more and more plausible. I do not believe in angels because of the sudden worldwide emphasis on the reality of Satan and demons. I do not believe in angels because I have ever seen one—because I haven't.

I believe in angels because the Bible says there are angels; and I believe the Bible to be the true Word of God.

I also believe in angels because I have sensed their presence in my life on special occasions.

So what I have to say in the chapters that follow will not be an accumulation of *my* ideas about the spirit world, nor even a reflection of my own spiritual experiences in the spirit realm. I propose to put forward, at least in part, *what I understand the Bible to say about angels.* Naturally, this will not be an exhaustive study of the subject. I hope, however, that it will arouse your curiosity sufficiently for you to dig out from the Bible all that you can find on this subject after you have read this book. More than that, it is my prayer that you will discover the reality of God's love and care for you as evidenced in the ministry of His angels on your behalf, and that you would go forth in faith each day trusting God's constant watch-care over you.

Spiritual forces and resources are available to all Christians. Because our resources are unlimited, Christians will be winners. Millions of angels are at God's command and at our service. The hosts of heaven stand at attention as we make our way from earth to glory, and Satan's BB guns are no match for God's heavy artillery. So don't be afraid. God is for you. He has committed His angels to wage war in the conflict of the ages—and they will win the victory. The apostle Paul has said in Colossians 2:15, "And having spoiled principalities and powers, he made a show of them openly, triumphing over them." Victory over the flesh, the world and the devil is ours now! The angels are here to help and they are prepared for any emergency.

As you read this book, therefore, I pray that God will open your eyes to the resources He has provided for all who turn to Him for strength. I pray also that God will use it to show you your constant need of Him, and how He has sent His Son, Jesus Christ, into the world to deliver you from both the guilt and power of sin.

The British express train raced through the night, its powerful headlight piercing the darkness. Queen Victoria was a passenger on the train.

Suddenly the engineer saw a startling sight. Revealed in the beam of the engine's light was a strange figure in a black cloak standing in the middle of the tracks and waving its arms. The engineer grabbed for the brake and brought the train to a grinding halt.

He and his fellow trainmen clambered down to see what had stopped them. But they could find no trace of the strange figure. On a hunch the engineer walked a few yards further up the tracks. Suddenly he stopped and stared into the fog in horror. The bridge had been washed out in the middle and ahead of them it had toppled into a swollen stream. If the engineer had not heeded the ghostly figure, his train would have plummeted down into the stream.

While the bridge and the tracks were being repaired, the crew made a more intensive search for the strange flagman. But not until they got to London did they solve the mystery.

At the base of the engine's headlamp the engineer discovered a huge dead moth. He looked at it a moment, then on impulse wet its wings and pasted it to the glass of the lamp.

Climbing back into his cab, he switched on the light and saw the "flagman" in the beam. He knew the answer now: the moth had flown into the beam, seconds before the train was due to reach the washed-out bridge. In the fog, it appeared to be a phantom figure, waving its arms.

When Queen Victoria was told of the strange happening she said, "I'm sure it was no accident. It was God's way of protecting us."

No, the figure the engineer saw in the headlight's beam was not an angel . . . and yet God, quite possibly through the ministry of His unseen angels, had placed the moth on the headlight lens exactly when and where it was needed. Truly "He will command his angels concerning you to guard you in all your ways" (Psalm 91:11, NIV).

2

Angels Are for Real

SPECULATION ABOUT THE nature of angels has been around since long before Queen Victoria's time, and it continues down to the present time. Yet through revelation in the Bible God has told us a great deal about them. For this reason, theologians through the ages have universally agreed about the importance of "angelology" (the orderly statement of biblical truth about angels). They judged it worthy of treatment in any book of systematic theology. They wrote at length, distinguishing between good angels and satanology (the study of fallen and thus evil angels). But today we have neglected the theme of good angels, although many are giving the devil and all of his demons rapt attention, even worshiping them.

Angels belong to a uniquely different dimension of creation that we, limited to the natural order, can scarcely comprehend. In this angelic domain the limitations are different from those God has imposed on our natural order. He has given angels higher knowledge, power and mobility than we. Have you ever seen or met one of these superior beings called angels? Probably not, for both the Bible and human experience tell us visible appearances by angels are very rare—but that in no way makes angels any less real or powerful. They are God's messengers whose chief business is to carry out His orders in the world. He has given them an ambassadorial charge. He has designated and empowered them as holy deputies to perform works of righteousness. In this way they assist Him as their creator while He sovereignly controls the universe. So He has given them the capacity to bring His holy enterprises to a successful conclusion.

Angels Are Created Beings

Don't believe everything you hear (and read!) about angels! Some would have us believe that they are only spiritual will-o'-the-wisps. Some view them as only celestial beings with beautiful wings and bowed heads. Others would have us think of them as effeminate wierdos.

The Bible states that angels, like men, were created by God. At one time no angels existed; indeed there was nothing but the Triune God: Father, Son and Holy Spirit. Paul, in Colossians 1:16, says, "For by him were all things created, that are in heaven, and that are in earth, visible and invisible." Angels indeed are among the invisible things made by God, for "all things were created by him, and for him." This Creator, Jesus, "is before all things, and by him all things consist" (Colossians 1:17), so that even angels would cease to exist if Jesus, who is Almighty God, did not sustain them by His power.

It seems that angels have the ability to change their appearance and shuttle in a flash from the capital glory of heaven to earth and back again. Although some interpreters have said that the phrase "sons of God" in Genesis 6:2 refers to angels, the Bible frequently makes it clear that angels are nonmaterial; Hebrews 1:14 calls them ministering "spirits." Intrinsically, they do not possess physical bodies, although they may take on physical bodies when God appoints them to special tasks. Furthermore, God has given them no ability to reproduce, and they neither marry nor are given in marriage (Mark 12:25).

The empire of angels is as vast as God's creation. If you believe the Bible, you will believe in their ministry. They crisscross the Old and New Testaments, being mentioned directly or indirectly nearly 300 times. Some biblical scholars believe that angels can be numbered potentially in the millions since Hebrews 12:22

speaks of "an innumerable [myriads—a great but indefinite number] company of angels." As to their number, David recorded 20,000 coursing through the skyways of the stars. Even with his limited vision he impressively notes, "The chariots of God are twenty thousand, even thousands of angels" (Psalm 68:17). Matthew Henry says of this passage, "Angels are 'the chariots of God,' his chariots of war, which he makes use of against his enemies, his chariots of conveyance, which he sends for his friends, as he did for Elijah . . . , his chariots of state, in the midst of which he shows his glory and power. They are vastly numerous: 'Twenty thousands,' even thousands multiplied."

Ten thousand angels came down on Mount Sinai to confirm the holy presence of God as He gave the Law to Moses (Deuteronomy 33:2). An earthquake shook the mountain. Moses was held in speech-bound wonder at this mighty cataclysm attended by the visitation of heavenly beings. Furthermore, in the New Testament John tells us of having seen ten thousand times ten thousand angels ministering to the Lamb of God in the throne room of the universe (Revelation 5:11). The book of Revelation also says that armies of angels will appear with Jesus at the Battle of Armageddon when God's foes gather for their final defeat. Paul in 2 Thessalonians says, "the Lord Jesus shall be revealed from heaven with his mighty angels" (1:7).

Think of it! Multitudes of angels, indescribably mighty, performing the commands of heaven! More amazingly, even one angel is indescribably mighty, as though an extension of the arm of God. Singly or corporately, angels are for real. They are better organized than were the armies of Alexander the Great, Napoleon, or Eisenhower. From earliest antiquity, when the angel guardians of the gates to the glory of Eden sealed the entrance to the home of Adam and Eve, angels have manifested their presence in the world. God placed angelic sentinels called cherubim at the east of the Garden of Eden. They were commissioned not only to bar man's return into Eden, but with "a flaming sword flashing back and forth to guard the way to the tree of life" (Genesis 3:24, NIV) lest Adam by eating of its fruit should live forever. If Adam had lived in his sin forever—this earth would long ago have been hell. Thus, in one sense death is a blessing to the human race.

Angels Serve God and Regenerate Men

Witness the unprecedented and unrepeated pageantry at Mt. Sinai. When God moves toward man, it is an event of the first magnitude and can include the visitation of angelic hosts. In the billowing clouds that covered Sinai an angelic trumpeter announced the presence of God. The whole mountain seemed to pulsate with life. Consternation gripped the people below. The earth seemed convulsed with a nameless fear. As God came to the mountaintop, He was accompanied by thousands of angels. Moses, the silent, lone witness, must have been overcome with even a limited vision of the forces of God. It staggers the imagination to wonder what kind of a headline would be prompted in the daily press for even a man-sided view of such a heavenly visitation. "And so terrible was the sight, that Moses said, I exceedingly fear and quake" (Hebrews 12:21).

The appearance of God was glorious. He shone like the sun when it goes to its strength. In his commentary Matthew Henry says, "Even Seir and Paran, two mountains at some distance, were illuminated by the divine glory which appeared on Mount Sinai, and reflected some of the rays of it, so bright was the appearance, and so much taken notice to set forth the wonders of the divine providence (Habakkuk 3:3,4; Psalm 18:7–9). The Jerusalem Targum has a strange gloss [note of explanation] upon this, that, 'when God came down to give the law, he offered it on Mount Seir to the Edomites, but they refused it, because they found in it, *Thou shalt not kill.* Then he offered it on Mount Paran to the Ishmaelites, but they also refused it, because they found in it, *Thou shalt not steal;* and then he came to Mount Sinai and offered it to Israel, and they said, *All that the Lord shall say we will do.'*" This account by the Jerusalem Targum is, of course, fictional, but it throws an interesting light on how some Jews later regarded this extraordinary and spectacular event.

Belief in Angels: A General Phenomenon

The history of virtually all nations and cultures reveals at least some belief in angelic beings. Ancient Egyptians made the tombs of their dead more impregnable and lavish than their homes because they felt angels would visit there in succeeding ages. Islamic scholars have proposed that at least two angels are assigned to each person: one angel records the good deeds and the other the bad. In fact, long before Islam arose, and even apart from contact with Scripture, some religions taught the existence of angels. But no matter what the traditions, our frame of reference must be the Scripture as our supreme authority on this subject.

Today some hard-nosed scientists lend credence to the scientific probability of angels when they admit the likelihood of unseen and invisible intelligences. Increasingly, our world is being made acutely aware of the existence of occult and demonic powers. People pay attention as never before to sensational headlines promoting films and books concerning the occult. News accounts of strange happenings around the world fascinate readers and TV viewers everywhere. Ought not Christians, grasping the eternal dimension of life, become conscious of the sinless angelic powers who are for real, and who associate with God Himself and administer His works in our behalf? After all, references to the holy angels in the Bible far outnumber references to Satan and his subordinate demons.

Cosmic Powers

If the activities of the devil and his demons seem to be intensifying in these days, as I believe they are, should not the incredibly greater supernatural powers of God's holy angels be even more indelibly impressed on the minds of people of faith? Certainly the eye of faith sees many evidences of the supernatural display of God's power and glory. God is still in business too.

Christians must never fail to sense the operation of angelic glory. It forever eclipses the world of demonic powers, as the sun does the candle's light.

If you are a believer, expect powerful angels to accompany you in your life experiences. And let those events dramatically illustrate the friendly presence of "the holy ones," as Daniel calls them.

Angels speak. They appear and reappear. They are emotional creatures. While angels may become visible by choice, our eyes are not constructed to see them ordinarily any more than we can see the dimensions of a nuclear field, the structure of atoms, or the electricity that flows through copper wiring. Our ability to sense reality is limited: The deer of the forest far surpass our human capacity in their keenness of smell. Bats possess a phenomenally sensitive built-in radar system. Some animals can see things in the dark that escape our attention. Swallows and geese possess sophisticated guidance systems that appear to border on the supernatural. So why should we think it strange if men fail to perceive the evidences of angelic presence? Could it be that God granted Balaam and his ass a new optical capacity to view the angel? *(See* Numbers 22:23, 31.) Without this special sense they might have thought him to be only a fragment of their imagination.

Reports continually flow to my attention from many places around the world telling of visitors of the angelic order appearing, ministering, fellowshiping and disappearing. They warn of God's impending judgment; they spell out the tenderness of His love; they meet a desperate need; then they are gone. Of one thing we can be sure: angels never draw attention to themselves but ascribe glory to God and press His message upon the hearers as a delivering and sustaining word of the highest order.

Demonic activity and Satan worship are on the increase in all parts of the world. The devil is alive and more at work than at any other time. The Bible says that since he realizes his time is short, his activity will increase. Through his demonic influences he does succeed in turning many away from true faith; but we can still say that his evil activities are countered for the people of God by His ministering spirits, the holy ones of the angelic order. They are vigorous in delivering the heirs of salvation from the stratagems of evil men. They cannot fail.

Believers, look up—take courage. The angels are nearer than you think. For after all (as we have already noted), God has given "his angels charge of you, to guard you in all your ways. On their hands they will bear you up, lest you dash your foot against a stone" (Psalm 91:11, 12, RSV).

3

Angels Visible
or Invisible?

THE SPIRIT WORLD and its activities are big news today. And the idea of the supernatural is not only seriously regarded, but is accepted as a fact. Many of the most recent books on the subject border on the sensational, or are purely speculative, or have been dreamed up in somebody's imagination. But those who take the Bible at full value cannot discount the subject of angels as speculation or hollow conjecture. After all, the Scriptures mention their existence almost three hundred times.

Have You Ever Seen an Angel?

I have already said that angels are created spirit beings who can become visible when necessary. They can appear and disappear. They think, feel, will and display emotions. But some people have questions about them that ought not concern us. The old debate about how many angels can dance on the head of a pin is foolish. And to ask how many angels can be crowded into a telephone booth or into a Volkswagen hardly merits our attention. On the other hand, we should know what the Bible teaches about them as oracles of God, who give divine or authoritative decisions and bring messages from God to men. To fulfill this function angels have not infrequently assumed visible, human form. The writer to the Hebrews asks, "Are they [angels] not all ministering spirits?" (1:14). Now, have you ever seen a pure spirit? I can't say that I have. Yet I do know that down through the ages God has chosen to manifest His own spiritual presence in different ways. At the baptism of Jesus, God the Holy Spirit was present in the form of a dove. So God has chosen also to manifest His presence through His angels, who are lesser beings to whom He has given the power to assume forms that occasionally make them visible to men.

Are Angels to Be Worshiped?

It is no mere accident that angels are usually invisible. Though God in His infinite wisdom does not, as a rule, permit angels to take on physical dimensions, people tend to venerate them in a fashion that borders on worship. We are warned against worshiping the creature rather than the Creator (Romans 1:24–25). It's no less than heretical, and indeed is a breach of the first commandment, to worship any manifestation of angelic presence, patron or blesser.

Paul has pointed out that while unusual manifestations may be deeply significant, Jesus Christ the incarnate God, the second person of the Trinity, who is creator of all things and by whom all things exist, is worthy of our worship (Colossians 2:18). We are not to pray to angels. Nor are we to engage in "a voluntary humility and worshiping" of them. Only the Triune God is to be the object of our worship and of our prayers.

Moreover, we should not confuse angels, whether visible or invisible, with the Holy Spirit, the third person of the Trinity and Himself God. Angels do not indwell men; the Holy Spirit seals them and indwells them when He has regenerated them. The Holy Spirit is all knowing, all present, and all powerful. Angels are mightier than men, but they are not gods and they do not possess the attributes of the Godhead.

Not angels, but the Holy Spirit convicts men of sin, righteousness and judgment (John 16:7). He reveals and interprets Jesus Christ to men, while angels remain messengers of God who serve men as ministering spirits (Hebrews 1:14). So far as I know, no Scripture says that the Holy Spirit ever manifested Himself in human form to men. Jesus did this in the incarnation. The glorious Holy Spirit can be everywhere at the same time, but no angel can be in more than one place at any given moment. We know the Holy Spirit as spirit, not flesh, but we can know angels not as spirits alone but sometimes also in visible form.

At the same time, both angels and the Holy Spirit are at work in our world to accomplish God's perfect will. Frankly, we may not always know the agent or means God is using—the Holy Spirit or the angels—when we discern God's hand at work. We can be sure, however, that there is no contradiction or competition between God the Holy Spirit and God's command of the angelic hosts. God Himself is in control to accomplish His will—and in that we can rejoice!

God uses angels to work out the destinies of men and nations. He has altered the courses of the busy political and social arenas of our society and directed the destinies of men by angelic visitation many times over. We must be aware that angels keep in close and vital contact with all that is happening on the earth. Their knowledge of earthly matters exceeds that of men. We must attest to their invisible presence and unceasing labors. Let us believe that they are here among us. They may not laugh or cry with us, but we do know they delight with us over every victory in our evangelistic endeavors. Jesus taught that "there is joy in the presence of the angels of God when our sinner repents" (Luke 15:10, TLB).

Angels Visible? Invisible?

In Daniel 6:22 we read, "My God hath sent his angel, and hath shut the lions' mouths." In the den, Daniel's sight evidently perceived the angelic presence, and the lions' strength more than met its match in the power of the angel. In most instances, angels, when appearing visibly, are so glorious and impressively beautiful as to stun and amaze men who witness their presence.

Can you imagine a being, white and dazzling as lightning? General William Booth, founder of the Salvation Army, describes a vision of angelic beings, stating that every angel was surrounded with an aura of rainbow light so brilliant that were it not withheld, no human being could stand the sight of it.

Who can measure the brilliance of the lightning flash that illuminates the countryside for miles around? The angel who rolled away the stone from the tomb of Jesus was not only dressed in white, but shone as a flash of lightning with dazzling brilliance (Matthew 28:3). The keepers of the tomb shook and became as dead men. Incidentally, that stone weighed several times more than a single man could move, yet the physical power of the angel was not taxed in rolling it aside.

Abraham, Lot, Jacob and others had no difficulty recognizing angels when God allowed them to manifest themselves in physical form. Note, for example, Jacob's instant recognition of angels in Genesis 32:1, 2. "And Jacob went on his way, and the angels of God met him. And when Jacob saw them, he said, This is God's host: and he called the name of that place Mahanaim."

Further, both Daniel and John described the glories of the angels (Daniel 10:6 and Revelation 10:1) visibly descending from heaven with immeasurable beauty and brilliance, shining like the sun. Who has not thrilled to read the account of the three Hebrew children, Shadrach, Meshach and Abednego? They refused to fall in line with the music of obeisance and worship to the king of Babylon. They learned that the angel presence can be observed on occasion by people in the unbelieving world on the outside. After they had refused to bow, the angel preserved them from being burned alive or even having the smell of smoke on their garments from the seven-times-hotter fire. The angel came to them in the midst of the flame without harm and was seen by the king who said, "I see four men . . . in the midst of the fire" (Daniel 3:25).

On the other hand, the Bible indicates angels are more often invisible to human eyes. Whether visible or invisible, however, God causes His angels to go before us, to be with us, and to follow after us. All of this can be fully understood only by believers who know that angelic presences are in control of the battlefield about us, so that we may stand with complete confidence in the midst of the fight. "If God be for us who can be against us?" (Romans 8:31).

What Do You See When You See an Angel?

God is forever imaginative, colorful and glorious in what He designs. Some of the descriptions of angels, including the one of

Lucifer in Ezekiel 28, indicate that they are exotic to the human eye and mind. Apparently angels have a beauty and variety that surpass anything known to men. Scripture does not tell us what elements make up angels. Nor can modern science, which is only beginning to explore the realm of the unseen, tell us about the constitution or even the work of angels.

The Bible seems to indicate that angels do not age, and never says that one was sick. Except for those who fell with Lucifer, the ravages of sin that have brought destruction, sickness and chaos to our earth have not affected them. The holy angels will never die.

The Bible also teaches that angels are sexless. Jesus said that in heaven men "neither marry, nor are given in marriage, but are as the angels of God in heaven" (Matthew 22:30). This may indicate that angels enjoy relationships that are far more thrilling and exciting than sex. The joy of sex in this life may be only a foretaste of something that believers will enjoy in heaven which is far beyond anything man has ever known.

How are we to understand "theophanies"? (This is a theological term for the visible appearances of Jesus Christ in other forms prior to His incarnation.) Some passages in the Old Testament tell us that the second person of the Trinity appeared and was called either "the Lord" or "the angel of the Lord." Nowhere is it clearer than in Genesis 18 where three men appear before Abraham. Their leader is clearly identified with the Lord, whereas the other two are merely angels. There are no grounds for questioning the very early and traditional Christian interpretation that in these cases there is a preincarnation manifestation of the second person of the Trinity, whether He is called 'the Lord' or 'the Angel of the Lord' (*Zondervan Pictorial Encyclopedia of the Bible*).

We must remember, then, that in some cases in the Old Testament God Himself appeared in human form as an angel. This reinforces the idea of the relationship between God and His angels. Nevertheless, in almost all of the cases where angelic personages appear they are God's created angelic beings and not God Himself.

Yes, angels are real. They are not the product of our imagination, but were made by God Himself. Think of it! Whether we see them or not, God has created a vast host of angels to help accomplish His work in this world. When we know God personally through faith in His Son, Jesus Christ, we can have confidence that the angels of God will watch over us and assist us because we belong to Him.

4

Angels—How They
Differ from Man

THE BIBLE TELLS us that God has made man "a little lower than the angels." Yet it also says angels are "ministering spirits, sent forth to minister for them who shall be heirs of salvation" (Hebrews 2:5–7;1:13, 14). This sounds like a contradiction: man lower—but eventually higher through redemption. How can we explain this?

First we must remember that this Scripture is speaking both of Jesus Christ and men. Jesus did "stoop" when He became man. And as a man He was a little lower than the angels in His humanity—although without losing in any sense His divine nature. But it also speaks about men other than Jesus. God has made men head over all the creatures of our earth world; but they are lower than angels with respect to their bodies and to their place while here on earth. In his *Institutes*, John Calvin said, "The angels are the dispensers and administrators of the Divine beneficence toward us; they regard our safety, undertake our defense, direct our ways, and exercise a constant solicitude that no evil befall us."

God commands angels to help men since they will be made higher than the angels at the resurrection. So says Jesus in Luke 20:36. God will alter the temporary lower position of man when the kingdom of God has come in its fullness. Now let us examine in detail how God says angels differ from men.

Although angels are glorious beings, the Scriptures make it clear that they differ from regenerated men in significant ways. How can the angels who have never sinned fully understand what it means to be delivered from sin? How can they understand how precious Jesus is to those for whom His death on Calvary brings light, life and immortality? Is it not stranger still that angels themselves will be judged by believers who were once sinners? Such judgment, however, apparently applies only to those fallen angels who followed Lucifer. Thus Paul writes in 1 Corinthians 6:3, "Know ye not that we shall judge angels?" But even the holy angels have limitations, though the Bible speaks of them as being superior to men in many ways.

Is God "Father" to Angels?

God is not called "Father" by the holy angels because, not having sinned, they need not be redeemed. All the fallen angels cannot call God "Father" because they cannot be redeemed. The latter case is one of the mysteries of Scripture: God made provision for the salvation of fallen men, but He made no provision for the salvation of fallen angels. Why? Perhaps because, unlike Adam and Eve, who were enticed toward sin by sinners, the angels fell when there were no sinners, so no one could entice them to sin. Thus, their sinful state cannot be altered; their sin cannot be forgiven; their salvation cannot be achieved.

The wicked angels would never want to call God "Father," though they may call Lucifer "father," as many Satan worshipers do. They are in revolt against God and will never voluntarily accept His sovereign lordship, except in that Day of Judgment when every knee will bow and every tongue confess that Jesus Christ is Lord (Philippians 2:9, 10). Yet even holy angels who might like to call God "Father" could do so only in the looser sense of that word. As Creator, God is the father of all created beings; since angels are created beings, they might think of Him this way. But the term is normally reserved in Scripture for lost men who have been redeemed. So in a real sense, even ordinary men cannot call God "Father" except as their Creator God—until they are born again.

Angels Are Not Heirs of God

Christians are joint heirs with Jesus Christ through redemption (Romans 8:17), which is made theirs by faith in Him based on His death at Calvary. Angels who are not joint heirs must stand aside when the believers are introduced to their boundless, eternal riches. The holy angels, however, who are ministering spirits, have never lost their original glory and spiritual relationship with God. This assures them of their exalted place in the royal order of God's creation. By contrast, Jesus identified Himself with fallen men in the incarnation when He was "made a little lower than the angels for the suffering of death" (Hebrews 2:9). That He chose to taste the death we deserve also shows that the holy angels do not share our sinfulness—nor our need of redemption.

Angels Cannot Testify of Salvation by Grace through Faith

Who can comprehend the overwhelming thrill of fellowship with God and the joy of salvation that even angels do not know? When the local church assembles as a group of Christian believers, it represents in the human sphere the highest order of the love of God. No love could go deeper, rise higher, or extend farther than the amazing love that moved Him to give His only begotten Son. The angels are aware of that joy (Luke 15:10), and when a person accepts God's gift of eternal life through Jesus Christ, angels set all the bells of heaven to ringing with their rejoicing before the Lamb of God.

Yet although the angels rejoice when people are saved and glorify God who has saved them, they cannot do one thing: testify personally to something they have not experienced. They can only point to the experiences of the redeemed and rejoice that God has saved them. This means that throughout eternity we humans alone will give our personal witness to the salvation that God achieved by grace and that we received through faith in Jesus Christ. The man who has never married cannot fully appreciate the wonders of that relationship. The person who has never lost a father or mother cannot understand what that loss means. So angels, great as they are, cannot testify to salvation the same way as those who have experienced it.

Angels Have No Experiential Knowledge of the Indwelling God

Nothing in the Bible indicates that the Holy Spirit indwells angels as He does redeemed people. Since He seals believers when they accept Christ, such sealing would be unnecessary for the angels who never fell and who therefore need no salvation.

But there is a second reason for this difference. Redeemed men on earth have not yet been glorified. Once God has declared them just and given them life, He embarks on a process of making them inwardly holy while they live here below. At death He makes them perfect. So the Holy Spirit takes His abode in the hearts of all believers while they are still on earth, to perform His unique ministry, one that angels cannot perform. God the Father sent Jesus the Son to die; Jesus performed His unique ministry as His part of God's saving process. Likewise, the Holy Spirit has a role, one different from the Son's. Sent by the Father and the Son, He not only guides and directs believers, but also performs a work of grace in their hearts, conforming them to the image of God to make them holy like Christ. Angels cannot provide this sanctifying power.

Furthermore, angels themselves do not need the ministry of the Holy Spirit the way believers do. The angels have already been endowed with authority by virtue of their relationship to God through creation and continuing obedience. They are unspoiled by sin. People, however, are not yet perfect and therefore need what the Holy Spirit alone can give. Someday we will be as perfect as angels are now.

Angels Do Not Marry or Procreate

I have already said that angels do not marry. In Matthew 22:30, Jesus points out that "in the resurrection they [men] neither marry,

nor are given in marriage, but are as the angels of God in heaven."
Because of this we can make a deduction: The number of angels
remains constant. For the obedient angels do not die. The fallen
angels will suffer the final judgment at the time God finishes dealing with them. While we cannot be certain, some scholars estimate that as many as one third of the angels cast their lot with
Satan when he mysteriously rebelled against his Creator. In any
event the book of Hebrews says the angels constitute an "innumerable company," vast hosts that stagger our imagination. A third
of them would likely be counted in the hundreds of thousands—
ones who are now desperate demons.

Just as angels differ from people with respect to marriage, so they
differ in other important ways. Nothing in Scripture says that
angels must eat to stay alive. But the Bible says that on certain
occasions angels in human form did indeed eat. David refers to the
manna eaten by the children of Israel in the wilderness as the bread
of angels. In Psalm 78:25, Asaph says, "Man did eat angels' food."
We can hardly disregard what happened to Elijah after he won a
great victory over the priests of Baal on Mount Carmel. Because
Jezebel threatened his life he needed help from God. So God's angel
came to the tired, discouraged prophet and set before him food and
drink. When he had eaten twice he was sent on his journey; the
food he had eaten was enough to keep him for forty days and forty
nights (1 Kings 19:5). Not without reason some have concluded
that Elijah indeed ate angels' food.

When Abraham was encamped in the plains of Mamre, three
angels visited him, of whom one may have been the Lord Jesus
(Genesis 18:1, 2). These heavenly beings ate and drank what he
provided for them by way of customary entertainment. Shortly
thereafter, when God decided to destroy Sodom and Gomorrah,
two angelic beings came to save backslidden Lot and his family.
Lot made them a feast and there again they ate food, including
unleavened bread (Genesis 19).

It is interesting that after His resurrection, Jesus ate with His
disciples. Luke's account says that the disciples "gave him a piece
of a broiled fish, and of an honeycomb. And he took it, and did
eat before them" (Luke 24:42, 43).

The Knowledge of Angels

Angels excel humankind in their knowledge. When King David was being urged to bring Absalom back to Jerusalem, Joab asked a woman of Tekoah to talk to the king. She said: "My lord is wise, according to the wisdom of an angel of God, to know all things that are in the earth" (2 Samuel 14:20). And angels possess knowledge that men do not have. But however vast is their knowledge, we can be sure they are not omniscient. They do not know everything. They are not like God. Jesus bore testimony to the limited knowledge of the angels when He was speaking of His second coming. In Mark 13:32 He said, "But of that day and that hour knoweth no man, no, not the angels which are in heaven."

Angels probably know things about us that we do not know about ourselves. And because they are ministering spirits, they will always use this knowledge for our good and not for evil purposes. In a day when few men can be trusted with secret information, it is comforting to know that angels will not divulge their great knowledge to hurt us. Rather, they will use it for our good.

The Power of Angels

Angels enjoy far greater power than men, but they are not omnipotent or "all powerful." In 2 Thessalonians 1:7, Paul refers to the "mighty angels of God." From the word translated "mighty" here we get the English word "dynamite." In material power, angels are God's dynamite! In Peter we read, "angels who are greater in might and power [than men] do not bring a reviling judgment against them before the Lord" (2 Peter 2:11, NASB). Peter's testimony here reinforces Paul's. We should also note that it took only one angel to slay the first born of Egypt in Moses' day, and one to shut the lions' mouths for Daniel.

In Psalm 103:20 David speaks about [God's] "angels that excel in strength." Nowhere in Scripture is that strength manifested more dramatically than in the climax of this age. Following the Battle of Armageddon, Scripture pictures what will happen to Satan: He is to be bound and cast into a bottomless pit. But what power, apart from God Himself, can do this to Satan, whose power we all know about and whose evil designs we have experienced? The Bible says that one angel will come from heaven. He will have a great chain in his hand. He will lay hold of Satan and bind him with that chain. And then he will cast him into the pit. How great is the power of one of God's mighty angels.

Do Angels Sing?

There has been much conjecture about angel choirs. We at least assume that angels can and do sing, even if the Scriptures do not pointedly say so. In *Hamlet*, William Shakespeare seemed to underscore the possibility that angels sing when he stated, "Now cracks a noble heart, Good night, sweet prince:/ and flights of angels sing thee to thy rest."

Some Bible students insist that angels do not sing. This seems inconceivable. Angels possess the ultimate capacity to offer praise, and their music from time immemorial has been the primary vehicle of praise to our all-glorious God. Music is the universal language. It is likely that John saw a massive heavenly choir (Revelation 5:11, 12) of many millions who expressed their praise of the heavenly Lamb through magnificent music. I believe angel choirs will sing in eternity to the glory of God and the supreme delight of the redeemed.

While it is partly speculative, I believe that angels have the capacity to employ heavenly celestial music. Many dying believers have testified that they have heard the music of heaven. Most of my close friends tease me because I cannot carry a tune. When I am singing beside people in a congregation I usually throw them off key. But from years of listening I recognize good music when I hear it—even if I can't produce it myself. And there have been times when I have seriously tried to understand and appreciate music I did not like, whether it was a difficult opera or rock. I think before we can understand the music of heaven we will have to go beyond our earthly concept of music. I think most earthly music will seem to us to have been in the "minor key" in comparison to what we are going to hear in heaven.

The Bible tells us of many who sang: Moses (Exodus 15:1), Miriam (Exodus 15:20, 21), David (Psalms), and many others. Thou-

sands of worshipers at the temple continually sang, praising the
Lord (2 Chronicles 5:12). Thousands of singers preceded the ark
of the covenant (1 Chronicles 15:27, 28). We all think of Psalms
as the hymn book of the Bible.

New Testament believers also sang with rapturous joy. Though
the Bible does not say it, it implies that angels, who are of a higher
creative order, are tuned to sing with no discordant note to God
and the Lamb. Paul reminds us that there is a language of man and
a language of angels (1 Corinthians 13:1). Angels have a celestial
language and make music that is worthy of the God who made
them. I believe in heaven we will be taught the language and music
of the celestial world. The wonderful hymn, "Holy, Holy Is What
the Angels Sing," by Johnson Oatman, Jr., and J. Sweney expresses
this thought in verse 4:

> So, altho' I'm not an angel,
> yet I know that over there
> I will join the blessed chorus
> that the angels cannot share;
> I will sing about my Saviour,
> who upon dark Calvary
> Freely pardoned my transgressions,
> died to set a sinner free.

Angels Worship before the Throne

Unquestionably angels ascribe honor and glory to the Lamb of
God. But angels do not spend all their time in heaven. They are
not omnipresent (everywhere present at the same time), so they
can be in only one place at a given time. Yet as God's messengers
they are busy around the world carrying out God's orders. Is it not,
therefore, obvious that when they are engaged in their ministry
here they cannot stand before God's throne? But when angels do
stand before the throne of God, indeed they worship and adore
their creator.

We can look for that future day when angels will have finished
their earthly ministry. Then they will gather with all the redeemed
before the throne of God in heaven. There they will offer their

praise and sing their songs. In that day the angels who veiled their faces and stood mute when Jesus hung on the cross will then ascribe glory to the Lamb whose work is finished and whose kingdom has come. The angels may also stop to listen as the redeemed children of God express their own thanksgiving for salvation. It may well be true as the hymn writer has said in verse 3 of the song, "Holy, Holy Is What the Angels Sing,"

> Then the angels stand and listen,
> For they cannot join that song,
> Like the sound of many waters,
> By that happy, blood-washed throng.

But the children of God will also stop to listen to the angels. They have their own reasons for singing, ones that differ from ours. They have given themselves to the service of God Almighty. They have had a part in bringing in the kingdom of God. They have helped the children of God in difficult circumstances. So theirs shall be a shout and a song of victory. The cause they represent has been victorious; the fight they fought is finished; the enemy they met has been conquered; their wicked companion angels who fell shall vex them no more. The angels sing a different song. But they sing; my, how they sing! And I believe that angels and those of us who have been redeemed will compete with each other for the endless ages of eternity to see who can best ascribe glory and praise to our wonderful God!

Do you have that hope of eternity in your heart right now? Do you know—beyond doubt—that some day you will join the angels in heaven in singing praises to God? If not, make your commitment to Christ today.

Without Christ you are separated from God and without hope of eternal life. You need to have your sins forgiven, and you need to be renewed and cleansed by the power of God. And this can happen, if you will give your life to Christ and trust Him as your personal Lord and Savior. Christ came to take away your sins by His death on the cross. You deserved to die—but He died in your place! "For Christ died for sins once for all, the righteous for the unrighteous, to bring you to God" (1 Peter 3:18, NIV). Right now

Billy Graham

by a simple prayer of faith you can invite Christ to come into your heart. When you do, He will make you part of His family forever and you can know that some day you will join with the angels and with millions of believers from across the ages in singing praises to God in heaven. Take that step of faith today.

5

Angelic Organization

WE CANNOT STUDY the subject of angels in the Bible without becoming aware of ranks among angelic beings. The evidence shows that they are organized in terms of authority and glory.

Though some see the ranking of celestial powers as conjectural, it seems to follow this pattern: archangels, angels, seraphim, cherubim, principalities, authorities, powers, thrones, might and dominion (Colossians 1:16; Romans 8:38).

Medieval theologians divided angelic beings into ten grades. Some people, however, have asked whether some of these grades—the principalities, authorities, powers, thrones, might and dominion—could not refer to human institutions and human beings. To answer, we must understand Colossians 1:16. Paul is speaking about creation of things both seen and unseen. On this verse Matthew Henry says that Christ "made all things out of nothing, the highest angel in heaven as well as men upon earth. He made the world, the upper and lower world, with all the inhabitants of both. . . . He [Paul] speaks here as if there were several orders of angels: 'Whether thrones, or dominions, or principalities, or powers,' which must signify either different degrees of excellence or different offices and employments." Perhaps any list that ranks angelic beings will err, but we can be sure they differ in power, some having authority others do not possess. While I do not wish to be dogmatic, I think there are different ranks of angels and that the list given in Colossians does refer to these celestial personalities. Let's look at four of them:

1. ARCHANGEL

While Scripture designates only Michael as an archangel (Jude 9), we have biblical grounds for believing that before his fall Lucifer was also an archangel, equal or perhaps superior to Michael. The prefix "arch" suggests a chief, principal or great angel. Thus, Michael is now the angel above all angels, recognized in rank to be the first prince of heaven. He is, as it were, the Prime Minister in God's administration of the universe, and is the "angel administrator" of God for judgment. He must stand alone, because the Bible never speaks of archangels, only *the* archangel. His name means "who is like unto the Lord."

In the Old Testament, Michael seems to be identified primarily with Israel as a nation. Thus, God speaks of Michael as prince of His chosen people, "the great prince which standeth for the children of thy people" (Daniel 12:1). He specially protects and defends God's people whoever they are.

Further, in Daniel he is referred to as "Michael, your prince" (Daniel 10:21). He is God's messenger of law and judgment. In this capacity he appears in Revelation 12:7–12 leading the armies that battle Satan, the great dragon, and all of his demons. Michael with his angels will be locked in the titanic struggle of the universe at the last conflict of the age, which will mark the defeat of Satan and all forces of darkness. Scripture tells us in advance that Michael will finally be victorious in the battle. Hell will tremble; heaven will rejoice and celebrate!

Bible students have speculated that Michael cast Lucifer and his fallen angels out of heaven, and that Michael enters into conflict with Satan and the evil angels today to destroy their power and to give to God's people the prospect of their ultimate victory.

Michael, the archangel, will shout as he accompanies Jesus at His Second Coming. Not only does he proclaim the matchless and exciting news that Jesus Christ returns, but he speaks the word of life to all who are dead in Christ and who await their resurrection. "For the Lord himself shall descend from heaven with a shout, with the voice of the archangel . . . and the dead in Christ shall rise first" (1 Thessalonians 4:16).

2. THE ANGEL GABRIEL

Gabriel is one of the most prominent angels mentioned in Scripture.

"Gabriel," in Hebrew, means "God's hero," or "the mighty one," or "God is great." Scripture frequently refers to him as "the messenger of Jehovah" or "the Lord's messenger." However, contrary to popular opinion and to the poet John Milton, it never calls him an archangel. Yet it refers to his work more often than to Michael's.

Ministry of Gabriel

Gabriel is primarily God's messenger of mercy and promise. He appears four times in the Bible, always bearing good news (Daniel 8:16, 9:21; Luke 1:19, 26). We may question whether he blows a silver trumpet, since this idea arises from folk music and finds only indirect support in Scripture. But the announcements of Gabriel in unfolding the plans, purposes and verdicts of God are of monumental importance.

In Scripture we gain our first glimpse of Gabriel in Daniel 8:15,16. There he announces the vision of God for the "end time." God has charged him to convey the message from the "situation room" of heaven that reveals God's plan in history. In verse 17 Gabriel says, "Understand, . . . the vision belongs to (events that shall occur in) the time of the end" (AB).

Daniel, while in prayer, records Gabriel's second appearance to him: "While I was speaking in prayer, the man Gabriel, whom I had seen in the former vision, being caused to fly swiftly, came near to me and touched me about the time of the evening sacrifice" (Daniel 9:21, AB). To Daniel he said, "Understand the vision" (9:23), and then revealed to him the magnificent sequence of events at the end time. Gabriel, sketching panoramically the procession of earthly kingdoms, assured Daniel that history would culminate in the return of Christ, "the prince of princes," (Daniel 8:25, AB) and conqueror of the "king of fierce countenance" (Daniel 8:23, AB). The prophetic announcement by Daniel in his prayer to God is twofold. He expressly refers to the more immediate judgment upon Israel (Daniel 9:16) and then to the awesome portent of "end time judgment" and "tribulation" which shall be for "seven years" (Daniel 9:27). In a later chapter, "Angels in Prophecy," we will trace how the angels supervise the fearsome events of the end time.

Gabriel in the New Testament

Gabriel first appears in the New Testament in Luke 1. He identifies himself to Zacharias (verse 19), announces the birth of John the Baptist and describes his life and ministry as the forerunner of Jesus.

But in his most important appearance, Gabriel informs the Virgin Mary about Jesus, the incarnate God! What a message to deliver to the world through a teenage girl! What a wonderfully holy girl she must have been, to be visited by the mighty Gabriel. He declares:

Fear not, Mary: for thou hast found favour with God. And, behold, thou shalt conceive in thy womb, and bring forth a son, and shalt call his name Jesus. . . . And he shall reign over the house of Jacob for ever; and of his kingdom there shall be no end (Luke 1:30–33).

Throughout all time, this divine declaration of Gabriel shall be the Magna Charta of the incarnation and the foundation stone of the world to come: God became flesh to redeem us.

3. SERAPHIM

It would appear from the Bible that celestial and extraterrestrial beings differ in rank and authority. The seraphim and cherubim follow in order after the archangel and angels. These may possibly define the angelic authority to which Peter refers when he speaks of Jesus, "Who is gone into heaven, and is on the right hand of God; angels and authorities and powers being made subject unto him" (1 Peter 3:22).

The word "seraphim" may come from the Hebrew root meaning "love" (though some think the word means "burning ones" or "nobles"). We find the seraphim only in Isaiah 6:1–6. It is an awe-inspiring sight as the worshiping prophet beholds the six-winged seraphim above the throne of the Lord. We can assume that there were several seraphim since Isaiah speaks about "each one" and "one cried unto another."

The ministry of the seraphim is to praise the name and character of God in heaven. Their ministry relates directly to God and His heavenly throne, because they are positioned above the throne—unlike the cherubim, who are beside it. Students of the Bible have not always agreed on the duties of the seraphim, but we know one thing: they are constantly glorifying God. We also learn from Isaiah 6:7 that God can use them to cleanse and purify His servants.

They were indescribably beautiful. "With two [wings] he covered his face, and with two he covered his feet, and with two he did fly" (implying that some angelic beings fly). The Scriptures do not, however, support the common belief that all angels have wings. The traditional concept of angels with wings is drawn from their ability to move instantaneously and with unlimited speed from place to place, and wings were thought to permit such limitless movement. But here in Isaiah 6 only two of the seraphim's wings were employed for flying.

The glory of the seraphim reminds us of Ezekiel's description of the four living creatures. He did not call them seraphim, but they too performed their service for God. Like seraphim they acted as both agents and spokesmen of God. In both cases the glory displayed was a witness to God, though only the seraphim, of course, hovered over the heavenly throne as functionaries and attendants, with a chief duty of praising God. In all these manifestations we see God willing that men should know of His glory. He determines to maintain an adequate witness to that glory in both terrestrial and celestial realms.

4. CHERUBIM

Cherubim are real and they are powerful. But the cherubim in the Bible were often symbolic of heavenly things. "At God's direction they were incorporated into the design of the Ark of the Covenant and the Tabernacle. Solomon's temple utilized them in its decoration" (*Zondervan Pictorial Encyclopedia*). They had wings, feet and hands. Ezekiel 10 pictures the cherubim in detail as having not only wings and hands, but being "full of eyes," encompassed by "wheels within wheels."

But Ezekiel sounds a somber note in chapter 10 also, and the cherubim provide the clue. The prophet presents his vision that prophesies the destruction of Jerusalem. In Ezekiel 9:3, the Lord has descended from His throne above the cherubim to the threshold of the temple, while in 10:1 He returns again to take His seat above them. In the calm before the storm, we see the cherubim stationed on the south side of the sanctuary. Being stationed in position toward the city, they witness the beginning of the gradual withdrawal of God's glory from Jerusalem. The fluttering of their wings indicates immensely important events to follow (10:5). Then the cherubim rise up in preparation for the departure.

While Ezekiel 10 is difficult to understand, one point comes across clearly. The cherubim have to do with the glory of God. This chapter is one of the most mysterious and yet descriptive passages of the glory of God to be found in the Bible, and it involves angelic beings. It should be read carefully and prayerfully. The reader gets a sense of God's greatness and glory as in few other passages in the Bible.

While the seraphim and the cherubim belong to different orders and are surrounded by much mystery in Scripture, they share one thing. They constantly glorify God. We see the cherubim beside the throne of God. "Thou that dwellest between the cherubim, shine forth" (Psalm 80:1). "He sitteth between the cherubim" (Psalm 99:1). God's glory will not be denied, and every heavenly being gives silent or vocal testimony to the splendor of God. In Genesis 3:24, we see cherubim guarding the tree of life in Eden. In the tabernacle in the wilderness designs representing the guardian cherubim formed a part of the mercy seat and were made of gold (Exodus 25:18).

The cherubim did more than guard the most holy place from those who had no right of access to God. They also assured the right of the high priest to enter the holy place with blood as the mediator with God on behalf of the people. He, and he alone, was permitted to enter into the inner sanctuary of the Lord. By right of redemption and in accordance with the position of believers, each true child of God now has direct access as a believer-priest to the presence of God through Jesus. Cherubim will not refuse the humblest Christian access to the throne. They assure us that we can come boldly—because of Christ's work on the cross! The veil in the temple has been rent. As Paul says, "Ye are no more strangers and foreigners, but fellow citizens with the saints, and of the household of God" (Ephesians 2:19). Further, Peter assures that "Ye are a chosen generation, a royal priesthood, an holy nation, a peculiar people; that ye should show forth the praises of him who hath called you out of darkness into his marvelous light" (1 Peter 2:9).

The inner sanctuary of God's throne is always open to those who have repented of sin and trusted Christ as Savior.

Many believe that the "living creatures" often mentioned in the book of Revelation are cherubim. But as glorious as the angelic and heavenly beings are, they become dim beside the inexpressible glory resident in our heavenly Lamb, the Lord of glory, to whom all powers in heaven and on earth bow in holy worship and breathless adoration.

6

Lucifer and the Angelic Rebellion

FEW PEOPLE REALIZE the profound part angelic forces play in human events. It is Daniel who most dramatically reveals the constant and bitter conflict between the holy angels faithful to God and the angels of darkness allied with Satan (Daniel 10:11–14). This Satan, or the devil, was once called "Lucifer, the son of the morning." Along with Michael he may have been one of the two archangels, but he was cast from heaven with his rebel forces, and continues to fight. Satan may appear to be winning the war because sometimes he wins important battles, but the final outcome is certain. One day he will be defeated and stripped of his powers eternally. God will shatter the powers of darkness.

Many people ask, "How could this conflict come about in God's perfect universe?" The apostle Paul calls it "the mystery of iniquity" (2 Thessalonians 2:7). While we have not been given as much information as we might like, we do know one thing for certain: The angels who fell, fell because they had sinned against God. In 2 Peter 2:4 the Scripture says, "God spared not the angels that sinned but cast them down to hell, and delivered them into chains of darkness, to be reserved unto judgment." Perhaps the parallel passage in Jude 6 puts the onus of responsibility more directly on the shoulders of the angels themselves. "The angels," wrote Jude, quite deliberately, "kept not their first estate, but left their own habitation."

Thus, the greatest catastrophe in the history of the universal creation was Lucifer's defiance of God and the consequent fall of perhaps one third of the angels who joined him in his wickedness.

When did it happen? Sometime between the dawn of creation and the intrusion of Satan into the Garden of Eden. The poet Dante reckoned that the fall of the rebel angels took place within twenty seconds of their creation and originated in the pride that made Lucifer unwilling to await the time when he would have perfect knowledge. Others, like Milton, put the angelic creation and fall immediately prior to the temptation of Adam and Eve in the Garden of Eden.

But the important question is not, "When were angels created?" but, "When did they fall?" It is difficult to suppose that their fall occurred before God placed Adam and Eve in the Garden. We know for a fact that God rested on the seventh day, or at the end of all creation, and pronounced everything to be good. By implication, up to this time even the angelic creation was good. We might then ask, "How long were Adam and Eve in the Garden before the angels fell and before Satan tempted the first man and woman?" This question must remain unanswered. All we can say positively is that Satan, who had fallen before he tempted Adam and Eve, was the agent and bears a greater guilt because there was no one to tempt him when he sinned; on the other hand Adam and Eve were faced with a tempter.

Thus, we pick up the story where it began. It all started mysteriously with Lucifer. He was the most brilliant and most beautiful of all created beings in heaven. He was probably the ruling prince of the universe under God, against whom he rebelled. The result was insurrection and war in heaven! He began a war that has been raging in heaven from the moment he sinned and was brought to earth shortly after the dawn of human history. It sounds like a modern world crisis!

Isaiah 14:12–14 records the conflict's origin. Prior to his rebellion, Lucifer, an angel of light, is described in scintillating terms in Ezekiel 28:12–17 (NASB): "You had the seal of perfection, full of wisdom and perfect in beauty. . . . You were the anointed cherub who covers, and I placed you there. You were on the holy mountain of God. You walked in the midst of the stones of fire. You were blameless in your ways from the day you were created, until unrighteousness was found in you. . . . Your heart was lifted up because of your beauty; you corrupted your wisdom by reason of your splendor." When the angel Lucifer rebelled against God and His works, some have estimated that as many as one third of the angelic hosts of the universe may have joined him in his rebellion. Thus, the war that started in heaven continues on earth and will see its climax at Armageddon with Christ and His angelic army victorious.

Leslie Miller in his excellent little book, *All About Angels*, points out that Scripture sometimes refers to angels as stars. This explains why prior to his fall Satan was called, "the star of the morning." And to this description John adds a qualifying detail, "His tail swept a third of the stars out of the sky and flung them to the earth" (Revelation 12:4, NIV).

Rebellion in Heaven

The apostle Paul understood and spoke of the war of rebellion in the heavens when he referred to the former Lucifer, now Satan, as "the prince of the power of the air, the spirit that now worketh in the children of disobedience" (Ephesians 2:2). He also says that in fighting the organized kingdom of satanic darkness, we struggle against "the worldforces of this darkness . . . the spiritual forces of wickedness in the heavenly places" (Ephesians 6:12, NASB).

We can describe all unrighteousness and transgression against God as "self-will" against the will of God. This definition applies to human beings today as well as to angels.

Lucifer's Five "I Wills"

Lucifer, the son of the morning, was created, as were all angels, for the purpose of glorifying God. However, instead of serving God and praising Him forever, Satan desired to rule over heaven and creation in the place of God. He wanted supreme authority! Lucifer said (Isaiah 14), "I will ascend into heaven." "I will exalt my throne above the stars of God." "I will sit also upon the mount of the congregation." "I will ascend above the heights of the clouds." "I will be like the most high." I . . . I . . . I . . . I . . . I.

Lucifer was not satisfied with being subordinated to his creator. He wanted to usurp God's throne. He exulted at the thought of being the center of power throughout the universe—he wanted to be the Caesar, the Napoleon, the Hitler of the entire universe. The "I will" spirit is the spirit of rebellion. His was a bold act to dethrone the Lord Most High. Here was a wicked schemer who saw himself occupying the superlative position of power and glory. He wanted to be worshiped, not to worship.

Satan's desire to replace God as ruler of the universe may have been rooted in a basic sin that leads to the sin of pride I have already mentioned. Underneath Satan's pride lurked the deadliest of all sins, the sin of covetousness. He wanted what did not belong to him. Virtually every war ever fought began because of covetousness. The warfare in heaven and on earth between God and the devil certainly sprang from the same desire—the lust for what belonged to God alone.

Today as always in the past, virtually no one can sin alone. The influences of sin are contagious. The Bible speaks of "the dragon . . . and his angels" (Revelation 12:7), indicating that along with Lucifer, myriads of angels also chose to deny the authority of God and subsequently lost their high position. They chose to participate in the "war program" of Lucifer. As a result of their fall, those angels have been "reserved unto judgment" (2 Peter 2:4) and have their part with Lucifer in the "everlasting fire, prepared for the devil and his angels" (Matthew 25:41). But until this happens they constitute a mighty force—capable of wreaking havoc among individuals, families and nations! Watch out, they are dangerous, vicious and deadly. They want you under their control and they will pay any price to get you!

Satan, the fallen prince of heaven, has made his decision to battle against God to the death. He is the master craftsman who has plotted destruction during all the ages since he first rebelled. His "I will" spirit has worked through his consuming hatred of God to write his tragic story in the annals of human history. In his warfare against God, Satan uses the human race, which God created and loved. So God's forces of good and Satan's forces of evil have been engaged in a deadly conflict from the dawn of our history. Unless world leaders and statesmen understand the true nature of this warfare, they will continue to be blind leaders of the blind. They can only patch a little here and patch a little there. We will find no final solution to the world's great problems until this spiritual warfare has been settled. And it will be settled in the last war of history—Armageddon. Then Christ and His angelic armies will be the victor!

Past, Present and Future in Perspective

Lucifer became Satan, the devil, the author of sin; and it is sin that has always deceived, disturbed, betrayed, depraved and destroyed all that it has touched.

Will there never be an end to this Battle of the Ages, this war against God lustfully conceived in Lucifer and perpetrated on earth?

Not only does the battle rage on earth, but it rages in heaven. "And there was war in heaven: Michael and his angels fought against the dragon; and the dragon fought and his angels . . . and the great dragon was cast out" (Revelation 12:7, 9).

Satan and his demons are known by the discord they promote, the wars they start, the hatred they engender, the murders they initiate, the opposition to God and His commandments. They are dedicated to the spirit of destruction. On the other hand the holy angels obey their Creator. No discordant note sounds among the angels of heaven. They are committed to fulfill the purpose for which all true children of God pray, "Thy kingdom come. Thy will be done . . . as it is in heaven" (Matthew 6:10).

The Bible refers to Lucifer and the fallen angels as those who sinned and did not keep their first position (Jude 6). They committed the sins of consummate pride and covetousness. The sin of pride particularly has caused the downfall of Lucifer in heaven; most certainly it can bring mortal man down too. We must be on guard against pride, or we are headed for a fall patterned after the fall of Lucifer and his angels, who turned into demons.

Could it be that God wanted to be sure that men would not question the existence of Satan and his demon-hosts? Perhaps He had this in mind when He inspired the writing of Ezekiel 28, which sets forth the typology of Satan in the earthly sense. This account by the prophet Ezekiel speaks of an earthly prince of the city of Tyre. He seems to be an earthly symbol of Satan. It is clear from the passage that the king of Tyre became a devil incarnate, and an earthly illustration of the heavenly Lucifer who became the devil.

We live in a perpetual battlefield—the great War of the Ages continues to rage. The lines of battle press in ever more tightly about God's own people. The wars among nations on earth are merely popgun affairs compared to the fierceness of battle in the spiritual, unseen world. This invisible spiritual conflict is waged around us incessantly and unremittingly. Where the Lord works, Satan's forces hinder; where angel beings carry out their divine directives, the devils rage. All this comes about because the powers of darkness press their counterattack to recapture the ground held for the glory of God.

Were it not for the angel hosts empowered by God to resist the demons of Satan, who could ever hope to press through the battlements of the fiendish demons of darkness to the Lord of eternal liberty and salvation? Paul speaks the truth when he says that the forts of darkness are impregnable. Yet they yield to the warfare of faith and light as angel hosts press the warfare to gain the victory for us (2 Corinthians 10:4, 5).

Satan on the Attack

Revelation 12:10 speaks of Satan as "the accuser of the brethren" and Ephesians 6:12 (NIV) describes the "rulers . . . authorities . . . the powers of this dark world . . . the spiritual forces of evil in the heavenly realms." Although Satan and his evil followers press their warfare in the heavens, it seems that their primary endeavor is to destroy faith in the world.

Isaiah 13:12–14 clearly points up Satan's objectives: he works to bring about the downfall of nations, to corrupt moral standards and to waste human resources. Corrupting society's order, he wants to prevent the attainment of order, and to shake the kingdoms of our God. He uses his destructive power to create havoc, fire, flood, earthquake, storm, pestilence, disease and the devastation of peoples and nations. The description of Satan's great power ends with the words, "who opened not the house of his prisoners" (Isaiah 14:17). This undoubtedly refers to the prison house of Satan, Hades or the abode of the dead so clearly pictured in Luke 16:19–31.

Satan has great power. He is cunning and clever, having set himself against God and His people. He will do everything in his power to hold people captive in sin and to drag them down to the prison of eternal separation from God.

Since the fall of Lucifer, that angel of light and son of the morning, there has been no respite in the bitter Battle of the Ages. Night and day Lucifer, the master craftsman of the devices of darkness, labors to thwart God's plan of the ages. We can find inscribed on every page of human history the consequences of the evil brought to fruition by the powers of darkness with the devil in charge. Satan never yields an inch, nor does he ever pause in his opposition to the plan of God to redeem the "cosmos" from his control. He forever tries to discredit the truthfulness of the Word of God; he coaxes men to deny the authority of God; and he persuades the world to wallow in the deluding comforts of sin. "He was a murderer from the beginning, not holding to the truth, for there is no truth in him. When he lies, he speaks his native language, for he is a liar and the father of lies" (John 8:44, NIV). Sin is the frightful fact in our world. It writes its ruin in vice and lust, in the convulsions of war, in selfishness and sorrow, and in broken hearts and lost souls. It remains as the tragedy of the universe and the tool of Satan to blunt or destroy the works of God.

Satanic Intrigue

God cannot tolerate sin forever if He is just. He will not permit the perversions of Lucifer to mock Him, for the inescapable answer to the evil of the world is found in the unalterable law of the Word of God that "the wages of sin is death; but the gift of God is eternal life through Jesus Christ our Lord" (Romans 6:23). Satan's attacks, which began at the dawn of history, will continue until God begins to bring down the curtain on this frightening drama at Armageddon.

Satan's ideology is based on the little word "if." Through all time he has sought to discredit God by making Him out a liar in the eyes of man. He never ceases trying to discredit the claims of the Word of God and to rob mankind of the strength and comfort of faith. The all-time tool of Lucifer is an "if," but God declares that there are no "ifs," "buts" or "ands" about His program for salvation. God's plan is unalterable; His antidote for the satanic "if" works and is unchangeable. God assures us that through the work of Christ and the labors of His angelic deputies we can look for the triumphant and victorious warfare over the armies of Lucifer.

It is not surprising that the fallen Lucifer hatched his plot to usurp the preeminence of God in His creation. In the first conversation in the Garden, the serpent embodying Lucifer asked, "Hath God said, Ye shall not eat of every tree of the garden?" (Genesis 3:1). To this question Eve replied, "But God did say, 'You must not eat fruit from the tree that is in the middle of the garden, and you must not touch it, or you will die" (Genesis 3:3, NIV).

Hear Lucifer reply, if you eat of the fruit of this tree "ye shall not surely die" (Genesis 3:4). He says in effect that God does not know what He is talking about. Satan often works by interjecting a question to raise doubts. It is deadly to doubt God's Word! Satan's strategy is to persuade us to rationalize. Eve probably began to reason with the enemy: Is it possible that God would be so unjust and unkind as to forbid this seemingly innocent thing?—"it was pleasant to the eyes" (Genesis 3:6).

Eve foolishly parleyed with the tempter. In her own mind she began to doubt the truth and the wisdom of God. How easily Satan covers with a light color ideas that are dark. His intrigue comes to us colored in the light of our own desires. Time after time he injects his subtle "ifs." "This tree is to be desired to make one wise." Eve listened; she reasoned with herself, she took, she tasted. Satan never fails to appeal to the appetites of the flesh and to the seeming sensual satisfactions that come from the inventions of sin.

Our senses are inlets through which Satan can work, prod and inject his deadly "ifs."

The Genesis account states that Eve ate first, and then gave some to Adam to eat. If they had fixed their minds on God and trusted His wisdom, recognizing the danger that lurked in the fruit He had forbidden, all history would have been radically different and had another ending. Had they only realized the consequences of disobedience, had they only seen the danger of the satanic "if," had they only envisioned the flaming sword barring them forever from the Garden! Had they only realized the terrible consequences of a single "innocent" moment, they would not have had to stand over the silent, lifeless form of their son Abel. His tragic death was the fruit of the seductive power of sin in their own lives. Apart from it our world would have been paradise today!

Had Adam and Eve resisted the devil, he would have fled, forever defeated. But they fell, and thus death passed upon all men (Genesis 3:13). This is where death began! Sin works the same with all of us, whatever our condition, nature or environment. We are depraved by nature because we inherited it from our parents (Romans 3:19). The stream has been polluted. We must bear the sentence of guilt and the stain of sin. Each must give account of himself to God.

Listen to Satan's "ifs" of death being injected into the minds of people today: "if" you live a good life, "if" you do what is right, "if" you go to church, "if" you work for the benefit of others—if, if, if. But the Bible teaches that these "ifs" are not enough to meet God's requirements for salvation. Our good works and intentions are not enough. Jesus said, "Ye must be born again" (John 3:7). Only when we turn to Christ in faith and trust, confessing our sins to Him and seeking His forgiveness, can we be assured of our salvation. Satan will do all in his power to make us trust ourselves instead of Christ. But only Christ can save us—and He will, if we will commit our lives to Him and trust His work on the cross for our salvation. "For God so loved the world that he gave his one and only Son, that whosoever believes in him shall not perish but have eternal life" (John 3:16, NIV).

These are Satan's approaches today. The hiss of the serpent is the "if" of death. The stench of death is everywhere today! As

C. S. Lewis points out, "War does not increase death—death is total in every generation." But we can find eternal life when we believe in Jesus Christ.

Have you made your personal commitment to Christ, and are you trusting Him alone for your salvation? If you have never taken that step of faith, or if you are unsure about your relationship to Christ, turn to Him today and receive Him as your personal Lord and Savior. "To all who received him, to those who believed in his name, he gave the right to become children of God" (John 1:12, NIV). This can be your experience today if you will ask Christ to come into your heart by faith.

7

Angels as Messengers of God

ANGELS MINISTER TO us personally. Many accounts in Scripture confirm that we are the subjects of their individual concern. In his book, *Table Talk*, Martin Luther said, "An angel is a spiritual creature created by God without a body, for the service of Christendom and the church."

We may not always be aware of the presence of angels. We can't always predict how they will appear. But angels have been said to be our neighbors. Often they may be our companions without our being aware of their presence. We know little of their constant ministry. The Bible assures us, however, that one day our eyes will be unscaled to see and know the full extent of the attention angels have given us (1 Corinthians 13:11, 12).

Many experiences of God's people suggest that angels have been ministering to them. Others may not have known they were being helped, yet the visitation was real. The Bible tells us that God has ordered angels to minister to His people—those who have been redeemed by the power of Christ's blood.

Daniel and the Angel

In the Old Testament, Daniel vividly describes the bitter conflict between the angelic forces of God and the opposing demons of darkness. Before the angel came to him he had spent three weeks mourning (Daniel 10:3). He ate no bread, meat or wine, nor did he anoint himself. As he stood by the Tigris River, a man appeared clothed in linen. His face looked like lightning and his eyes like flaming torches. His voice sounded like the roar of a crowd.

Daniel alone saw the vision. The men who were with him did not. Yet a great dread came upon them, and they ran away to hide. Left alone with the heavenly visitor, Daniel's strength departed from him, so great was the effect of this personage on him.

Daniel was held in the bonds of a great sleep, yet he heard the voice of the angel. A hand touched him and the angel described an experience he himself had just had. The angel had started to come to Daniel from the moment he began to pray, but en route was waylaid by a demon prince who engaged him in conflict and delayed him. Then Michael came to help this subordinate angel, freeing him to fulfill his mission to Daniel.

The angel had a message. He was to show Daniel what God foresaw would befall the world—especially Israel in the latter days. Daniel then found himself weak and unable to speak, so the angel touched his lips and also restored his strength. Having finished his mission, the angel told Daniel he was returning to fight with the demon prince in the unending struggle of the forces of good versus the forces of evil. In all this Daniel was having no hallucination or dream. It was a genuine experience with a real person, and no one could ever have persuaded Daniel otherwise.

He had pleaded with God for the sons of Israel. His prayer session, accompanied by fasting, had lasted for three weeks. At that moment he received the news from the "angel visitor" sent from heaven that his prayer had been heard. This incident makes it clear that delays are not denials, and that God's permissive will is involved in all of life.

Unseen Forces at Work

During several world crises I have had the privilege of talking with some heads of state or secretaries of state. During the 1967 Middle East war, for example, Secretary of State Dean Rusk, who was visiting my home town of Montreat, North Carolina, invited me to his room. While we were discussing the war that had just broken out, I told him I believed "supernatural forces are at work."

On the eve of one of his missions abroad during the Ford Administration, Secretary of State Kissinger briefed me on some of the staggering problems facing the world. I told him I believed the world was experiencing an unseen spiritual war in which the powers of darkness were attacking the forces of God. As we have moved through the turbulent events of the past decade, I have become more convinced than ever that the activities of the unseen demonic forces are increasing. A well-known television newscaster said to me in his office, "The world is out of control." It seems incredible that such a warfare is taking place—but the Bible says it is!

Dr. A. C. Gaebelein has called it "the conflict of the ages." It will be resolved only when Jesus Christ returns to earth. This is why the world is crying for "a leader." The Anti-Christ, who will be Satan's "front," will arrive on the scene for a brief time and seemingly be The Answer. But after only a few months the world will be thrown back into chaos and conflict. He will prove to be "The Lie" (2 Thessalonians 2:3–10). Then the One whom God chose and anointed before time began will return to earth with His mighty, holy angels. At the end of the age He will throw the devil and his demons into the lake of fire. Thus, for the true believer the conflict now raging will end as God intends. Righteousness will prevail.

Jacob's Experience

The experience of Jacob with angels is a splendid illustration of their ministry for God to men. In some ways Jacob was a cheat. He had stolen the birthright from his brother. He lied to his father and deceived him when his sight was almost gone. He fled from his brother, who would have killed him. He married his Uncle Laban's two daughters, and when their father and brothers no longer looked on him with favor he took his family and flocks back to Canaan.

Though Jacob was a cunning schemer and skilled in deception, God was concerned for him as the one who was in "the line of promise." From him the twelve tribes of Israel were to come. While he was en route home the Scripture tells us that "the angels of God met him." So overcome was he by what happened that he said, "This is God's army!" (verse 2, Genesis 32, AB), and called the place Mahanaim, meaning "two camps." He called the angels, "God's hosts." But the story does not end there. Having formerly cheated his brother Esau, he now feared him, not knowing whether he would be welcomed or killed. So Jacob prayed, admitting he was not worthy of the least of God's mercies. He asked to be delivered from the hand of his brother Esau.

The night before Jacob met Esau he was alone, his family and servants having gone ahead. Suddenly a man appeared and wrestled with him until daybreak, when he finally touched Jacob's thigh, "and the hollow of the thigh was out of joint." At this, Jacob realized the man was a heavenly visitor, and would not let him go until the man had blessed him. When he had told the stranger his name, the man said, "Thy name shall be called no more Jacob, but Israel: for as a prince hast thou power with God and with men and hast prevailed." When Jacob asked the man to identify himself, he received no reply. But the man blessed him there. Jacob called the place Peniel, meaning "face of God" saying, "I have seen God face to face, and my life is preserved" (Genesis 32:24–30).

It may well be that the wrestler was Jesus, appearing fleetingly in human form. In the former part of the story many angels were surrounding Jacob. Through the two experiences, God revealed His will for Jacob's life more fully, and promised that he would be a prince. The next day he therefore went forward cheerfully to meet Esau; everything turned out well for him and his family. Centuries later Hosea testified to this incident, saying that the God of heaven had appeared to Jacob, ministering to him in the person of an angel (Hosea 12:3–6).

Moses and Abraham are perhaps the two greatest Old Testament characters; angels were involved in their lives on important occasions. We have already seen how angels ministered to Abraham. We must look at the experience of Moses at the burning bush (Exodus 3).

Moses Meets an Angel

The background is important. For forty years Moses had lived amid the splendors of Egypt, coming to know its language, customs and laws. He lived a life of luxury and occupied an impor-

tant position in the social structure. Then because of the misad-
venture of slaying an Egyptian he fled to the desert. For forty years
more he was tutored as a sheepherder in the "university of solitude." Scripture says little about that period, but it represented a
great change in circumstances to go from the court of Pharaoh to
a field of grazing sheep. It was not exactly an occupation that
ranked high in the social order. He was an outcast, a lonely figure
compared to his former life. And it took God forty years to bring
him to the place where he was serviceable for the job God had in
mind for him. So it was that at eighty years of age when the life
work of most people has already been completed, Moses was ready
for God's call.

One day as he was going about his duties, Moses saw a bush
burning. It struck him as peculiar because the bush was not consumed. More than that, "the angel of the Lord appeared to him in
a flame of fire out of the midst of the bush." Since we have no
reason to suppose that Moses had ever seen an angel before, this
must have been an extraordinary visitation to him. Further, his
curiosity was aroused. Then it was that God Himself spoke to
Moses out of the bush.

Moses was profoundly moved. Having told him to remove his
shoes because he was standing on holy ground, God identified
Himself as the God of Abraham, Isaac and Jacob. At this Moses
was awestruck, and hid his face, fearing to look at God. God then
disclosed to Moses His plan to release the Israelites from their
captivity in Egypt, using Moses as their leader. When asked by
Moses whom he should say had told him this when he approached
the Israelites, God responded, "Say I AM hath sent me unto you."

Moses was not at all enthusiastic about what God told him to
do. He began to offer what he thought were compelling reasons
to be excused from that service. First he said that the people of
Israel would never believe him, and therefore would not accept his
leadership. In answer, God asked him what he had in his hand.
Moses said, "a rod." "Cast it on the ground," God said, and suddenly it became a serpent. But when Moses picked it up, it again
became a rod. Then at God's command he put his hand in his robe,
and withdrawing it found it leprous. But putting it back a second
time and withdrawing it, he found it free of all disease. By such

signs, God said, would He show the people Moses' divine commission.

Then Moses made another excuse: He said he couldn't talk, professing to be slow of speech. Perhaps this was the result of forty years in virtual silence on the backside of the desert, but God even refused this excuse, saying He would send Aaron to be his voice. And so Moses went from the desert to Egypt to begin the work of deliverance. But the incident is important in our study because it is tied closely to the angel of the Lord in the burning bush. This again shows that God used angels (or appeared as an angel) to make His will known and communicate His decisions to men.

The presence of angels became part of "the Exodus experience." Thus, in Numbers 20:16 the Bible says, "When we cried unto the Lord, he heard our voice, and sent an angel, and hath brought us forth out of Egypt." Isaiah says that "In all their affliction he was afflicted, and the angel of his presence saved them: in his love and in his pity he redeemed them; and he bare them, and carried them all the days of old" (63:9). It may well be that some of these instances involved angelic forms taken by Jesus Christ, the second person of the Trinity. We can only speculate. In that event, it makes alive the thrilling testimony of Paul who declared that "Jesus Christ [is] the same yesterday, and today, and forever" (Hebrews 13:8).

The Mystery of Angels

Therefore, just as Jesus is with us now through the Holy Spirit, revealing Himself and His will, so was He with His people in ages past, and so shall He be for all time to come, the angel of God's presence who leads us. To His "faithful" of past ages, God the Father revealed His presence through angels; through the angel of the Lord, God the Son, Jesus Christ, He revealed Himself and redeemed us by the Son's crucifixion, death and resurrection. Here is mystery too deep for any of us to fathom fully.

Jewish scholars called the angel of the Lord by the name, "Metatron," "the angel of countenance," because He witnesses the countenance of God continuously and, therefore, works to extend the program of God for each of us.

God has given us the fullest revelation—Jesus Christ in the flesh—so He no longer needs to manifest Himself in the form of "the angel of the Lord" in this age of grace. Consequently, the angels who appear in the New Testament or even today are always "created spirits" and not God in that special angel form He used now and then in the Old Testament. The appearance of God the Son in physical form (a theophany) in the Old Testament is no longer necessary. Consider the presence of angels in the New Testament subsequent to the thrilling account of the birth of God the Son in the flesh through His incarnation at Bethlehem. The angels then were to minister the message of God and to establish the message of the gospel of Christ, but never to supplant it or to detract from it.

Angels Are Ministering Spirits

God uses both men and angels to declare His message to those who have been saved by grace. "Are they [angels] not all ministering spirits, sent forth to minister for them who shall be heirs of salvation?" (Hebrews 1:14.) What a glorious honor it will be for angels to know us by name because of our faithful witness to others. Angels will share our rejoicing over those who repent (Luke 15:10), even though they cannot preach the gospel themselves.

In this regard, consider Philip the deacon, whom God was using as a minister of revival in Samaria. An angel appeared with instructions for him to go to the desert (Acts 8:26), and by God's appointment he met the Ethiopian to whom he became the voice for God in preaching the word of truth.

Angels visited John, too. As he looked out upon the lonely seas from the Isle of Patmos and wondered why he was isolated from all but heaven, the angel of the apocalypse came to announce the message that formed the book of Revelation with its prophecies of the end time (Revelation 1:1–3).

An angel ministered in a somewhat similar way in an incident in Daniel's life. Chapter 5 describes a great feast ordered by Belshazzar in Babylon. It had been prepared ostensibly to show the glory of the kingdom, but in reality Belshazzar meant it to parade his own personal greatness. It was a feast for the thousands of his kingdom's greatest nobles. But on this occasion they desecrated the sacred vessels taken from the Temple at Jerusalem by using them for an ignoble purpose: They ate, drank and offered homage to idols of wood and stone, silver and gold. The god of materialism was in power. Suddenly the fingers of a man's hand appeared and traced on the wall a record of God's judgment on Babylon. "Mene, Mene, Tekel, Upharsin," the hand wrote—"You have been weighed in the balances and been found wanting. Your kingdom is finished" (verses 25–27). It was one of God's angels sent to announce the impending judgment. Not only were the days of King Belshazzar numbered, but God was finished with him.

Later Daniel prayed for the people, "And he [Gabriel] informed me, and talked with me, and said, O Daniel, I am now come forth to give thee skill and understanding. . . . therefore, understand the matter, and consider the vision" (Daniel 9:22–23). In answer to Daniel's prayer, God gave him a panoramic view of the future "history" of the human race. It is my belief that the world is now possibly reaching the climax of those great visions that God gave Daniel.

The scene in the time of Belshazzar seems almost contemporary, those times and conditions resembling so closely what we see and hear today. It may even be that God is writing another story of impending judgment through the crises of the hour. He is telling men everywhere that unless they repent for their sins, their days like Belshazzar's are numbered and they are finished.

Let us conclude this study of the personal ministry of angels by noting some further incidents when God used angels to declare His plan to men.

The Angel Gabriel

At the beginning of the New Testament, Zacharias the priest saw the angel of the Lord, receiving from him the message that proclaimed the birth of John, who was to prepare the way for the promised Messiah. The angel (Gabriel in this instance, a special angelic minister of promise) encouraged Zacharias to believe the miracle surrounding the birth of John.

Later Gabriel appeared to the Virgin Mary, announcing to her the divinely conceived plan of the incarnation by which God's Son, Jesus Christ, should be conceived miraculously in her womb by the power of the Holy Spirit. Whatever Mary's questions may have been, they were answered by the angel's witness, "The Holy Ghost shall come upon thee, and the power of the Highest shall over-shadow thee: therefore also that holy thing which shall be born of thee shall be called the Son of God" (Luke 1:35). Not only did Gabriel, the special angel of ministry and revelation, bring this message to Mary, but either he or another angel also confirmed to Joseph that he should take Mary as his wife, "For that which is conceived in her is of the Holy Ghost" (Matthew 1:20). He also told Joseph the plan of God that Jesus should "save his people from their sins" (Matthew 1:21).

The special angels of proclamation having faithfully bridged the centuries, carrying the message of God's will in times of oppression, discouragement and waning endurance. God's restoring servants, His heavenly messengers, have encouraged, sustained and lifted the spirits of many flagging saints; and they have changed many hopeless circumstances into bright prospect. Angels have ministered the message, "All is well," to satisfy fully the physical, material, emotional and spiritual needs of His people. They could testify, "The angel of the Lord came unto me."

8

Angels Protect and Deliver Us

THE ENEMIES OF Christ who attack us incessantly would often be thwarted if we could grasp God's assurance that His mighty angels are always nearby, ready to help. Tragically, most Christians have failed to accept this fact so frequently expressed in the Bible. I have noticed, though, that in my travels the closer I get to the frontiers of the Christian faith the more faith in angels I find among believers. Hundreds of stories document extraordinary divine intervention every year: God is using His angels as ministering spirits.

Angels Are Divine Protectors

God's angels often protect His servants from potential enemies. Consider 2 Kings 6:14–17. The king of Syria had dispatched his army to Dothan, learning that Elisha the prophet was there. Upon dressing in the morning, the prophet's helper exclaimed excitedly to Elisha that the surrounding countryside bristled with armies and implements of war. Elisha assured him, "Don't be afraid! . . . our army is bigger than theirs" (verse 16, TLB). Elisha then prayed that God would open the eyes of the young man to see the hosts of protective angels: as He did so, the young man "could see horses and chariots of fire everywhere on the hills surrounding the city."

This passage has been one of the great assurances and comforts to me in my ministry.

The angels minister to God's servants in time of hardship and danger. We find another outstanding illustration of this in Acts 27:23–25. Paul on his way to Rome faced shipwreck with more than two hundred others on board. Speaking to the fear-ridden crew he said, "Last night an angel of the God whose I am and whom I serve, stood beside me and said, 'Do not be afraid, Paul. You must stand trial before Caesar; and God has graciously given you the lives of all who sail with you'" (verses 23, 24, NIV).

Some believe strongly that each Christian may have his own guardian angel assigned to watch over him or her. This guardianship possibly begins in infancy, for Jesus said, "See that you do not look down on one of these little ones. For I tell you that their angels in heaven always see the face of my Father in heaven" (Matthew 18:10).

Angels at Work for Us

The most important characteristic of angels is not that they have power to exercise control over our lives, or that they are beautiful, but that they work on our behalf. They are motivated by an inexhaustible love for God and are jealous to see that the will of God in Jesus Christ is fulfilled in us.

David says of angels, "He who dwelleth in the secret place of the Most High shall abide under the shadow of the Almighty. . . . For he shall give his angels charge over thee, to keep thee in all thy ways. They shall bear thee up . . . lest thou dash thy foot against a stone" (Psalm 91:1,11,12).

My wife, Ruth, tells of a strange incident in a Christian bookroom in Shanghai, China. She learned of it through her father, the late Dr. L. Nelson Bell, who served in the hospital in Tsingkiangpu, Kiangsu province. It was at this store that Dr. Bell bought his gospel portions and tracts to distribute among his patients.

The incident occurred in 1942, after the Japanese had won control of certain areas of China. One morning around nine o'clock, a Japanese truck stopped outside the bookroom. It was carrying five marines and was half-filled with books. The Christian Chinese shop assistant, who was alone at the time, realized with dismay that they had come to seize the stock. By nature timid, he felt this was more than he could endure.

Jumping from the truck, the marines made for the shop door; but before they could enter, a neatly dressed Chinese gentleman entered the shop ahead of them. Though the shop assistant knew practically all the Chinese customers who traded there, this man was a complete stranger. For some unknown reason the soldiers seemed unable to follow him, and loitered about, looking in at the four large windows, but not entering. For two hours they stood around, until after eleven, but never set foot inside the door. The stranger asked what the men wanted, and the Chinese shop assistant explained that the Japanese were seizing stocks from many of the bookshops in the city, and now this store's turn had come. The two prayed together, the stranger encouraging him, and so the two hours passed. At last the soldiers climbed into their truck and drove away. The stranger also left, without making a single purchase or even inquiring about any items in the shop.

Later that day the shop owner, Mr. Christopher Willis (whose Chinese name was Lee), returned. The shop assistant said to him, "Mr. Lee, do you believe in angels?"

"I do," said Mr. Willis.

"So do I, Mr. Lee." Could the stranger have been one of God's protecting angels? Dr. Bell always thought so.

Corrie ten Boom writes of a remarkable experience at the terrible Nazi Ravensbruck prison camp:

"Together we entered the terrifying building. At a table were women who took away all our possessions. Everyone had to undress completely and then go to a room where her hair was checked.

"I asked a woman who was busy checking the possessions of the new arrivals if I might use the toilet. She pointed to a door, and I discovered that the convenience was nothing more than a hole in the shower-room floor. Betsie stayed close beside me all the time. Suddenly I had an inspiration, 'Quick, take off your woolen underwear,' I whispered to her. I rolled it up with mine and laid the bundle in a corner with my little Bible. The spot was alive with cockroaches, but I didn't worry about that. I felt wonderfully relieved and happy. 'The Lord is busy answering our prayers, Betsie,' I whispered. 'We shall not have to make the sacrifice of all our clothes.'

"We hurried back to the row of women waiting to be undressed. A little later, after we had had our showers and put on our shirts and shabby dresses, I hid the roll of underwear and my Bible under my dress. It did bulge out obviously through my dress; but I prayed, 'Lord, cause now Thine angels to surround me; and let them not be transparent today, for the guards must not see me.' I felt perfectly at ease. Calmly I passed the guards. Everyone was checked, from the front, the sides, the back. Not a bulge escaped the eyes of the guard. The woman just in front of me had hidden a woolen vest under her dress; it was taken from her. They let me pass, for they did not see me. Betsie, right behind me, was searched.

"But outside awaited another danger. On each side of the door were women who looked everyone over for a second time. They felt over the body of each one who passed. I knew they would not see me, for the angels were still surrounding me. I was not even surprised when they passed me by; but within me rose the jubilant cry, 'O Lord, if Thou dost so answer prayer, I can face even Ravensbruck unafraid.'"

Divine Surveillance

Every true believer in Christ should be encouraged and strengthened! Angels are watching; they mark our path. They superintend the events of our lives and protect the interest of the Lord God, always working to promote His plans and to bring about His highest will for us. Angels are interested spectators and mark all we do, "for we are made a spectacle unto the world, and to angels, and to men" (1 Corinthians 4:9). God assigns angelic powers to watch over us.

Hagar, Sarah's maid, had fled from the tents of Abraham. It is ironic that Abraham, after having scaled such glorious heights of faith, should have capitulated to his wife's conniving and scolding, and to the custom of that day, to father a child by Hagar. And it is ironic that Sarah his wife should have been so jealous that when their own son, Isaac, was born years later, she wanted to get rid of both Hagar and the earlier child, Ishmael. So Abraham's self-indulgence led to sorrow and he thrust Hagar out of his home.

Nonetheless, God sent His angel to minister to Hagar. "And the angel of the Lord found her by a fountain of water in the wilderness, by the fountain in the way to Shur" (Genesis 16:7). The angel spoke as an oracle of God, turning her mind away from the injury of the past with a promise of what she might expect if she placed her faith in God. This God is the God not only of Israel but the God of the Arab as well (for the Arabs come from the stock of Ishmael). The very name of her son, Ishmael, meaning "God hears," was a sustaining one. God promised that the seed of Ishmael would multiply, and that his destiny would be great on the earth as he now undertook the restless pilgrimage that was to characterize his descendants. The angel of the Lord revealed himself as the protector of Hagar and Ishmael. Hagar in awe exclaimed, "Thou God seest me" (Genesis 16:13), or as it may be better translated, "I have seen Thou who seest all and who sees me."

Psalm 34:7 underscores the teaching that angels protect and deliver us, "The angel of the Lord encampeth round about those who fear him, and delivereth them." We also find this idea reflected in one of Charles Wesley's songs:

> Angels, where ere we go,
> Attend our steps whate'er betide.
> With watchful care their charge attend,
> And evil turn aside.

Miraculous Deliveries

The great majority of Christians can recall some incident in which their lives, in times of critical danger, have been miraculously preserved—an almost plane crash, a near car wreck, a fierce temptation. Though they may have seen no angels, their presence could explain why tragedy was averted. We should always be grateful for the goodness of God, who uses these wonderful friends called angels to protect us. Evidence from Scripture as well as personal experience confirms to us that individual guardian, guiding angels attend at least some of our ways and hover protectively over our lives.

The Scriptures are full of dramatic evidences of the protective care of angels in their earthly service to the people of God. Paul admonished Christians to put on all the armor of God that they may stand firmly in the face of evil (Ephesians 6:10–12). Our struggle is not against flesh and blood (physical powers alone), but against the spiritual (superhuman) forces of wickedness in heavenly spheres. Satan, the prince of the power of the air, promotes a "religion" but not true faith; he promotes false prophets. So the powers of light and darkness are locked in intense conflict. Thank God for the angelic forces that fight off the works of darkness. Angels never minister selfishly; they serve so that all glory may be given to God as believers are strengthened. A classic example of the protective agency of angels is found in Acts 12:5–11.

As the scene opened, Peter lay bound in prison awaiting execution. James, the brother of John, had already been killed, and there was little reason to suppose that Peter would escape the executioner's axe either. The magistrates intended to put him to death as a favor to those who opposed the gospel and the works of God. Surely the believers had prayed for James, but God had chosen to deliver him through death. Now the church was praying for Peter.

As Peter lay sleeping an angel appeared, not deterred by such things as doors or iron bars. The angel came into the prison cell, shook Peter awake and told him to prepare to escape. As a light shone in the prison Peter's chains fell off, and having dressed, he followed the angel out. Doors supernaturally opened because Peter could not pass through locked doors as the angel had. What a mighty deliverance God achieved through His angel!

Angelic Intervention

Many experiences in both Old and New Testaments grew out of the imprisonment of God's saints, calling either for God to deliver directly, or to intervene through angels acting in His name. Many today who are captive in the chains of depression can take courage to believe in the prospect of deliverance. God has no favorites and declares that angels will minister to all the heirs of faith. If we, the sons of God, would only realize how close His ministering angels are, what calm assurance we could have in facing the cataclysms of life. While we do not place our faith directly in angels, we should place it in the God who rules the angels; then we can have peace.

Hebrews 11 contains a long list of men and women of faith. For most of them God performed miracles, delivering them from disease, calamity, accidents and even death. Someone has called this chapter, "God's Hall of Fame." Angels helped these great men and women to subdue kingdoms, obtain promises, stop the mouths of lions, quench the violence of fire, escape the edge of the sword, and when they were weak, stand with the help of angels to defeat entire armies.

But the tempo changes in verse 35, with the opening words, "and others were tortured, not accepting deliverance." Those now mentioned were of equal faith and courage: they had to endure the trial of cruel mockings and scourgings. They suffered bonds and imprisonment. They were stoned, they were sawn asunder, they were slain with the sword. They wandered about in goatskins, being destitute, afflicted and tormented. Time after time they must have called on God to send His mighty angels to help. No delivering angel came. They suffered and endured almost as though there were no God.

God's Winners

Why? We find a clue when our Lord faced Calvary as He prayed, "If it be possible let this cup pass from me" (Matthew 26:39); but then He added, "nevertheless not my will, but thine, be done" (Luke 22:42). In the sufferings and death of these great saints not physically delivered, God had a mysterious plan, and was performing His will. Knowing this, they suffered and died *by faith*. This latter part of Hebrews 11 indicates that those who received no visible help in answer to prayer will have a far greater heavenly reward because they endured by "faith" alone. But having died, they did enjoy the ministry of angels who then escorted their immortal souls to the throne of God. If the first part of Hebrews 11 is called "God's Hall of Fame," the second should be called, "God's Winners of the Medal of Honor."

Once when I was going through a dark period I prayed and prayed, but the heavens seemed to be brass. I felt as though God had disappeared and that I was all alone with my trial and burden. It was a dark night for my soul. I wrote my mother about the experience, and will never forget her reply: "Son, there are many times when God withdraws to test your faith. He wants you to trust Him in the darkness. Now, Son, reach up by faith in the fog and you will find that His hand will be there." In tears I knelt by my bed and experienced an overwhelming sense of God's presence. Whether or not we sense and feel the presence of the Holy Spirit or one of the holy angels, by faith we are certain God will never leave us nor forsake us.

9

Angels—God's Agents in Judgment

THE BIBLE SAYS that throughout history angels have worked to carry out God's judgments, directing the destinies of nations disobedient to God. For example, God used angels in scattering the people of Israel because of their sins. He also used angels in bringing judgment on Sodom and Gomorrah, and eventually on Babylon and Nineveh. Further, at "the end of the age" angels will execute judgment on those who have rejected God's love.

The writer of Hebrews speaks of angelic forces as executors of God's judgments: "Who maketh his angels spirits, and his ministers a flame of fire" (Hebrews 1:7). The flaming fire suggests how awful are the judgments of God and how burning is the power of the angels who carry out God's decisions. Angels administer judgment in accord with God's principles of righteousness.

Unknown to men they have undoubtedly in the past helped destroy evil systems like Nazism, because those governments came to the place where God could no longer withhold His hand. These same angels will carry out fearful judgments in the future, some of which the book of Revelation vividly describes.

We often get false notions about angels from plays given by Sunday school children at Christmas. It is true that angels are ministering spirits sent to help the heirs of salvation. But just as they fulfill God's will in salvation for believers in Jesus Christ, so they are also "avengers" who use their great power to fulfill God's will in judgment. God has empowered them to separate the sheep from the goats, the wheat from the chaff, and one of them will blow the trumpet that announces impending judgment when God summons the nations to stand before Him in the last great judgment.

Angels Warn of Judgment

In the case of Sodom and Gomorrah, there was no way judgment could be averted. Their wickedness had become too great. God had judged them; they had to be destroyed. But before God sends judgment, He warns. In this case, He used angels to point out to Abraham the approaching doom of Sodom and Gomorrah for their wickedness (Genesis 18). Abraham, whose nephew, Lot, and his family lived among these wicked people, began to plead with God to spare the two cities. Abraham asked God if He would avert judgment if fifty righteous people lived in Sodom. God told Abraham He would not destroy the city if there were fifty such people. Then Abraham asked for a stay of execution if there were only forty-five righteous people. God agreed. Then Abraham asked for deliverance if there were thirty righteous people. God agreed. Abraham then asked for twenty; then for ten. God agreed to withhold judgment if as many as ten righteous people could be found in Sodom. But not even ten such people lived there. Notice that God answered Abraham every time he asked. And He did not leave off answering until Abraham left off asking.

After this, God ordered the angelic ministers of judgment to rain destruction on these two wicked cities and all their inhabitants. Prior to the destruction of the cities, however, two unidentified heavenly messengers visited Sodom to warn Lot and his family to flee from the wrath about to come. So evil were the inhabitants of Sodom that they wanted to molest the angels physically. The angels blinded them and prevented them from carrying out their iniquitous conduct. In his book, *All About Angels*, C. Leslie Miller states, "It is significant that although Lot, Abraham's nephew, had drifted far from the holy standards of his uncle and had sought the companionship and material benefits of an unholy alliance, yet the angels of the Lord were there to spare his life and assist him in avoiding the consequences of his own poor judgment."

Thus, we see something of the mercy, grace and love of God

toward even those who profess His name and try sincerely to live a God-honoring life in the midst of the most difficult circumstances.

The Angel Who Destroyed the Assyrian Army

In 2 Kings 19, Scripture dramatically underscores God's use of angels to execute His judgments. King Hezekiah had received a letter from the commander of the Assyrian forces and immediately sought God's counsel. God gave Isaiah the answer, saying that not one Assyrian arrow would be fired into the city. He promised to defend Jerusalem on that occasion for David's sake. Dramatically, that night, just one angel struck the Assyrian encampment and 185,000 soldiers were found dead on the field of battle the next morning (verse 35).

The Angel Who Almost Destroyed Jerusalem

Nowhere in the Old Testament is there a more significant use of angelic power in judgment against God's own people than when David defied God's command by numbering Israel. God sent a pestilence among the Israelites and 70,000 died. He also sent a single angel to destroy the city of Jerusalem. David "saw the angel of the Lord stand between the earth and the heaven, having a drawn sword in his hand stretched out over Jerusalem" (1 Chronicles 21:16).

When David pleaded for mercy, the angel told him to set up an altar on the threshing floor of Araunah the Jebusite. God then accepted David's sacrifice there and said to the destroying angel, "It is enough: stay now thine hand" (2 Samuel 24:16). The Scripture significantly says that the same angel had already slain the 70,000 men (verse 17). Indeed angels are God's agents in judgment.

New Testament history also records incidents where avenging angels judged the unrighteous acts of men and nations.

The Angel Who Smote Herod Agrippa

We have already referred to the case of Herod. Dressed in his royal apparel, he appeared before the people to make a speech.

When he finished the people shouted, "It is the voice of a god, and not of a man" (Acts 12:22). Instead of disclaiming any such thing Herod delighted in the impact he had made. God's response to this idolatrous act was prompt, and for Herod, disastrous. "Because he gave not God the glory," he "was eaten of worms, and gave up the ghost" (verse 23). "The angel of the Lord smote him."

The Angel Who Destroyed the Egyptian First Born

One fateful night in Egypt just before the Exodus, the destroying angel was about to sweep over the land with a visitation of death (Exodus 12:18–30). How deeply must anxiety have etched itself upon the hearts of the Israelites. Believing Jews had offered sacrifices and generously sprinkled the blood over doorposts and lintels of their homes. Then in accord with God's time schedule, judgment fell on Egypt as the dark and awesome moment of midnight arrived. The destroying angel (1 Corinthians 10:10; Hebrews 11:28) was God's minister of judgment, leaving death in his wake. The first born of every unbelieving Egyptian or Israeli household died under the judgment of a holy God who, however, had respect for the blood.

Down through the centuries this heart-rending account has been the theme of Jews and Christians alike: "When I see the blood, I will pass over you." It has been the text of thousands of sermons by rabbis and Christian clergymen. It was not the quality of life of the people in the blood-sprinkled houses that counted. It was their faith, apart from works, that they showed by sprinkling the blood. God had respect for only one thing: the blood sprinkled by faith.

How fearful it is to have these mighty angels carry out the judgments of an all-powerful God.

The Angel Who Stopped Abraham

In Genesis 22, God, wanting to test the reality of Abraham's faith, told him to sacrifice his beloved "son of promise," Isaac. God said, "Abraham . . . take now thy son, thine only son Isaac, whom thou lovest, and get thee into the land of Moriah; and offer him there for a burnt offering upon one of the mountains which I will tell thee of" (Genesis 22:1–2). What great suffering must have haunted and hurt the heart of Abraham through the long night as he considered what this supreme sacrifice entailed. Nevertheless, with nothing to go on but God's Word, Abraham by sheer, naked faith took fire, wood and his son, and set off to do God's bidding. The Bible records no greater act of faith.

Having prepared the altar, Abraham placed Isaac, bound hand and foot, on the altar; then, unsheathing his knife, he raised his face toward the heaven in submission to the Father's will. As Abraham lifted the knife in the air to plunge it into the heart of Isaac, "the angel of the Lord called unto him out of heaven, and said, Abraham, Abraham . . . Lay not thine hand upon the lad, neither do thou any thing unto him; for now I know that thou fearest God, seeing thou hast not withheld thy son, thine only son from me" (Genesis 22:11–12).

The double use of the name always implies the importance of the message about to be given. When he heard his name called, faithful Abraham responded immediately, and God rewarded him for his unqualified obedience. "Abraham lifted up his eyes, and looked, and, behold, behind him a ram caught in a thicket by his horns: and Abraham went and took the ram, and offered him up for a burnt offering in the stead of his son" (Genesis 22:13).

Many scholars believe, as I do, that the angel here is a "theophany," an appearance of the Lord Jesus Christ Himself. He assumed the role of an angel and God showed the principle of substitutionary atonement: God had demanded of Abraham the death of his son. The demand for the burnt offering had to be met, and it was met. But in the place of Isaac, God through an angel accepted the animal substitute. That same principle applies to us. True judgment demands that we die. And the judgment must be executed. But Jesus Christ Himself was the substitute offering. He died so that we do not have to die. He took our place so that the words used here, "in the stead of," can be wonderfully applied to every person who trusts in Christ. He died "in the stead of" all who believe on Him.

How could God have asked for a human sacrifice? How could He have asked Abraham to slay Isaac when He had forbidden the killing of people (Genesis 9:6)? Is not this inconsistent with the nature of God? He gives us the answer to these questions about judgment by death in the Epistle to the Romans. "He that spared not his own Son, but delivered him up for us all, how shall he not with him also freely give us all things?" (Romans 8:32). God could ask Abraham to slay Isaac because He Himself was willing to let His own Son die. He was not asking Abraham to do anything more than He was willing to do with His only begotten Son.

Neither Abraham nor Isaac had to drink the cup God presented. Isaac did not die and Abraham did not slay him. But when we come to another cup in the Garden of Gethsemane, the picture is startlingly different. Jesus has now come; as the guiltless one for the guilty, as the sinless one for sinners, He was willing to accept the condemnation of God for the world's guilt, identifying Himself with it through His own death on Calvary.

Neither man nor angel could ever understand what was implied in the "cup" Jesus took in the Garden of Gethsemane that was to lead to His awful suffering, condemnation and death (Mark 14:36; Luke 22:42). In the Garden as He wrestled over the cup He was to drink, no ministering angel could spare Him from it or alleviate His suffering. It was His and His alone. It settled down on the Savior as a cup of judgment He accepted and took upon Himself as the righteous one bearing the guilt of the wicked. The angels would have helped Him in that hour, but Christ did not call for their help. This one who said No to angel help said, in effect, "I will die for the sins of men because I love them so much." And in dying He was forsaken by men, by angels, and by the Father who is of purer eyes than to look upon sin and who in His Son's atoning agony turned His face from Him. That is why Jesus cried from the cross, "My God, my God, why hast thou forsaken me?" (Matthew 27:46). He died alone. Angels were ready to rescue Him, but He refused.

Angels and Those Who Reject Jesus

It is clear in Scripture that angels will be God's emissaries to carry out His judgment against those who deliberately reject Jesus Christ and the salvation God offers through Him. While all men

are sinners by nature, choice and practice, yet it is their deliberate rejection of Jesus Christ as Savior and Lord that causes the
judgment of eternal separation from God.

God has assigned angels at the end of the age to separate the
sheep from the goats, the wheat from the tares, the saved from the
lost. We are not called upon to obey the voice of angels. But we
are to heed and obey the Word of God and the voice of God that
calls upon us to be reconciled to Him by faith in Jesus Christ. If
not, we will have to pay the penalty of unforgiven sin. The angels
will administer that penalty. They "shall cast them into the furnace of fire" (Matthew 13:50). I am constantly astounded that
God's decrees and warnings are considered so lightly in our modern world—even among Christians.

Angels and Eternal Life

Every son of Adam's race is confronted with two ways of life:
one, to eternal life; the other, to eternal death. We have seen how
angels execute God's judgment on those who reject Jesus; the
angels cast them into the furnace of fire. But there is a totally different judgment: It is the good and wonderful judgment unto everlasting life. God gives the angels a place in this too. He commis-
sions them to escort each believer to heaven and to give him a
royal welcome as he enters the eternal presence of God. Each of
us who trusts Christ will witness the rejoicing of angelic hosts
around the throne of God.

In the story of the rich man and Lazarus (Luke 16), Jesus told of
a beggar who died in the faith. He had never owned many of this
world's goods, but he was rich in faith that counts for eternity.
When he died he was "carried by the angels into Abraham's
bosom." Here were angelic pallbearers who took his immortal
spirit to the place of glory where he was to be eternally with God—
the place the Bible calls "heaven."

Another beautiful account of this kind comes from the life of
the martyr Stephen (Acts 6:8–7:60). The "council, looking
stedfastly on him, saw his face as it had been the face of an angel."
Then Stephen in a powerful sermon declared that even unbelievers "received the law by the disposition of angels, and have not

kept it" (Acts 7:53). When he had finished his discourse Stephen saw the glory of God and Jesus at the Father's right hand. Immediately his enemies stoned him to death and he was received into heaven. Even as the angels escorted Lazarus when he died, so we can assume that they escorted Stephen; and so they will escort us when by death we are summoned into the presence of Christ. We can well imagine what Stephen's abundant entrance to heaven was like as the anthems of the heavenly host were sung in rejoicing that the first Christian martyr had come home to receive a glorious welcome and to gain the crown of a martyr.

Do you fear the judgment of God? Or do you know that Christ has taken your judgment upon Himself by His death on the cross? When you know Christ you need not fear God's judgment, for He has fully and completely purchased your salvation. Don't delay your decision for Christ, but open your heart to Him and you too will know the joy of sharing in His fellowship throughout all eternity in heaven.

10

Angels and the Gospel

WHILE GOD HAS delegated angels to make special pro-
nouncements for Him, He has not given them the privilege of
proclaiming the gospel message. Why this is so, Scripture does not
say. Perhaps spirit-beings who have never experienced the effects
of separation from fellowship with God because of sin would be
unable to preach with understanding.

But notice what the writer says in "Holy, Holy Is What the
Angels Sing:"

> Holy, Holy is what the angels sing,
> And I expect to help them make the
>   courts of heaven ring.
> And when I sing redemption's story,
> They will fold their wings,
> For angels never felt the joy
>   that our salvation brings.

Down through the ages man's heart has remained unchanged.
Whatever the color of his skin, whatever his cultural or ethnic
background, he needs the gospel of Christ. But who has God
ordained to bring that gospel to fallen men? Fallen angels cannot
do it; they cannot even be saved from their own sins. Yet unfallen

angels cannot preach the gospel either. Presumably they do not hear the gospel the way we do; in their purity they have escaped the effects of sin and are unable to comprehend what it means to be lost.

Rather, God has commanded the church to preach. This great task is reserved to believers. God has no other means. Only man can speak salvation's experience to man.

God has, however, assigned angels to assist those who preach. Their assistance includes the use of miraculous and corroborating signs. Missionaries of the eighteenth and nineteenth centuries have reported many wonderful incidents where angels seemed to help them proclaim the gospel. My wife, whose parents were missionaries to China, can remember many instances in her life where angels must have intervened in the ministry of her father and his fellow missionaries.

At any rate, you and I have the privilege of conveying a message to men from God in heaven, a message that angels cannot speak. Think of that! The story is told of a question asked of God: "In the event that men fail to preach the gospel as you have commanded, what other plan have you in mind?" "I have no other plan," He said.

No angel can be an evangelist. No angel can pastor a church, although angels watch over particular churches. No angel can do counseling. No angel can enjoy sonship in Jesus or be partaker of the divine nature or become a joint heir with Jesus in His kingdom. You and I are a unique and royal priesthood in the universe, and we have privileges that even angels cannot experience.

The Angel and Zacharias

The birth of John the Baptist was dynamically connected with the "evangel" (a term meaning the gospel, the good news of God's salvation in Jesus Christ). His parents, Zacharias and Elizabeth, were both old, Elizabeth being beyond the age to bear children. She and her husband were descendants of Aaron and thus connected with the priesthood. Both walked blameless before the Lord and kept His commandments. They illustrate how God works through godly parents; not infrequently we find that some of His greatest servants have enjoyed the benefits of a godly home. John and Charles Wesley, founders of the Methodist Church, came from a godly home and were profoundly influenced by their mother. Adoniram Judson, the great missionary to Burma, came from a minister's home. Jonathan Edwards, pastor, evangelist and educator in early America, was from a line of godly forebears.

When the angel appeared to Zacharias to announce the good news that Elizabeth would, despite her age, give birth to a son, his words were immersed in the evangel. He predicted John's ministry: "Many of the children of Israel shall he turn to the Lord their God" (Luke 1:16). Thus, we learn that no one should presume that any person is saved, not even one born to a believing home, who has believing forebears, and grows up in a believing church. Moreover John was "to make ready a people prepared for the Lord" (verse 17).

How great the message of the angel was and how seriously Zacharias regarded it can be seen from events some months later. Zacharias lost his ability to speak following the angel's visit; he did not regain it until the birth of John. But at that time his tongue was loosed and he was filled with the Holy Spirit. His thinking—curing the long months while Elizabeth awaited the birth of the baby—now burst out in his first words, which reflect the angel's visit and concern for the evangel. Zacharias says, "Blessed be the Lord God of Israel; for he hath visited and redeemed his people, and hath raised up an horn of salvation for us in the house of his servant David." A moment later he added, "And thou, child, [that is, John] shalt . . . give knowledge of salvation unto his people by the remission of their sins, through the tender mercy of our God; whereby the dayspring from on high hath visited us, to give light to them that sit in darkness and in the shadow of death, to guide our feet into the way of peace" (Luke 1:76–79).

Now that was really a message! And all of it rises from the visit of the angel, who told Zacharias about God's intention for John. But notice especially that the angel came, not simply to announce the birth of John, but to make it clear that John was to live his life as the forerunner of the Messiah, and as one who would bring the knowledge of salvation and the remission of sins to his fellow Israelites.

The Angel and the Evangel in the Birth of Jesus

The announcement to Mary that she was to be the mother of Jesus was made by no ordinary angel. It was Gabriel, one of three angels whose names have been given us in Scripture, who made the announcement. And it was connected with the evangel. This was true both of the words Gabriel spoke and the words Mary spoke while she was pregnant and looking toward the birth of her son. The angel told Mary that Jesus would be the Son of the Highest, that He would inherit the throne of His father David, would reign over the house of Jacob forever, and would be an everlasting kingdom. This was something far different from anything promised anyone else in Scripture. It was not promised to Abraham, or David, or Solomon. Only Jesus' name is connected with these promises, and all of them are inextricably connected with both personal and national salvation.

After Mary became pregnant she visited Elizabeth and sang one of the sweetest songs known to literature. In it she makes evident that she has grasped what the angel told her. And what he told her she describes as salvation and the remission of sins: "My spirit hath rejoiced in God my Saviour" (Luke 1:47). Here was the news that Mary herself needed a Savior, and had found Him. The very baby who was encased in her womb would one day offer Himself as a propitiation for her and for all men. And that baby in her womb was God Almighty who had humbled Himself in order to dwell among us in the flesh.

Indeed she cries out that God's "mercy is on them that fear him from generation to generation." What is this but the glorious evangel, gospel, that God was in Christ reconciling the world to Himself? And this was the message Gabriel brought to Mary. He could not preach it himself, but he could bear witness to the gospel that was to be preached by Jesus Christ and His followers through all ages.

The Angel, the Evangel and Joseph

Joseph, the husband of Mary, was caught up in a seemingly abysmal situation. He was legally engaged to a girl who was pregnant.

He knew he was not the father because they had not yet consummated their forthcoming marriage. Yet Mary was apparently guilty of adultery under Jewish law, unless Joseph was willing to believe her story that the Holy Spirit had come upon her, and that she had never engaged in sexual relations with a man. As the innocent party, Joseph was thinking seriously of putting Mary away according to the custom of that day. The Scripture says that "while he thought on these things" (Matthew 1:20), an angel appeared to him in a dream and told him the true story of the incarnation and the role of Mary. Responding, Joseph believed the angel. But the announcement contained more than the simple fact that Mary was innocent of any transgression and that Joseph was the chosen vessel of God in affording her protection in this extraordinary event.

The angel also told Joseph something that was to witness to the gospel. Though the angel could not preach to Joseph, he struck at the root of the matter when he proclaimed, "He shall save his people from their sins" (Matthew 1:21). Here was the gospel in all of its beauty, simplicity and purity. According to the witness of the angel, sins can be forgiven. There is someone who can forgive sins. This is Jesus the Christ. The Savior has a people about whom He is concerned and guarantees that their sins will be forgiven. In the midst of the wonder of the incarnation we should not overlook the fact that the angel was here bearing witness to the "evangel," the gospel. Jesus was not coming simply as God. He was coming as Redeemer and Savior to make men right with His Father and to assure them of the gift of everlasting life.

Gabriel, the Evangel and Daniel

Long before the days of Zacharias, Elizabeth, Mary, Joseph and John the Baptist, the angel Gabriel had borne witness of the evangel to the prophet Daniel. He had done this in connection with the prophecy of the seventy weeks. Daniel was deep in prayer, confessing both his sin and that of his people. While he was praying, Gabriel appeared to him. Notice again that Gabriel did not preach the word of salvation, but he bore eloquent testimony to it. He said that the seventy weeks were designed "to finish the transgression, to make an end of sins, and to make reconciliation for iniquity" (Daniel 9:24). Then he foretold the cutting off of the

Messiah, an event that Isaiah 53 had prophesied and depicted so dramatically.

The Jews had had difficulty understanding the notion of a suffering Messiah, rather picturing Him as one who would come in power and glory to overthrow their enemies and to reign triumphantly over them. But Gabriel told Daniel that sin is a reality, and must be paid for. The Messiah will do this by being cut off; that is, He will die for the sins of men. Then the power of sin to separate us from God will end, and men will be reconciled to Him. We see that though Gabriel could not preach, he could prophesy! And how beautifully the prophecies of the Old Testament are linked together with the fulfillment in the New Testament. How gracious God was to use His angels as agents to make it plain to all they visited in all ages that their business was to witness to the evangel.

The Angel, the Evangel and the Shepherds

Does it not seem mysterious that God brought the first message of the birth of Jesus to ordinary people rather than to princes and kings? In this instance, God spoke through His holy angel to the shepherds who were keeping sheep in the fields. This was a lowly occupation, so shepherds were not well educated. But Mary in her song, the Magnificat, tells us the true story: "He hath put down the mighty from their seats, and exalted them of low degree. He hath filled the hungry with good things, and the rich he hath sent empty away" (Luke 1:52, 53). What a word for our generation!

What was the message of the angel to the shepherds? First, he told them not to be afraid. Over and over again the presence of angels was frightening to those to whom they came. But unless they came in judgment, the angels spoke a word of reassurance. They calmed the people to whom they came. This tells us that the appearance of angels is awe-inspiring, something about them awakening fear in the human heart. They represent a presence that has greatness and sends a chill down the spine. But when the angel had quieted the fears of the shepherds, he brought this message, one forever to be connected with the evangel:

"For behold I bring you good tidings of great joy, which shall be to all people. For unto you is born this day in the city of David a

Saviour, which is Christ the Lord" (Luke 2:10, 11). I could preach a dozen sermons on those two verses for they contain so many important theological themes. But note once more that the angel does not preach the gospel. Rather, he witnesses to it and demonstrates again the overwhelming concern angels have for it.

What did the angel say? First, he brought good tidings, not bad ones. The shepherds already knew the bad news—the human race had sinned and was lost. But the angel had come to tell them that God was doing something about their lostness. And he pointed out that the good news was not simply for the people of one nation, but for the whole world. Isaiah said, "The God of the whole earth shall he be called" (Isaiah 54:5). Jonah learned the same truth when he was sent to preach repentance to the people of Nineveh. The angel told the shepherds that the good tidings were for all people.

The good tidings were that the Savior had come. They needed somebody who could bring them back into fellowship with God, because the blood of bulls and goats could not do this in any permanent way. But the blood of the Savior could. The angel message was that God had come, redemption was possible, the Lord had visited His people with salvation. What a testimony to the evangel this was. And it was further validated when the angel who was accompanied by "a multitude of the heavenly host" began to chant or sing, "Glory to God in the highest, and on earth peace, good will toward men." Where could there be sweeter music? What hymn writer could match those words?

Angels and the Evangel in the Book of Acts

We might call two wonderful instances "case studies" of how angels see to it that unbelievers hear the gospel, respond to it and become saved. It shows again the concern of angels for the evangel and the steps they take to implement it.

The first case is that of the Ethiopian nobleman, a man of great authority. While reading the Old Testament Scriptures, he came to Isaiah and, unable to understand what the prophet meant, needed someone to interpret the Scripture to him. An angel knew of this situation. But the angel did not and could not do what the Ethiopian needed. He could not preach the gospel. But he could assist the Ethiopian eunuch by sending someone to him who could.

So the Scripture tells us that the angel spoke to Philip and specifically instructed him to go "toward the south unto the way that goeth down from Jerusalem unto Gaza, which is desert" (Acts 8:26). Philip obeyed the angel and approached the chariot. Then he interpreted the Scripture for him. Later the angel led him up and took him away. And the Ethiopian went on his way rejoicing. If the angel had been unconcerned about the evangel he would not have sent Philip to preach the gospel to this interested inquirer.

The second instance has to do with Peter and the conversion of Cornelius. In this case the situation is reversed. The angel had told Philip what to do so the Ethiopian could be saved. In this case he did not tell Peter what to do, but rather ordered Cornelius to send for Peter, who would then tell him the story of the gospel so he could be saved. Would it not have been much easier for the angel to have preached the gospel to Cornelius than to have had him send for Peter? After all, Peter was not a willing witness. He had the notion that it was wrong to preach the gospel for the salvation of Gentiles. Cornelius, however, followed the word of the angel and sent for Peter. Then God had to appear in a dream and convince Peter that it was all right for him to witness to a Gentile. Peter finally went and Cornelius was wonderfully saved. But it was done through the auspices of the angel who was deeply concerned with the evangel, and for the salvation of this Roman soldier.

One other story in the Acts of the Apostles is somewhat different, though no less worthy of consideration. It has to do with Paul on his way to Rome. He was shipwrecked en route. But while it appeared that the ship would sink with all hands lost, an angel of the Lord appeared to Paul at night. He told those aboard the ship that they would all be saved. Then he said something that illuminates the concern of angels for the salvation of men and the witness of Christians to the unsaved. "Fear not, Paul; thou must be brought before Caesar" (Acts 27:24). Here we see that same principle. The angel could not witness to Caesar, but Paul could. And God in His providence was sending him to Rome for precisely this purpose. If Paul had not fully known the will of God before, it was clear at this moment. God intended that Caesar should hear the gospel. And the angel, by bringing the message, revealed his own interest in the evangel.

The Sound of Angel Voices

The keynote of evangelism is couched in the heavenly proclamation I have mentioned, "Unto you is born this day. . . a Saviour which is Christ the Lord." And the task of world evangelization will be completed by men and women whom the Holy Spirit uses. But wherever and whenever we see the gospel working in its power to transform, there is a possibility that in some ways angels may be involved. This is a mystery that we will never quite understand until we get to heaven.

It is not unreasonable to ask, "What did the angel voices sound like?" And "What did they say when they spoke?" Angels seemed to communicate terse commands. Often the angel messengers urged haste, and this is understandable since they were communicating a directive from God. Dr. Miller points out that the contemporary expression, "Hurry up," would fit most angel commands. The words, "Get up," were sometimes literally used. The angel said to Peter, "Rise quickly." The angel said to Gideon, "Arise and go in this thy might." The angel said to Joseph, "Go quickly," and to Philip, "Arise and go."

In the same way any evangelistic ministry sounds the note of urgency concerning the gospel. We have no time to waste because we can never reclaim this moment. We may never have a second chance to witness if we neglect the first.

We can illustrate this from the sinking of the *Titanic*. The greatest ship of its day, weighing 46,000 tons, it was considered unsinkable. But on the night of 14 April 1912, while moving through the ocean at 22 knots, it struck an iceberg. Because it carried only half as many life jackets as passengers, when it sank 1,513 people drowned. Even though this event occurred more than 70 years ago, there is still a great fascination about it. The recent discovery of the hulk of the *Titanic* has revived our interest in the whole tragic story.

Out of tragedy, however, God can still bring triumph.

One passenger, John Harper, was on his way to preach at Moody Church in Chicago. Trying to stay afloat in the ocean he drifted toward a young man holding onto a plank. Harper asked, "Young man, are you saved?" The man said, "No." A wave separated them. After a few minutes they drifted within speaking distance of each other, and again Harper called to him, "Have you made your peace with God?" The young man said, "Not yet." A wave overwhelmed John Harper and he was seen no more, but the words, "Are you saved?" kept ringing in the young man's ears.

Two weeks later a youth stood up in a Christian Endeavor meeting in New York, told his story and said, "I am John Harper's last convert."

11

Angel Ministries
in the Life of Jesus

I T WOULD TAKE an entire book to spell out in detail how
the life of Jesus was intertwined with the attending ministry of
angels. Before He was here they followed His orders. And since He
ascended into heaven they have worshiped Him before the throne
of God as the Lamb slain for our salvation.

To prepare for the coming of Jesus an angel appeared to Zacharias
to inform him that his wife would be the mother of John the Baptist (Luke 1:13). Gabriel, one of the mighty angels of God, announced to Mary that she would give birth to the Messiah. An
angel and a multitude of the heavenly host spread the good news
of Jesus' coming to the shepherds in the field (Luke 2:9). These
angelic incidents preceded and accompanied His birth, but when
Jesus began His public ministry angels were intimately involved
in His life as well.

Perhaps the most difficult period in the life of Jesus before His
crucifixion was His temptation by the devil in the wilderness. After
He had fasted forty days and nights, Satan tried to break Him
down. In Christ's weakened human condition, Satan began his
attack, seeing this as his greatest opportunity to defeat the program of God in the world since his victory in the Garden of Eden.
He was out to shipwreck the hope of the human race. Wishing to
prevent the salvation of sinners, he struck at the moment when
Christ's physical weakness made Him most susceptible to temp-

tation. Satan always directs his sharpest attack at his victim's weakest point. He knows where the Achilles' heel may be and he does not fail to strike at the opportune time.

Three times Satan attempted to defeat Jesus. Three times Jesus quoted Scripture, and three times Satan went down to defeat. Then the Bible declares that "he [Satan] departed from him [Jesus] for a season" (Luke 4:13). It was at this point that angels came to His assistance—not to help Him resist Satan as they help us, for He did that by Himself, but to help Him after the battle was won. The angels "ministered" to Jesus. The Greek word *diakoneo* says it well, for they served Him as a deacon would serve. "Behold, angels came and ministered unto him" (Matthew 4:11). Angelic ambassadors supported, strengthened and sustained Him in that trying hour. From that moment on our Lord Jesus Christ, "who has been tempted in every way, just as we are—yet was without sin" (Hebrews 4:15, NIV), could sympathize and help Christian believers for the ages to come, and lead them to victory in their hour of temptation.

The Angel with Jesus in the Garden of Gethsemane

The night before His crucifixion Jesus was in the Garden of Gethsemane. Only a short time later He was to be seized by the soldiers, betrayed by Judas Iscariot, set before the rulers, beaten and at last crucified. Before He was hung on the cross He went through the terrible agony in the Garden which made Him sweat, as it were, drops of blood. It was in this situation that the Son of man needed inner strength to face what no other being in heaven, hell or earth had ever known. In fact, He was to face what no created being could have faced and gone through in victory. He was about to take upon Himself the sins of men. He was to become sin for us.

Jesus had taken Peter, James and John with Him to the Garden. They could have provided Him with reinforcement and encouragement, but instead they fell asleep. The Son of man was all alone. He prayed, "Father, if thou be willing, remove this cup from me: nevertheless not my will, but thine, be done" (Luke 22:42). Then it was at that crucial moment that the angel came to assist Him, "strengthening Him." The Greek word for strengthening is *eniskuo*, which means to make strong inwardly. Where the disciples of the Lord Jesus had failed to share His agony, as they slept the angel came to help.

Angels Waiting at the Cross

The tragedy of sin reached its crescendo when God in Christ became sin. At this point He was offering Himself as the sacrifice required by the justice of God if man was to be redeemed. At this moment Satan was ready to try his master stroke. If he could get Christ to come down from the cross, and if Christ allowed the mockery of the crowd to shame or anger Him, then the plan of salvation would be jeopardized. Again and again they shouted, "If thou be the Son of God, come down from the cross" (Matthew 27:40). He knew He could come down if He chose; He knew He could get help from more than twelve legions of angels who hovered about with drawn swords.

Yet for our salvation He stayed there. The angels would have come to the cross to rescue the King of kings, but because of His love for the human race and because He knew it was only through His death that they could be saved, He refused to call for their help. The angels were under orders not to intervene at this terrible, holy moment. Even the angels could not minister to the Son of God at Calvary. He died alone to take the full death penalty you and I deserved.

We can never plumb the depths of sin, or sense how terrible human sin is, until we go to the cross and see that it was "sin" that caused the Son of God to be crucified. The ravages of war, the tragedy of suicide, the agony of the poverty-stricken, the suffering and irony of the rejected of our society, the blood of the accident victim, the terror of rape and mugging victims of our generation—these all speak as with a single voice of the degradation that besets the human race at this hour. But no sin has been committed in the world today that can compare with the full cup of the universe's sin that brought Jesus to the cross. The question hurled toward heaven throughout the ages has been, "Who is He and why does He die?" The answer comes back, "This is my only begotten Son, dying not only for your sins but for the sins of the whole world." To you sin may be a small thing; to God it is a great and awful thing. It is the second largest thing in the world; only the love of God is greater.

When we comprehend the great price God was willing to pay for the redemption of man, we only then begin to see that something is horribly wrong with the human race. It must have a Savior, or it is doomed! Sin cost God His very best. Is it any wonder that the angels veiled their faces, that they were silent in their consternation as they witnessed the outworking of God's plan? How inconceivable it must have seemed to them, when they considered the fearful depravity of sin, that Jesus should shoulder it all. But they were soon to unveil their faces and offer their praises again. A light was kindled that day at Calvary. The cross blazed with the glory of God as the most terrible darkness was shattered by the light of salvation. Satan's depraved legions were defeated and they could no longer keep all men in darkness and defeat.

The Angels at the Resurrection

On the third day after His death the Bible says, "And behold there was a great earthquake; for the angel of the Lord descended from heaven, and came and rolled back the stone from the door, and sat upon it. His countenance was like lightning, and his raiment white as snow: And for fear of him the keepers did shake, and became as dead men" (Matthew 28:2–4).

Though some Bible students have tried to estimate how much this stone weighed, we need not speculate because Jesus could have come out of that tomb whether the stone was there or not. The Bible mentions it so that generations to come can know something of the tremendous miracle of resurrection that took place. I have often wondered what those guards must have thought when, against the brightness of the rising sun, they saw the angel rolling away the gigantic boulder with possibly the lightest touch of his finger! The guards, though heavily armed, were paralyzed with fear.

As Mary looked into the tomb she saw "two angels in white sitting, the one at the head, and the other at the feet, where the body of Jesus had lain" (John 20:11, 12). Then one of the angels who was sitting outside the tomb proclaimed the greatest message the world has ever heard: "He is not here, but is risen" (Luke 24:6). Those few words changed the history of the universe. Darkness and despair died; hope and anticipation were born in the hearts of men.

Angels and the Ascension of Jesus

We find the story of the ascension of Jesus in Acts 1. Verse 9 says, "And when he had spoken these things, while they beheld, he was taken up; and a cloud received him out of their sight." Jesus had been accompanied to earth by an angelic host. I believe that the word "cloud" suggests that angels had come to escort Him back to the right hand of God the Father.

The watching disciples were sad and despondent. Tears filled their eyes. But again two angels, looking like men and dressed in white raiment, appeared and said, "Ye men of Galilee, why stand ye gazing up into heaven? This same Jesus, which is taken up from you into heaven, shall so come in like manner as ye have seen him go into heaven" (Acts 1:11).

Thus, the angels escorted the resurrected Lord of glory back to be seated at the Father's right hand; then even the morning stars ascribed honor, glory and praise to Him as the Son of the Living God. On the other hand, some angels remained behind to assure those early disciples that they would always be near, ready to help God's people throughout the ages to come—until Christ returns in person with the angelic host.

12

Angels in Prophecy

ANGELS HAVE AN important role in future events! Human history began at Eden where God planted a garden and made man for His eternal fellowship. Angels were there. They have never failed to attend the human scene. And they will continue on the scene throughout the succeeding ages till time runs into eternity.

Just as millions of angels participated in the dazzling show when the morning stars sang together at creation, so will the innumerable hosts of heaven help bring to pass God's prophetic declarations throughout time and into eternity.

When God decrees it, Satan (Lucifer) will be removed from the world of disorder so God can establish righteousness everywhere, and a true theocracy. Not until that event takes place will the human race know perfect peace on earth. Paul tells us in Romans 8 that the whole creation groans and travails as it awaits the day of Christ's victory.

The prophets spoke of a wonderful day when God would lift the curse, when lion and lamb would lie down together, and when nations would learn war no more (Isaiah 2:4; 11:6). Angel hosts will fulfill His royal decrees and oversee God's purpose in the universe. Christ is coming in great power, and all His holy angels will be with Him. In Acts 1:10, 11 angels gave counsel to the disciples after Jesus had ascended to heaven. As we have already seen, when He had left the Mount of Olives, angels appeared, saying, "Ye men of Galilee, why stand ye gazing up into heaven? This same Jesus

... shall so come in like manner as ye have seen him go into heaven" (Acts 1:11). Angels encouraged those downcast believers who had seen Jesus Christ disappear from their view into a cloud. After this, angels figure prominently in the prophetic plan of God that continued on into the future events of Bible prophecy.

In every age, the true believers have asked, "Will this conflict of the ages ever end?" Each period of history seemingly has its own trials and convulsions. Each generation seems to have to "fight it out." Behind it all is the unseen struggle of the ages. We thought that modern technology would solve many of the great problems of the human race. In some ways it has, by eliminating the fear of diseases like polio and smallpox. But it has also given us Frankenstein weapons of destruction. Poverty, hunger, greed, injustice, prejudice, terrorism, lust, war and death are still with us. This is the same war that began mysteriously in the heart of Lucifer. It seems that our world is on a suicidal course; but God has other plans. Light shines at the end of the tunnel. Someday Satan and his demons will go down in defeat. The Bible declares that righteousness will eventually triumph, Utopia will come to earth, the kingdom of God will ultimately prevail. In bringing all this about angels will have a prominent part.

A little girl heard a clock strike thirteen times. Breathlessly she ran to her mother and said, "Mother, it's later than it's ever been before." Almost everyone throughout the world will agree. It's later than it's ever been before. The human race is rushing madly toward some sort of climax, and the Bible accurately predicts what the climax is! A new world is coming. Through modern technology and scientific achievement we are catching glimpses of what that new world is. If it were not for depraved human nature, man could achieve it himself. But man's rebellion against God has always been his stumbling block. The penalty for man's rebellion is death. The best leaders and the best brains have many times been stopped by death. The Bible teaches that "it is appointed unto men once to die" (Hebrews 9:27). Today the world longs for a leader such as Abraham Lincoln—but death took him from us.

God will use the angels to merge time into eternity, creating a new kind of life for every creature. Even today's intellectual world speaks of a point when time will be no more. Most scientists agree that the clock of time is running out. Ecologically, medically, scientifically, morally, time seems to be running out. In almost every direction we look, man's time on earth seems to be running out. Self-destruction is overtaking us as a human race.

Will man destroy himself? No! God has another plan!

Since the beginning of time, man has been interested in what lies beyond the short span of life. Modern man is turning to the occult, Eastern mysticism, palm readers and every other kind of help available to tell him about the future. Strangely, only a minority turn to the Bible, the only book that accurately foretells the future. The Bible teaches that Jesus Christ is coming back again with His holy angels. It refers to His coming as like "a thief in the night" (2 Peter 3:10), a day of wrath (Romans 2:5), and the judgment of the great day (Jude 6), with many other references both direct and indirect. The Age of Utopia will be preceded by unparalleled events of suffering for the human race—totalitarianism, poverty, disease, earthquakes, moral collapse, war—until men's hearts will fail them for fear (Luke 21:26).

Luke 21 says there will be "wars and commotions . . . Nation shall rise against nation, and kingdom against kingdom: And great earthquakes shall be in divers places, and famines, and pestilences; and fearful sights and great signs shall there be from heaven" (verses 9–11).

Believing Christians and believing Jews alike will be persecuted. Men will deliver "you up to the synagogues, and into prisons, being brought before kings and rulers for my name's sake. . . . And ye shall be betrayed both by parents, and brethren, and kinsfolk, and friends; and some of you shall they cause to be put to death. And ye shall be hated of all men for my name's sake. . . . And when ye shall see Jerusalem compassed with armies, then know that the desolation thereof is nigh. . . . And there shall be signs in the sun, and in the moon, and in the stars; and upon the earth distress of nations, with perplexity; the sea and the waves roaring; Men's hearts failing them for fear, and for looking after those things which are coming on the earth: for the powers of heaven shall be shaken" (verses 12–26).

Jesus continued in verse 27, "And then shall they see the Son of man coming in a cloud with power and great glory."

Even as in the beginning of time angelic forces waged war in heaven (Revelation 12:7–9), so in the very last days angels will wage still another war; Satan will make his last stand. As the time draws near he intensifies his activities.

But it will be a victorious day for the universe, and especially planet earth, when the devil and his angels are thrown into the lake of fire, never again to tempt and destroy man. To the angels God has assigned this task, and Scripture assures us that they will be victorious (Matthew 13:41, 42).

Angels Will Gather God's Elect

Linked to this idea Jesus says that "When the Son of man shall come in his glory, and all the holy angels with him, then shall he sit upon the throne of his glory" (Matthew 25:31). In other words, when Jesus returns, He will be accompanied by the hosts of heaven. The holy angels will be with Him! As He says in Matthew 13:41–42, "The Son of man shall send forth his angels, and they shall gather out of his kingdom all things that offend, and them which do iniquity; And shall cast them into a furnace of fire: there shall be wailing and gnashing of teeth."

Earlier in this same chapter, Jesus has related a significant little story commonly called the Parable of the Tares and Wheat (Matthew 13:24–30, 36–43). Both had been allowed to grow together until the harvest, but then the reapers were to gather them up in bundles. The tares were to be burned; the wheat gathered. We often wonder why God permits so much sin in the world, why He withholds His right arm of judgment. Why doesn't God put an end to sin now? We can give an answer from this text where Jesus said, "Let both grow together," the evil with the good (verse 30). If we were to try to wipe all evil from the face of the earth, who could count on justice? Pure justice does not exist here, because everyone is guilty, including the judges who sit in judgment. We are all guilty of sin.

Man must do his best in meting out justice, but his best is not complete justice. To angels will be delegated the ministry of separating the good from the bad, discerning even attitudes. God's judgment will be so pure that even those who are condemned will bow their knee and confess, "Thou art just." As someone has said, "When I die I do not want justice—I want mercy!" That mercy has been provided by the Lord Jesus Christ.

So angels will not only accompany Christ when He returns, but will be assigned the responsibility of gathering out of His kingdom all things that offend and work iniquity, that they might be judged (Matthew 13:47–50).

It boggles the mind to try to imagine the kind of earth this is going to be when God eliminates the devil and sin. Our minds are staggered at the thought of "Christ on the throne." The great southward-moving Sahara Desert of Africa will bloom and blossom. Mankind will be able to grow new foods; land that today is useless will grow twelve crops a year. The urge in man's heart toward immorality will have vanished. In that day the great drive in man will be a thirst for righteousness. It takes a great deal of faith in these days of despondency to believe this, but it is the clear teaching of the Bible. Without this hope of the future I do not know what modern man does, except turn to drugs and alcohol.

Today we have the choice of whether or not to receive the ministry of angels. In choosing to follow Jesus Christ we also choose the protective watch and care of the angels of heaven. In the time of the Second Coming, we will no longer be afforded the privilege of choice. If we delay now, it will be too late, and we forfeit forever the gracious ministry of angels and the promise of salvation to eternal life.

Angels in Our Future

Dr. Miller asks the question, "What does the future hold for this weary old world? . . . for the physical earth? The answers to such questions are not to be found in astrology or necromancy but in the divinely inspired Word of God. And we may be certain that, as the passing of time fulfills the prophetic Scriptures, the holy angels will be deeply involved in the fulfillment." God will renovate the earth, order the New Jerusalem to descend from heaven, and give redeemed man a position above the angels—what a future!

Elijah was one of the greatest prophets, suddenly appearing on the scene in one of Israel's darkest hours (1 Kings 17). He was a strong, suntanned son of the desert. At times he could be bold as a lion, and at times crushed with frustration. On one occasion he challenged the prophets of the heathen god Baal to a duel to see who was the true God (1 Kings 18:19). When the prophets of Baal could get no answer from their false god, and Elijah's God answered by fire, Queen Jezebel, unable to accept the prophet's verdict, determined to take his life and pursued him with her chariot for many miles. Elijah, weary from his flight and desperately hungry, lay down under a juniper tree to rest. Feeling extremely sorry for himself, he went to sleep, to be wakened by an angel's touch. Then food was set before him to eat, and the angel said, "Arise, eat."

"And he looked, and, behold, there was a cake baken on the coals, and a [jar] of water at his head. And he did eat and drink, and laid him down again. And the angel of the Lord came again the second time, and touched him, and said, Arise and eat; because the journey is too great for thee. And he arose, and did eat and drink, and went in the strength of that meat forty days and forty nights unto Horeb the mount of God" (1 Kings 19:6–8).

God did not let his faithful prophet down. He provided just what he needed physically, psychologically and spiritually. Many of us despair of coping with the pressures of our lives, but if we are living Spirit-filled and Spirit-directed lives, we can claim God's promises. The prophetic Scriptures give us "hope." Without Scripture's plan of God for the future and the hope it brings, I do not know what the average thinking person does. Certainly a person will not find the answer by wringing his hands, or by committing suicide, or by turning to the occult. We find the answer to the future in Holy Scripture. It is summed up in the person of Jesus Christ. God has centered all our hopes and dreams on Him. He is the Commander-in-Chief of these angelic armies that will accompany Him on His return.

Angel Authority

New Testament writers have reaffirmed the badge of authority given to angels to fulfill the prophetic dictates of God. The apostle Peter emphasized this truth when speaking of Christ, who was at the right hand of God, having gone into heaven after "angels and authorities and powers [had been] made subject unto him" (1 Peter 3:22). The time is coming when the twenty-four elders of His angelic creation will fall down before the Lamb and sing their new song (Revelation 5:9–10). Thereafter, the holy angels will gather round the throne and join in a great testimony to the Lamb, expressing praise with such words as, "Worthy is the Lamb that was slain to receive power and riches and wisdom and might and honor and glory and blessing" (Revelation 5:12, NASB). While angels have tremendous authority, it is limited to doing only the will of God. They never deviate from God's message, never dilute His message, never change God's plan. Throughout the ages they have glorified only Him, never themselves.

The Bible teaches that the demons are dedicated to controlling this planet for their master, Satan. Even Jesus called him "the prince of this world" (John 12:31). He is the master-organizer and strategist.

Many times throughout biblical history, and possibly even today, angels and demons engage in warfare. Many of the events of our times may very well be involved in this unseen struggle.

We are not left in doubt about who will ultimately triumph. Time after time Jesus has assured us that He and the angels would be victorious. "When the Son of man shall come in his glory, and all the holy angels with him, then shall he sit upon the throne of his glory" (Matthew 25:31). The apostle Paul wrote, "The Lord Jesus shall be revealed from heaven with his mighty angels in flaming fire . . ." (2 Thessalonians 1:7, 8).

Jesus also taught that "Whosoever shall confess me before men, him shall the Son of man also confess before the angels of God" (Luke 12:8). It is impossible to comprehend one's suffering of eternal loss when he learns that angels do not acknowledge him because he has been false in his claims to know Christ. But what a moment it is going to be for believers throughout all the ages, from every tribe, nation and tongue, when they are presented in the Court of Heaven. Scripture calls it, "the marriage supper of the Lamb" (Revelation 19:9). This is the great event when Jesus Christ is crowned King of kings and Lord of lords. Both believers of all ages, and all the angelic hosts will join in bowing their knees and confessing that He is Lord.

The book of Revelation, from chapter four to nineteen, gives us a picture of judgments to befall the earth such as the world has never known. Angels will be involved in all of these judgments. But after these terrifying events, Christ will come with His holy angels to set up His kingdom.

Whether the battle between the forces of Satan and the forces of God involve other planets and galaxies we do not know. But we do know that the earth is the scene of the conflict; however, it is a gigantic struggle that affects the entire universe. It is mind-boggling that you and I, with such a short period of time on this planet, play a part in this battle of the ages. It is almost incredible to us that supernatural beings from outer space are engaged in a struggle for this planet.

It all started in the Garden of Eden, a place located somewhere between the Tigris and the Euphrates rivers in the Middle East. It is significant that the nations prominent in early history are once again becoming prominent: Israel, Egypt, Syria, Iran, and so on. In that Garden God gave a great promise, "And I will put enmity between thee and the woman, and between thy seed and her seed; it shall bruise thy head, and thou shalt bruise his heel" (Genesis 3:15). As we approach the end of the age, the head of Satan is being battered and bruised as the forces of God gain momentum. Under the command of God, Michael the archangel is now organizing his forces for the last battle—Armageddon. The last picture in the Bible is one of heaven.

Many years ago I was visiting the dining room of the United States Senate. As I was speaking to various people, one of the senators called me to his table. He said, "Billy, we're having a discussion about pessimism and optimism. Are you a pessimist or an optimist?" I smiled and said, "I'm an optimist." He asked, "Why?" I said, "I've read the last page of the Bible."

The Bible speaks about a city whose builder and maker is God, where those who have been redeemed will be superior to angels. It speaks of "a pure river of water of life, clear as crystal proceeding out of the throne of God and of the Lamb" (Revelation 22:1). It says, "And they shall see his face; and his name shall be in their foreheads. And there shall be no night there; and they need no candle, neither light of the sun; for the Lord God giveth them light: and they shall reign for ever and ever" (verses 4, 5).

The next verse has a thrilling last word to say about angels: "These sayings are faithful and true: and the Lord God of the holy prophets sent his angel to shew unto his servants the things which must shortly be done."

Christian and non-Christian alike should meditate on the seventh verse where God says, "Behold I come quickly: blessed is he that keepeth the sayings of the prophecy of this book."

13

The Angels and Death

THE ANGEL WHO came to the garden where Jesus' body lay, rolled away the stone and permitted fresh air and morning light to fill His tomb. The sepulcher was no longer an empty vault or dreary dormitory; rather it was a life-affirming place that radiated the glory of the living God. No longer was it a dark prison but a transformed reminder of the celestial light that sweeps aside the shadows of death. Jesus' resurrection changed it.

An unknown poet has said of the tomb, "'Tis now a cell where angels used to come and go with heavenly news." No words of men or angels can adequately describe the height and depth, the length and breadth of the glory to which the world awakened when Jesus came forth to life from the pall of death. As Charles Wesley says in his hymn:

> 'Tis mystery all! Th' Immortal dies!
> Who can explore His strange design?
> In vain the first-born seraph tries
> To sound the depths of love Divine!
> 'Tis mercy all! Let earth adore!
> Let angel minds inquire no more.

In contrast to Jesus, we all still have to die. Yet just as an angel was involved in Christ's resurrection, so will angels help us in death. Only one thin veil separates our natural world from the spiritual world. That thin veil we call death. However, Christ both vanquished death and overcame the dark threats of the evil fallen angels. So now God surrounds death with the assurance of angelic help to bring pulsing life out of the darkness of that experience for believers. We inherit the kingdom of God.

Christians at Death

Death for the Christian cuts the cord that holds us captive in this present evil world so that angels may transport believers to their heavenly inheritance. Death is the fiery chariot, the gentle voice of the King, the invitation to non-stop passage into the banquet house of the world of glory.

In another connection I have already mentioned Lazarus, whom angels escorted to Abraham in heaven. This story has always been a tremendous comfort to me as I think about death. I will actually be taken by angels into the presence of God. These ministering spirits who have helped me here so often will be with me in my last great battle on earth. Death is a battle, a profound crisis event. Paul calls it "the last enemy" (1 Corinthians 15:26). While the sting of death has been removed by the work of Christ on the cross, and by His resurrection, yet the crossing of this valley still stimulates fear and mystery. However, angels will be there to help us. Could not the "rod and staff," which help us in the valley of the shadow of death (Psalm 23:4), be these holy angels?

We who have made our peace with God should be like the evangelist D. L. Moody. When he was aware that death was at hand, he said, "Earth recedes, heaven opens before me." It appeared as though he was dreaming. Then he said, "No, this is no dream . . . it is beautiful, it is like a trance. If this is death, it is sweet. There is no valley here. God is calling me, and I must go."

After having been given up for dead, Moody revived to indicate that God had permitted him to see beyond that thin veil separating the seen from the unseen world. He had been "within the gates, and beyond the portals," and had caught a glimpse of familiar faces whom he had "loved long since and lost awhile." Then he could remember when he had proclaimed so vociferously earlier in his ministry, "Some day you will read in the papers that D. L. Moody of East Northfield is dead. Don't you believe a word of it. At that moment I shall be more alive than I am now. I shall have gone up higher, that is all—out of this old clay tenement into a house that is immortal; a body that death cannot touch, that sin cannot taint, a body fashioned like unto His glorious body. . . . That which is born of the flesh may die. That which is born of the Spirit will live forever" (*The Life of Dwight L. Moody*, by W. R. Moody). If Moody were to witness to us now, he would surely tell us of the glowing experience that became his as the angelic hosts ushered him into the presence of the Lord.

Phillips Brooks, the writer of "O Little Town of Bethlehem," was one of the greatest pulpit orators and best loved preachers of the nineteenth century. No greater tribute could be paid him than the words of a five-year-old Boston girl, who exclaimed after her mother had told her that the beloved Mr. Brooks had died, "Mother, how happy the angels will be!"

Death is not natural, for man was created to live and not to die. It is the result of God's judgment because of man's sin and rebellion. Without God's grace through Christ, it is a gruesome spectacle. I have stood at the bedside of people dying without Christ; it was a terrible experience. I have stood at the bedside of those who were dying in Christ; it was a glorious experience. Charles Spurgeon said of the glory that attends the death of the redeemed, "If I may die as I have seen some die, I court the grand occasion. I would not wish to escape death by some by-road if I may sing as they sang. If I may have such hosannas and alleluias beaming in my eyes as I have seen as well as heard from them, it were a blessed thing to die."

Death is robbed of much of its terror for the true believer, but we still need God's protection as we take that last journey. At the moment of death the spirit departs from the body and moves through the atmosphere. But the Scripture teaches us that the devil lurks then. He is "the prince of the power of the air" (Ephesians 2:2). If the eyes of our understanding were opened, we would probably see the air filled with demons, the enemies of Christ. If Satan could hinder the angel of Daniel 10 for three weeks on his mission to earth, we can imagine the opposition a Christian may encounter at death.

But Christ on Calvary cleared a road through Satan's kingdom. When Christ came to earth, He had to pass through the devil's territory and open up a beachhead here. That is one reason He was accompanied by a host of angels when He came (Luke 2:8–14). And this is why holy angels will accompany Him when He comes again (Matthew 16:27). Till then, the moment of death is Satan's final opportunity to attack the true believer; but God has sent His angels to guard us at that time.

In telling the story in Luke 16 Jesus says that the beggar was "carried by the angels." He was not only escorted; he was *carried*. What an experience that must have been for Lazarus! He had lain begging at the gate of the rich man until his death, but then suddenly he found himself carried by the mighty angels of God!

Once I stood in London to watch Queen Elizabeth return from an overseas trip. I saw the parade of dignitaries, the marching bands, the crack troops, the waving flags. I saw all the splendor that accompanies the homecoming of a queen. However, that was nothing compared to the homecoming of a true believer who has said good-by here to all of the suffering of this life and been immediately surrounded by angels who carry him upward to the glorious welcome awaiting the redeemed in heaven.

The Christian should never consider death a tragedy. Rather he should see it as angels do: They realize that joy should mark the journey from time to eternity. The way to life is by the valley of death, but the road is marked with victory all the way. Angels revel in the power of the resurrection of Jesus, which assures us of our resurrection and guarantees us a safe passage to heaven.

Hundreds of accounts record the heavenly escort of angels at death. When my maternal grandmother died, for instance, the room seemed to fill with a heavenly light. She sat up in bed and almost laughingly said, "I see Jesus. He has His arms outstretched toward me. I see Ben [her husband who had died some years earlier] and I see the angels." She slumped over, absent from the body but present with the Lord.

When I was a student in a Bible school a godly young mission-ary volunteer was suddenly taken ill. The physician said she had only a few hours to live. Her young husband and one or two fac-ulty members were in the room when she suddenly exclaimed, "I see Jesus. I can hear the singing of the angels."

The Reverend A. A. Talbot, missionary to China, was at the bedside of a dying Chinese Christian. Suddenly the room was filled with heavenly music. The Chinese Christian looked up with a radiant smile exclaiming, "I see Jesus standing at the right hand of God, and Margaret Gay is with Him." (Margaret Gay was the Talbot's little daughter who had died months before.)

Susanna Wesley said, "When I am gone, sing a song of praise to God."

Dying patients are given so many drugs today that we do not hear as many of these stories now. But to those who face death in Christ it is a glorious experience. The Bible guarantees every believer an escorted journey into the presence of Christ by the holy angels.

The angelic emissaries of the Lord are often sent not only to catch away the redeemed of the Lord at death, but also to give hope and joy to those who remain, and to sustain them in their loss. He has promised to give "the oil of joy for mourning, the garment expressive of praise instead of a heavy, burdened and failing spirit . . . (Isaiah 61:3, AB).

Today man has been overtaken by an increasing sense of gloom about life. In his *Responding to Suicidal Crisis*, Doman Lum quotes Minna Field on the inadequacy of the counsel and treat-ment given by those who merely "attempt to escape what is to them an unbearable prospect by a pat on the back and by telling the patient that he is talking nonsense." Death seminars are now being held in major medical centers, and teams of psychiatrists, psychologists and therapists are constantly encouraged to become involved. Robert J. Lifton, in studying the cessation of life, points out in the same book some interesting views held by survivors of the atomic destruction of Hiroshima. He says that "There was a lasting sense of an overwhelming and permanent encounter with death. As a result, there was a breakdown of faith or trust in any human structure, a psychological closure in which people literally numbed themselves to any emotional feelings regarding death, and an overwhelming sense of guilt and self-condemnation as if they were responsible for the tragedy. . . . We are obsessed with the fear of sudden death . . . and recognize the unpredictable nature of life."

In popular thinking you and I have heard people speaking of death as "crossing the Jordan." It is found in spirituals and in some hymns of the Christian faith. It comes, of course, from the victorious march of the Israelites who crossed the Jordan to enter the Promised Land. They passed over Jordan on dry ground. By analogy we can consider that the ministering angels will see us safely across the Jordan River of death as we enter the promised land of heaven. So the Christian does not sorrow as those who have no hope (1 Thessalonians 4:13).

When the apostle Paul spoke of his own approaching death, he said, "We are confident, I say, and willing rather to be absent from the body, and to be present with the Lord" (2 Corinthians 5:8). When that glorious physical and spiritual separation takes place, the angels will be there to escort us into the presence of our Savior with abounding joy, and it will mean "life everlasting."

The Wonderful Welcome to Come

I believe that death can be beautiful. I have come to look forward to it, to anticipate it with joy and expectation. I have stood at the side of many people who died with expressions of triumph on their faces. No wonder the Bible says, "Precious in the sight of the Lord is the death of his saints" (Psalm 116:15). No wonder David said, "Even though I walk through the valley of the shadow of death, I will fear no evil, for you are with me . . ." (Psalm 23:4, NIV).

You may be filled with dread at the thought of death. Just remember that at one moment you may be suffering, but in another moment, you will be instantly transformed into the glorious likeness of our Savior. The wonders, beauties, splendor and grandeur of heaven will be yours. You will be surrounded by these heavenly messengers sent by God to bring you home where you may rest from your labors, though the honor of your works will follow you (Revelation 14:13).

No wonder the apostle Paul said, "Therefore, my dear brothers, stand firm. Let nothing move you.

Always give yourselves fully to the work of the Lord, because you know that your labor in the Lord is not in vain" (1 Corinthians 15:58, NIV).

Are you ready to face life? Are you ready to face death? No one is truly ready to die who has not learned to live for the glory of God. You can put your confidence in Jesus because He died for you, and in that last moment—the greatest crisis of all—He will have His angels gather you in their arms to carry you gloriously, wonderfully into heaven.

14

Angel Spectators

HOW WOULD YOU live if you knew that you were being watched all the time, not only by your parents, wife, husband or children, but by the heavenly host? The Bible teaches in 1 Corinthians 4:9 that angels are watching us. Paul says we are a "spectacle" to them. A. S. Joppie points out that the word referred to the arenas where first-century crowds went to see animals killed for sport, men battle to the death and, later, Christians torn apart by lions. In using the word spectacle, Paul is picturing this world as one vast arena. All true Christians participate in this great drama as they seek to obey Christ since this throws them into severe conflict with the forces of evil, who are bent on humiliating them. Yet Scripture says, "They did not love their lives so much as to shrink from death" (Revelation 12:11, NIV).

During this conflict, which was not limited to the arena, the angels were watching them, longing to hasten to their rescue to set free those men and women who often went joyfully to their death. Yet God forbade the angels to rush in as armies of deliverance. Nor had He allowed them to rescue Jesus at the cross when He tasted the death of separation from God the Father. The angel spectators were poised and ready to intervene; the attack order never came. Why? Because God's moment of final victory over the vicious forces of evil had not yet come.

As I mentioned earlier we face many perplexing questions today, such as: Why does God permit evil? Why doesn't God intervene and punish sin? Why does God allow disease? Why does God permit catastrophe? Yet God's timing is precise! Angel hosts who witness everything that transpires in our world are not free to bear up the righteous and deliver the oppressed until God gives the signal. One day He will. Christ has reminded us that the wheat and the tares, the righteous and the unrighteous, are to grow in the field together until the harvest time when the holy angels gather God's elect and bring them into His kingdom.

Angels at Attention

As God's angels have watched the drama of this age unfolding they have seen the Christian church established and expand around the world. They miss nothing as they watch the movements of time, "To the intent that now unto the principalities and powers in heavenly places might be known by the church the manifold wisdom of God" (Ephesians 3:10). Dr. Joppie reminds us that the word "now" actually covers the vast expanse of this Church age. Angel hosts have witnessed the formation of the Church of Christ Jesus, and have watched the walk of each believer as the Lord worked His grace, love and power into each life. The angels were observing firsthand the building of the body of the true Church in all places of His dominion this very hour.

But what are they thinking as we live in the world's arena? Do they observe us as we stand fast in the faith and walk in righteousness? Or may they be wondering at our lack of commitment? These two possibilities seem evident from Ephesians 3:10: "(The purpose is) that through the church the complicated, many-sided wisdom of God in all its infinite variety and innumerable aspects might now be made known to the angelic rulers and authorities (principalities and powers) in the heavenly sphere" (AB).

Our certainty that angels right now witness how we are walking through life should mightily influence the decisions we make. God is watching, and His angels are interested spectators too. The Amplified Bible expresses 1 Corinthians 4:9 this way: "God has made an exhibit of us ... a show in the world's amphitheater—

with both men and angels (as spectators)." We know they are watching, but in the heat of the battle, I have thought how wonderful it would be if we could hear them cheering.

Incentives for Righteousness

The charge to live righteously in this present world sobers us when we realize that the walk and warfare of Christians is the primary concern of heaven and its angelic hosts. Paul said, "I solemnly charge you in the presence of God and of Christ Jesus and of the chosen angels, that you guard and keep (these rules) . . ." (1 Timothy 5:21, AB). Paul was stirring up Timothy to remember that the elect angels were constantly watching how he served the Savior and lived the Christian life. What fact could provide a greater motivation to righteous living than that? I must say to myself, "Careful, angels are watching!"

It must give the angels great satisfaction to watch the Church of Jesus Christ minister the unsearchable riches of Christ to lost men everywhere. If the angels rejoice over one sinner who repents (Luke 15:10), then the angel hosts are numbered among the spectators in the heavenly grandstands. They are included among those who are referred to as "so great a cloud of witness" (Hebrews 12:1); and they never miss any of the details of our earthly pilgrimage. Yet they do not jeer as did the Greek crowds of Paul's day. Rather as we declare the gospel and see our friends saved, they rejoice with us.

In his book, *Though I Walk Through the Valley*, Dr. Vance Havner tells of an old preacher who worked into the night on a sermon for his small congregation. His wife inquired why he spent so much time on a message that he would give to so few. To this the minister replied, "You forget, my dear, how large my audience will be!" Dr. Havner adds that "Nothing is trivial here if heaven looks on. We shall play a better game if, 'seeing we are encompassed,' we remember who is in the grandstand!"

Our valleys may be filled with foes and tears; but we can lift our eyes to the hills to see God and the angels, heaven's spectators, who support us according to God's infinite wisdom as they prepare our welcome home.

15

Angels in
Our Lives Today

IN THE EARLY days of World War II, Britain's air force saved it from invasion and defeat. In her book, *Tell No Man*, Adela Rogers St. John describes a strange aspect of that weeks-long air war. Her information comes from a celebration held some months after the war, honoring Air Chief Marshal Lord Hugh Dowding. The King, the Prime Minister and scores of dignitaries were there. In his remarks, the Air Chief Marshal recounted the story of his legendary conflict where his pitifully small complement of men rarely slept, and their planes never stopped flying. He told about airmen on a mission who, having been hit, were either incapacitated or dead. Yet their planes kept flying and fighting; in fact, on occasion pilots in other planes would see a figure still operating the controls. What was the explanation? The Air Chief Marshal said he believed angels had actually flown some of the planes whose pilots sat dead in their cockpits.

That angels piloted planes for dead men in the battle for Britain we cannot finally prove. But we have already seen from Scripture some of the things angels have certainly done, can do, and are yet going to do as history approaches its climax. The important question for each of us is how angels can assist us in our lives here and now: How do they help us attain victory over the forces of evil? What is our continuing relationship to them?

We know that God has given His angels charge over us so that without their help we could never get the victory over Satan. The apostle Paul said, "For we wrestle not against flesh and blood, but against principalities, against powers, against the rulers of the darkness of this world, against spiritual wickedness in high places" (Ephesians 6:12). Let's consider how we can gain help from God through angels.

The God of This Age

Lucifer, our archenemy, controls one of the most powerful and well-oiled war machines in the universe. He controls principalities, powers and dominions. Every nation, city, village and individual has felt the hot breath of his evil power. He is already gathering the nations of the world for the last great battle in the war against Christ—Armageddon. Yet Jesus assures us that Satan is already a defeated foe (John 12:31; 16:11). In 2 Timothy 1:10 Paul says that Jesus Christ has abolished death and brought life and immortality to light through the gospel. Peter declares that Jesus "has gone into heaven and is at God's right hand—with angels, authorities and powers in submission to him" (1 Peter 3:22, NIV).

The Defeat of Satan

While Satan is a defeated foe in principle, obviously God has not yet eliminated him from the world scene. The Bible teaches, however, that God will use angels to judge and totally eliminate him from the universe. In Revelation 12 we read of Satan's earlier defeat: "Michael and his angels fought against the dragon; and the dragon fought and his angels, And prevailed not; neither was their place found any more in heaven. And the great dragon was cast out, that old serpent, called the Devil, and Satan, which deceiveth the whole world: he was cast out into the earth, . . ." (verses 7–9). In chapter 20 John describes how Satan's present earthly rule will be temporarily restricted: "And I saw an angel come down from heaven, having the key of the bottomless pit and a great chain in his hand. And he laid hold on the dragon, that old serpent, which is the Devil, and Satan, and bound him a thousand years, And cast him into the bottomless pit, and shut him up, and set a seal upon him, that he should deceive the nations no more, . . ." John then tells us that after a temporary release followed by the last great battle, God will cast Satan into the lake of fire and brimstone, there to be tormented forever (Revelation 20:10).

Some will say, "It is well and good to talk about the final defeat of the devil but until that happens it doesn't help me because I have to contend with him every day." But this is not the whole story. We have been given specific instructions in Scripture about how to get victory over the devil.

We are told, for example, "Do not give the devil a foothold" (Ephesians 4:27, NIV). In other words, don't leave any vacant places in your heart for him. The apostle Peter taught, "Be sober, be vigilant; because your adversary the devil, as a roaring lion, walketh about, seeking whom he may devour" (1 Peter 5:8). Thus, we cannot be too careful. This includes the injunction to join God's resistance movement: "Whom resist stedfast in the faith" (1 Peter 5:9). And James says, "Resist the devil, and he will flee from you" (James 4:7).

But these admonitions to be vigilant and to resist tell only part of the story. We are not in the battle alone, nor must we rely on our strength alone. Instead, we are to rely on the Holy Spirit, who dwells within us and is willing and able to help us in every situation if we will turn to Him. In addition we can count on the powerful presence of angels many times more numerous and powerful than Satan and his demons. As Increase Mather wrote centuries ago in *Angelographia*, "Angels both good and bad have a greater influence on this world than men are generally aware of. We ought to admire the grace of God toward us sinful creatures in that He hath appointed His holy angels to guard us against the mischiefs of wicked spirits who are always intending our hurt both to our bodies and to our souls."

We have already considered Elisha at Dothan, ringed by apparently overwhelming enemy forces. Yet if we, like his servant, had open spiritual eyes, we would see not only a world filled with evil spirits and powers—but also powerful angels with drawn swords, set for our defense.

At Dothan thousands of soldiers surrounded the city and intended to do Elisha harm. Yet he had peace. His servant, however, did not, and needed his eyes opened. We, who are troubled, confused, fearful, frustrated Christians need God to open our eyes this very moment. As Vance Havner says, "Our primary problem is not light, but sight. Light is of no value to a blind man. Reading books galore on the subject will not reveal the angels unless our eyes are touched by faith."

We must not get so busy counting demons that we forget the holy angels. Certainly we are up against a gigantic war machine. But we are encompassed by a heavenly host so powerful that we need not fear the warfare—the battle is the Lord's. We can boldly face Satan and his legions with all the confidence of the old captain who, when told that his outfit was completely surrounded, shouted, "Good, don't let any of them escape." If your valley is full of foes, raise your sights to the hills and see the holy angels of God arrayed for battle on your behalf.

When Abraham sent his eldest servant back to his blood relations to look for a bride for Isaac he urged him to go confidently because of God's angel: "he shall send his angel before thee, . . . and prosper thy way" (Genesis 24:7, 40). Isaiah the prophet said, "In all their affliction he [the Lord] was afflicted, and the angel of his presence saved them" (63:9). God promised Moses in the midst of all his exasperations, "Mine angel shall go before thee" (Exodus 23:23). The Bible also says we may see the angels God has sent, but fail to recognize them: "Be not forgetful to entertain strangers: for thereby some have entertained angels unawares" (Hebrews 13:2). Angels, whether noticed by men or not, are active in our twentieth-century world too. Are we aware of them?

It was a tragic night in a Chinese city. Bandits had surrounded the mission compound sheltering hundreds of women and children. On the previous night the missionary, Miss Monsen, had been put to bed with a bad attack of malaria, and now the tempter harassed her with questions: "What will you do when the looters come here? When firing begins on this compound, what about those promises you have been trusting?" In his book, *1,000 New Illustrations*, Al Bryant records the result. Miss Monsen prayed, "Lord, I have been teaching these young people all these years that Thy promises are true, and if they fail now, my mouth shall be forever closed; I must go home."

Throughout the next night she was up, ministering to frightened refugees, encouraging them to pray and to trust God to deliver them. Though fearful things happened all around, the bandits left the mission compound untouched.

In the morning, people from three different neighborhood families asked Miss Monsen, "Who were those four people, three sitting and one standing, quietly watching from the top of your house all night long?" When she told them that no one had been on the housetop, they refused to believe her, saying, "We saw them with our own eyes!" She then told them that God still sent angels to guard His children in their hour of danger.

We have also noted the provision of angels. On occasion they have even given food, as we know from the life of Elijah, following his triumph over the priests of Baal. Fearful, tired and discouraged, "As he lay and slept under a juniper tree, behold, then an angel touched him, and said . . . Arise and eat" (1 Kings 19:5–7). God has promised, "Are they not all ministering spirits, sent forth to minister for them who shall be heirs of salvation?" (Hebrews 1:14). Need we think this provisioning by angels ceased thousands of years ago?

When I was visiting the American troops during the Korean War, I was told of a small group of American marines in the First Division who had been trapped up north. With the thermometer at twenty degrees below zero, they were close to freezing to death. And they had had nothing to eat for six days. Surrender to the enemy seemed their only hope of survival. But one of the men, a Christian, pointed out certain verses of Scripture, and taught his comrades to sing a song of praise to God. Following this they heard a crashing noise, and turned to see a wild boar rushing toward them. As they tried to jump out of his way, he suddenly stopped in his tracks. One of the soldiers raised his rifle to shoot, but before he could fire, the boar inexplicably toppled over. They rushed up to kill him only to find that he was already dead. That night they feasted on meat, and began to regain their strength.

The next morning just as the sun was rising they heard another noise. Their fear that an enemy patrol had discovered them suddenly vanished as they found themselves face to face with a South Korean who could speak English. He said, "I will show you out." He led them through the forest and mountains to safety behind their own lines. When they looked up to thank him, they found he had disappeared.

Angels in Judgment

As we continue to study how to gain the help of angels in our lives today, we need to look soberly once again at the relation of angels to judgment.

Just before fire and brimstone fell on Sodom because of its sins, the angel said, "For we will destroy this place . . . the Lord hath sent us to destroy it" (Genesis 19:13).

In Daniel 7:10 the Word of God says, "A fiery stream issued and came forth from before him . . . the judgment was set, and the books were opened." In scores of places in the Bible God tells us that He will use angels to execute His judgments on all those who have refused to obey His will by failing to receive Christ as Savior and Lord. As Jesus said, "The Son of man shall send forth his angels, and they shall gather out of his kingdom all things that offend, and them which do iniquity; and shall cast them into a furnace of fire: there shall be wailing and gnashing of teeth" (Matthew 13:41, 42). Jesus also said, "It shall be more tolerable for Tyre and Sidon at the day of judgment, than for you" (Matthew 11:22). And again, "every idle word that men shall speak, they shall give account thereof in the day of judgment" (Matthew 12:36). "For there is nothing covered, that shall not be revealed; neither hid, that shall not be known" (Luke 12:2).

God is recording not only the words and actions but all the thoughts and intents of our hearts. Someday you and I will have to give an account, and at that time our final destiny will be determined by whether we have received or rejected Jesus. Paul said that God would give "to you who are troubled rest with us, when the Lord Jesus shall be revealed from heaven with his mighty angels, in flaming fire taking vengeance on them that know not God and that obey not the gospel of our Lord Jesus Christ" (2 Thessalonians 1:7–8).

Justice demands that the books of life be balanced, but without a final judgment this would be impossible. Laws too are meaningless unless accompanied by a penalty for those who break them.

Reason alone should tell us that there must come a time when God will call upon the Hitlers and the Idi Amins of the world for an accounting. Otherwise there is no justice in the universe.

Thousands of wicked men have lived evil lives and perpetrated their evil designs upon others without seeming to pay any penalty for their misdeeds in this life. However, the Bible says that a time will come when the crooked places will be made straight (Isaiah 45:2). In the great day of God's judgment men will call on Him for mercy, but it will be too late. In that day if men were to seek God, they would not be able to find Him. It would be too late. They could cry out for angels to deliver them, but it would be of no avail.

Angels Rejoice in the Salvation of Sinners

While angels will play an important role in executing the judgment of God on those who refuse Jesus Christ as Savior and Lord, yet at the same time the Bible informs us that they also rejoice in the salvation of sinners. Jesus tells several striking stories in Luke 15. In the first, a man had a hundred sheep. When one was lost, he left the ninety-nine in the wilderness to seek him. When he found the sheep he slung it over his own shoulders and brought it back to the fold. At home he summoned all his friends, saying, "Rejoice with me: for I have found my sheep which was lost" (verse 6). Jesus said, "I say unto you, that likewise joy shall be in heaven over one sinner that repenteth, more than over ninety and nine just persons, which need no repentance" (verse 7).

His second story is that of a woman who lost a valuable silver coin. She looked everywhere. She swept her house carefully. At last when she recovered the coin she called all her friends and neighbors saying, "Rejoice with me; for I have found the piece which I had lost" (verse 9). "Likewise, I say unto you, there is joy in the presence of the angels of God over one sinner that repenteth" (Luke 15:10).

In these two parables is not Jesus telling us that the angels of heaven have their eyes on every person? They know the spiritual condition of everybody on the face of the earth. Not only does God love you, but the angels love you too. They are anxious for you

to repent and turn to Christ for salvation before it is too late. They
know the terrible dangers of hell that lie ahead. They want you
to turn toward heaven, but they know that this is a decision that
you and you alone will have to make.

A rich young ruler came running to kneel before Christ one day,
and asked, "Good Master, what shall I do that I may inherit eternal life?" (Mark 10:17). When Peter had preached his great sermon
at Pentecost, Luke says the people were "pricked in their heart,
and said unto Peter, . . . what shall we do?" (Acts 2:37).

The African nobleman riding in the chariot across the desert
talked with Philip the evangelist. Suddenly the nobleman stopped
his chariot and said, "What doth hinder me to be baptized?" (Acts
8:36). At midnight the Philippian jailer asked Paul and Silas, "Sirs,
what must I do to be saved?" (Acts 16:30). Modern man forever
asks this same question. It is old, but always new. It is just as relevant today as it was in the past.

Just what must you do to cause the angels to rejoice? How do
you become reconciled to God? How do you repent of your sin?
A simple question demands a simple answer. Jesus made everything so simple, and we have made it so complicated. He spoke
to people in short sentences, using everyday words, illustrating His
message with never-to-be-forgotten stories. He presented the message of God in such simplicity that many were amazed at what
they heard. They could hardly believe their ears, because the message was so simple.

In the Acts of the Apostles, the Philippian jailer asked the apostle
Paul, "What must I do to be saved?" Paul gave him a very simple
answer, "Believe on the Lord Jesus Christ, and thou shalt be saved"
(Acts 16:30, 31). This is so simple that millions stumble over it.
The one and only way you can be converted is to believe on the
Lord Jesus Christ as your own personal Lord and Savior. You don't
have to straighten out your life first. You don't have to try to give
up some habit that is keeping you from God. You have tried all
that and failed many times. You can come "just as you are." The
blind man came just as he was. The leper came just as he was. The
thief on the cross came just as he was. You can come to Christ
right now wherever you are and just as you are—and the angels of
heaven will rejoice!

Some of the greatest and most precious words recorded in all of Scripture were spoken by Satan himself (not that he intended it to be so). In his discussion with God about Job, he said, "Hast not thou made an hedge about him, and about his house, and about all that he hath on every side? thou hast blessed the work of his hands, and his substance is increased in the land" (Job 1:10).

As I look back over my life I remember the moment I came to Jesus Christ as Savior and Lord. The angels rejoiced! Since then I have been in thousands of battles with Satan and his demons. As I yielded my will and committed myself totally to Christ—as I prayed and believed—I am convinced that God "put a hedge about me," a hedge of angels to protect me.

The Scripture says there is a time to be born and a time to die. And when my time to die comes an angel will be there to comfort me. He will give me peace and joy even at that most critical hour, and usher me into the presence of God, and I will dwell with the Lord forever. Thank God for the ministry of His blessed angels!

How to
Be Born Again

CONTENTS

PREFACE

TODAY BEING "BORN again" is big news. *Time* magazine carries a feature story on "Born Again Faith." Political candidates give the subject as much attention as the latest economic statistics or the energy crisis. A former Black Panther leader and radical of the 1960s returns from exile and announces, "My life has turned 180 degrees. I have been born again." A man who was deeply involved in one of the most publicized political scandals of our time writes a best seller explaining the change in his life as a result of being born again. A Gallup poll comes up with the astonishing conclusion that "more than one-third of those who are old enough to vote have experienced 'born again' religious conversions."

Born again!

Is it possible? Can life be transformed?

What's it all about? What does it mean?

Is it real? Will it last?

How is a person "born again"?

The expression "born again" is not a new term, invented by modern journalists to describe recent religious trends. The term "born again" is almost two thousand years old. One dark night, in the ancient city of Jerusalem, Jesus turned to one of the best-known intellectuals of his time and said, "I say to you, unless one is born again, he cannot see the kingdom of God" (John 3:3). In those words Jesus told us of both the necessity and the possibility of new birth—of spiritual transformation. Since that time untold millions throughout the ages have attested to the reality and the power of God in their lives through being born again.

A young Marine Corps officer, a veteran of the Vietnam War, described publicly the night battle in Vietnam when he and his troops came under enemy attack. Only a few were lifted out alive by helicopter. The sixteen surgical operations he endured had helped to restore his physical powers, but now he was speaking of the spiritual rebirth he had received since returning home. He said, "We bear an allegiance to the flag of our country, but unless we have been born again through faith in Christ, all our religion is worth nothing."

This lieutenant had been born again.

I think of the great Dutch Christian, Corrie ten Boom, who is now in her 80s. Her story of courage in the midst of Nazi persecution has inspired millions. She tells of an experience when she was only five years old when she said, "I want Jesus in my heart." She described how her mother took her little hand in hers and prayed with her. "It was so simple, and yet Jesus Christ says that we all must come as children, no matter what our age, social standing, or intellectual background."

Corrie ten Boom, at the age of five, had been born again.

I have had countless people tell me, in person and by letter, how they were born again and their lives were changed. A man from Milwaukee wrote, "Tonight my wife and I had come to the brink of ending our marriage. We felt we could no longer stay together under the conditions in which we were living. Both of us admitted that we thought we no longer loved each other. I no longer enjoyed her company nor appreciated my home life. We made bitter statements about each other. We could make no compromise, nor could we agree on how to improve our marriage even if we were to try.

"I believe it was God's will that I turned on the television and listened to your message about spiritual rebirth. As my wife watched with me, we began to search our hearts and felt a new life within us. I prayed that God would come into my heart and truly make me a new man and help me begin a new life. Our troubles seem rather slight now."

Both this man and his wife were born again.

What does it mean to be born again? It is not just a remodelling job, performed somehow by us on ourselves. Today we hear a lot about recycling, reconstruction, and reshaping. We renovate houses and add on more rooms. We tear down old buildings and build new ones in our cities, calling it urban renewal. Millions and millions of dollars are spent every year on health spas, beauty resorts, and exotic cosmetics—all by people hoping to reshape their faces or renew their bodies.

In like manner, people frantically pursue all sorts of promised cures for the renewal of their inner lives. Some people hunt for renewal at the psychiatrist's office. Others search for spiritual renewal in exotic oriental religions or processes of inward meditation. Still others seek for inner peace and renewal in drugs or alcohol. Whatever the path, however, they eventually come to a dead end. Why? Simply because man cannot renew himself. God created us. Only God can recreate us. Only God can give us the new birth we so desperately want and need.

I believe this is one of the most important subjects in the entire world. Governments may be elected or may topple. Military machines may advance and retreat. Men may explore outer space or probe the ocean depths. All of these events are part of the grand plan for humans on this planet.

But the central theme of the universe is the purpose and destiny of every individual. Every person is important in God's eyes. That is why God is not content to stand with His arms folded (as it were) and simply watch the human race wallow in misery and destruction. The greatest news in the universe is that we can be born again! "For God so loved the world, that He gave His only begotten Son, that whoever believes in Him should not perish, but have eternal life" (John 3:16).

This new birth happens in all kinds of ways. It may seem to happen over a period of time or in a moment. The paths which people take to reach that point of decision may be very direct or very circuitous. Whatever the path, we always find Christ at the end to welcome us. And that encounter with Christ, that new birth, is the beginning of a whole new path in life under His control. Lives can be remarkably changed, marriages excitingly improved, societies influenced for good—all by the simple, sweeping surge of individuals knowing what it is to be born again.

It may be that down inside you sense an unnamed need you cannot describe. Perhaps you have been consciously searching all your life to fill a void in your heart and to find a purpose for living. Perhaps outwardly you have been very successful in life, but you know it has not brought you peace and true happiness. Perhaps your life is an unbroken chain of heartaches and shattered dreams. Maybe you are just curious.

Whatever your background may be, I pray that God will use this little book to give you hope—to show you that you, too can be born again.

How to be Born Again is not for the theologians or the philosophers. There are many learned works of theology which probe the meaning of the new birth (or "regeneration," as theologians often call it). I know there have been different emphases among theologians concerning the new birth. Some have stressed the importance of what God does to bring us to faith. Some have stressed the importance of man's search for faith. Some have thought of the new birth as a single event in time, while others use the term to speak of all God wills to do in our lives. Ultimately there is a mystery about the new birth; we cannot understand everything about it, for our minds are finite.

However much the theologians may disagree about fine points of doctrine, the central truth of the new birth is clear: Man apart from God is spiritually dead. He needs to be born again. Only by God's grace through faith in Christ can this new birth take place.

My concern has been to make this book practical. Although we may not be able to say everything possible about the new birth, I have wanted to say everything that was necessary to help people who really want to know God. I want to help them come to have this life-changing experience. I want them—I want you—to be born again. I believe God wants you to be born again.

I was already working on this book when the term "born again" became big news. I have sensed the blessing of God as I have continued writing, and have sensed also that God may have led me to write this book at just the right time as millions wonder about being born again.

I gave my original manuscript to my friends Paul Fromer and Carole Carlson—and asked for help. Then with the added help of my wife and of Cliff and Billie Barrows, we finished it in a little apartment provided by dear Mexican friends while I recuperated from an illness.

Thus, my deepest appreciation to Bill and Vivian Mead of Dallas, Texas, and our wonderful friends the Servitje family in Mexico for making our working, recuperating period possible; to Paul Fromer, professor at Wheaton College, and to my secretary Stephanie Wills, who typed and retyped the manuscript, for the wonderful encouragement and help from my wife, Ruth, for the comments of Dr. John Akers and Mrs. Millie Dienert; but especially to Carole Carlson for the magnificent work she did in helping to simplify what may have been too deep and theological for people all over the world who I pray will read this book and experience "the new birth."

BILLY GRAHAM

Montreat, North Carolina

Author's Note. I am using the words *born again* and *regeneration* in their widest possible terms in this book. I recognize that in one sense they can be narrowly defined theologically, and in another sense cover the whole range of what we mean by "salvation." (The term *new birth* has been used in a wide and in a restricted sense; it may signify the whole process of salvation including the preparatory work of conviction and the concluding work of discipleship and, ultimately, glorification; or it can be used only for that act of imparting spiritual life, excluding the preparation phase and the lifetime phase.

I recognize that different denominations have slightly different interpretations. For example, the Roman Catholic Church regards regeneration as meaning everything in the transition from a position of condemnation on earth to a state of salvation in Heaven. The Augsburg Confession and the Formula Concordie use the new birth or regeneration in the wide meaning but distinguish between justification and sanctification. In the Reformed Churches, such as the Presbyterians, the term is used in the wide significance, but also distinguishes between justification and sanctification. Thus reformed theologians include not only the new birth but all that comes from it. Calvin taught that the new birth was the restoration of the Divine image within us. He believed that the new birth came not only by an instantaneous act of Divine life being infused to the spiritually dead, but also the various processes of spiritual growth that followed. The Westminster Confession of Faith never used the term regeneration, but used the term *effectual calling.* This meant the entire work of the Holy Spirit in the application of total redemption.

Sometimes these uses of the terms *new birth* and *regeneration* have led to semantic differences. In this book I am not making these distinctions but simply stating what most denominations basically believe historically—that man needs regeneration and to be born again—and how he may go about it if he lacks the assurance or if he has never made this commitment, whether he is a church member or not.

I
MAN'S PROBLEM

1

Why Am I So Empty?

WHEN THE VIKING landed on Mars, the world exclaimed, "Unbelievable! Magnificent!" The mysterious Red Planet had been penetrated. An ingeniously designed robot which was the result of one billion dollars and the probing minds of hundreds of scientists had accomplished a task that man had dreamed about for generations.

Exploring the great mysteries of the universe, trying to predict the quirks of nature, attempting to predict a trend in society or politics are all modern concerns.

In the business world, for instance, men search for ways to improve their efficiency. On office walls and on bulletin boards of sales organizations we see slogans like "Plan Ahead" or "Plan Your Work and Work Your Plan." Corporations hire firms at large fees to determine how they can improve their planning. Business, world politics, and economics change so fast that in a few days the direction of an entire country can change. Companies called "Think Factories" project thinking a decade or more in advance to keep abreast of the changing times.

In our daily lives we keep a calendar, trying to mark down appointments and schedule our days. If there were no planning, children would never get to the dentist, mothers would never make the community meeting, businesses and labor unions would collapse. We are always searching for ways to streamline our lives, to simplify daily living.

But what about the greater issues of life and death? Do we plan? Do we need to search for answers to the deep moral and spiritual questions so that our lives are more orderly? Man has always thought so, which is why we have philosophers, psychologists, and theologians. Today, however, much of the world in search of knowledge and fulfillment ignores God!

I knew a brilliant young lawyer who did not seem to find a need for God during his intense years of concentration as a student. Later, he began to write a book about a famous person. While he was working on this book we had a conversation during the course of which I detected that he was on a personal spiritual quest. He hoped to find somewhere in the life of the man who was the subject of his book a spiritual fulfillment which he himself wanted. He knew this person believed in God and had accepted Christ into his heart. He also seemed reassured that the one about whom he was writing had doubts from time to time.

This young man who has been searching for so long has now become interested in spiritual things. In my earlier contacts with him I thought he was an agnostic, interested only in gaining knowledge at the university and later at law school. Now I suspect that all through adolescence and his twenties he was searching for God without knowing it.

The Self-made Man

We are taught to be independent, to make it on our own. As we look at an individual we may say, "Now there's someone who's made it!" We admire him and respect his ability to "pull himself up by his bootstraps."

We have even had a well-known TV commercial that says, "Please, mother, I'd rather do it myself."

And yet within each of us is a deep-seated frustration: "I ought to be better. I believe I was made for something more; there must be more to life than this. Why am I so empty?"

Such feelings, often subconscious, cause us to struggle toward some unknown, unnamed goal. We may try to evade this quest, we may detour into a fantasy world, we may even regress to lower levels of life and seek to escape. We may throw up our hands in disgust and say, "What's the use? I'm O.K. just working and keeping out of trouble." But somehow, deep inside is a compulsion which invariably leads us to take up the search again.

This is one of the reasons the nation became fascinated by *Roots*, the product of Alex Haley's ten-year search for identity. My friend Rod McKuen felt rootless and a strange "vacuum" in his heart as he began his search for his true father. The oldest book in the possession of the human race is *Job*, and Job once exclaimed "Oh that I knew where I might find Him" (Job 23:3).

This search transcends race, age, economic status, sex, and educational background. Either man began nowhere and is looking for some place to go, or he began somewhere and lost his way. In either case, he's searching. None of us will ever find "total satisfaction" until we find that our roots are in eternity.

A famous scientist at an eastern university asked to see me. Somewhat surprised, I met him in a quiet room at the Student Union. Suddenly this brilliant man, admired by many and respected as a leader in his field, broke down. When he regained his composure he told me: "I'm at the point of ending my life. . . . My home is a wreck, I'm a secret alcoholic, my children don't respect me. I've never really had a guiding principle in my life except to be recognized in my field of physics. I've come to realize that I don't really know the true values of living. I've watched you on TV and although I don't understand all you're trying to communicate, I have a conviction that you know what the real meaning of life is."

He hesitated, and I'm sure the next thing this famous, self-made man said was very difficult for him: "I've come to you for help." It was a desperate cry.

From every culture, every country—from those who cannot read to Nobel Prize winners—there is the age-old phenomenon, the mystery of *anthropos*, the "upward-looking one," the one who is searching, inquiring for life's deeper and often hidden meaning.

In airports, on planes, in hotel lobbies across the world, people have come to me with serious questions about broken family relationships, ill health, or financial catastrophes. But more often they reveal empty souls. On an airplane flight a man poured out his life story to me. It was a saga of shattered dreams, broken hopes, and emptiness. Before we parted he had said "yes" to Christ. Tremendous relief came over his face as he whispered, "Thank you."

When we landed, I watched him embrace his wife and talk excitedly to her at the same time. I don't know what their conversation was, but from his expression he was evidently telling her of his new relationship with the Lord. I can only imagine how amazed she must have been at the change, because he had told me how his temper and unfaithfulness had just about broken their marriage.

I don't know if his marriage was put back together, because I never saw him again, but his direction was certainly changed on that plane trip.

Fame and Fortune

One of our best known show biz personalities asked me to come to his dressing room after a show on which I had appeared. He motioned me in and said, "I make people laugh . . . but inside I feel like hell. I've been married twice; both marriages have broken up. It's been mostly my fault, I guess, but I don't think I could make a go of a third marriage unless I could find some sort of fulfillment which I don't know how to get."

He stopped and looked at me. "Do you think what I'm really looking for is summed up in the word *God?*"

All of his fame and money had not satisfied his searching heart.

A man who was destined to be very influential in the life of Charles Colson, of Watergate fame, was Tom Phillips. Colson writes in his book, *Born Again,* that Phillips said: "'It may be hard to understand . . . but I didn't seem to have anything that mattered. It was all on the surface. All the material things in life are meaningless if a man hasn't discovered what's underneath them. . . .

"'One night I was in New York on business and noticed that Billy Graham was having a Crusade in Madison Square Garden,' Tom continued. 'I went—curious, I guess—hoping maybe I'd find some answers. What Graham said that night put it all into place for me. I saw what was missing—the personal relationship with Jesus Christ, the fact that I hadn't ever asked Him into my life, hadn't turned my life over to Him. So I did it—that very night at the Crusade.'"[1]

Once again a man was forced to examine his soul.

I was in another country at one time and was invited to have lunch with a man who, materially speaking, had everything this world could offer. In fact, he expressed to me how he could buy anything he wanted. He had traveled extensively in business; everything he touched seemed to turn to gold. He was leader of his social set, and yet in his own words he said, "I'm a miserable old man, doomed to die. If there is a hell, that's where I'm headed."

I looked through the beautiful old windows at the snow falling gently on the manicured lawn and thought about others, like him, who had expressed to me similar thoughts about the emptiness of life without God—the meaninglessness of life for a man who has everything to live with, but nothing to live for. My attention came back with a start as I heard him say, "I've asked you here today to read the Bible to me and to talk to me about God. Do you think it's too late? My father and mother were strong believers in God and often prayed for me."

The verse from Matthew 4:4 flashed across my mind: "Man shall not live on bread alone." And Luke 12:15 tells us, "Not even when one has an abundance does his life consist of his possessions."

We read every day about the rich, the famous, the talented, who are disillusioned. Many of them are turning to the occult, or Transcendental Meditation, or Eastern religions. Some are turning to crime. The questions they thought were answered are left dangling: What is man? Where did he come from? What is his purpose on this planet? Where is he going? Is there a God who cares? If there is a God, has He revealed Himself to man?

Is the Intellectual Searching?

The men and women who are considered part of the intellectual community are searching for the same meaning, the same sense of fulfillment, but many are hampered by their own sense of pride. They would like to save themselves, because pride nourishes self-esteem, making us believe we can manage ourselves without God.

The famous English writer and philosopher, Bertrand Russell, wrote prolifically concerning ethics, morals, and human society, trying to prove what he believed were fallacies in the Bible. When it came to the pride of the intellectual, Russell wrote, "Every man would like to be God, if it were possible; some few find it difficult to admit the impossibility."[2]

From the very beginning of time, man has said, like Lucifer, "I will be like the Most High" (Isa. 14:14, kjv).

The search continues. The heart needs filling, and most intellectuals come to a point in their lives when the academe, the scientific community, the business or political activities are no longer enough.

A brilliant analyst of the cultural scene wrote: "Man, being human, however, tries again and again to evade the logic of his own position, and searches for his true self, his humanity, his freedom, even if he can only do so by means of sheer irrationality or completely unfounded mysticism."[3]

We see the results of man searching for his true self in mystic experiences, new cults, and what is called the New Consciousness. "Man today wants to experience God. It is not faith or knowledge which is the key word, but experience."[4]

As the desire for this experience increases, the false philosophies and false gods become acceptable. A European intellectual says: "For centuries there has been the search for the attainment of that ideal which the Greeks called ataraxia, the idea of quiet calm, of deep inner contentment, beyond the restlessness, frustrations, and tensions of normal living. Many searched for this via philosophy and religion, but always there has been the parallel search for short cuts."[5]

An American scholar writes, "As man's search for new experiences, new leaders, new hopes, increases in intensity, there will be that continued desire to find an alternative route into what appears to be a dark future."[6]

Men desperately want peace, but the peace of God is not absence from tension or turmoil, but peace in the midst of tension and turmoil.

In Calcutta, India, I wanted to see a great woman of God who is known to the world as Mother Theresa. I arrived early in the evening and the sisters hated to disturb Mother Theresa, because three men had died in her arms that day and she had just gone to her room to get a bit of rest. However, the official who brought me there sent a note to Mother Theresa, and in a few minutes she was there. I immediately had the impression of this saintly woman as a person who has peace in the midst of turmoil. It's the peace that passes all understanding, and all misunderstanding, too.

How desperately we need that kind of peace during a generation which is being torn apart by internal unrest and despair. The daily newspapers are classics in negative outlook. Terrorism, bombings, suicide, divorce, general pessimism are the diseases of the day because in his pride man refuses to turn to God!

The honest intellectual, however, the one who keeps an open mind along with his searching heart, is the one who makes a thrilling discovery. Dr. Rookmaaker says: "We cannot understand God fully, nor know His work completely. But we are not asked to accept in blind faith. On the contrary: we are asked to look around us, and know that the things He tells us through His Son and His prophets and apostles are true, real, and of this world, the cosmos He has made.

"Therefore our faith can never be just 'out of the box,' irrational. Faith is not a sacrifice of the intellect if we believe in the biblical account of history."[7]

Who Needs Help?

In the rash of disaster movies in the middle 70s there was one called *Earthquake*. When the devastating quake hit, two of the main characters in the movie found shelter under a sturdy car from the flying debris and the terror of unleashed nature. At that moment they didn't reason about what had happened; they didn't analyze what they were going to do; they knew they needed help and dove for shelter.

The person who is on the bottom of life's circumstances wants help immediately. He doesn't need to analyze and examine how help comes; he only knows he needs to be saved.

When it comes to the disasters of our inner earthquakes some intellectuals want to know the source of help and all the details concerning that source. The intellectual has a certain set of beliefs which are self-sufficient and he believes his system is complete. Other intellectuals accept blindly the counterfeits which may be veiled in such complex language and thought patterns that the denial of their premises would sound ignorant. It's very difficult for some to say, "That doesn't really make good sense and I don't understand what is being said."

Nevertheless, many intellectual searchers have opened their minds and hearts to the truth of the Good News and found new life.

A young Hindu who was doing graduate study in nuclear medicine at UCLA was just beginning her second year of study when she came to a Crusade. At the end of the service she accepted Christ as her Savior and was born again.

A brilliant surgeon who came to a Crusade heard me say that if gaining Heaven depended upon good deeds I wouldn't expect to get there. He had devoted his life to helping humanity, but at that moment he realized his training, his years of hard work and devotion, his sleepless nights with patients, and his love for his profession wouldn't earn him a place with God. This man, who had seen many births himself, knew what it was to be born twice.

Many people think Christ talked only to down-and-outers or children. One of His greatest encounters during His teaching ministry was with an intellectual. This man, whose name was Nicodemus, had a very rigid philosophical and theological system, and it was a good plan, with God at the center. However this "intellectual" structured his philosophical religious system without the new birth—found only in Jesus Christ!

What did Jesus, the carpenter from Nazareth, tell this well-educated man? He said, in words like these, "Nicodemus, I'm sorry I can't explain it to you. You have seen something that troubles you, that doesn't fit your system. You admit I am more than an ordinary man, that I act with the power of God. This may not make sense to you, but I can't explain it to you because your assumptions do not allow for a starting point. Nicodemus, to you it's not 'logical.' Nothing in your thought patterns permits it. You cannot see with spiritual insight until you are born spiritually. You will just have to be born again."

Nicodemus was baffled. "'And how can a man who's getting old possibly be born?' replied Nicodemus. 'How can he go back into his mother's womb and be born a second time?'" (John 3:4, Phillips).

The intellectual asks, "How can a man be born twice?"

If anyone is to find the answer to his search he must reject much of his old system and plunge into a new one. He will see the possibility of what he thought was impossible.

"That is also why only this uniquely 'impossible' faith—with a God who is, with an Incarnation that is earthly and historical, with a salvation that is at cross-purposes with human nature, with a Resurrection that blasts apart the finality of death—is able to provide an alternative to the sifting, settling dust of death and through a new birth open the way to new life."[8]

In the mountains near our home there was a small plane lost with four people on board. At the same time a fifteen-year-old girl was lost in approximately the same area in the Great Smoky Mountains. It was a sad time for our little community because the four were killed and the girl was never found.

As my wife talked to a man who helps us about the tragic events of these people, he told her a story from his own experience. He was born and raised in these mountains, he said, and thought he could never get lost. The mountains were his playground as a child and his hunting area as an adult. One day, however, he found himself groping through the brush and clambering over the rocks, hopelessly confused. He wandered and retraced his steps and suddenly, to his relief, came upon an old man in a mountain cabin. He told Ruth that he would never forget the advice the old man gave him: "When you find yourself lost in the mountains, never go down—always go up. At the top of the ridge you can get your bearings and find your way again."

We can become lost in the mountain of life. We have two choices: we can either go down and get caught in drugs, depression, emptiness, and confusion, or we can keep heading up. The direction we go will determine whether we find ourselves or not.

In this Age of Quest the most important is our personal search for answers concerning life and about God. That search will propel us in the only true direction, in only one way, and we will be embarked on that journey when we are born again.

2

Can Anyone Tell Me
Where to Find God?

ADRUNK WAS LOOKING for something on the sidewalk one night under a street light. He groped along the ground, feeling the cement, occasionally grabbing the pole for support. A passerby asked what he was looking for. "Lost my wallet," the drunk replied. The passerby offered to help him look, but with no success.

"Are you sure you lost it here?" he asked the drunk.

"'Course I didn't!" the drunk replied. "It was half a block back there."

"Then why aren't you looking back there?"

"Because," answered the drunk with baffling logic, "there ain't no street lights back there."

Searching is important, but it doesn't do any good unless we search in the right places.

The governor of one of our states entertained us in his home and after dinner asked to talk to me privately. We went into his study and I could see that he was struggling with his emotions, but finally he said, "I'm at the end of my rope. I need God. Can you tell me how to find Him?"

A young man, toughened in the Green Berets, so strong that his hands had been insured as lethal weapons, fell upon the floor of his room one night, weeping like a helpless child. "God, God, where are you?"

From the ghetto to the mansion, from community leader to

prisoner on death row, man wonders if there is a God. And if there is, what is He like?

A remarkable fact for all seekers of God is that belief in some kind of God is practically universal. Whatever period of history we study, whatever culture we examine, if we look back in time we see all peoples, primitive or modern, acknowledging some kind of deity. During the past two centuries archaeology has unearthed the ruins of many ancient civilizations, but none has ever been found that did not yield some evidence of a god who was worshiped. Man has worshiped the sun and carved idols. Man has worshiped a set of rules, animals, and other men. Some seem to worship themselves. Man has made gods out of his imagination, although basically through a fog of confusion he believes that God does exist.

Some people give up the pursuit of God in frustration, calling themselves "atheists" or "agnostics," professing to be irreligious. Instead they find it necessary to fill the vacuum left within them with some other kind of deity. Therefore man makes his own "god"—money, work, success, fame, sex, or alcohol, even food.

Today many use their nation as an object of worship, espousing the gospel of nationalism. They mistakenly attempt to displace the true and living God with the religion of nationalism. Others make a god of their cause. Although many radical groups deny faith in God, thousands willingly lay down their lives and suffer privation and poverty because of their belief in "the cause" or "the revolution."

Failing to find the true God, millions declare their allegiance to lesser gods and causes. They find no ultimate answers or satisfaction, however. Just as Adam was made for fellowship with God, so are all men. Jesus commented on the First Commandment by saying, "And you shall love the Lord your God with all your heart, and with all your soul, and with all your mind, and with all your strength" (Mark 12:30).

He meant that man, unlike a stone or an animal, has the capacity to love God.

Two-Way Search

Although the wise person seeks God, we have seen that he doesn't have the intellectual capacity to reason his way through to God. He must raise a serious personal question: "Is there any hope of being successful in this search? Can I really know God?"

Once when being interviewed by Ludovic Kennedy on BBC in London, I was asked, "Who made God?" The answer was simple. "No one made God." God is self-existent.

"In the beginning God" are the words which build the cornerstone of all existence. Without God there would have been no beginning and no continuing. God was the creating power and the cohesive force that brought cosmos out of chaos. By divine fiat He brought form out of shapelessness, order out of disorder, and light out of darkness.

Scientists cannot see God in a test tube or a telescope. God is God and the mind of man is too small!

Blaise Pascal, the celebrated seventeenth century French physicist, said, "A unit joined to infinity adds nothing to it any more than one foot added to infinite length. The finite is swallowed up by the infinite and becomes pure zero. So are our minds before God."

As we seek this great God, what route are we to take? How can a created, finite human being, limited by time and space, understand an infinite God?

Our failure to comprehend God fully should not strike us as strange. After all, we live surrounded by mysteries we cannot explain—mysteries far simpler. Who can explain why objects are always attracted to the center of the earth? Newton formulated the law of gravity, but he couldn't explain it. Who can explain reproduction? For years scientists have tried to reproduce a living cell and solve the mystery of procreation. They believe they are coming close, but as yet they are without success.

We have become accustomed to accepting as fact many mysteries we cannot explain. I am amazed when my wife mixes corn meal, shortening, eggs, baking powder, and buttermilk, and I see the soupy mixture slowly rise in the oven and come out light and fluffy with a crispy brown crust. I don't understand it, but I accept the results.

God is far more complex than some of the earthly phenomena we cannot understand. However, we could present many arguments before a very skeptical jury which would suggest the existence of God. In the scientific realm we know that whatever is in motion must be moved by something else, since motion is the response of matter to power. Yet in the world of matter there can be no power without life, and life presupposes a being who produces the power to move such things as tides and planets.

Another argument says that nothing can be the cause of itself. It would be prior to itself if it caused itself to be, and that is an absurdity!

Consider the law of life. We see objects that have no intellect, such as stars and planets, moving in a consistent pattern, cooperating ingeniously with one another. It is evident that they achieve their movements not by accident but by design.

Whatever lacks intelligence cannot move intelligently. What gives direction and design to these inanimate objects? It is God. He is the underlying, motivating force of life.

Many evidences and arguments suggest God's existence, yet the plain truth is that God cannot be proved by intellectual arguments alone. If the human mind could fully prove God, He would be no greater than the mind that proves Him!

Ultimately you must come to God by faith. Faith is the link between God and man. The Scriptures say you must believe that *He is*. "Faith" is used many times in the Bible, and God has taken it upon Himself to encourage that faith. God continues to pursue man—just as man is searching for Him.

In spite of man's repeated rebellion, God loves man with an everlasting love. Some earthly fathers give up on their children when they fall into habits and company that are despicable. A father might order his son or daughter out of the house and tell them never to return. On the other hand, some fathers and even mothers deny their children before they are born. We know young people—even grown ones—whose lives are scarred by parental rejection. The only way such a person can be healed is to accept the fact and ask the Lord to supply the lack. The Bible says, "When my father and my mother forsake me, then the Lord will take me up" (Ps. 27:10, KJV).

God has never forsaken man. The most dramatic quest of the centuries is God's loving and patient pursuit of man.

When man chose in the Garden of Eden to defy God's law, to break the line of communication between himself and God, they could no longer have fellowship. Light and darkness could not live side by side. Why did this barrier come between God and His creation? The cause is a characteristic of God that the average person does not comprehend. God is absolute "holiness."

Long ago God said to Israel, "I the Lord your God am holy" (Lev. 19:2).

In the book of Revelation the cry in heaven night and day is, "HOLY, HOLY, HOLY, is THE LORD GOD, THE ALMIGHTY, who was and who is and who is to come" (Rev. 4:8).

A holy God recoils from our evil; He cannot look upon sin because it is ugly and revolting to Him. Because man was stained with sin, God could no longer have fellowship with him. However, *God loves us—in spite of ourselves!*

God had a plan to restore fellowship with man, in spite of his sin. If God didn't have a plan, certainly no one else can! He had said to Adam and Eve at the very beginning when they broke His law, "You shall surely die" (Gen. 2:17). In a later chapter we will discuss the three dimensions of death. Man had to die or God would have had to go back on His word, and God cannot be a liar or He would no longer be God.

We can see that because man still sins, still defies authority and still acts independently of God, a great gulf exists between him and God. Twentieth-century man and woman are no different from Adam and Eve. We may have added some sophisticated technology, built a few skyscrapers, and written several million books, but there is still a chasm between sinful man and holy God. Yet across this dark, barren abyss, God calls, even pleads, with man to be reconciled to Him.

God loves us.

The Apostle John said that "God is love" (1 John 4:8).

The prophet Jeremiah quotes God as saying, "'I have loved you with an everlasting love; therefore I have drawn you with loving-kindness'"(Jer. 31:3).

Another prophet, Malachi, said, "'I have loved you,' says the Lord" (Mal. 1:2).

In every good novel or play there must be conflict. But even Shakespeare could not have created a more powerful plot than the divine dilemma. We know that man is sinful and separated from God. Because God is holy, He couldn't automatically forgive or ignore man's rebellion. Because God is love, He couldn't completely cast man aside. Conflict. How could God be just and the justifier? This is the question Job posed: "But how can a man be in the right before God?" (Job 9:2).

God Speaks

Radio was just coming of age when I was a boy. We would gather around a crude homemade set and twist the three tuning dials in an effort to establish contact with the transmitter. Often all the sound that came out of the amplifier was the squeak and squawk of static. It wasn't very exciting to listen to all those senseless sounds, but we kept at the controls with anticipation. We knew that somewhere out there was the unseen transmitter, so if contact was established and the dials were in adjustment we could hear a voice loud and clear. After a long time of laborious tuning the far distant sound of music or a voice would suddenly break through and a smile of triumph would brighten the faces of everyone in the room. At last we were tuned in!

Perhaps you have been puzzled that the prophets said God spoke to them. Does He speak to us? Does He tell us where He is—how we can find Him—how we can be right with Him? How God has answered these questions in His Word is the subject of part 2 of this book, which deals with the kind of person Jesus Christ was and the work He did. God has solved the problem, He does tell us about Himself and his loving concern. The key is a line of communication which is "revelation."

Revelation means "to make known" or "to unveil." Revelation requires a "revealer," who in this case is God. It also requires "hearers"—the chosen prophets and apostles who recorded in the Bible what He told them. Revelation is communication in which God is at one end and man is at the other.

In the revelation that God established between Himself and us we can find a new dimension of living, but we must "tune in." Levels of living we have never attained await us. Peace, satisfaction, and joy we have never experienced are available to us. God is trying to break through. The heavens are calling and God is speaking!

Have you heard God's voice? At the same time you are searching for God, He is speaking to you.

3

Does God Really Speak to Us?

GOD HAS SPOKEN to us from the beginning. Adam heard the voice of the Lord in the Garden of Eden. God also spoke to Eve, and she knew who was speaking and must have trembled because she knew she had disobeyed Him.

Two people, a man and a woman, chose to disobey God and plunged into a world that was spiritually dark and dead—and physically unproductive except by hard work and suffering. The world was under the judgment of God. The Bible teaches that man is in a period of spiritual blackout. "The god of this world has blinded the minds of the unbelieving" (2 Cor. 4:4).

Isaiah, the great Hebrew prophet, said, "We grope along the wall like blind men, we grope like those who have no eyes; we stumble at midday as in the twilight, among those who are vigorous we are like dead men" (Isa. 59:10).

Isaiah was giving a vivid description of what sounds like physical blindness, but which is the darkness of the spirit.

To be trapped in physical darkness can be an uncanny experience. When Cliff Barrows and I were in England just after World War II we drove down the streets in fog so thick that one of us had to walk in front of the car to prevent it from running into the curb. This was a new experience, a type of "blackout" which was frightening.

How much worse it is to be forever spiritually blacked out and trapped! There are those who have physical blindness and yet are able to "see" better than a sighted person.

There is a beautiful Korean girl with a voice that has been described as "electric." She also plays the piano beautifully, and yet she is physically blind. Kim sees more than many with 20-20 vision and does not consider her blindness a handicap, but a gift from God. I have found her to have mental, psychological, and spiritual insights which are absolutely amazing.

Man is also spiritually deaf. Another great prophet said, people have "ears to hear but do not hear" (Ezek. 12:2). Jesus said it with more force: "If they do not listen to Moses and the Prophets, neither will they be persuaded if someone rises from the dead" (Luke 16:31).

The difference between physical deafness and spiritual deafness is illustrated to me vividly at the Crusades. We have a section for the deaf and I have often stopped to shake hands with these men and women. At one Crusade about a dozen deaf persons were brought to see me in my office and I sat and talked to them through an interpreter. The light of Christ was quite obvious on the faces of many of them.

The world of the physically deaf is one which those of us with normal hearing find difficult to comprehend. But we walk in the world of the spiritually deaf every day.

Spiritually, many men and women are more than deaf and blind, they are dead. "You were dead in your trespasses and sins" (Eph. 2:1).

For the spiritually dead there is no communication with God. Millions of persons long for a world of joy, light, harmony, and peace, instead they are engulfed in a world of pessimism, darkness, discord, and turmoil. They search for happiness, but it eludes them, just as a sunbeam or a shaft of light eludes a child who tries to catch it.

Many give up and give in to pessimism. Often their despondent attitude leads to a circle of cocktail parties or bars where they obliterate the reality of their world with the unreality of alcohol. Sometimes they are led to drugs or an all-consuming pursuit of a hobby or a sport. All these are symptoms of the great escapist disease caused by an insidious infection called sin.

Many persons want to dissect God under their own microscopes. After establishing their own methods of analysis they come to no conclusions. God remains the great cosmic silence, unknown and unseeing. However, God does communicate with those who are willing to obey Him. He penetrates the dark silence with free, life-giving discoveries in nature, the human conscience, Scripture, and the Person of Jesus Christ.

God Speaks in Nature

I was present when our youngest son was born, and our three sons-in-law and our oldest son were present at the births of their children. We all felt that we had experienced a miracle. As one of the doctors said, "How can anyone deny the existence of God after witnessing birth?"

In its own language, nature speaks of God's existence, whether it is the cry of a baby or the song of a meadowlark. It is the language of order, beauty, perfection, and intelligence. The intricacies of a flower are God's work; the instincts of the birds are within His plans. God speaks in the regularity of the seasons; in the movements of the sun, moon, and stars; in the balance of the elements which allow us to breathe. "The heavens are telling of the glory of God; and the firmament is declaring the work of His hands. Day to day pours forth speech, and night to night reveals knowledge" (Ps. 19:1,2).

The very size of the universe has always been incomprehensible to man, but as twentieth century exploration has taken man into space our minds have become boggled. Every scientist who lacks belief in God must be completely baffled when he surveys how small man is on this earth—part of an estimated 100 billion galaxies, with 100 billion stars and planets in each galaxy.

With the exploration of the universe this generation has also looked at the other end of the scale. The electron microscope and biochemical research have enabled investigators to examine cells which have been magnified up to 200,000 times. There are so many molecules in one drop of water that if they could be transformed into grains of sand there would be enough sand to pave a road from Los Angeles to New York!

The Apostle Paul said, "For since the creation of the world His invisible attributes, His eternal power and divine nature, have been clearly seen, being understood through what has been made" (Rom. 1:20).

God says that we can learn a great deal about Him just by observing nature. Since He has spoken through His universe men and women are without excuse for not believing Him. This is the reason the Psalmist writes, "The fool has said in his heart, 'There is no God'" (Ps. 14:1).

God speaks in nature but we cannot know Him simply by sitting under a tree and gazing at the sky. He has another avenue of revelation for us which is often called that "still small voice."

God Speaks in Our Conscience

What is a conscience? A dictionary definition is "the sense of right and wrong; ideas and feelings within a person that tell him when he is doing right and warn him of what is wrong."

"Let your conscience be your guide" is sometimes wise advice, but not always. God shows Himself in our conscience. Sometimes it is a gentle teacher, prodding us in the right direction like the usher in a darkened theater leading us to our seats. Other times our conscience is our worst enemy, torturing us day and night with agonizing unrest.

Paul describes the working of conscience in this way: "For when Gentiles who do not have the Law do instinctively the things of the Law, these, not having the Law, are a law to themselves, in that they show the work of the Law written in their hearts, their conscience bearing witness, and their thoughts alternately accusing or else defending them" (Rom. 2:14,15).

"A man's conscience is the Lord's searchlight exposing his hidden motives" (Prov. 20:27, *The Living Bible*).

When we realize that God takes a powerful light and shines it into the darkest recesses of our minds, examining not just our actions, but the motives behind those actions, it becomes clear that God does indeed speak through our conscience.

Even people who are not Christians realize the existence of something within themselves which is a guiding force. Thomas

Jefferson wrote almost two hundred years ago that "the moral sense, or conscience, is as much a part of man as his leg or arm. It is given to all human beings in a stronger or weaker degree, as force of members is given them in a greater or less degree."

Some persons, even without God, have a stronger sense of conscience than others. But the one with a seared or dead conscience is like an airplane without a pilot or a boat without a rudder—confused and directionless, on a collision course with circumstances. Through sin the conscience can become hardened, and even dead.

God Speaks in Scripture

The Bible is the textbook of revelation. In God's great classroom there are three textbooks—one called nature, one called conscience, and one named Scripture. The laws God revealed in nature have never changed. In the written textbook of revelation—the Bible—God speaks through words. The Bible is the one book which reveals the Creator to the creature He created! No other book that man has conceived can make that statement and support it with fact.

The Bible is unique in its claims, its teachings, and its survival. Today there are many persons who are looking at books which are supposed to give the answers to the great questions of life and death; many of these books are products of Eastern religions or humanistic philosophy. In his book *Evidence That Demands a Verdict*, Josh McDowell quotes a former professor of Sanskrit who spent forty-two years studying Eastern books and said this in comparing them with the Bible: "Pile them, if you will, on the left side of your study table; but place your own Holy Bible on the right side—all by itself, all alone—and with a wide gap between them. For, . . . there is a gulf between it and the so-called sacred books of the East which severs the one from the other utterly, hopelessly, and forever . . . a veritable gulf which cannot be bridged over by any science of religious thought.'"[1]

Skeptics have attacked the Bible and retreated in confusion. Agnostics have scoffed at its teaching, but are unable to produce an intellectually honest refutation. Atheists have denied its validity, but must surrender to its historical accuracy and archae-ological verification.

I picked up a reputable news magazine and read that a certain head of state made a remark about the economic trends. Nothing very startling about that. You and I read statements made by men and women every day. If we hear them from several different sources, we are inclined to believe that they're true and to tell someone else.

If we were confronted with a book which said in hundreds of different situations that, for instance, the Queen of England spoke, we would believe that she actually had been making statements. No doubt about it!

The writers of the Bible spoke in many ways to indicate that God gave them their information. In the Old Testament alone they said 3000 times that God spoke! Just in the first five books of the Bible we find such phrases as these:

"The Lord God called to the man"
"The Lord God said to the woman"
"The Lord said to Noah"
"God spoke unto Israel"
"God said"
"The Lord spoke saying"
"The Lord commanded"
"Hear the words of the Lord"
"Says the Lord"

Did God speak to these men as they were inspired to write? If He didn't, then they were the most blatant and consistent liars the world has ever known, or they were mentally deranged. Would a variety of men from different areas, many of them not knowing each other, tell more than 3000 lies on one subject? If they were mistaken in this area why should we believe anything they said? If we cannot believe that God spoke to men in the Bible, then we cannot believe that the prophecies of these great men came true—and yet they did!

If someone lies to you two or three times, you begin to distrust him. You find it difficult, if not impossible, to believe anything he says. However, we would have to negate everything in the Bible if we thought that the Bible writers lied when they said God spoke.

Jesus quoted frequently from the Old Testament. He knew it well and never doubted the Scriptures. He said, "Scripture cannot be broken" (John 10:35).

The Apostles often quoted the Old Testament Scriptures. Paul said, "All Scripture is inspired by God" (2 Tim. 3:16). Peter said, "For no prophecy was ever made by an act of human will, but men moved by the Holy Spirit spoke from God" (2 Pet. 1:21).

Many people get their belief about the Bible from secondhand sources. A smattering of biblical movie epics, some television reruns, hearsay, and courses on comparative religion give them man's view of Scripture. In high school or college classes students take courses in "the Bible as Literature." Many times these classes are used to undermine the faith of young people unless there is a teacher who understands the Bible and has a strong faith in God. I know students who have studied such topics as the "Myths and Discrepancies of the Bible."

Secondhand sources will not do.

A verse or a story in the Bible may speak to someone in a way someone else could not imagine. It was a firsthand source in a secondhand bookstore that changed the lives of an entire family.

My wife has a weakness for books—especially old, choice religious books which are now out of print. At one time Foyles in London had a large secondhand religious book department. One day during the 1954 London Crusade she was browsing through the books in Foyles when a very agitated clerk popped out from behind the stacks and asked if she was Mrs. Graham. When she told him that she was, he began to tell her a story of confusion, despair, and frustrations. His marriage was on the rocks, his home was breaking up, and business problems were mounting. He explained that he had explored every avenue for help and as a last resort planned to attend the services at Harringay arena that night. Ruth assured him that she would pray for him, and she did. That was in 1954.

In 1955 we returned to London. Again my wife went into Foyles' secondhand book department. This time the same clerk appeared from behind the stacks, his face wreathed in smiles. After expressing how happy he was to see her again, he explained that he had gone to Harringay that night in 1954 as he had said he would, that he had found the Savior, and that the problems in his life had sorted themselves out.

Then he asked Ruth if she would be interested in knowing what verse it was that "spoke to him." She was. Again he disappeared behind all the books and reappeared with a worn Bible in his hand. He turned to Psalm 102, which I had read the night that he had attended the Crusade. He pointed out verse 6, "I am like a pelican of the wilderness; I am like an owl of the desert" (KJV). This had so perfectly described to him his condition that he realized for the first time how completely God understood and cared. As a result he was soundly converted to the Lord Jesus Christ. And subsequently so was his entire family.

My wife was in London during 1972 at the time of a Harringay reunion. As the ceremonies closed, a gentleman came up to speak to her, but he didn't have to introduce himself. She recognized the clerk from Foyles. He was radiantly happy, introduced his Christian family, and explained how they were all now in the Lord's work—all because God spoke to him when he was "an owl of the desert!"

Make use of this tool of communication by which God speaks to us—namely, the Bible! Read it, study it, memorize it. It will change your entire life. It is not like any other book. It is a "living" book that works its way into your heart, mind and soul.

Speaking In Dark Places

In places where there is easy accessibility to the Bible, it may gather dust on the shelf. In countries where the Bible is subversive literature, God speaks in unusual ways.

A famous violinist was invited years ago by Chow En Lai to teach at one of the famous universities in the People's Republic of China. He was told that if he wanted to leave he would be able to do so. After seven years this violinist was completely disillusioned.

When he went to the exit permit office to apply for the right to leave, he was refused. However, he returned every day, and one day a piece of paper was slipped into his pocket. On returning home he found it there and pulled it out, only to discover that it was a page from the Bible. He read it with interest and found that it strangely spoke to his heart. On one of his subsequent visits a man came up to him and asked if he would like another page from the Bible. He said he would.

Each day when he returned to the exit permit office he was supplied with another page from the Bible. There in the People's Republic of China he was soundly converted to Jesus Christ. Ultimately he received his exit permit and went to Hong Kong. He is now a professor in another country.

When Corrie ten Boom was in Ravensbruck prison camp it was the studying and teaching of the Word of God which kept her mind clear so that when she was released she was mentally alert. Many inmates upon their release were little more than vegetables and had to be cared for until they regained some form of normalcy.

A similar story is told of a missionary who was imprisoned by the Japanese in China. At this concentration camp the penalty for owning even a portion of the Scriptures was death. However, a small Gospel of John was smuggled to her in a winter coat. At night when she went to bed she pulled the covers over her head and with her flashlight read a verse and then put herself to sleep memorizing that verse. In this way, over a period of time, she memorized the entire Gospel of John.

When she went to wash her hands she would take one page at a time, dissolve it in the soap and water, and flush it down the drain. "And that is the way," she said, "that John and I parted company."

This little missionary was interviewed by a *Time* reporter just before the prisoners were released. The reporter happened to be standing at the gates when the prisoners came out. Most of them shuffled along, eyes on the ground, little more than automatons. Then out came the little missionary, bright as a button. One of the reporters was heard to ask, "I wonder if they managed to brainwash her?"

The *Time* reporter overheard the remark and said, "God washed her brain!"

The Word of God hidden in the heart is a stubborn voice to suppress. Ruth had another experience in London which emphasizes this fact. During the meetings in Earls Court in 1966 she made friends with a little Cockney beatnik. Each night as we arrived, this thoroughly likable, irrepressible little rebel would be waiting for Ruth. During the Earls Court Crusade she would frequently sit with Ruth, or sometimes just walk with her to her seat. They began an unusual, but lasting friendship.

Ruth learned that the girl had, previous to her conversion, been on drugs. Ruth told her to memorize several verses which she felt would be important to her, like John 3:16, 1 John 1:8, and the last two verses of Jude. One night she even warned her that, because of her past background, when she hit a snag in life she would have two choices: one was to go back on drugs, the other was to go forward with the Lord Jesus Christ.

One night during the service the usher gave my wife a note saying, "I am on drugs and I need you. Please come help me." It was signed by this young friend.

Ruth slipped out of the meeting and found her waiting—white-faced, hollow-eyed, and obviously drugged. Ruth, having had little previous experience with drug-users, thought that they were handled as drunks and took her to a coffee stand to get her a cup of coffee. She didn't realize that was the last thing she should have done. On the way she asked the girl why she had done this, only to receive the reply, "Me best friend died on an overdose today."

Ruth wanted her to hear the sermon, and they sat down on a step within earshot of the service. The girl was in no condition to hear. Realizing that her little friend was fast passing out, Ruth wrote on the little card found at the bottom of a pocket package of Kleenex, something to this effect: "God loves me. Jesus died for me. No matter what I have done, He will forgive me if I repent and ask Him to forgive me."

The following year, 1967, we were back in London at Earls Court for another series of meetings. One evening Ruth was having tea with her young beatnik friend. The girl fished into her sack and brought out the crumpled Kleenex card on which Ruth had written the words the previous year. She asked Ruth when she had written these words. Ruth told her, but the girl had no recollection of what had happened that night. Then she repeated the verses of Scripture that Ruth told her to learn and asked when it was that she had learned them. Ruth explained to her, but she didn't remember the occasion. It is interesting that the drugs could cause amnesia up to a certain point, but they had not been able to take away the Word of God which she had hidden away in her heart.

A similar situation happened when Ruth fell out of a tree while trying to build a pipeslide for our grandchildren. She suffered a severe concussion and was unconscious for the better part of a week. As she regained consciousness, the thing that concerned her the most was that she could remember so little. Her greatest loss was that of the Bible verses which she had memorized down through the years.

In her notebook she has written how one night as she was fuzzily praying about this fact, out of nowhere came the words, "I have loved thee with an everlasting love, therefore with loving kindness have I drawn thee." There was no recollection of when or where she had memorized the verse, for her mind was still foggy. And yet—there it was!

God Speaks in Jesus Christ

God speaks most clearly in the person of His Son Jesus Christ. "God, . . . in these last days has spoken to us in His Son" (Heb. 1:1,2).

Throughout the ages many people have believed that God is a spirit within everyone. Tolstoi, the great Russian writer, said, "Every man recognizes within himself a free and rational spirit, independent of his body. This spirit is what we call God."

Philosophers have found God in everything. In the first century the Roman philosopher Seneca set the stage for belief throughout the ages when he wrote, "Call it nature, fate, fortune: all are but names of the one and same God."

Seneca was, of course, wrong. But so have millions of men throughout the ages been equally mistaken.

In most religions of the world we find some references to a belief that God would visit the earth. There have been many men who have come claiming they are God. One man from Korea during our time has drawn many followers by claiming to be the "Lord of the Second Advent."

However, it was not until the "fulness of time" when all the conditions were right, when all the prophecies were fulfilled, that God "sent forth His Son, born of a woman" (Gal. 4:4).

In a little town in the Middle East almost 2000 years ago, the prophecy in Micah 5:2 was fulfilled when God "was revealed in the flesh" (1 Tim. 3:16). This revelation came in the person of Jesus Christ.

The Scripture says about Christ, "In Him all the fulness of Deity dwells in bodily form" (Col. 2:9).

This revelation is the most complete God ever gave to the world. Do you want to know what God is like? All you have to do is look at Jesus Christ.

Nature has perfection and beauty; we see order, power, and majesty in the physical world around us. All of these descriptions apply to Jesus Christ. In the working of our conscience and the magnificence of the written Scriptures we find justice, mercy, grace and love. These are attributes of Jesus Christ. "The Word [logos] became flesh, and dwelt among us" (John 1:14).

To His disciples and to all of us living in this twentieth-century world, Jesus said, "Believe in God, believe also in me" (John 14:1). This sequence of faith is inevitable. If we believe in what God made and what God said, we must believe in the One whom God sent.

How can we believe? The means of understanding these facts of salvation is "faith." We are not always challenged to understand everything, but we are told to believe. "But these have been written that you may believe that Jesus is the Christ, the Son of God; and that believing you may have life in His name" (John 20:31).

Every need to know God, every expectation of eternal life, every desire for a new social order—all must be tied to the only One who can accomplish these goals—Jesus Christ. When we come to Jesus Christ, the unknown becomes known; we experience God Himself.

When our groping darkened lives experience the light of the eternal presence of God, we are able to see that another world stretches beyond the confusion and frustration of the world we live in.

A small child, not even old enough for school, went into one of those mirrored mazes at an amusement park. When her father discovered that she had slipped away he saw her trying to find her way out and beginning to cry in fear. She became increasingly confused by all the paths, until she heard her daddy call out, "Don't cry, darling. Put your hands out and reach all around. You'll find the door. Just follow my voice."

As he spoke the little girl became calm and soon found her way out and ran to the security of her father's outstretched arms.

God has revealed Himself to the human race on this little planet through nature, conscience, the Bible—and fully in the person of Jesus Christ.

4

But I'm Not Religious!

THE QUESTION IS often heard, "What about all the other religions of the world? Isn't one religion just as good as another?"

Few terms in the language of man have been so distorted and misunderstood as that of "religion." The 18th century German philosopher Immanuel Kant described religion as "morality or moral action." Hegel, the philosopher who influenced Hitler's thinking, said religion was "a kind of knowing."

"Religion" has many meanings for many people. It can mean the sadistic symbolism of the Manson girls, who cut an "x" on their foreheads; it can be the rituals of Transcendental Meditation or the chants of various cults; or it can suggest quiet meditation within the comforting walls of a church.

Many people say rather proudly, "I'm not very religious," but in spite of some of his own objections man is a religious being. The Bible, anthropology, sociology, and other sciences teach us that people long for some sort of religious experience.

My major in college was anthropology, which the dictionary explains as a science dealing with the races, customs, and beliefs of mankind. I have also had the privilege of traveling extensively on every continent. I have found from personal experience that what I learned from anthropology is true: man has naturally and universally a capacity for religion—and not only a capacity, for the vast majority of the human race practices or professes some form of religion.

Religion can be defined as having two magnetic poles, the biblical and the naturalistic. The biblical pole is described in the teachings of the Bible. The naturalistic pole is explained in all the man-made religions. In humanistic systems there are always certain elements of truth. Many of these faiths have borrowed from Judeo-Christianity; many use portions and incorporate their own fables. Other religions or faiths have in fragments what Christianity has as a whole.

The Apostle Paul described the naturalistic pole when he said that men "exchanged the glory of the incorruptible God for an image in the form of corruptible man and of birds and four-footed animals and crawling creatures" (Rom. 1:23).

All false religions cut away parts of God's revelation, add ideas of their own, and come out with various viewpoints that differ from God's revelation in the Bible. Natural religion does not come from God, but from the natural world He created and that turned away from Him in its pride.

A false religion is like the imitation of high fashion. I've read that after an exclusive showing of original designs in one of the fashion centers of the world like Paris, copies will soon appear in the mass merchandising stores under different labels. The very presence of counterfeits prove the existence of the real. There would be no imitations without a genuine product.

God's original design has always had imitators and counterfeits!

The Birth of Religion

How did all the religions of the world get started? A famous military conqueror from the past was able to state a truth, without realizing that he had charged right past the real Truth. Napoleon Bonaparte stated, "I would believe in a religion if it existed ever since the beginning of time, but when I consider Socrates, Plato, Muhammad, I no longer believe. All religions have been made by man."

Paul Bunyan once said, "Religion is the best armor that a man can have, but it's the worst cloak."

When did man invent this maze of religion? It began with a couple of fellows who are rather well known. When Adam and Eve had their sons, we might have thought they would have been able to instill in both of them the importance of a right relationship with God. However, Cain wanted to do it his own way. He approached the first altar with his offering of "the fruit of the ground," trying to regain "paradise" without accepting God's plan of redemption. Cain brought what he had grown, the distinctive elements of his own culture. Today we would call Cain's gift his attempt at salvation by works. But God never said we could work our way to heaven.

His brother, Abel, obeyed God and humbly offered the first of his flock in a sacrifice of blood. Abel agreed with God that sin deserved death and could be covered before God only through the substitutionary death of a guiltless sacrifice. Cain deliberately rejected this plan. God demanded a blood sacrifice.

The Bible writers knew that blood was absolutely essential for life. A person or an animal might get along without a leg or an eye, but no animal or man could live without blood. That is why the Old Testament said, "For the life of the flesh is in the blood" (Lev. 17:11).

Thus, the Bible teaches that atonement for sin comes only through the shedding of blood. "In fact, the law requires that nearly everything be cleansed with blood, and without the shedding of blood there is no forgiveness" (Heb. 9:22, NIV).

When we speak of the blood of Christ, therefore, we are saying that He died for us. Blood sacrifice underlined the seriousness of sin. Sin was a life-and-death matter. Only the shedding of blood could atone for sin. The death of Christ also underlined the principle of substitution. In the Old Testament a sacrificed animal was seen as a substitute; the innocent animal took the place of the guilty person. In the same way, Christ died in our place. He was innocent, but He freely shed His blood for us and took our place. We deserved to die for our sins, but He died in our place.

Because of Christ's death for us, we can know His life—now and eternally. "Knowing that you were not redeemed with perishable things . . . but with precious blood . . . of Christ" (1 Pet. 1:18,19).

When Cain chose to go his way, not God's way of blood, something bitter happened to his heart. He began to hate his brother, Abel. Just as the true Christian believer will often not be accepted by those who have their man-made religion, Abel was not accepted by Cain, and this hatred festered until Cain killed his brother.

Pride, jealousy, and hatred have been in the human heart in all cultures and all ages. Many years ago when I was a student in Florida a young man killed his older brother in a fit of jealousy. His father and mother had both been killed in an automobile crash, and when the will was read it indicated that the older brother had received two-thirds of an orange grove, leaving only a third to the younger brother. He became moody and depressed, angry at his deceased parents, and intensely jealous of his brother. Then the older brother disappeared, and about six weeks later his body was found tied with wire to the trunk of a cypress tree in a river.

Times haven't changed. Millions want salvation, but on their own terms; they want to chart their own courses and devise all kinds of routes to lead to God.

If Christianity is true, it is not a religion. Religion is man's effort to reach God. The dictionary describes religion as a "belief in God or gods . . . or worship of God or gods." Religion can be anything! But true Christianity is God coming to man in a personal relationship.

The modern interest in the occult and in Eastern religions is indicative of man's eternal search for God. We cannot escape the fact that man is instinctively religious, but God has chosen to reveal Himself to us through nature, conscience, the Scriptures, and through Jesus Christ. The Scripture says there is no excuse for a person not to know God!

In the Name of "Religion"

It's no wonder that people say with satisfaction, "I'm not religious." Extreme cruelties and great injustices have been perpetrated in the name of religion.

In China when my wife was growing up, frequently babies who died before cutting their teeth were thrown out to be eaten by pariah dogs. The people feared that if evil spirits thought they cared too much for the children they would come and take another one. They tried to prove their indifference in this crude way. "Religion" impressed Ruth as being grim and joyless, and often cruel.

I once saw a man in India lying on a bed of spikes. He had been there for many days, eating no food and drinking little water. He was attempting to atone for his sins. Another time in Africa I saw a man walk on coals of fire. Supposedly, if he came through unscathed, he was accepted by God; if he was burned, he was considered to be a sinner in need of more repentance.

In India a missionary who passed the banks of the Ganges noticed a mother sitting by the river bank with two of her children. On her lap was a beautiful new baby and whimpering beside her was a painfully retarded child of about three. On her return home that night, the missionary saw the young mother still sitting at the river bank, but the baby was gone and the mother was trying to comfort her little retarded child. Horrified at what she thought might be true, the missionary hesitated a moment and then walked over to the mother and asked her what had happened. With tears streaming down her cheeks, the mother looked up and said, "I don't know about the god in your country, but the god in mine demands the best." She had given her perfect baby to the god of the Ganges.

People have made human sacrifices in the name of religion. They have worshiped all types of idols, from brass monkeys to trees. In some of the Pacific islands, for instance, some of the islanders believe that the souls of their ancestors are in certain trees. Offerings are made to the tree, and they believe that if any injury occurs to the tree, some misfortune will come upon the village. They fear that if the tree were cut down, the village and all its inhabitants would inevitably perish.

In the name of religion, kings, emperors, and leaders of nations and tribes have been worshiped as gods. One English scholar wrote, "At a certain stage of early society the king or priest is often thought to be endowed with supernatural powers or to be an incarnation of a deity; . . . he is held responsible for bad weather, failure of the crops, and similar calamities."[1]

An example of the class of monarchs worshiped as deity was the Mikado, the spiritual emperor of Japan. In an official decree he received the title of "manifest or incarnate deity." An early account says of the Mikado: "It was considered as a shameful degradation for him even to touch the ground with his foot. . . . None of the superfluities of the body were ever taken from him, neither his hair, his beard, nor his nails were cut."[2]

Many people will shrug at "religion" and agree with the philosophy professor from a prestigious American university who wrote: "The term 'religion' has come into use as a label for referring all at once to Judaism, Christianity, Islam, Buddhism, Hinduism, Taoism, and Confucianism, as well as a great many other siblings, some of whom have proper names and some of whom do not, but all of whom are taken to be sufficiently similar to the seven mentioned here to make it useful to lump them together."[3]

Can we really lump Christianity with every "religion" of the world?

Without Excuse

From the very beginning of time, "natural" religion was introduced onto the human stage as a substitute for God's plan. The Apostle Paul describes this phenomenon in his letter to the Romans, using references to images resembling birds, animals, and serpents to illustrate man-made religion. But this doesn't describe all its forms. Today there are many new and more sophisticated religious expressions—especially at some universities—but they are really from the same root: man seeking God consciously or unconsciously.

Paul describes man's corruption of God's revelation: "For since the creation of the world His invisible attributes, His eternal power and divine nature, have been clearly seen, being understood through what has been made, so that they are without excuse. For even though they knew God, they did not honor Him as God, or give thanks; but they became futile in their speculations, and their foolish heart was darkened. Professing to be wise, they became fools. . . . For they exchanged the truth of God for a lie, and worshiped and served the creature rather than the Creator, who is blessed forever" (Rom. 1:20–25).

Paul is simply saying that all men everywhere possess at least a primitive knowledge of God. Some people greet this idea with cynicism, which initiates the inevitable question: What about the pagans who have never heard of Jesus?

What about the pagans on Main Street, U.S.A., or the pagans at Oxford or the Sorbonne? God created all of us in His image; everyone is answerable to the light that He revealed to them. How can a just God condemn people who have never had the opportunity of hearing the Gospel? The answer is in Genesis 18:25: "Shall not the Judge of all the earth do right?" (KJV).

God's nature will bear witness of a divine power and person to whom everyone will answer. On the other side, God's justice will be exhibited against those who fail to live up to the light that He has given them.

In my lifetime, I have heard of many instances in which people have been given insight into the "eternal power and divine nature" of God, without benefit of a Bible or an evangelistic crusade.

In the middle 1950s, we held a major Crusade in Madras, India. One man walked over 120 miles to attend these meetings. I was told that this man came from a village that had never had a missionary and, so far as anyone knew, the gospel of Christ was completely unknown. Yet he longed with all his heart to know the true and living God. He heard that a "guru" from America was going to be speaking, and his desire for God was so intense that he came and found Christ. Eight months later when Bishop Newbigin of the Church of South India (who told me the story) visited the village, he found the entire community had been turned into a church. Everyone had been led to Christ by this one man.

When we were preaching in northeast India in 1972, people walked for as much as ten days, carrying all their belongings on their shoulders, bringing their entire families from such places as Nepal, Sikkim, and Burma. We were told that a number of those people had never heard the name of Jesus Christ. They just heard that a religious meeting was going to be held and they wanted to come and see what it was about. Many stayed to find Christ.

I am convinced that when a man sincerely searches for God with all his heart, God will reveal Himself in some way. A person, a Bible, or some experience with believers will be used by God to reach the one who seeks.

A famous Bible teacher, Dr. Donald Barnhouse, told about a boat trip he had to take through the middle of Africa on a river. When he got into the boat, he noticed a chicken and thought it was probably for their next meal. After two or three hours he heard a roar in the distance and realized that they were approaching very turbulent water. The nationals who were rowing the boat steered it over to the bank, got out, and took the chicken into the woods. There they made a very crude altar. Preparatory to sacrificing the chicken, they chopped off its head and sprinkled the blood over the front of the boat. Dr. Barnhouse said he realized once more that even without a missionary and without God's Word having been taught to those people, they knew a sacrifice was necessary.

So Paul says that God has seen to it that all people everywhere possess basic knowledge of Him, His attributes, power, and divine nature. Through what they can observe, and through their consciences, they can respond to Him if they wish.

But humankind has turned away from Him. Their minds did not love the truth enough, their wills didn't desire to obey Him, their emotions were not excited by the prospect of pleasing Him.

What happened? What is still happening? Man suppresses the truth, mixes it with error, and develops the religions of the world.

Humanistic religions are often offended by biblical faith, which is the belief that accepts the Bible as the authoritative source of what sin is, and how through the life and atoning death of Christ, God can declare sinners "just." Natural religion contains just enough truth to make it deceptive. It may contain elements of the truth, or high ethical standards. Some of its followers at times use terms which sound like the language of the Bible. The English scholar C. S. Lewis said that all religions are really a preview or a perversion of Christianity.

Religion of man may have a very pleasant sound. Thomas Paine wrote, "The world is my country, all mankind are my brethren, and to do good is my religion." While morality or "do-goodness" may win the approval of men, it is not acceptable to God, nor does it reflect His full moral demands. In fact, some of the crudest immorality in human history has had the approval of natural religion.

There is a great counterfeiter who adapts himself to every culture, even deceiving true believers at times. He doesn't charge on the scene clothed in red and wearing a hideous mask but charms his way as an "angel of light." This is how Satan operates. Thousands of people have entered churches without discovering a vital experience with Jesus Christ. The substitutes have been handed them in the guise of religious rituals, good works, community effort, or social reform, all of which are commendable actions in themselves, but none of which can gain a person a right relationship with God.

There are many people who say, "I guess I'm a Christian," or "I try to be a Christian." There's no guess or "try to" in the Christian life. Even some of the great intellects of our time have not come to grips with this truth: The simplicity of the gospel can reach the mentally retarded as well as the geniuses.

The Compromisers

Where there is truth and error there is always compromise. Within some churches there is a movement to reshape the Christian message to make it more acceptable to modern man. A view held by many is that "the Christian churches have been, and still are, fountainheads of anti-intellectualism and opposition to critical thinking."[4]

Books are written and sermons preached scoffing at the Bible and the basic beliefs of the Christian faith. One thick volume is called *Bible Myths* and the chapter titled "The Miracles of Christ" starts this way: "The legendary history of Jesus of Nazareth, contained in the books of the New Testament, is full of prodigies and wonders. These alleged prodigies, and the faith which the people seem to have put in such a tissue of falsehoods, indicate the prevalent disposition of the people to believe in everything, and it was among such a class that Christianity was propagated."[5]

Time magazine, in a lengthy article on the Bible, said, "Questions about the Bible's truth are nothing new; they have arisen from its earliest days."[6]

There was an archaeology professor I knew at Wheaton College who was also studying at the University of Chicago. Frequently the Chicago professor would bring up some point to undermine the trustworthiness of the Scriptures. On each occasion the archaeology teacher would bring out some archaeological find which proved the authenticity of the Scriptures. At one point that professor at the University of Chicago exclaimed in exasperation, "That's the trouble with you evangelical archaeologists! You're always digging up something to prove us wrong and the Bible right!"

Archaeology has never uncovered anything that disproved the Scriptures.

Among some of those who are theologians but who fail to agree among themselves on which part of the New Testament to retain and which part to reject. Some of them seem to agree that the miracles were myths. They regard the resurrection as a subjective experience of the disciples rather than an objective historical event. They question that Jesus Christ was supernatural and reject any explanation that says part of His excellence came from the fact that He was God as well as man.

C. S. Lewis was baffled by biblical critics who would pick and choose among the supernatural events they accepted. "He wondered at the selective theology of the Christian exegete who, 'after swallowing the camel of Resurrection, strains at such gnats as the feeding of the multitudes.'"[7]

The Deceivers

From compromise to deceit is a small step. All through the Bible we are warned about false prophets and false teachers. Jesus said, "Beware of the false prophets, who come to you in sheep's clothing, but inwardly are ravenous wolves. . . . So then, you will know them by their fruits" (Matt. 7:15,20).

Sometimes the "sheep's clothing" is a clergyman's robe. He may be a liberal or a fundamentalist. The liberal is like the Sadducees of old, denying biblical truth. The extreme fundamentalists, like the Pharisees of old, may accept sound theology but add so much nonbiblical material to it. Other times the clothing may be worn by someone with a string of degrees, who speaks with logical-sounding phrases. It's difficult sometimes for a Christian to discern a false teacher, since in some ways he resembles the true teacher. Jesus spoke of false prophets who "show great signs and wonders, so as to mislead, if possible, even the elect" (Matt. 24:24).

The person behind the Great Deception is Satan himself. He is crafty and clever, working in such subtle and secretive ways that no Christian should brag that he is beyond the assaults of Satan.

The Apostle Paul warned Timothy, "But evil men and imposters will proceed from bad to worse, deceiving and being deceived" (2 Tim. 3:13). He also warned the church at Ephesus, "Let no one deceive you with empty words" (Eph. 5:6); and again, "As a result, we are no longer to be children, tossed here and there by waves, and carried about by every wind of doctrine, by the trickery of men, by craftiness in deceitful scheming" (Eph. 4:14).

A woman who now leads hundreds of women each week in a Bible class in California said that for years her pseudo-intellectualism had her grabbing onto every "religious thought" that was presented. After accepting Jesus Christ as her Savior and being born again spiritually, she said, "I'm no longer a child . . . carried about by every wind of doctrine."

This is a time when more false teachers will appear. We may be living in a time in history when this age may be drawing to an end. The Apostle Peter said: "But false prophets also arose among the people, just as there will also be false teachers among you, who will secretly introduce destructive heresies, even denying the Master who bought them, bringing swift destruction upon themselves. And many will follow their sensuality, and because of them the way of the truth will be maligned; and in their greed they will exploit you with false words; their judgment from long ago is not idle, and their destruction is not asleep" (2 Pet. 2:1–3).

When we realize that the heresies and the deceptions are secretly introduced, it should make us even more alert. The Sunday school, the Bible class, the pulpit, the classroom, and the mass media are being invaded en masse. Some of the terms of Christianity are even being used, for example, *peace, love, born again.* Watch for the words which pepper secular literature and have entirely different meanings; *messiah, a christ, redemption, regenerate, genesis, conversion, mercy, salvation, apostle, prophet, deliverer, savior, a spiritual leader.* Even great theological terms like *evangelical, infallible Bible,* etc. are rapidly losing their former meaning.

Thousands of untaught Christians are being deceived today, as are millions of people who are rejecting or ignoring the true Christ. Deceivers with intellectual arguments which sound like the epitome of scholarship are beguiling many.

Paul is not gentle with the false teachers. He says, "But the Spirit explicity says that in later times some will fall away from the faith, paying attention to deceitful spirits and doctrines of demons, by means of the hypocrisy of liars" (1 Tim. 4:1,2).

The Bible is very clear that many have turned away because they listened to Satan's lies and deliberately chose to accept the doctrines of devils rather than the truth of God.

Back to Basics

Church members and spiritually thirsty non-church members have been hungry for a personal, vital experience with Jesus Christ. Many have been turning to other forms of worship in addition to the church service.

In 1965 I wrote in my book *World Aflame* that "unless the church quickly recovers the authoritative biblical message, we may witness the spectacle of millions of Christians going outside the institutional church to find spiritual food." This is exactly what has happened.

We now estimate that there are over two million prayer groups and Bible study groups meeting in homes and churches in the United States that were not meeting ten years ago. One of the great hopes we see is that denominational leadership is beginning to recognize this and promote Bible studies conducted on a lay level with adequate leadership.

Our own Crusade preparation has revealed in recent years a far greater increase in actual home prayer meeting groups. In our most recent Crusades we established a prayer group on every block in the city. The result is that thousands of additional prayer meeting groups are being held in connection with the Crusades—in some cities as many as 5,000.

With nearly 50 million adult Americans having experienced "born again" religious conversions, I believe it is important to have a clear understanding of what this is all about.

An Old Cliché

Nothing could be more grossly wrong than the old cliché that "any religion will do, as long as you're sincere." What if the same line of reasoning were used with a baby? The mother would say,

"I don't have any milk, but I truly want my baby to be fed, so I'll just put some coke or a little wine in the bottle. After all, they're all liquids." Ridiculous as that may sound, it is no more so than the old "sincerity" answer.

Who invented religion? Let's go back to the brothers again. The two altar fires outside Eden illustrate the difference between true and false religion. One belonged to Abel, who made an offering to the Lord God from the first-born of his flock. Abel acted in love, adoration, humility, reverence, and obedience. And the Bible says that the Lord held Abel and his offering in high regard.

His older brother, Cain, brought a bloodless, cheap offering to the altar, and the Bible says of God that "for Cain and for his offering He had no regard" (Gen. 4:5).

Was God being unfair? After all, didn't Cain attempt to please God? Wasn't he sincere?

This story was put in the Bible to teach us there is a right way and a wrong way to make contact with God. Abel brought a sacrifice of blood as God had instructed; Cain made his vegetable sacrifice selfishly and superficially, disobeying God by coming without faith. When God didn't bless his sacrifice, Cain killed his brother. Cain's worship was empty religiosity, hollow as his whole life became. He left his family and walked the earth as a bitter man, crying out to the Lord, "My punishment is too great to bear" (Gen. 4:13).

Cain was sincere—but wrong.

Humanistic religion emerges under the very noses of great men of God. While Moses was on Mount Sinai receiving the tablets of stone "written with the finger of God," false religion was erupting in the camp of Israel. The people said to Aaron, "Come, make us a god who will go before us." Aaron was carried along with the idea of a new religion and said, "Tear off the gold rings which are in the ears of your wives, your sons, and your daughters, and bring them to me." Out of this gold he made a molten calf and the people said, "This is your god, O Israel, who brought you up from the land of Egypt" (Exod. 32:1–4).

Throughout time other idolatrous beliefs have eroded the foundations of truth. Whether ancient or modern, all have posed alternatives to the biblical way of approaching God.

Men and women may devise plans to satisfy their inner long-ings, but in the midst of all the "religions" of the world God's way is available in the Bible for all who will come to Him on His terms.

For the person who searches, the answers are available.

5

What Is This Thing Called Sin?

THERE'S A STORY about a jet which was traveling from Chicago to Los Angeles. As the gigantic plane leveled out at 40,000 feet, the passengers heard a voice over the loud speaker.

"This is a recording. You have the privilege of being the first to fly in a wholly electronic jet. This plane took off electronically. It is now flying at 40,000 feet electronically. It will land in Los Angeles electronically.

"This plane has no pilot, no co-pilot, no flight engineer. But don't worry. Nothing can go wrong . . . go wrong . . . go wrong . . . go wrong . . . go wrong . . ."

Something has gone wrong with our jet age. It's supposed to be scientifically sophisticated and morally liberated. But it isn't. What's gone wrong?

In every major city in America and Europe crime is up. The crime wave has hit the world with hurricane force. A news magazine reported that in the U.S. "in the past 14 years, the rate of robberies has increased 255%, forcible rape 143%, aggravated assault 153% and murder 106%."[1]

Statistics are cold until they happen to you. I was told that at a fine private university in a small town in the West the girls don't go out of their rooms at night for fear of mugging or rape. The father who told me this said he had sent his daughter there to get her away from the dangerous areas of the large cities. This was worse.

There is no longer a safety zone in any city. A woman may be pistol-whipped while parking her car in an underground structure, or a man beaten on his way out of his office. Criminals have no respect for age, with older citizens living in many areas in a nightmare of fear. In New York City, police charged a gang of six teenagers—one of whom was thirteen—with murdering three elderly and penniless men by asphyxiation. One man died with his prayer shawl stuffed into his mouth.

Man is a contradiction. On one side is hatred, depravity, and sin; on the other side is kindness, compassion, and love. Man is a helpless sinner on one hand and has capacities which would relate him to God on the other. No wonder Paul spoke of man's disease as "the mystery of iniquity."

Some people don't like the word *sin*. They believe this is for the other person, not them. But everyone recognizes that the human race is sick and that whatever the disease is, it has affected all of life.

What is this thing called sin? The Westminster Confession defines it as "any want of conformity to or transgression of the law of God." Sin is anything contrary to the will of God.

The Beginning of Sinning

Where did sin begin and why did God allow it? The Bible hints at the answer to this riddle when it teaches that sin did not originate with man, but with the angel whom we know as Satan. This was no ordinary angel, but the most magnificent of creatures!

The prophet Ezekiel describes this noble being this way: "'You were the anointed cherub who covers; and I placed you there. You were on the holy mountain of God. . . . You were blameless in your ways from the day you were created, *until unrighteousness was found in you*'" (Ezek. 28:14,15, emphasis mine). Here is a glimpse of where it started. In some unknown past, sin was found in the heart of this magnificent creature of heaven.

The prophet Isaiah gives us another hint of the origin of evil: "'How you have fallen from heaven, O star of the morning [Lucifer], son of the dawn! You have been cut down to the earth, you who have weakened the nations! But you said in your heart, "*I will* ascend to heaven; *I will* raise my throne above the stars of God, and *I will* sit on the mount of assembly in the recesses of the north. *I will* ascend above the heights of the clouds; *I will* make myself like the Most High." Nevertheless you will be thrust down to Sheol, to the recesses of the pit'" (Isa. 14:12–15, emphasis mine).

There's the picture. Lucifer's sin was that of the five "I wills." He fell and became Satan because of his undue ambition. He wanted to be like God! He wanted to be equal to God. This was conceit in its strongest form. The New Testament gives us a glimpse of the sin of pride or conceit when it speaks of a person who might "become conceited and fall into the condemnation incurred by the devil" (1 Tim. 3:63).

From Satan to Sinners

Sin began with the revolt of Lucifer and continued with man's revolt against God. In place of "living for God," sin substitutes "living for self."

The Bible makes it quite clear how sin entered the human race. In that luscious garden of Eden there were many trees. One tree symbolized the knowledge of good and evil, and God in His wisdom said, "You shall not eat." Adam and Eve with one or two bites violated what they knew to be God's will (see Rom. 5:12–19; Gen. 3:1–8; 1 Tim. 2:13,14).

God could have created us as human robots who would respond mechanically to His direction. Obviously this would be a response over which man had no control. But instead, God created us in His image, and He desires that the creature worship the Creator as a response of love. This can be accomplished when "free will" is exercised. Love and obedience which are compelled do not satisfy. God wanted sons, not machines.

A pastor friend who was having dinner with us one evening told us about his son who was attending a state university and becoming "very wise." "Dad," he said to his father one day, "I'm not sure that when I get out of school I will be able to follow you in your simple Christian faith." Our friend looked his son in the eyes and replied, "Son, that is your freedom—your terrible freedom."

And that is what God gave Adam and Eve—and what he gives us—our freedom to choose. Our "terrible freedom." God gave humankind the gift of freedom. Our first parents had the choice: whether to love God or rebel and build their world without Him. The tree of the knowledge of good and evil was their test—and they flunked.

Sin Is Rebellion

Why did Adam and Eve, with all Paradise to enjoy, choose to rebel? The cause of rebellion was "the lust of the flesh and the lust of the eyes and the boastful pride of life" (1 John 2:16). And this is the type of lust to which Eve submitted. "When the woman saw that the tree was good for food, and that it was a delight to the eyes, and that the tree was desirable to make one wise, she took from its fruit and ate; and she gave also to her husband with her, and he ate" (Gen. 3:6).

Centuries later, Christ faced the same three temptations in the wilderness. He overcame all of them and thereby showed us that it is possible to resist the temptations of Satan (Matt. 4: 1–11).

The Ten Commandments tell us not to covet or lust. However, all moral law is more than a test; it's for our own good. Every law which God has given has been for our benefit. If a person breaks it, he is not only rebelling against God, he is hurting himself. God gave "the law" because he loves man. It is for man's benefit. God's commandments were given to protect and promote man's happiness, not to restrict it. God wants the best for man. To ask God to revise His commandments would be to ask Him to stop loving man.

Children usually accuse their parents of "not understanding" and being too strict. When a father says to his teen-ager, "Be in at 11 o'clock, and let me know exactly where you are going to be," he is protecting his child, not punishing him. God is a loving father.

When Adam and Eve broke God's commandment, they died spiritually and faced eternal death. The consequences of that act were immediate and fearful. Sin became and is the stubborn fact of life.

In our universe we live under God's law. In the physical realm, the planets move in split-second precision. There is no guesswork in the galaxies. We see in nature that everything is part of a plan which is harmonious, orderly, and obedient. Could a God who made the physical universe be any less exacting in the higher spiritual and moral order? God loves us with an infinite love, but He cannot and will not approve of disorder. Consequently, He has laid down spiritual laws which, if obeyed, bring harmony and fulfillment, but, if disobeyed, bring discord and disorder.

What were the results of Adam and Eve's sin? When both Satan and Adam challenged God's law, they did not break it; they broke themselves upon it. The life of beauty, freedom, and fellowship that Adam had known was gone; his sin resulted in a living death. Nature became cursed and the poison of sin infected the entire human family. The whole of creation was thrown into disharmony and the earth was now a planet in rebellion!

Missing the Target

One of the translations of the term *sin* in the New Testament means "a missing of the target." Sin is failure to live up to God's standards. All of us miss the target; there is not one person who is capable of fulfilling all of God's laws at all times.

For some people, even the standards of the world seem unattainable. One of the most intense and exciting spectacles we ever view is the World Olympics. Athletes who have trained for years, disciplining their minds and bodies to attain greater and greater goals, often fall short of their target. One of the finest figure skaters said she was particularly afraid that a fall would ruin her performance. She said, "Think how much time I've put into this, and how much other people have to help me. With one mistake, it could all go down the drain."[2]

In our spiritual lives we are constantly falling. There is no way we can turn in a perfect performance. King David said, "They have all turned aside; together they have become corrupt; there is no one who does good, not even one" (Ps. 14:3).

The prophet Isaiah confessed, "All of us like sheep have gone astray, each of us has turned to his own way" (Isa. 53:6).

We have all been touched by the sin of Adam. David said, "Behold, I was brought forth in iniquity, and in sin my mother conceived me" (Ps. 51:5). This doesn't mean that he was born out of wedlock, but that he inherited the tendency to sin from his parents.

"Why do we have to be punished for what Adam did?" Think about it. Would you have done any better than Adam? I know I wouldn't have.

We are all sinners by choice. When we reach the age of accountability and face the choice between good and evil, we will slip. We may choose to get angry, to lie, or to act selfishly. We will gossip or slander someone's character. None of us can really trust his heart, any more than we can trust a lion. In an animal preserve in East Africa the lions are allowed to roam around as if they were in their native habitat. People drive their cars or jeeps through the area, watching the lions, but are warned not to get near them. One woman rolled down the window in her car to get a better look, and without warning a lion charged, critically mauling her. That lion looked so tame, acted so docile, and yet became ferocious in one frightening instant.

The Bible applies this principle like this: "Sin is crouching at the door" (Gen. 4:7). Most of us are capable of almost anything, given the right circumstances. David was a classic example. Under circumstances of fleshly desire he took a woman who belonged to another man, then saw to it that her husband was murdered by putting him in the front line of battle.

You may be saying, "You make everyone out to be so rotten, and that isn't really true." Of course it isn't. A person may be a very moral individual and yet lack the love for God which is the fundamental requirement of the law.

Because we fail to meet God's requirements, we are guilty and under condemnation. Being guilty means that we deserve punishment. The very holiness of God reacts against sin: "For the wrath of God is revealed from heaven against all ungodliness and unrighteousness of men . . ." (Rom. 1:18).

Guilty of What?

The Bible says that sin is falling short of the glory of God. Many people are unaware of the nature of the target, so they can't understand why they are told that they are missing it.

Let's imagine that someone puts a blindfold around your eyes and ties it so tight you are completely in the dark. Then you are told there is a dart board across the room and you are to hit it with a dart. You throw in exactly the direction you are told, but when the blindfold is removed you find that your dart is stuck in a lampshade, three feet from the target. You aimed in the right direction, but you missed.

This is where the world is today, missing the target. It's what Solomon meant when he said, "There is a way which seems right to a man, but its end is the way of death" (Prov. 14:12).

When God begins to open our blindfolds so that a small amount of light begins to seep through, we may begin to see an outline, at least, of the target. We can see, for instance, how God was beginning to reveal a general sense of direction to a girl who wrote me: "I'm not in any serious trouble or anything, but I do need the help of Jesus Christ. This is my first attempt to reach out to Him. I'm seventeen, and seriously want to consider myself a Christian. I'm reaching out . . . please don't disappoint me."

Her letter shows that she senses "something" is wrong with her present life. Just what is wrong in her life and right in Christ's life she isn't yet able to say, but her life without Christ carries a kind of odor of death to it, and she wants to replace it by the fragrance of Christ. When she says she isn't in any "serious trouble," she means that she hasn't been arrested, or shamed before the community. But she has an uneasiness in her heart.

To help us see that something is terribly wrong in our lives and that death—spiritual death—will result, God gives us "the law," that is, a set of standards to sharpen our moral judgment so that we can recognize sin. The Ten Commandments form the backbone of the law. They are a giant x-ray machine to reveal the bone structure of our sinfulness. The first four x-ray plates concern our direct relation to God. The last six concern our relationships with others.

Reading the X-rays

"You shall have no other gods before Me" (Exod. 20:3). Another god is not necessarily a brass Buddha or a carved totem pole. Whatever captures our highest interest is our god. Sports can be a

god—or work, or money. Sex may be a god to some, while travel may be a god to another. But our highest interest should be God. He alone is worthy of our worship. Jesus said that the great commandment was to love God with all our heart, soul, mind, and strength. If we were able to do this, we would be demonstrating that we have no other god except the Lord.

"*You shall not make for yourself an idol*" (Exod. 20:4). The first commandment dealt with whom we worship. This one concerns how. We are told to worship sincerely, with a heart for God. "Man looks at the outward appearance, but the Lord looks at the heart" (1 Sam. 16:7). When we sit in a church, full of piety, but ignoring God, we make an idol of the church building.

"*You shall not take the name of the Lord your God in vain*" (Exod. 20:7). This does not just apply to swearing, but even using the name for deity, such as God or Lord, without thinking of God Himself. If we vaguely mouth the words of a hymn, or call ourselves Christians without knowing Christ personally, we take the name of God in vain.

There is a story of Alexander the Great who met a disreputable character whose name was also Alexander. Alexander the Great said, "Either change your way of life or change your name."

"*Remember the sabbath day, to keep it holy*" (Exod. 20:8). A day in seven set apart for special worship and rest is called for in Scripture. Jesus said, "The Sabbath was made for man, and not man for the Sabbath" (Mark 2:27). This means that we need that special day. God in His wisdom tells us that our bodies need it for rest, just as our spirits need it for worship.

The practice of turning weekends into long periods of leisure and entertainment to the exclusion of worship means that we lose the advantage of both leisure and worship.

We know that a nation or an individual that works seven days a week, suffers physically, psychologically, and spiritually. All machinery needs occasional rest.

"*Honor your father and your mother*" (Exod. 20:12). This passage sets no age limit on such honor. In addition, it does not say they must be honorable to be honored. This doesn't necessarily mean that we must "obey" parents who may be dishonorable. Not only while we are children, but as long as our parents live, we must honor them if we are to obey God. Honor has many shapes: affection, humor, financial aid, respect. And yet, harsh words are often heard in the home more than anywhere else. We say things to our parents that we would never say to our friends at work or in church.

"You shall not murder" (Exod. 20:13). In the older translation of this command the word *kill* was used, but the original Hebrew properly refers to murder. The outward act of murder is the final act of many emotions. Behind it are the attitudes of irritation, envy, and hatred. Jesus said, "You have heard that men were told in the past, 'Do not murder; anyone who commits murder will be brought before the judge.' But now I tell you: whoever is angry with his brother will be brought before the judge; whoever calls his brother 'You good-for-nothing!' will be brought before the Council; and whoever calls his brother a worthless fool will be in danger of going to the fire of hell" (Matt. 5:21–22).

Is anyone able to say that he has never been angry with someone else? We all stand condemned before such a law, even if we have never forcefully taken someone's life.

"You shall not commit adultery" (Exod. 20:14). One scholar said: "One of the extraordinary things is that in the non-Christian religions time and time again immorality and obscenity flourish under the very protection of religion. It has often been said and said truly that chastity was the one completely new virtue which Christianity brought into this world."[3] Although that may be true, this commandment goes beyond chastity. It involves more than dishonoring a wife or husband by having sexual relations with others; it deals with the mentality which is occupied with sex. It means even looking at a man or woman with an attitude of desire or lust. To God, purity is first a matter of the heart, then of action.

Put in those terms you might say, "That's ridiculous. No one can live up to that commandment." And you would be right.

"You shall not bear false witness against your neighbor" (Exod. 20:16). We think of a witness as one being in court. If we were to lie on a stand and say, "But, your honor, my dog was provoked into biting my neighbor. He started to hit my animal with a large

stick and so he attacked in self-defense," when, in fact, your dog had taken a chunk out of your neighbor's leg without provocation, then you would be bearing false witness.

But what if you gossip in a "harmless" way? The commandment is just as shattered!

"You shall not covet" (Exod. 20:17). When we take something that belongs to another, that's stealing. It is an act. Coveting is an attitude. When we desire something which belongs to someone else, that's coveting. How many marriages have ended in divorce because a man replaced thoughts about his own wife with thoughts about the desirability of his neighbor's wife? We are told not to covet anything, and that means our neighbor's new house, his car, his TV set, or the camper in his driveway.

Results of the X-Rays

Can anyone read the Ten Commandments with insight and not feel condemned by them? They reveal our hearts. The Apostle James made the comment that even one commandment broken would be enough to destroy us. If we are suspended over a pit by a chain of ten links, how many links have to break for us to fall into the pit? "For whoever keeps the whole law and yet stumbles in one point, he has become guilty of all" (James 2:10).

The Bible and our consciences tell us that we have seriously missed the target and are sinners. What does a holy God do? How does God deal with our sin?

We see a glimpse of this in the words of a young man who became painfully aware of the commandment, "You shall not steal." He said, "My life was not a rosy one. Before I was thirteen years old I was a thief in heart, word, and action. I had been arrested many times. I spent time in a boy's reformatory and less than a week after I left I was stealing again." He said that his family gave up on him and thought that his future was destroyed. One night he heard the gospel on television, found a Bible, and started to read it. As a result he asked Christ to forgive him for his past. He is now looking to Christ to build a new foundation and give him a new future.

How can God forgive us? What happens if sin becomes a pattern in our lives? What if we are really caught up in the sin syndrome? Is there any hope?

If there weren't any hope I wouldn't be writing this book! If there weren't answers, you probably wouldn't be reading!

6

Does God Have a Cure for Spiritual Disease?

A DOCTOR IN Australia told me of a conversation between a man and his barber. As the scissors worked, the barber said, "Hmm—see you have a sore on your lip."

"Yep," said the man. "My cigarettes have done that."

"Well," said the barber, "it doesn't seem to be healing."

"Oh, it will—it will," replied the man confidently.

A month later he came into the shop again. His lip was split and ugly.

"Don't worry about it," he told the barber, "I've switched to a cigarette holder. It'll heal soon."

The barber had been concerned about his customer so he obtained some medical photographs that showed what lip cancer looked like. He urged his friend to compare them in the mirror with his own lip.

"Well, they look a lot alike," admitted the man, "but I'm not worried."

On the third month the man failed to come for his regular haircut. When the barber called his friend's home to inquire about him he was told, "Oh, didn't you know? He died of cancer two days ago."

Sin is like cancer. It destroys step by step. Slowly, without realizing its insidious onslaught, it progresses until finally the diagnosis is pronounced: sick to death.

A man was describing to us how he had been brought up in a godly European home, had come to this country as a young man to seek his fortune, had been converted to Christ, and then had gotten sidetracked. Temptation yielded to another temptation until finally he found himself in what he thought was a hopeless condition. I'll never forget how he described the process. "It was like being in the ocean when there is a strong undertow," he said. "You don't realize how far you're drifting from shore until all of a sudden you find yourself beyond your depth, trying desperately to swim, but unable to hold your own against the outgoing tide."

But, unless we know some of the signs of danger, how can we seek help? We can find the help the Bible provides when we know the parts of a person that sin strikes and corrupts.

Mind Attack

A person may be brilliant in some areas, but inadequate about spiritual realities. The Bible teaches us that a veil lies over our minds and that before we can know Christ this veil must be lifted. Without this spiritual sight we cannot come to God.

You may have heard someone ask, "How can any intelligent person believe in the Bible and all those myths and contradictions?" (implying that the gospel of Jesus Christ is anti-intellectual). The implication is contrary to truth. Understanding demands the use of the mind, but when the mind is diseased by sin it is clouded and confused.

Joel Quinones was a living example of a person whose mind was under attack. I met him in San Diego and heard his amazing story.

Joel was first thrown into prison at the age of eight for trying to kill a sadistic man who had beaten him and burned him with cigarettes. When Joel was released, he came out a bundle of hatred and from then on did everything he could to show his scorn to society. As a result Joel found himself in San Quentin at the age of nineteen and spent the next eleven years there. He was turned over to the prison psychiatrists who examined him, gave him shock treatments, and finally diagnosed him as "criminally insane."

Joel was placed in with the incorrigibles. When they were fed, the food was placed on what appeared to be a large shovel with the handle long enough to push it under two separate security doors. "You don't even feed a tiger that way," Joel told us, "but that's the way they fed us."

After all those years in San Quentin, it was decided to get rid of the undesirable aliens, and Joel, along with a number of other Mexicans, was taken across the border and turned loose. He had a godly mother, a cook at a Bible school, who had been in the courtroom when Joel had been convicted for the first time. She had said to him then, "Joel, this isn't the end. Jesus has work for you to do."

When he was released in Mexico, his mother was there to greet him. Putting her arms around him, she said, "Joel, you need the Lord Jesus; you need to ask Him to forgive your sins, to give you a new heart and a new life."

Joel struggled with this, but before the Lord was finished with him he was a transformed person. He went to Bible school, married one of the graduates, and is today a prison chaplain in Mexico. He has won so many prisoners to Christ that he is busy trying to build a halfway house, a "City of Refuge" to which these prisoners can come for rehabilitation before returning to normal life.

Sin had affected Joel's mind, but the transforming power of Christ had given him new gifts.

As I write this, I'm looking at a bone-handled knife with a five-inch blade that once belonged to Joe Medina. Joe's story is one of the most unbelievable, comic, awe-inspiring demonstrations of the power of God in what the ordinary person would have termed a hopeless life that I have ever heard. Mind attack? Joe simply couldn't think straight.

Joe was brought up in a Bronx ghetto. His mother and both of his grandmothers were spirit mediums. The streets of New York had been his home since babyhood, and gang warfare, knife fighting, stealing, and lying were simply a way of life. He was one of those disenchanted, rebellious youths of the sixties—a drug-user and accomplished thief.

Joe, however, went to a meeting at which Akbar Haqq, one of our associate evangelists, was speaking. Before the evening was over, Joe had given his heart to Jesus Christ. The day after his conversion, one of his best buddies was trying to induce Joe to go with him to get drugs and Joe didn't want to be bothered. The friend pulled a knife and threatened to cut Joe up. That was a big mistake. Joe was small, but like lightning, with a knife, and before he knew what had happened, he had plunged the knife (yes, the one on my desk) into his buddy. The boy he attacked was in the hospital for two weeks.

Joe had no Christian background to fall back on and he had many ups and downs in his spiritual life. He enrolled in a small college near us but quit school before the year was up. I'm still not sure what his reason was, but I think he had some vague notion that he had to get back to share his faith with his buddies in the Bronx.

My wife talked to Joe before he left and urged him to come to Madison Square Garden, where we were having a meeting. I found out later that Joe had rounded up some of his tough buddies and gotten to the Garden at 7:30, only to find it closed because it was full, and the policeman wouldn't let him in. There had been a threat on my life that night and the policemen were taking a dim view of any suspicious-looking characters. Joe and his friends qualified for that description.

They went into a huddle and decided to rush the police. They succeeded in getting to the top floor of the Garden but suddenly found themselves face to face with a wall of plainclothes men advancing on them. Turning to run the other way, they confronted another formidable wall of police. They were thrown out of the Garden without further ceremony. When I heard about this later I thought, "Oh no! Just the ones we were trying to reach!"

However, Joe was undaunted and brought his sister and brother the next night. They both came forward to receive Christ.

Joe had a lot of trouble for a while getting values straightened out. He called Ruth one time and said he had to see her. When he arrived, she could tell something was wrong. "What have you done now, Joe?" she asked.

"Ruth, I robbed a filling station."

"Oh, Joe, why did you do that?"

"Well, it's this way—I have this buddy, you know. Well, he needed some money and he'd never robbed a filling station before. Golly, Ruth, I just felt it was my Christian duty to help him."

Ruth asked him how much he had taken and then asked him if his buddy were a Christian. He was not, Joe said. Ruth explained to Joe that he would have to be responsible for returning the entire amount. Joe looked as if she had hit him in the stomach with her fist. She then asked him point-blank if he had anything else in his possession that he had stolen. He looked at her in amazement and exclaimed, as if that were the dumbest question ever asked, "Everything I own!"

Joe returned all the stolen goods. After more advances and retreats in his Christian growth than I care to relate, he was finally admitted to Columbia Bible College. In his senior year he became vice president of the student body and is today a graduate student there with an amazing knowledge and love of the Bible.

On a recent weekend he came to visit us, and the Presbyterian pastor of our community, Calvin Thielman, asked him to give his testimony and talk about his ministry. Joe told how he related to the drug-users, the dropouts, the rebels. His story was full of such wit, humor, and compassion that the audience was left with the reassurance that "nobody's hopeless."

Only those who knew Joe from the beginning can fully appreciate the marvels of the new birth in this young man's life. His mind had been so attacked by sin that it took a long time for the healing process. We are born again as babies, not mature Christians, and babies need a lot of love and patience!

The Bible teaches that sin affects the mind, whether that mind is of superior intelligence or average. A person may be intellectually brilliant, but spiritually ignorant. "A natural man does not accept the things of the Spirit of God; . . . and he cannot understand them, because they are spiritually appraised" (1 Cor. 2:14).

An intellectual mind can be turned into a first-class mind when Christ penetrates the heart. Gerhard Dirks, one of the most brilliant men in the world, is reported to have an IQ of 208. He has over 140 patents with IBM and has even attempted theoretically to reconstruct the human brain. He became completely bewildered and shaken, however, when confronted with the complexity and utter impossibility of such a reconstruction. He didn't know what to do or where to run. His choice was two-fold: either the human brain came about by a fantastic chance or by intelligent planning. When faced with the alternative he knew he had only one choice, and he became a believer in God as it was revealed to him through Jesus Christ, whose intellect he could not surpass.

Dr. Boris Botsenko, a brilliant Russian physicist-mathematician, was attending a conference of scientists in Edmonton, and in his hotel picked up a Gideon Bible. He read it and through it accepted Jesus Christ and was born again. He is now in the research department of the University of Toronto.

Attack on the Will

Sin attacks another facet of our being—will. Jesus said, "Every one who commits sin is the slave of sin" (John 8:34). Even in countries where there is political freedom, there are millions who live under the tyranny of pride, jealousy, or prejudice. Countless others are slaves to alcohol, barbiturates or narcotics. They possess traits or are consumed by desires they hate but are powerless in their grip. They want to be free, and some search for freedom through avenues offered by other men. But Christ said, "You shall know the truth, and the truth shall make you free" (John 8:32). Christ is the truth.

I have known many persons who found freedom from the bondage of will and desire. On May 9, 1972, in a little church outside of Nashville, Tennessee, a pastor gave a Gospel invitation and a man named Johnny Cash got up and went down the aisle and knelt at the altar of the church. Johnny Cash says that he gave his life to Jesus Christ that day. Here is a man whose life had been hurt by drugs and imprisonment, and who has become a hero to the world of country music. He is now a force for good in the world and is being used in the cause of Christ.

I have in my possession a hashish pipe as a reminder of a young man who was a slave to drugs. He had made a terrible mess of his life and also the life of the girl he loved. As a result, he drove to a lonely, deserted parkway where he slit his wrists. Evidently he didn't do a very good job, because the blood wasn't coming out fast enough and he thought at that rate it was going to take him too long to die. So he crawled under the tailpipe of his car with the motor still going, covered himself with a blanket, and proceeded to inhale the fumes.

He said that while he became drowsy from the fumes he uttered a prayer asking God to forgive him for what he was doing. Suddenly a horrible black feeling came over him and he knew that what he was about to do did not please God. In his weakness, with bleeding wrists and drugged mind, he drove to a pastor's home. The pastor took him to the hospital. After the young man was treated, the pastor explained to him that Christ alone can make atonement for our sins and give us release from guilt and the joy of being forgiven.

This young man is now happily married and is a positive influence on the lives of others.

Unresolved hatred is a tyranny which can make anyone a slave to sin as it attacks the will. Just a few years ago Dr. William P. Wilson, then Professor of Psychiatry at Duke University Medical Center, systematically took Bibles away from his patients at the center. But his life and medical practice have been transformed by the power of Jesus Christ, and he now uses the insights he has gained from the gospel in treating his patients. He keeps copies of the Bible in his office and gives them out. Dr. Wilson says, "One of the greatest causes of mental illness is unresolved guilt. Feelings of shame, inadequacy, missing the mark, not measuring up, are some sources of guilt feelings. The answer to guilt is grace and the new birth. The new birth leads to the forgiveness of sin."

Forgiveness is hard for many to believe. Dr. Warren Wiersbe of Chicago calls forgiveness "the greatest miracle in the Bible."

I have a letter from a young man who said, "In 1971 I was a drug-dealing dropout from Northwestern University. During your Chicago Crusade I came forward at the invitation and prayed for the Lord to save me, even though I personally didn't feel bad about my ungodly practices. I also asked that He forgive me my sins (I could intellectually conceive of them, but not personally feel them) and that He would make Himself known in a personal way.

"I was expecting a lightning bolt from heaven to knock me down, or for God to put me through a mental breakdown so He could straighten out my mind and use it for His glory. Needless to say, He didn't do that. I began to feel quite disappointed and also somewhat scared and thought this God thing might easily turn out to be a hoax after all. At that instant a middle-aged, short-haired, suit-wearing, Bible-carrying counselor came up to me and put a Jesus sticker on my shirt and shook my hand. 'God bless you, young man,' he said. Think of it! This establishment dude shaking my hand—me, a freaked-out hippie. The love of God coming through him showed me that Jesus loved me regardless of how I dressed or abused society. That simple act hit me and I suddenly realized the simplicity of God's salvation. He didn't want to put me through pain of a mental breakdown—all He wanted me to do was to receive His Son as I had just done!"

When Conscience Fails

Sin not only affects the mind and the will, but also the conscience. A person becomes very slow to detect the approach of sin. It's like telling an untruth: the first time you tell a story it really bothers you; but with repetition your conscience is no longer your guide, and soon the lie is woven so strong that you are convinced it's the truth. You no longer have sensitivity to things you know are wrong.

One day Joe Medina, to whom I referred earlier in the chapter, called Ruth from a telephone booth and said, "Ruth, I'm not drunk, but I just wanted to tell you something."

Ruth asked him what he was doing in a phone booth. He explained that he was riding around with a buddy who had a fifth of whiskey with him. Joe explained that his friend didn't have a North Carolina driver's license and shouldn't drive the car, especially while drinking. So Joe said, with his typical logic, "Ruth, I felt it was my Christian duty to drink that fifth of whiskey for him."

The patience of my wife never ceases to amaze me. She said, "Joe, you drank that fifth of whiskey because you wanted to drink that fifth of whiskey."

There was a long pause. Then, "Ruth, you're exactly right."

Joe had been trained in calling badness "good." He knew how to lie, cheat, and rationalize out of any situation. But for the grace of God, he would still be that way today.

The results of the infection of no longer knowing the difference between good and evil are reflected in every part of the Scriptures. When David first looked at Bathsheba, a train of events began which led from adultery to deceit to murder. David was forgiven for his sins, but he had to pay the natural consequences. He reaped a bitter harvest and his reign was clouded with constant trouble.

In view of the way we allow our consciences to become dulled, it is amazing that God is so patient. The Bible says, "The Lord is not slack concerning his promise, as some men count slackness, but is longsuffering toward us, not willing that any should perish, but that all should come to repentance" (2 Pet. 3:9, KJV).

No matter how patient God is, He is also just. When man hardens his heart, God continues to speak. But man cannot hear. Genesis 6:3 says, "My Spirit shall not always strive with man." Eventually, if God sees that man won't repent, "There is a sin unto death" (1 John 5:16, KJV). This refers to blasphemy against the Holy Spirit, which is final rejection of God's plan of salvation, and it is also described in Hebrews 6:4–6:

"For in the case of those who have once been enlightened and have tasted of the heavenly gift and have been made partakers of the Holy Spirit, and have tasted the good word of God and the powers of the age to come, and then have fallen away, it is impossible to renew them again to repentance, since they again crucify to themselves the Son of God, and put Him to open shame."

When a man's conscience is gone he uses all kinds of excuses to justify his action. He blames his family, his business associates, his bad breaks, anything. He can cheat on his income tax because the laws are unjust. He can cheat on his wife (or a wife can be unfaithful to her husband) because the other one is cold—or thoughtless. The good and bad are gone and life is lived in grey tones.

In Athens the columns and statues of the Parthenon have been eroding in recent years at an accelerated rate. It hasn't been storms or time which have caused the imminent destruction of these priceless ancient works of art, but the pollution of the wastes of modern society. In the same way, it's not the heavy storms of life that erode us, but the insidious, gradual pollution of sin which leads to our destruction.

Sick to Death

Crime requires punishment and sin has a penalty. Although this may be a subject we would like to ignore, it is an unavoidable fact.

Not only does everyone suffer as a result of sin in this life, but everyone must face the judgment to come. "For the wages of sin is death" (Rom. 6:23).

First, there is *physical death*. The Bible says, "It is appointed for men to die once" (Heb. 9:27). Incidentally, this completely rules out the possibility of reincarnation.

Death is inevitable and unpredictable in many cases. For each of us there is a day, an hour, a minute, when physically we are no longer earth beings. If God had not given the judgment of physical death, the earth would soon become uninhabitable, because men would live forever in their sins.

Because life is brief, the Bible teaches that we must "Prepare to meet [our] God" (Amos 4:12). In the course of my life I have known many people who are thoroughly prepared to meet God. There is a startling difference between them and people who have lived a life without God.

I will never forget the summer of 1973. That was the year that one of the greatest Christians I ever knew entered heaven. He was my father-in-law, Dr. L. Nelson Bell. Dr. Bell served Christ for years in China as a missionary surgeon. In 1972 he had been Moderator of the Presbyterian Church in the United States, the highest honor his denomination could bestow. The night before he died he spoke for the World Missions Conference in a large auditorium in Montreat.

At the end of his talk he said, "Before I pray I have a few words today. After hearing that singing, no one can deny that our Presbyterian Church is waking up. Now in this place there are two groups of people. There are those who know they are saved and love the Lord Jesus Christ, and there are those here who as yet may not know Christ. My hope is that before you leave this place you will come to know Him as your personal Lord and Savior. The Lord said, 'Behold, I stand at the door and knock; if any man hears my voice, and open the door, I will come in to him, and will sup with him and he with me."

Those were the last words that Dr. Bell said in public. That night he went to sleep and when he awoke he was in the presence of his Lord. His life had come full circle. His favorite hymn was "All the Way My Saviour Leads Me," and when I saw him that morning, it was a great comfort to see the face of one so peaceful.

He was prepared to meet God.

I remember hearing of the last words said by Pearl Goode, a wonderful woman who through the years was one of our most faithful prayer supporters, often going into seclusion and praying night and day for the Crusade team wherever they were. She walked in such close fellowship with God that when it was her time to go, she sat up in bed and said, "Well, there He is. There's Jesus!" She was prepared to meet God.

In the summer of 1976 there was a flash flood in Colorado that took the lives of a great many people. Among the victims were some young Christian girls who had been at a retreat in the mountains. The men who had the job of searching out the bodies of those who were killed reported later that most of the people had expressions of horror on their faces, but they were astounded to see that every one of the girls appeared to be at peace. They were prepared to meet their God.

Life is so short. The Bible says that we must be prepared to meet God at all times. We never know when we step into our car, walk out the door of our home, or just open our eyes to a new day, what lies ahead. "'Since his days are determined, the number of his months is with Thee, and his limits Thou hast set so that he cannot pass'" (Job 14:5).

The second dimension of death is *spiritual death*. Millions of people on earth are walking around physically alive, but spiritually dead. When your eyes and ears become attuned to the cries of others, you hear those who say they are empty and lost. They are separated from the source of life and like a lamp which is unattached, they are dark and lifeless. The lamp may be very expensive, may have a beautiful shade which draws attention, but has no light without being plugged into the source of energy. Jesus said, "I am the life."

Newspapers and magazines throughout the world carried the story of the suicide of Freddie Prinze. At the age of twenty-two he had attained one of the highest status roles in show business. He was the darling of television and had just performed for an incoming president at the Inaugural gala in Washington. Yet something was terribly wrong in the life of this talented comedian. A close friend, comedian David Brenner, explained to *Time* magazine,

"There was no transition in Freddie's life. It was an explosion. It's tough to walk off a subway at age 19 and then step out of a Rolls Royce the next day." Producer Komack, also a close confidant, said, "Freddie saw nothing around that would satisfy him. He would ask me 'Is this what it is? Is this what it's all about?'" Mr. Komack said, "His real despondency, whether he could articulate it or not, concerned the questions: 'Where do I fit in? Where is my happiness?' I would tell him, 'God, Freddie, your happiness is right here. You're a star.' He'd say, 'No. That's not happiness for me any more.'" As *Time* magazine commented at the end of the story, "For one of the most singular escape stories in ghetto history, escape was not enough."

We may be physically alive, but spiritually dead, like the woman who is described as "dead even while she lives" (1 Tim. 5:6).

The third dimension of death is *eternal death*. This may be a subject which most try to avoid. We hear a lot about "hell on earth," but there is another hell which is more real and certain, and that's the hell of eternal death. Jesus Himself spoke frequently about hell. He warned of a hell to come. The Scripture teaches us that we'll be in hell alone and bearing pain alone. There is no fellowship in hell except fellowship with darkness. I have heard some people say, "If I thought my father [or some other loved one] were in hell, that's where I want to be, too!" What an illusion! Hell is the loneliest place imaginable.

Jesus warned men, "And these will go away into eternal punishment" (Matt. 25:46). He also said, "The Son of Man will send forth His angels, and they will gather out of His kingdom all stumbling blocks, and those who commit lawlessness, and will cast them into the furnace of fire; in that place there shall be weeping and gnashing of teeth" (Matt. 13:41,42).

There is never such an urgency to talk about eternity as there is when physical death confronts us. A friend of mine told me that the day after her son was killed in an airplane accident, while their house was full of people offering love and consolation, something went wrong with the furnace. A repair man was called. After looking at the heater, he said, "Lady, if you had waited a little while longer to call me that furnace might have blown up." In the midst of her own grief she paused, looked the repair man squarely in the eyes. "There's only one thing that's important right now," she said. "If that furnace had exploded while you were working on it, do you know for sure where you would spend eternity?"

Before he left the house he learned how to have assurance of his eternal destiny.

Two Faces of Man

Man has two faces. One shows his ingenuity, his capacity to create, to be kind, to honor truth. The other face reveals him using his ingenuity maliciously. We see him doing kind acts in a shrewd manner in order to forward a private desire. We see one side of him enjoying a sunset, but at the same time working in a job that fills the atmosphere with waste products that nearly obscure the sunset. His search for truth often degenerates into a rat race to discover a scientific fact so the credit will be his.

Man is both dignified and degraded.

The need for spiritual rebirth is evident to the most casual observer of human nature. Man is fallen and lost, alienated from God. From the very beginning, all attempts to recover man from his lostness have revealed one or the other of two ways.

Plan A and Plan B

Remember Cain and Abel? The sons of Adam and Eve represent Plan A and Plan B of salvation. One of them, Cain, came his own way: he initiated Plan A; the other, Abel, was obedient and came God's way, Plan B.

Cain was the self-sufficient materialist and religious humanist. He brought to the altar an expression of his own labors; he became the prototype of all who dare approach God without the shedding of blood.

Cain's way didn't work for him. It has never worked for anyone, and it will not work today. Only God can properly diagnose our disease and provide the cure. God chose blood as the means of our redemption. The Apostle John wrote that Jesus Christ "washed us from our sins in his own blood" (Rev. 1:5, KJV).

When Jesus Christ, the perfect God-man, shed His blood on the cross, He was surrendering His pure and spotless life to death as an eternal sacrifice for man's sin. Once and for all, God made complete provision for the cure of man's sins. Without the blood of Christ, it is a fatal disease.

Each of us makes his choice between the two ways—man's way or God's way. Which?

II

GOD'S ANSWER

7

The Man Who Is God

〜

IT'S JUST AFTER Christmas as I write this chapter. The cards are still coming in each day, bulging the mailbox and dazzling the eye. Many of them have pictures of Jesus, some as a baby in a rough-hewn cradle, others as a shepherd, surrounded by children. The world is fascinated with how He might look. From the magnificent cathedrals of Europe to Sunday school classrooms in the U.S.A., we see pictures of artists' conceptions of Jesus. I was in Africa a few days before Christmas and saw Jesus depicted as a black baby. Last year we were in the Orient just before Christmas and saw Him depicted as an Oriental.

What is the image the world has of Jesus Christ? Some visualize him as a pale, blue-eyed man, smiling rather weakly beneath an ethereal halo. In America, the new popular Jesus is a handsome, virile type with robust charm and appeal. Probably Jesus looked Middle Eastern, with a swarthy colored skin—we really don't know. And it's just as well that we don't know what He really looked like physically—because today He belongs to the world!

No matter how we imagine Him to be, Jesus Christ has no stronger portrait than the one in the Bible. It is a picture of the man who is God. The claim that Jesus Christ is deity is the focal point for all belief. It is the foundation of Christianity. Since the quickest way to destroy any edifice is to tear out or weaken its base,

men have always tried to disprove, ignore, or scoff at the claims
of Christ. However, our hope of redemption from sin is dependent
upon the deity of Christ.

Who is He?

Jesus: Unique in All Ways

We know that Jesus lived. He was a man in history, as well as a
man for all times. Tacitus, perhaps the greatest Roman historian
born in the first century, speaks of Jesus. Josephus, a Jewish historian born A.D. 37, tells of the crucifixion of Jesus. A contemporary
Bible scholar said that "the latest edition of the *Encyclopaedia
Britannica* uses 20,000 words in describing this person, Jesus. His
description took more space than was given to Aristotle, Cicero,
Alexander, Julius Caesar, Buddha, Confucius, Mohammed or Napoleon Bonaparte."[1]

Rousseau said, "It would have been a greater miracle to invent
such a life as Christ's than to be it."

Jesus lived, taught, and died on earth in a small area of the
Middle East, mostly in what is in Israel today. That is a confirmed
fact of history.

His Intellect

Many men in history have been admired and many have been
given honors for their intellectual achievements, but no man has
had the incisive intellect of Jesus. In all circumstances, whether
tired from a long journey, or plagued by his enemies, Jesus was able
to confound some of the greatest minds of His day.

He had three years of intellectual encounters with the religious
leaders of His day. These men often tried to put Him on the spot
by asking questions which were difficult to answer. On one occasion, when He was teaching in the temple, the chief priests and
elders questioned Him belligerently. They asked, "By what authority are You doing these things, and who gave You this authority?"
(Matt. 21:23).

Here were the men who had control of all the religious teaching, and this Jesus, a carpenter from Nazareth, who was not their pupil, was teaching in their territory. Can you imagine what would happen at one of our prestigious seminaries if the janitor suddenly stepped onto the platform and began to instruct the students?

Jesus answered the question of the religious authorities with another question. "I will ask you one thing too, which if you tell Me, I will also tell you by what authority I do these things. The baptism of John was from what source, from heaven or from men?"

Now John the Baptist had not been ordained by them either, and he had urged his followers to obey Jesus. The religious leaders were thrown into confusion. They knew if they said "From heaven," that Jesus would say, "Then why didn't you believe him?" On the other hand, if they answered "From men," they feared that the people would become irate, because they believed John was a prophet. So they simply said, "We don't know."

Jesus replied, "Neither will I tell you by what authority I do these things" (Matt. 21:27).

Jesus possessed a mental agility that has astounded scholars for 2,000 years.

His Frankness

No matter what the consequences, Jesus was very open and frank. The members of the religious establishment of His day were meticulously following certain rites for cleansing the dishes they ate from each day. Using this practice as an illustration, Jesus said, "Woe to you, scribes and Pharisees, hypocrites! For you clean the outside of the cup and of the dish, but inside they are full of robbery and self-indulgence. You blind Pharisee, first clean the inside of the cup and of the dish, so that the outside of it may become clean also" (Matt. 23:25,26).

The charge Jesus made is just as applicable today. True belief in God is inward and has to do with a personal commitment and attitude, rather than strict observance of rituals and rules. Most of us would be reticent to speak so frankly to church leaders of our time. Jesus, however, was a man who was frank, bold and honest in every situation.

His Openness

Jesus had the ability to understand all people, no matter what their position in society. On one occasion He was dining with a prominent religious leader named Simon. While they were eating, a repentant prostitute came into the hall where the meal was being served and began to wash the feet of Jesus with her tears and to dry them with her hair. The religious leader was shocked and began to look at Jesus with doubt. He thought, "If this man were a prophet He would know who and what sort of person this woman is who is touching Him . . ."

Jesus, sensing his thoughts, told him this story: "A certain money-lender had two debtors; one owed five hundred denarii [a denarius was then a day's wage], and the other fifty. When they were unable to repay, he graciously forgave them both. Which of them therefore will love him more?"

Simon must have wondered, what's the purpose of this story? He probably shrugged as he answered, "I suppose the one to whom he forgave more."

Jesus told him that was the right answer. Then He reminded Simon that when He had come into his house as a guest, Simon had ignored all the normal courtesies of the day. "You gave Me no water for My feet, but she has wet My feet with tears, and wiped them with her hair. You gave Me no kiss; but she, since the time I came in, has not ceased to kiss My feet."

Then Jesus turned to the woman and reassured her that her sins had been forgiven.

The other guests at the dinner party were astounded. They asked, "Who is this man who even forgives sins?" (Luke 7).

We know that Jesus often dined with the social elite but defended the social outcasts.

His Forgiving Spirit

His opponents were powerful and persistent. They mocked Him, plotted against Him, and finally maneuvered the crowds to support His death by crucifixion.

As He was hanging on the cross, bleeding and suffering from the pain and the hot sun, many jeered at Him, saying, "Save Yourself, and come down from the cross!" (Mark 15:30).

Under such extreme circumstances, Jesus exhibited a trait that was beyond our comprehension. He spoke to God the Father and said, "Father forgive them; for they do not know what they are doing" (Luke 23:34).

How many mere men could forgive their persecutors under such brutal circumstances?

His Moral Authority

The pictures of Jesus as a vague, colorless man do not fit the true account of His strength and moral authority. At the end of His life the establishment, both religious and political, had united together to end His work by sending officers to arrest Him. The burly henchmen approached Jesus, but stopped to listen to what He was saying. They returned to their superiors without Him.

"Why didn't you bring Him?" they were asked.

The officers replied in astonishment, "Never did a man speak the way this man speaks" (John 7:45,46). They were experiencing what the crowds of ordinary people already knew. "The multitudes were amazed at His teaching," Matthew reported, "for He was teaching them as one having authority, and not as their scribes" (Matt. 7:28,29).

Jesus Christ lived the type of life He taught. There are many men we know who are noble, intelligent, frank, open, and who speak with authority. But only in Jesus do we find the human characteristics which we would expect God to display if He were to become a man.

Jesus' claim to deity is fully supported by His character. He was unique in history.

More Than Just a Man

If this were all we had to say about Jesus Christ, He would have very little more to offer than many great men of history. However, the uniqueness of Christ is that in His life on earth He displayed every known attribute or characteristic of deity.

What is an attribute? One Bible scholar offered this simple definition: "The attributes of God are those distinguishing characteristics of the nature of God which are inseparable from the idea of deity, and which constitute the basis and grounds for His various manifestations to His creatures."[2]

Jesus Christ was the supreme manifestation of God. "God was in Christ reconciling the world to Himself" (2 Cor. 5:19).

He was no ordinary man. Several hundred years before He was born, Isaiah, the prophet, said, "Behold, a virgin will be with child and bear a son" (Isa. 7:14). No other man in all history could say that his mother was a virgin. The Scriptures teach that He did not have a human father; if He had, He would have inherited the sins and infirmities that all men have, since "that which is born of the flesh is flesh" (John 3:6). Since He was conceived not by natural means, but by the Holy Spirit, He stands as the one man who came forth pure from the hand of God. He could stand before His fellowmen and ask, "Which of you can truthfully accuse Me of one single sin?" (John 8:46, *The Living Bible*). He was the only man since Adam who could say, "I am pure."

If we honestly probe our minds, we have to admit that there are mysteries about the incarnation that none of us can ever understand. In fact, Paul speaks of God, manifest in the flesh, as a "mystery" (1 Tim. 3:16).

Paul explained the Man who is God in another epistle: "Have this attitude in yourselves which was also in Christ Jesus, who, although He existed in the form of God, did not regard equality with God a thing to be grasped, but emptied Himself, taking the form of a bond-servant, and being made in the likeness of men" (Phil. 2:5–7).

First, *God is holy*. This is a characteristic possessed by Jesus Christ which is central to the entire Christian faith. What does "holiness" mean? It is a term used in reference to people, places, and sometimes circumstances. However, this very common word, often misused and misunderstood, means "self-affirming purity." No mere human being now or ever could possess pure holiness and moral perfection.

In the Old Testament, God is described as "holy in all His ways" (Ps. 145:17) and the prophet Isaiah, in his vision of the Lord God, declares "Holy, holy, holy, is the Lord of hosts" (Isa. 6:3). In the New Testament this unique attribute is possessed by Jesus Christ, the holy child, the sinless man. Thus Jesus Christ had a characteristic that only God could possess.

Second, *God is also just.* In order to guard His holiness, God must exercise justice. Since all sin is an offense to God, the principle of God's justice is vital to an orderly universe, just as a nation must have certain laws and codes. But unlike human government, which uses justice in ways that are suitable to the rulers or heads of government, God's justice is pure; no mistake is ever made.

Jesus Christ was just. During His earthly career He exhibited this characteristic when He drove the racketeers out of the temple with a whip. He is also described as faithful and just in forgiving us our sins. When He died for our sins it was "the Just" dying for the unjust.

Third, *God is mercy.* This characteristic of deity was seen in the entire life of Jesus Christ. When the woman who was an adulteress was brought before the authorities and condemned to be stoned, Jesus defended her with the charge, "Let him who is without sin cast the first stone." Her accusers retreated in embarrassment. Jesus Christ, exhibiting God's mercy, told her to go and sin no more. The love, mercy, and compassion of Jesus comes out time after time throughout His public ministry. In the opening address that Jesus gave at His hometown of Nazareth, He had quoted Isaiah the prophet, "The Spirit of the Lord is upon Me, because He anointed Me to preach the gospel to the poor. He has sent Me to proclaim release to the captives, and recovery of sight to the blind, to set free those who are downtrodden, to proclaim the favorable year of the Lord" (Luke 4:18).

Fourth, *God is love.* The first songs children learn in Sunday school, when they are barely able to carry a tune, are about God's love. A child can understand God's love, but the depths are so infinite that an adult finds it difficult to fathom. God's love is the continuing result of His holiness, justice, and mercy.

As a holy God, He hates sin and can have no fellowship with sin. Because the Bible tells us that the soul that sins must surely die, we can see that separation from God is a result of sin. However, because God is also mercy, He longs to save the guilty sinner and must then provide a substitute which will satisfy His divine justice. He provided that substitute in Jesus Christ. There is God's love: "For God so loved the world, that He gave His only begotten Son, that whoever believes in Him should not perish, but have eternal life" (John 3:16).

God and Jesus Christ the Same

Fifth, Jesus Christ possesses the three great "omni's" of God. This prefix means "completely or all" and when used within the word *omnipotent* it means that the possessor has all power. The dictionary has one word to describe the Omni-potent, and that is God.

While a man on earth, Jesus Christ performed many miracles. He raised people from the dead; He took a few loaves and fishes and multiplied them to feed thousands; He cured the chronically sick and healed the crippled. But why should this be surprising? Jesus said, "All power is given unto me in heaven and in earth" (Matt. 28:18, KJV). That is a startling statement if it were made by any ordinary man. Only God could make such a claim.

Jesus Christ was *omniscient*. This means that He knew all things, and He still knows all things. The Scriptures say, "Jesus knowing their thoughts" (Matt. 9:4); "He knew all men . . . He Himself knew what was in man" (John 2:24,25); "In whom are hidden all the treasures of wisdom and knowledge" (Col. 2:3).

Do you know anyone of your acquaintance, or any person in history who knew everything? Have you ever heard of a person who could know, without a mistake, the minds of men? Only an all-powerful God knows everything, and Jesus Christ was omniscient.

Probably no idea is more difficult for man to comprehend than the thought of *omnipresence*. How can God be everywhere at once? From our viewpoint we are bound by time and space. We are physical creatures who can only be one place at a time. We frequently complain, "I can't be everyplace at once!" God transcends time and space, and so does Jesus Christ. He existed before time began. "Before Abraham was born, I AM" (John 8:58). "He is before all things" (Col. 1:17).

Jesus is not earthbound. He said, "Wherever two or more of you are gathered together in My Name there am I in the midst of you." He can be with a gathering of believers in a primitive hut in New Guinea or a businessman's luncheon in Dallas. He can be at the supper table of a family or in the banquet hall of royalty. Jesus Christ is omnipresent.

Jesus Christ claimed to be God. He said, "I and the Father are one" (John 10:30) and, "He who beholds Me beholds the One who sent Me" (John 12:45). He made it very clear when He spoke to the religious leaders of his time who He was. "I am He who bears witness of Myself, and the Father who sent Me bears witness of Me." Members of the local church hierarchy said to Him, "Where is Your Father?" Jesus answered, "You know neither Me, nor My Father; if you knew Me, you would know My Father also."

Christ represents Himself as having been "sent from God" and being "not of this world." He declares that He is "the light of the world," "the way, the truth, and the life," and "the resurrection and the life." He promises eternal life to everyone who believes in Him as Lord and Savior.

Knowing the claims of Jesus Christ, you are faced with this vital decision—

What Will You Do With Jesus?

Question: Who do you think Jesus Christ is? If He is not who He claimed to be, He is a deceiver or an egomaniac. We cannot settle for a middle-of-the-road answer that He was "a good man," or the modern form of adulation as a "superstar." He Himself eliminates a neutral answer. Either we decide He is a liar or a lunatic, or we must declare Him to be Lord.

In light of the evidence of Scripture and the physical fact of the Resurrection, the only wise conclusion is that He is God, worthy of our worship and trust. When I decide to be a Christian, I am deciding who Jesus Christ is. Trust in Him makes me a believer in Him and leads to being truly alive!

Out of His Private Wilderness

We heard about a young couple who were separated during World War II. While the father was gone the mother gave birth to a baby girl. The months passed and the mother kept a large picture of her husband on the desk so that the little girl would grow up knowing what her daddy looked like. She learned to say "Daddy" and associated the name with the picture on the desk. Finally the day came when her father returned home from the war. The whole family gathered to watch the little girl when she saw her father for the first time. Imagine their disappointment when she would have nothing whatever to do with him. Instead, she ran to the photograph on the desk, saying, "That's my daddy." Day after day the family had to blink back the tears as they saw the young father on his knees trying his best to get acquainted with his little daughter, explaining as simply as he could that he was her daddy. But each time she would shake her head, then run to the picture on the desk and exclaim, "That's my daddy." This went on for some time, but one day something happened. The little girl, having gone repeatedly to the picture on the desk, returned to her father and looked carefully into his face. Then she went back to the picture on the desk and studied it. The family held their breath. After several trips the little face lit up as the child exclaimed excitedly, "They're both the same daddy!"

C. S. Lewis describes his experience: "You must picture me alone in that room in Magdalen, night after night, feeling, whenever my mind lifted even for a second from my work, the steady unrelented approach of Him whom I so earnestly desired not to meet. That which I greatly feared had at last come upon me. In the Trinity Term of 1929 I gave in, and admitted that God was God, and knelt and prayed: perhaps, that night, the most dejected and reluctant convert in all England. I did not then see what is now the most shining and obvious thing; the Divine humility which will accept a convert even on such terms. The Prodigal Son at least walked home on his own feet. But who can duly adore that Love which will open the high gates to a prodigal who is brought in kicking, struggling, resentful, and darting his eyes in every direction for a chance of escape? The words *compelle intrare*, compel them to come in, have been so abused by wicked men that we shudder at them; but, properly understood, they plumb the depth of the Divine mercy. The hardness of God is kinder than the softness of men, and His compulsion is our liberation."[3]

A certain professor said that in over forty years on campus he had never been asked, "Are you a Christian?" When he was a student he had read books that explained away Christ's miracles; he considered himself well informed and sophisticated on the subject. As a result, on the one hand he disbelieved the deity of Jesus Christ while on the other hand he kept some vague belief in God.

In practice, however, he said, "I usually chose to ignore Him in my early post-college days. This started the path into my own personal wilderness. I tried to satisfy my inner needs by reading and studying literature and science. These studies often confirmed my opinion that I could leave Christ out of my life because He was just another prophet."

Then one day a student entered this professor's "private wilderness" to invite him to hear a campus talk on the deity of Christ. The professor later recalled, "I was confronted with the positive side of Christ's deity for the first time since I was a child. I didn't expect to have my disbelief in the deity of Christ changed.

"As I listened that evening, partly in skepticism, partly in hope, I admit I also yearned to be convinced. The speaker had scarcely completed half of his remarks before I was convinced of the deity of Christ. A lifetime's assumption that Jesus was just another gifted teacher was destroyed. The turnabout in my convictions was simple."

I must agree with the professor. It is simple. Jesus is God. Our earthly lives and eternal destinies depend on our belief in that fact.

8

What Happened at the Cross

IN JEWELRY STORES from Fifth Avenue to the airport in Rome one piece of jewelry is universally displayed—the cross. Clerical robes have this emblem sewn on the front or back. Churches display the cross in wood, bronze, concrete, or brass. The last month of the year some office buildings light certain windows at night to form a cross which can be seen for miles.

What does the cross of Jesus mean? If we stopped people on the street and asked that question we might hear, "It's a symbol for Christianity, I guess." Or, "Jesus was a martyr and was nailed to a cross." Others might say it was a myth, or a history major might say it was an example of Roman justice.

Another answer to the question "What does the cross mean?" was given by the poet, Thomas Victoria. He tried to express how Jesus Himself might speak of the cross if we asked Him. The poet pictured Jesus on the cross, surrounded by men who were intent upon killing him.

Jesus looks at them and says:

> Oh, how sweet the wood of the cross,
> How sweet the nails,
> That I could die for you.

This deeply personal, intimate view of the cross is what the Apostle Paul taught when he said, "In human experience it is a rare thing for one man to give his life for another, . . . though there have been a few who have had the courage to do it. Yet the proof of God's amazing love is this: that it was *while we were sinners* that Christ died for us" (Rom. 5:7,8, Phillips).

The focus of Paul's whole ministry to the great commercial city of Corinth was summed up when he said, "For I determined to know nothing among you except Jesus Christ, and Him crucified" (1 Cor. 2:2).

The average person in Corinth would have answered a question about the cross in the same way as the man on the street in the USA or any European, African, or Asian country. Corinthians lived in a city which was known for its depraved moral character. It was the kind of town in which we wouldn't want to raise our families. The Corinthians were a sophisticated, sexually dissolute bunch, who thought that the cross was ridiculous, foolish, and even idiotic. Commenting on this view, Paul said, "The foolishness of God is wiser than men, and the weakness of God is stronger than men" (1 Cor. 1:25).

In Corinth the preaching of the Cross of Christ was a stumbling block to the Jews, and idiocy to the philosophic Greeks. The philosophers believed they could unravel divine mysteries because they were overconfident of their own mental capacities. However, Paul said that the natural man (meaning the man who does not have the Spirit of God indwelling him) cannot understand the things of God. He meant that sin has twisted our understanding of truth so that we cannot recognize the truth about God.

Before the teaching in the Bible about the cross can mean anything to us, the Spirit of God must open our minds. The Scriptures teach that a veil covers our minds as a result of our separation from God.

To an "outsider" the cross must appear to be ridiculous. But to those who have experienced its transforming power, it has become the only remedy for the ills of each person, and of the world.

In spite of this available power, the gospel about Christ who was crucified is still unimportant to millions. They reflect the failure Paul analyzed when he questioned, "What have the philosopher, the writer and the critic of this world to show for all their wisdom? Has not God made the wisdom of this world look foolish?

For it was after the world in its wisdom had failed to know God, that he in his wisdom chose to save all who believe by the 'simple-mindedness' of the gospel message" (1 Cor. 1:20,21, Phillips).

How can we brand the message of the cross as foolishness? Have we done so well with our private lives, with our families, and with our society that we can claim wisdom? It's time we abandoned the pretense of being intellectual and recognize that our best minds are baffled by life.

God successfully changes men and women by the message that centers in the cross. His approach recognizes our disease and presents the right medicine. He offers His wisdom as an alternative to our failures.

In our everyday life we profit from many helps that we can't understand. We go to the sink and turn on the water tap, never stopping to figure out the source of the water, or how it was carried through the pipes to us. What about a prescription from a doctor? We can't read it or analyze it. We pay a sum we may think is too much because we rely on the doctor's knowledge and authority to make us well.

In the same way we may not be able to fully comprehend the deep significance of the cross, but we can benefit from it because the Bible gives us the authoritative answer to the problem of sin.

What Happened at the Cross?

The cross is the focal point in the life and ministry of Jesus Christ. Some think that God didn't want Christ to die, but was forced to adjust His plans to adapt to it. Scripture makes it very clear, however, that the cross was no afterthought with God. Christ was "delivered up by the predetermined plan and foreknowledge of God" (Acts 2:23).

God designed the cross to defeat Satan, who by deception had obtained squatters' rights to the title deed of the world. When Satan with all of his clever promises separated man from God in the Garden of Eden, he was more than the deceiver of Adam and Eve. In some mysterious manner he began to exert a kind of pseudosovereignty over man. In his arrogant violence, Satan unleashed his fiercest attack to stop Christ's ministry by seeing that He was murdered. But Satan was stopped by God and caught in his own trap. He hadn't realized that God loved the world so intensely that He could let His own Son be subjected to the worst Satan could do. Satan miscalculated. He didn't comprehend the greatness of God's love and the wisdom of His plan.

Satan's power was broken at the cross. "The Son of God appeared for this purpose, that He might destroy the works of the devil" (1 John 3:8).

What a blow was dealt to Satan! Although he is still a wily pretender, his destruction was made certain by the victory of Christ at the cross. "That through death he might render powerless him who had the power of death, that is, the devil" (Heb. 2:14). What seemed to be the biggest defeat of history turned into the greatest triumph.

Through the cross, God not only overpowered Satan but brought Himself and man together. Christ rescued the slaves that Satan held captive and reconciled them to Himself. The Bible describes this amazing divine plan in these words: "We speak God's wisdom in a mystery, the hidden wisdom, which God predestined before the ages to our glory; the wisdom which none of the rulers of this age has understood; for if they had understood it, they would not have crucified the Lord of Glory" (1 Cor. 2:7,8).

The cross revealed an eternal secret. This was "the mystery which has been kept secret for long ages past, but now is manifested" (Rom. 16:25,26).

If it were possible for one man, Adam, to lead mankind to ruin, why shouldn't it be possible for one man to redeem it? The Bible says, "For as in Adam all die, so also in Christ all shall be made alive" (1 Cor. 15:22).

What Did the Cross Cost God?

As human beings filled with our own hurts and desires and emotions, we find it almost impossible to stretch our minds enough to conceive the cost to God in allowing His only Son to go to the cross. If He could have forgiven our sins by any other method, if the problems of the world could have been solved in any other way, God would not have allowed Jesus to die.

In the garden of Gethsemane on the night before He was killed, Jesus prayed, "My Father, if it is possible, let this cup pass from Me" (Matt. 26:39), in other words, if there is any other way to redeem the human race, Oh God, find it! There was no other way. And then He prayed, "Not as I will, but as Thou wilt" (Matt. 26:39).

It's important to understand that when Jesus prayed that prayer, He was not just considering the simple act of dying. Just as His life was unique, so was His death. What happened to Him when He died had never happened to any person in the past and would never happen to anyone in the future. To be able to understand this we need to look into God's revelation before Christ's earthly ministry, back to the Old Testament.

The orthodox Jewish religion was founded on God's grace. God entered into a covenant relationship with Israel, declaring Himself to be their God and stating in a special way that they were to be His people (Deut. 7:6). With this type of relationship, how were they to express their love for Him? The answer was by doing His will as it was described in the Old Testament law. But the people could not keep the law perfectly, and when they broke it, they sinned. As the Bible says, "Sin is the transgression of the law" (1 John 3:4 KJV).

The sacrifices in the temple were meant by God to show graphically that a person's guilt and penalty for sin could be transferred from him to another. In the case of the Old Testament, a perfect animal symbolically bore the penalty and was killed.

Why did God give the law if He knew people couldn't possibly keep it? The Bible teaches that the law was given as a mirror. When we look into it, we see what true righteousness is. The Ten Commandments describe the life that pleases God. If we are separated from God by sin, the law exposes our sin and faces us with our true spiritual condition. The mirror does not reveal a very attractive image!

Sin had to be paid for, so in the beginning God instituted the sacrificial system by which we finally could be brought into a right relationship with God. In Old Testament times, those who had sinned brought sacrifices of animals and offered them to God. These sacrifices were shadows of The Great Sacrifice who was yet to come.

In Leviticus 4, Moses describes a situation in which a leader needs to offer a sacrifice. We can think of it in seven steps:

1. "When a leader sins . . .
2. he shall bring for his offering a goat,
3. a male without defect.
4. And he shall lay his hand on the head of the male goat,
5. and slay it . . . ; it is a sin offering.
6. Then the priest is to take some of the blood of the sin offering . . . and put it on the horns of the altar. . . .
7. Thus the priest shall make atonement for him in regard to his sin, and he shall be forgiven" (vv. 22–26).

Notice the sequence. Man sinned and wants forgiveness of God. He brings an animal, a perfect specimen, to the priest and lays his hand on its head. Symbolically, at that point the guilt and punishment he bears because of his sin passes to the animal. He then kills it as a sin offering, and the priest places some of the blood on the altar.

What is the significance? It is an atonement for the man in regard to his sin. In place of a broken relationship between God and the sinner, "atonement" results and "he shall be forgiven" by God.

The sacrifices were visual aids to show sinners that there was hope because the punishment for sin could be transferred to another. However, they were only symbols, because, "It is impossible for the blood of bulls and goats to take away sins" (Heb. 10:4). But God could forgive them in the light of what He would one day do at the cross. Jesus, "having offered one sacrifice for sins for all time, sat down at the right hand of God" (Heb. 10:12).

God did not initiate the sacrifices because He was bloodthirsty or unjust. He wanted us to zero in on two things: first, the loathsomeness of sin, and second, the cross on which God Himself would satisfy forever the demands of His justice. "Not through the blood of goats and calves, but through His own blood He [Jesus] entered the holy place once for all, having obtained eternal redemption" (Heb. 9:12).

When Christ atoned for sin, He stood in the place of guilty men and women. If God had forgiven sin by a divine decree, issuing some sort of a heavenly document written across the sky, without the atonement which involved the personal shame, agony, suffering, and death of Christ, then we might assume that God was indifferent to sin. Consequently we would all go on sinning, and the earth would become a living hell.

In the suffering of Jesus we have the participation of God in the act of atonement. Sin pierced God's heart. God felt every searing nail and spear. God felt the burning sun. God felt the scorn of His tormenters and the body blows. In the cross is the suffering love of God bearing the guilt of man's sin. This love alone is able to melt the sinner's heart and bring him to repentance for salvation. "He [God the Father] made Him who knew no sin [Jesus] to be sin on our behalf" (2 Cor. 5:21).

The Reason for Communion

Many people do not understand communion. For them, the communion service has no mystical meaning. And yet the cross is what communion is all about. In the Lord's Supper, Jesus likens Himself to the Lamb that was offered in the sacrifice or atonement and says to His disciples and to all who will believe in Him, "This is my body broken for you." This is symbolic of what He did on the cross. When the cup is offered the emphasis is upon the fact that His blood is shed for the remission of sins. The elements of bread and wine convey to us the reality of atonement and forgiveness. We can touch them, taste them and see them. We have bread in our hands, but we have Christ in our hearts. We have the cup in our hand, but we have the benefits of forgiveness through His blood in our hearts.

One of the most famous Scottish theologians was John Duncan of New College in Edinburgh. As communion was being held in a Church of Scotland on one occasion, when the elements came to a little sixteen-year-old girl, she suddenly turned her head aside. She motioned for the elder to take the cup away—that she couldn't drink it. John Duncan reached his long arm over, touched her shoulder, and said tenderly, "Take it, lassie, it's for sinners!"

How Can I Understand All This?

There is a mystery to the death of Christ that is beyond our human understanding. The depths of God's love in sending His Son to pay such an awful price is beyond the measure of the mind of man. But we must accept it on faith or we will continually bear the burdens of guilt. We must accept the atonement which Christ has made to try to make our own atonement, and this we can never do. Salvation is by Christ alone through faith alone, and for the glory of God alone.

Christ took the punishment which was due us.

My friend and associate, Cliff Barrows, told me this story about bearing punishment. He recalled the time when he took the punishment for his children when they had disobeyed. "They had done something I had forbidden them to do. I told them if they did the same thing again I would have to discipline them. When I returned from work and found that they hadn't minded me, the heart went out of me. I just couldn't discipline them."

Any loving father can understand Cliff's dilemma. Most of us have been in the same position. He continued with the story: "Bobby and Bettie Ruth were very small. I called them into my room, took off my belt and my shirt, and with a bare back, knelt down at the bed. I made them both strap me with the belt ten times each. You should have heard the crying! From them, I mean! They didn't want to do it. But I told them the penalty had to be paid and so through their sobs and tears they did what I told them."

Cliff smiled when he remembered the incident. "I must admit I wasn't much of a hero. It hurt. I haven't offered to do that again, but I never had to spank them again, either, because they got the point. We kissed each other when it was over and prayed together."

In that infinite way that staggers our hearts and minds, we know that Christ paid the penalty for our sins, past, present, and future.

That is why He died on the cross.

9

The King's Courtroom

THE UNITED STATES has a Presidential election every four years. Changes are usually made in the White House, the Congress, and in many governor's mansions. When one elected leader is about to step down for his successor, he may grant some pardons to prisoners under his jurisdiction. It's always interesting to see who might benefit from these last-minute gestures.

If you or I were in prison and were told, "You're free. The President just granted you a pardon," we would certainly pack up and get out fast! That pardon would change our lives.

In the courtroom of the King of kings, a pardon means much more. At the cross, God not only delivered the believer in Christ from punishment, He also welcomed Him with open arms into His family. He opens His home to us.

At the cross we have not only acquittal, but also justification (just-as-if-I'd-never-sinned); not only pardon, but also acceptance. We saw in the last chapter that God Himself bore the burden of our sin and suffered for us. Now we must see that the cross offers us more than a pardon.

The issue involved is not just in Jesus' blood, which cleanses us from sin, but also in His righteousness. The key is in the word "justified." We are "justified as a gift by His grace through the redemption which is in Christ Jesus" (Rom. 3:24).

Several years ago I was to be interviewed at my home for a well-known television show and, knowing that it would appear on nationwide television, my wife took great pains to see that everything looked nice. She had vacuumed and dusted and tidied up the whole house but had gone over the living room with a fine-tooth comb since that was where the interview would be filmed. When the film crew arrived with all the lights and cameras, she felt that everything in that living room was spic and span. We were in place along with the interviewer when suddenly the television lights were turned on and we saw cobwebs and dust where we had never seen them before. In the words of my wife: "I mean, that room was festooned with dust and cobwebs which simply did not show up under ordinary light."

The point is, of course, that no matter how well we clean up our lives and think we have them all in order, when we see ourselves in the light of God's Word, in the light of God's holiness, all the cobwebs and all the dust do show up.

Picture a courtroom. God the Judge is seated in the judge's seat, robed in splendor. You are arraigned before Him. He looks at you in terms of His own righteous nature as it is expressed in the moral law. He speaks to you:

GOD: John (or) Mary, have you loved Me with all your heart?
JOHN/MARY: No, Your Honor.
GOD: Have you loved others as you have loved yourself?
JOHN/MARY: No, Your Honor.
GOD: Do you believe you are a sinner and that Jesus Christ died
    for your sins?
JOHN/MARY: Yes, Your Honor.
GOD: Then your penalty has been paid by Jesus Christ on the cross
    and you are pardoned.

I have my pardon, but there is much more. When the Bible says that the person who believes in Jesus is justified as a gift by His grace (see Romans 3:24), this sounds like more than a mere pardon. And it is. If I'm a criminal whom the president or the governor pardons, everyone knows I'm still guilty. I simply don't have to serve my sentence. But if I'm justified, it's *just-as-if-I'd* never sinned at all.

Both pardon and justification come to us when we believe in

Jesus. On the one hand God pardons our sin because of the death of Christ. He paid our penalty. On the other hand God actually declares us "righteous" (a word which means the same as "just").

GOD: Because Christ is righteous, and you believe in Christ, I now declare you legally righteous.

How can God do that and remain "just" Himself—when He attached the penalty of death to sin? The answer is in the righteousness of Jesus Christ. He lived an unblemished, perfect life. His character perfectly supported His claim to deity, as we saw in chapter 7, "The Man Who Is God." It's easy to see God the Father declaring Jesus just, because He was. But how does that help me, a sinner? Paul gives the answer in 2 Corinthians 5:21. To make it clear we'll substitute the words *God* and *Christ* where the words *He* and *Him* appear. "God made Christ who knew no sin to be sin on our behalf, that we might become the righteousness of God in Christ."

God put my sin on Christ, who had no sin; He punished Him in my place, as we have seen. But He did one other thing, according to this verse. By God's action the righteousness of Christ was put on us who believe, "that we might become the righteousness of God in Him."

The Judge, God, has transferred Christ's righteousness to your legal account if you have believed in Christ. Now He examines you according to law. What does He see? All of your past evil deeds and thoughts? Your sinful actions of the present?

No. He doesn't see your sin because that has been transferred to Christ when God made Christ to be sin. Rather He looks at you carefully and sees the righteousness of Christ.

But you may say, "Look, am I not still a sinful person?"

The answer is "Yes and No." If you mean that you have the legal status of a sinner before God, the answer is "No." To Him, legally, you are just. You are in right standing before Him, and "standing" is the issue in the courtroom.

Do you still have the capacity to sin? The answer is "Yes." Of course you are not perfect. You may still at times think and act in ways contrary to God's desires. But your character and mine aren't the issue here. Our legal standing is. And legally we are declared just.

Am I Free to Sin?

"Love God and live as you please!" Now are we free to sin without restraint? Can we run out of the courtroom, pardoned and justified, and do anything we want? Yes. But you are now "born again." You don't want to do the same old wrong things; your desires are changed.

If you have trusted Jesus and seen what depth of concern He had for you at the cross, you can say with the Apostle Paul, "It is Christ's love that controls me" (2 Cor. 5:14, Goodspeed). The inner changes God begins to achieve in our character will be the subject of a later chapter. But they are all based on a change in status. We who were properly condemned are now properly declared just if we have trusted Christ.

Can you imagine what a newspaper man would do with this event?

SINNER PARDONED—GOES
TO LIVE WITH JUDGE

It was a tense scene when John and Mary stood before the Judge and had the list of charges against them read. However, the Judge transferred all of the guilt to Jesus Christ, who died on a cross for John and Mary.

After John and Mary were pardoned the Judge invited them to come to live with Him forever.

The reporter on a story like that would never be able to understand the irony of such a scene, unless he had been introduced to the Judge beforehand and knew His character.

Pardon and Christ's righteousness come to us only when we totally trust ourselves to Jesus as our Lord and Savior. When we do this, God welcomes us into His intimate favor. Clothed in Christ's righteousness we can now enjoy God's fellowship and "come boldly unto the throne of grace, that we may obtain mercy, and find grace to help in time of need" (Heb. 4:16, KJV).

Conclusions from the Testimony

If I were a lawyer, I'm sure I would study the procedures of great trials of the past, the evidences presented, and the conclusions reached by the findings.

There are some vital conclusions we can draw from the death of Christ. First, at the cross we see the strongest evidence of the guilt of the world. Here sin reached its climax when its terrible display occurred. Sin was never blacker or more hideous than on the day Christ died.

Some people have said that man has improved since then and that if Christ returned today He wouldn't be crucified but might even be given a glorious reception. I am convinced that if Christ came today He might be tortured and put to death even more quickly than He was two thousand years ago, though perhaps in different, more sophisticated ways. But sinful people would still shout, "Away with Him."

Human sinful nature has not changed. As we look at the cross we see clear proof that all men have "sinned and fallen short of the glory of God." This is God's inescapable verdict.

The second conclusion we see at the cross is that God hates sin and loves righteousness. He has told us repeatedly that the soul that sins shall die, and that He cannot forgive our sin unless our debt has been paid. The Scripture says, "Without the shedding of blood there is no forgiveness of sins" (Heb. 9:22, RSV).

God will not tolerate sin. As the moral judge of the entire universe, He cannot compromise if He is to remain just. His holiness and His justice demand the penalty for broken law. There are some schools of thought which feel that such a view of God is too severe. Sin, they say, has its psychological basis. Some time ago a young man was executed for killing two other young men. The newspapers were full of the legal arguments, the debates over the death penalty, and the frequent postponements of the execution date. Why did he do it? What events or people in his past influenced his twisted mind?

Many say they are not responsible for what they do. Poor parents, bad environment, the government are all blamed. But God says that we are responsible. When we look at the cross, we see how drastically God deals with sin. The Bible says, "He who did not spare His own Son, but delivered him up for us all, how will He not also with Him freely give us all things?" (Rom. 8:32). "For our sake he [God] made him [Christ] to be sin who knew no sin" (2 Cor. 5:21, RSV).

If God had to send His only Son to the cross to pay the penalty for sin, then sin must be terrible indeed in His sight.

However, we see that God loves righteousness and clothes the believer in His righteousness because of the cross. It is amazing to think about! We are clothed, we are covered, protected, shielded. A wonderful old hymn says, "Jesus, thy blood and righteousness, My beauty are, my glorious dress."[1] This is not self-righteousness, but "the righteousness which comes from God on the basis of faith" (Phil. 3:9).

God is now at work through the Holy Spirit to make the believer righteous in his inner character. Peter shows how intimately this is based on the cross also when he says of Christ that "He Himself bore our sins in His body on the cross, that we might die to sin and live to righteousness" (1 Pet. 2:24).

What other conclusion must we reach from the testimony of the cross? We see the greatest demonstration of God's love. "For God so loved the world, that He gave His only begotten Son, that whoever believes in Him should not perish, but have eternal life" (John 3:16).

In our own weakness as humans, we tend to grade sins. Here's a little sin on our scale, but over here there's a very, very heavy sin. We may see God as able to forgive the small sin, but incapable of forgiving and accepting the gross sinner. I recall a story out of World War II that illustrates this graphically. Hitler and his Third Reich had gone down to defeat at the hands of the Allies. Many of the men who had been Nazi leaders in some of the most infamous crimes known to man were brought to trial in Nuremberg. The world watched as sentences of imprisonment and death were brought against these war criminals.

However, out of the Nuremberg trials came an amazing account by Chaplain Henry Gerecke. He was called upon to be prison chaplain to the former Nazi high command. He described himself as a humble preacher, a one-time Missouri farm boy, and then he was given this extremely difficult assignment.

Chaplain Gerecke recalls the sincere conversion to faith in Jesus Christ by some of these men who had committed despicable crimes. One of them was a former favorite general of Hitler. At first the chaplain was very leery of confessions of faith. He said the first time he saw this criminal reading his Bible he thought, "a phony." However, as he spent time with him he wrote; "But the longer I listened, the more I felt he might be sincere. He said he had not been a good Christian. He insisted he was very glad that a nation which would probably put him to death thought enough of his eternal welfare to provide him with spiritual guidance." With this Bible in his hand he said, "I know from this book that God can love a sinner like me."[2]

What an amazing love God exhibited for us at the cross!

The fourth conclusion we can reach from the testimony at the cross is that it is the basis for true world brotherhood. There are many groups which espouse the brotherhood of man and make appeals in behalf of peace. Only when we are brought into the family of God through the Fatherhood of God can there be any true brotherhood of man. God is not our Father automatically (except by creation) when we are born; He must become our Father spiritually.

The Bible teaches that we can experience glorious brotherhood and Fatherhood through the cross. "For He Himself is our peace, who made both groups into one, and broke down the barrier of the dividing wall, by abolishing in His flesh the enmity, which is the Law of commandments contained in ordinances, that in Himself He might make the two into one new man, thus establishing peace" (Eph. 2:14,15).

Outside the work of the cross we see bitterness, intolerance, hatred, prejudice, lust, and greed. Within the powerful working of the cross grow love, new life, and new brotherhood. The only human hope for peace lies at the cross of Christ, where all men, no matter what their background of nationality or race, can become a new brotherhood.

You are probably familiar with the story of Hansei. Her book *Hansei* describes vividly her absolute dedication to Adolph Hitler and the Nazi movement as a member of the Hitler Youth; her subsequent disenchantment and disillusionment; then her conversion to Jesus Christ. My wife has a letter from Hansei telling of her first meeting with Corrie ten Boom, whose book *The Hiding Place* tells of the ten Boom family's experiences during World War II. The family was arrested and put in prison for hiding Jews, and Corrie's father and sister died there.

One day Hansei and Corrie were at a convention and were seated in the same building, autographing their books. Hansei waited as long as she could, then made her way to Corrie because she simply had to ask forgiveness for what she had done. Hansei pushed through those standing in line with their books for Corrie to sign, knelt in front of Corrie with tears streaming down her cheeks and said, "Corrie, I'm Hansei." Corrie's reaction was not only absolute forgiveness, but love and acceptance. This could only happen between Christians and illustrates what the cross does.

Captain Mitsuo Fuchida was the Japanese Naval air commander who led the bombing attack on Pearl Harbor. He relates that when the Japanese war prisoners were returning from America he was curious as to what kind of treatment they had received. An ex-prisoner he questioned told him what made it possible for those in the camp to forget their hate and hostility toward their captors. One young girl had been extremely kind and helpful and had shown such love and tenderness for them that their hearts were touched. They wondered why she was so good to them and were amazed when she told them it was because her parents had been killed by the Japanese army! She explained that her parents had been Christian missionaries in the Philippines at the beginning of the war but when the Japanese landed they were forced to flee to the mountains. They were later found by the Japanese, accused of being spies and put to death. But before they were killed they had asked for thirty minutes of time to pray, which was granted. The girl was convinced that her parents had spent that thirty minutes praying for forgiveness for their executioners, and because of this she was able to allow the Holy Spirit to remove the hate from her heart and replace it with love.

Captain Fuchida could not understand such love. Several months passed and one day in Tokyo he was given a leaflet as he left a railroad station. This told the story of Sergeant Jacob DeShazer who was captured by the Japanese, tortured, and held prisoner of war for forty months. While in prison camp he received Christ through reading the Bible. God's Word removed the bitter hatred for the Japanese from his heart and replaced it with such love that he was compelled to return to tell the Japanese people of this marvelous love of Christ.

Captain Fuchida bought a Bible and began to read. He faced the scene of the crucifixion of Christ and was struck by Jesus' words "Father forgive them; for they do not know what they are doing" (Luke 23:34). Jesus prayed for the very soldiers who were about to thrust the spear into His side. In his book *From Pearl Harbor to Golgotha* Captain Fuchida tells how he found the source of this miracle love that can forgive enemies, and how he could now understand the story of the American girl whose parents had been slain and the transformation in Jake DeShazer's life.

Personal Questions the Cross Answers

"Why can't I seem to solve my problems?" This question reminds me of a Peanuts cartoon. It pictures Lucy in her psychiatrist's booth giving counsel to Charlie Brown. Charlie has lost another ball game and feels depressed and defeated. Lucy, the psychiatrist, is explaining to him that life is made of ups and downs. Charlie goes away screaming, "But I hate downs, all I want is ups."

I'm afraid that often those of us who teach the Christian message give the impression that once we have accepted Jesus Christ we will never again have any problems. This isn't true, but we do have Someone to help us face our problems. I have a paraplegic friend who has been that way for over thirty years. In spite of overwhelming problems for which there is no solution, she has learned not only to live with her condition, but to be radiant and triumphant, blessing and winning others to Christ.

Paul Tournier, one of the great Swiss psychiatrists, has stated that the Christian life we have to realize that each day will present new circumstances and there will always be adjustments that have to be made. If I drive my car into a city, I can't rigidly place my hands on the steering wheel and drive at a set rate of speed. I have to stop and start and turn to make adjustments. The same thing is true in daily living. There is always a price to being a person; part of that price is pain and problems, but we have the promise Christ made that He will always be with us.

In Psalm 34 there are three great statements about our problems:

"This poor man cried and the Lord heard him; and saved him out of all his troubles" (v. 6).

"The righteous cry and the Lord hears, and delivers them out of all their troubles" (v. 17).

"Many are the afflictions of the righteous; but the Lord delivers him out of them all" (v. 19).

The Christian life is not a way "out" but a way "through" life. The "out of" in these verses refers to deliverance not from but through difficulty. The English scholar Dr. Arthur Way phrased it, "Deliverance out of, not from the crisis of trial. So that the sense appears to be, 'bring me safely out of the conflict'" and, "not simply keep me from entering into it."

Another question: "I feel so guilty—how can I find relief?"

Guilt is a very debilitating feeling. It can destroy our attitude, our personal relationships, and our outreach. Sometimes we feel guilty because we've done things that are wrong for which we must accept the responsibility and also accept God's forgiveness.

I have been told by doctors that a large percentage of the patients in psychiatric hospitals could be released if only they could be assured of the fact that they had been forgiven.

It's so easy to blame someone or something else. Anna Russell, the British comedienne, has an interesting little poem about guilt:

I went to my psychiatrist to be psychoanalyzed.
To find out why I kicked the cat, and blacked my wifey's eyes.
He laid me on his downy couch to see what he could find,
And this is what he dredged up from my subconscious mind.
When I was one my mama hid my dolly in a trunk,
And so it falls naturally that I am always drunk.
When I was two I suffered from ambivalence toward my
    brothers,

And so it falls naturally I poisoned all my lovers.
Now I am so glad that I have learned the lessons this has taught,
That everything I do that's wrong is someone else's fault.

For some people guilt is an excuse. They won't accept the forgiveness that is offered to them; it is so hard to believe. It seems too good to be true that God should let us go eternally scot-free from our sins—and yet that is the message that the Gospel brings to us. When we cling to our guilt we do not honor God and we handicap our own lives terribly.

Forgiveness is an opportunity that Christ extended to us on the cross. When we accept His forgiveness and are willing to forgive ourselves, then we find relief.

After the sewage plants of London have reclaimed all that is usable of sewage, sludge barges on the river Thames collect the residue and carry it out to sea a certain number of miles and dump it. Apparently it is only a matter of minutes before the sea water is as pure as it was before! This is a beautiful illustration of how He has buried our sins in the depths of the sea.

Corrie ten Boom tells a story of a little girl who broke one of her mother's treasured demitasse cups. The little girl came to her mother sobbing, "Oh, mama, I'm so sorry I broke your beautiful cup."

The mother replied, "I know you're sorry and I forgive you. Now don't cry any more." The mother then swept up the pieces of the broken cup and placed them in the trash can. But the little girl enjoyed the guilty feeling. She went to the trash can, picked out pieces of the cup, brought them to her mother and sobbed, "Mother, I'm so sorry that I broke your pretty cup."

This time her mother spoke firmly to her, "Take those pieces and put them back in the trash can and don't be silly enough to take them out again. I told you I forgave you so don't cry any more, and don't pick up the broken pieces any more."

Guilt is removed with confession and cleansing. "If we confess our sins, he is faithful and just to forgive us our sins, and to cleanse us from all unrighteousness" (1 John 1:9, KJV).

However, the story of David's sin (Ps. 51) shows that forgiveness does not preclude the natural consequences of our sin. Murder can be forgiven, but that does not bring the dead to life again.

There is a well-known story of some fishermen in Scotland who had spent the day fishing. That evening they were having tea in a little inn. One of the fishermen, in a characteristic gesture to describe the size of the fish that got away, flung out his hands just as the little waitress was getting ready to set the cup of tea at his place. The hand and the teacup collided, dashing the tea against the whitewashed walls. Immediately an ugly brown stain began to spread over the wall. The man who did it was very embarrassed and apologized profusely, but one of the other guests jumped up and said, "Never mind." Pulling a pen from his pocket, he began to sketch around the ugly brown stain. Soon there emerged a picture of a magnificent royal stag with his antlers spread. That artist was Landseer, England's foremost painter of animals.

This story has always beautifully illustrated to me the fact that if we confess not only our sins but our mistakes to God, He can make out of them something for our good and for His glory. Somehow it's harder to commit our mistakes and stupidities to God than it is our sins. Mistakes and stupidities seem so dumb, whereas sin seems more or less to be an outcropping of our human nature. But Romans 8:28 tells us that if they are committed to God He can make them work together for our good and His glory.

When you bake a cake, you put in raw flour, baking powder, soda, bitter chocolate, shortening, etc., none of which taste very good in themselves, but which work together to make a delicious cake. And so with our sins and our mistakes—although they are not good in themselves, if we commit them in honest, simple faith to the Lord, He will work them out His own way and in His own time make something of them for our good and His glory.

Question: "Do I have to understand all this about Christ's death?"

The depths of God's love in sending His Son to pay such an awful price is beyond the measure of the mind of man. We must accept it on faith or we will continually bear the burden of guilt. Salvation is by Christ alone, through faith alone, for the glory of God alone.

Jesus never said, "Only understand." He said, "Only believe."

10

Jesus Christ Is Alive

IN A MAUSOLEUM in Moscow's Red Square lie the em-
balmed remains of Lenin. A crystal casket in that tomb has been
viewed by millions of people. On the casket it says: "For he was
the greatest leader of all people of all time. He was the lord of the
new humanity; he was the savior of the world."

The tribute to Lenin is stated in past tense. What a startling
contrast to the triumphant words of Christ. "I am the resurrection, and the life; he who believes in Me shall live even if he dies"
(John 11:25).

The basis for our belief in Jesus Christ is in His resurrection. Karl
Barth, the great Swiss theologian, said that without belief in the
physical resurrection of Jesus Christ there is no salvation.

If Christ were entombed someplace in a grave near Jerusalem
where the millions who visit Israel each year could walk by a grave
and worship Him, then Christianity would be a fable. The Apostle
Paul said, "If Christ has not been raised, then our preaching is in
vain and your faith is in vain. . . . If Christ has not been raised,
your faith is futile and you are still in your sins" (1 Cor. 15:14,17,
RSV).

We usually hear a sermon about the resurrection every Easter,
and that's about all. But when the early apostles preached, the cross
and resurrection were their constant themes. Without the resurrection, the cross is meaningless.

Shall Man Live Again?

Some say we are nothing but bone, flesh, and blood. After we have died, nothing happens—we don't go anywhere. Or if we do go somewhere it is to a nebulous location, devised by the imagination to represent almost anything.

Does science help? I have questioned scientists concerning life after death and most of them say, "We just don't know." Science deals in formulas and test tubes; the spiritual world is beyond its reach.

Many who do not believe in life after death fill their writings with tragedy and pessimism. Gore Vidal, Truman Capote, Dalton Trumbo, and many others write with almost unrelieved pessimism. How different are the words of Jesus Christ, who said, "Because I live, you shall live also" (John 14:19). We must base our hope of immortality on Christ alone—not on any longings, arguments, or instinctive feelings of immortality.

The Bible speaks of the resurrection of Jesus as something which could be examined by the physical senses. The disciples saw Him under many different conditions after He had been raised. A single disciple saw Him on one occasion, five hundred on another. Some saw Jesus separately, some together; some for a moment, some for a long time.

The disciples heard Him in conversation. They were told to touch Him to verify His physical reality. They touched Him, walked with Him, conversed with Him, ate with Him, and examined Him. This took the resurrection appearances of Jesus out of the realm of hallucination and put them into the realm of demonstrable physical fact.

Historical fact provides the basis for our belief in the bodily resurrection of Christ. We have more evidence for it than for any other event of that time, secular or religious.

What about the Other Religions?

Most of the world religions are based upon philosophical thought, except for Judaism, Buddhism, Islam, and Christianity. These four are based upon personalities. Only Christianity claims resurrection for its founder.

Abraham, the father of Judaism, died about nineteen centuries before Christ. There are no evidences for his resurrection.

Buddha lived about five centuries before Christ, and taught principles of brotherly love. It is believed that he died at the age of eighty. There are no evidences for his resurrection.

Muhammad died A.D. 632, and his tomb at Medina is visited by thousands of devout Mohammedans. His birthplace at Mecca sees many pilgrims each year. However, there are no evidences for his resurrection.

Evidences of Christ's Resurrection

There is something called "the swoon theory" which says that Jesus didn't actually die, but only fainted. Since there could be no resurrection without a death, this thought denies His resurrection. Yet the evidence for His death is strong.

The soldiers were positive Jesus was dead, so they didn't need to induce death by shock through breaking His legs, which they did to the two thieves beside Him. It was not the friends of Jesus, but His enemies who vouched for His death. Also, they made certain when they thrust a spear into His heart.

One of the wealthiest men in the world, Howard Hughes, died recently. The events and circumstances surrounding his death are still shrouded in mystery, and yet he had an entourage of men who followed and guarded him for years.

In a city in the Middle East, however, there is more historical evidence for the death of one man, alone on a cross between two thieves, than any other in history. The great Bible student Wilbur Smith said, "Let it simply be said that we know more about the details of the hours immediately before, and the actual death of Jesus, in and near Jerusalem, than we know about the death of any other one man in all the ancient world."[1]

Jesus was buried. We know more about the burial of Jesus than we know of the burial of any character in ancient history. His body was taken from the cross and wrapped in fine linen with spices. Joseph of Arimathea, a rich man and a secret disciple of Jesus, mustered up his courage and asked Pilate for the body of Jesus. When his request was granted, we are told, he took Him down from the cross and wrapped Him in a linen sheet (Matt. 27:59).

We are told that Nicodemus (the same religious leader who had asked Jesus how to be born again) came and brought a very expensive mixture of myrrh and aloes to wrap in with the linens, as was the custom of Jewish burial.

The body of Jesus was placed in Joseph's own tomb, which was located in the garden. This burial procedure shows that it was the body of Jesus which was buried, not His spirit. Spirits are immaterial and cannot be buried.

After Jesus was buried, a huge stone was placed against the face of the tomb and a seal placed upon that. Anyone trying to move the stone from the entrance to the tomb would have had to break the Roman seal and face the consequences of the harsh Roman law.

To make sure that His disciples didn't steal His body, a Roman guard was then placed in front of the sealed stone. The enemies of Jesus didn't want to take any chances that the prophecy about his resurrection would take place.

What about the Roman guards? These men weren't cowards. Their discipline was so severe that the punishment for quitting their post, or even falling asleep on the job, was death.

Historians say there were probably four guards on watch at the tomb, all of them outfitted with strong weapons and shields. No chances were taken that this Jesus would be removed from the tomb.

The empty tomb. It was the third day, the day Jesus said he would arise. Around the tomb the earth began to shake, and along with it the armor of the Roman soldiers must have clattered wildly. And then an angel of the Lord came from heaven and easily rolled away the stone and sat on it. He didn't even have to say, "Hi, fellas!" The guards just looked at him and became like dead men. The angel spoke to Mary Magdalene and Mary, too, but the Bible says that they took action and ran to tell the disciples that He had risen.

When Peter and John came running to the tomb, John peeped in and saw the linen clothes Christ had been wrapped in lying there empty. Peter, who, true to his character, blundered right in, saw that Jesus' body was missing. He was gone.

The bodily resurrection was a fact attested to by hundreds of eyewitnesses. We have records of thirteen different appearances of

Jesus under widely different circumstances. His body was both similar and dissimilar to the one nailed to the cross. It was so similar to an ordinary human body that Mary mistook Him for the caretaker of the garden by the tomb when He appeared to her. He could eat, speak to people, and occupy space.

However, his body was not like a normal body. He could pass through closed doors or vanish in a moment. Christ's body was physical, and also spiritual. Why should this be surprising? Paul said to King Agrippa, "Why should it be thought a thing incredible with you, that God should raise the dead?" (Acts 26:8, KJV).

Over and over again the Bible affirms the fact of the bodily resurrection of Christ. Luke says it very directly in the book of Acts. He reports that Jesus "presented Himself alive, after His suffering, by many convincing proofs, appearing to them over a period of forty days" (Acts 1:3).

In speaking about those "convincing proofs," C. S. Lewis says, "The first fact in the history of Christendom is a number of people who say they have seen the Resurrection. If they had died without making anyone else believe this 'gospel' no gospels would ever have been written."[2]

The Resurrection Essential

There is a series of events that form links in a chain from eternity to eternity. These include the incarnation of Jesus, His crucifixion, resurrection, ascension, and return. Any missing link and the chain is destroyed.

All of Christianity as a system of truth collapses if the resurrection is rejected. As Paul said, "If Christ has not been raised, then our preaching is vain, your faith also is vain" (1 Cor. 15:14).

In addition to breaking the chain of redemptive events, if the resurrection were not essential, then the good news of salvation would be flat, lifeless, and negative. Resurrection is central to the gospel. Paul said: "Now I make known to you, brethren, the gospel which I preached to you, which also you received, in which also you stand, by which also you are saved, if you hold fast the word which I preached to you, unless you believed in vain. For I delivered to you as of first importance what I also received, that

Christ died for our sins according to the Scriptures, and that He was buried, and that He was raised on the third day according to the Scriptures" (1 Cor. 15:1–4).

In my book *World Aflame*, I told the story about Auguste Comte, the French philosopher, and Thomas Carlyle, the Scottish essayist. Comte said he was going to start a new religion that would supplant the religion of Christ. It was to have no mysteries and was to be as plain as the multiplication table; its name was to be positivism. "Very good, Mr. Comte," Carlyle replied, "very good. All you will need to do will be to speak as never a man spake, and live as never a man lived, and be crucified, and rise again the third day, and get the world to believe that you are still alive. Then your religion will have a chance to get on."

Today many "new religions" are springing up, like toadstools after a summer rain. I wonder how many could meet the criteria that Carlyle told his friend?

We have been emphasizing throughout this book the experience of being born again. A personal salvation experience is directly related to belief in the resurrection. Paul gave the formula for saving faith and showed that it centered in this belief: "If you confess with your mouth Jesus as Lord, and believe in your heart that God raised him from the dead, you shall be saved; for with the heart man believes, resulting in righteousness, and with the mouth he confesses, resulting in salvation" (Rom. 10:9,10).

It couldn't be clearer in the Scriptures. Yet there are churches where ministers say they believe in the resurrection, but that this means Jesus immediately rose from death into spiritual life with God. They say they believe in a "spiritual" but not a "physical" resurrection. This is what some modern preachers proclaim on Easter morning—though I am thankful they are diminishing in number.

No wonder there are many who sit in some churches week after week, year after year, without hearing the whole gospel and knowing what it is to be born again. They hear a gospel which is incomplete, and consequently not good news at all. The resurrection was not disembodied, it was physical. Eyewitnesses said, "We saw his glory"; "You will see him"; "He appeared"; "I have seen Jesus the Lord."

Within the short span of three days both events, the death and resurrection, took place bodily and not symbolically—tangibly, not spiritually—watched by men of flesh and blood, not fabricated by hallucination.

The resurrection was also the pledge and the promise of our own resurrection.

To understand this we need to see that, in the Bible, death affects both personality and body. (Remember the three dimensions of death?) The body, too, has to be retrieved from condemnation. Only by resurrecting the body could God make a complete conquest of death. He started with the body of Jesus, but He will also work in a similar manner with the bodies of all who believe. As the judgment of death was total, so salvation from its penalty is total, involving the physical, spiritual, and eternal.

Obviously our resurrection bodies will be recognizable, but they can't possibly be the exact bodies we have here. However, they must be like Christ's resurrected body. He had the nail prints and the wound in His side, and yet he could pass through closed doors. When it was time for Him to go to heaven He was able to ascend.

What a promise this is! "For if we believe that Jesus died and rose again, even so God will bring with Him those who have fallen asleep in Jesus (1 Thess. 4:14).

Jesus staked everything upon His rising from the dead. By His resurrection He would be judged true or false.

What Does the Resurrection Mean to Us Today?

Christ lives with every person who puts his trust in Him. The resurrection means the presence of the living Christ. He said, "Lo, I am with you always, even unto the end of the world" (Matt. 28:20, KJV). This is Christ's own guarantee: life has a new meaning. After the crucifixion, the disciples were in despair. They said, "We had hoped that he was the one to redeem Israel" (Luke 24:21, RSV). They were full of anguish because they thought of Christ's death as such a tragedy. Life had lost its meaning for them. But when he rose from the grave, they saw the living Christ, and life took on purpose once more.

We can also claim the prayers of the living Christ. The Bible says, "Christ Jesus is He who died, yes, rather who was raised, who is at the right hand of God, who also intercedes for us" (Rom. 8:34). We don't have to think that our prayers are bouncing off the ceiling. The living Christ is sitting at the right hand of God the Father. God the Son retains the same humanity He took to save us, and is now living in a body that still has nail prints in its hands. He is our great High Priest, interceding for us with God the Father.

The resurrection presence of Christ gives us power to live our lives day by day and to serve Him. "Truly, truly, I say to you, he who believes in Me, the works that I do shall he do also; and greater works than these shall he do; because I go to the Father" (John 14:12).

The resurrected body of Jesus is the design for our bodies when we are raised from the dead also. No matter what afflictions, pain, or distortions we have in our earthly bodies, we will be given new bodies. What a glorious promise of things to come! "For our citizenship is in heaven, from which also we eagerly wait for a Savior, the Lord Jesus Christ; who will transform the body of our humble state into conformity with the body of His glory, by the exertion of the power that He has even to subject all things to Himself" (Phil. 3:20,21).

Thousands of people today are excited about Bible prophecy. The revelation of what the Bible says about events past, present, and future, has become more prominent in the themes of books, sermons, and conferences. The Second Coming of Christ is becoming a closer and closer reality for those of us who study the Bible and the world scene.

The entire plan for the future has its key in the resurrection. Unless Christ was raised from the dead, there can be no kingdom and no returning King. When the disciples stood at the place Jesus left this earth, which is called the place of ascension, they were given assurance by angels that the Christ of resurrection would be the Christ of returning glory. "Men of Galilee, why do you stand looking into the sky? This Jesus, who has been taken up from you into heaven, will come in just the same way as you have watched Him go into heaven" (Acts 1:11).

The resurrection is an event which prepares us and confirms for us that future event when He will return again.

Yes, Jesus Christ is alive.

Obviously Christ's physical resurrection is an essential part of God's plan to save us. Have you given yourself to this living Christ?

A woman wrote us this: "Last evening I was alone and watching television. I had no *TV Guide*. Something urged me to turn the dial to the station where the gospel was being preached. I had been really wrestling with a great problem. I was and am facing death, and may or may not be helped through surgery. I had been putting off the operation because I was afraid I had been cut off from God.

"I began to really seek the Lord. The message I heard was God's way of speaking to me and answering my prayers. Now I feel entirely at peace in my soul."

If you trust the resurrected Christ as your Lord and Savior, He will be with you when you die, and will give you life with Him forever. Because of the resurrection, you can be "Born Again."

III

MAN'S RESPONSE

11

The New Birth
Is for Now

THE COFFEE SEEMS bitter and the toast cold when the morning newspaper is finished. Another riot in Egypt. Africa torn apart by rival factions. The Middle East seemed quiet until another border incident set off new hostilities. Three coeds murdered on the campus of a prominent state university.

What can the average person do? He feels inadequate, powerless. All of the committees, the resolutions, the changes in governments don't seem to change society.

We see that if mankind is to be saved, something radical needs to be done quickly. The forces building up in our world are so overwhelming that men and women everywhere are beginning to cry out in desperation. They feel like the man John Bunyan describes in the beginning of *Pilgrim's Progress*. ". . . he was greatly distressed in his mind, he burst out, as he had done before, crying, 'What shall I do to be saved?'"

So much in our world seems to improve, but man doesn't. We can send a spaceship to the moon and take close-up pictures of Mars, but we can't walk safely on the streets at night. The subtle sins of selfishness and indifference are everywhere. Seemingly upright men and women admit to desires of the grossest sort. (And who is shocked any more?) Human viciousness breaks out as people steal, cheat, lie, murder, and rape.

Someone in the movie industry said that all we would have to do is contrast the titles of some of the old movie classics with current movie offerings to see the change in morality during the past generation. It's a long way from *Indian Love Call* to *Deep Throat*.

Man has made many attempts to change himself. We have tried without success to achieve moral goals by improvement in our environment and many are disillusioned with the results.

How can we change human nature?

From the Outside In

Studies in anthropology, psychology, and sociology to discover the laws of human behavior are an important part of educational research. Too often however, the researchers themselves ignore the fact of human sin and see a human being as proceeding from a combination of genes and chromosomes, and then shaped by his environment. At a meeting of the American Anthropological Association a new discipline was introduced to the academic community by a Harvard zoologist. He calls it "sociobiology," and it is described as "the study of the biological basis for social behavior in every species; its practitioners believe that some—and perhaps much—of human behavior is genetically determined."[1]

The sociobiologists imply that "a good deal more of mankind's morality may be genetically based."[2] They fail to give a proper place to the inborn twist toward selfishness, viciousness, and indifference to God, so many of their conclusions are only pseudo-scientific.

If we are shaped by our genes, and molded by our environment, then all we need to do is develop a way to alter genetic bases in humans or cure man's environment in terms of bad housing, slums, poverty, unemployment, and racial discrimination.

A best-selling author said this: "Many ministers today 'keep their cool' about questions of the sin and repentance of individuals and have turned their attack on the sin of society, in an attempt to make society squirm. This 'attack' varies from a mild sociology lecture to an angry assault against social injustice. However, slums and ghettos and put-downs are not going to disappear in society unless slums and games disappear from the hearts of people."[3]

But as Christians we need to do something about social injustice, slums and ghettos. We cannot sit back with the attitude that the problems are too overwhelming or insoluble. We need to get involved in helping to make this world a better place to live for the unfortunate whose standard of living is so low as to defy imagination, and for those who live under terrible political oppression. Ultimately, however, society is not going to be changed with coercion and force because when it is changed that way, man usually loses his freedom. It can be changed by a complete transformation of the human heart.

Man also attempts to change himself by *chemistry*. Scientists have developed methods to control behavior by drugs, which in some cases have been helpful. A great deal of research is being done that may benefit the mentally ill. The danger is that these same drugs in the hands of a world dictator could control an entire population of normal people. Stories from prisoners in oppressed countries verify how present-day mind manipulators misuse drugs to influence human actions.

One of them wrote: "I personally witnessed the treatment undergone by political prisoners in psychiatric hospitals when they tried to protest by refusing the food and the 'treatments' inflicted upon them. They were tied up, injected with paralyzing sulphur and force fed. . . . [They] have invented a powerful means to get rid of those who do not think as they do. Not only do they not hesitate to confine them in hospital-prisons, but they also compound their crime by injecting prisoners with chemical substances in order to destroy their personality and intellect."[4]

Changes in our body chemistry may benefit us or damage us permanently. The determining question is, "Who administers the drugs and for what purpose?"

Experiments are being made to try to give one person the intellectual capacities of another by what the mind-manipulators call "artificial reincarnation." In a study that came out of Russia, it was reported that one of the country's top physicists had experimented with "tuning one mind to another telepathically." The scientist explained, " 'When this happens, the teacher can teach a student beyond the normal capacity of his mind by broadcasting over the defense mechanism into the normally empty 90 percent of the brain.'" He continues to explain that he "reincarnated a European mathematical genius in a college math student."[5]

Another human attempt to solve man's problems concerns *microbiology*. The increasing success with organ transplants may in time lead to a vast movement to change people by replacing certain organs connected with thinking, conscience, and emotions. However, the gospel of microbiology, administered by scientists who themselves are sinners, and who have access only to the substance of a fallen world, must likewise fail.

Many writers of science fiction consider their *interplanetary speculations* as the only source for solving man's problems. But the fundamental difficulty is that sin is too deeply ingrained in human nature to be rooted out by such influences. When God is ignored, the problem-solvers themselves participate in the problems. The superpowers are now frantically preparing for a "space" war. As a newspaper editorial says, "Whoever wins this race could control the world."

Many people today are trying to find a solution to man's problems by turning to *the occult world*. They seek knowledge and power from sources the Bible says we should wholeheartedly resist. The Apostle Paul says, "For our struggle is not against flesh and blood, but against the rulers, against the powers, against the world-forces of this darkness, against the spiritual forces of wickedness in the heavenly places" (Eph. 6:12). The occult world is a source only of terror and destruction.

The methods men use to change themselves from the outside in are truly varied, and sometimes amazing.

From the Inside Out

Jesus said that God can change men and women from the inside out. It was a challenge—a command. He didn't say, "It might be nice if you were born again," or, "If it looks good to you you might be born again." Jesus said, "You *must be* born again" (John 3:7).

It has always astounded me that He made this statement to a devout religious leader, Nicodemus, who must have been shocked by it. After all, Nicodemus was a good, moral, religious man. His neighbors probably said of him, "He's a wonderful man. You could trust him with your life. He's a great theologian." Nicodemus fasted two days a week; he spent two hours a day in prayer at the temple and tithed all his income. He was a professor of theology at the local seminary. If a pastor-seeking committee were looking for the best man they could get for their local church, they would seek a man like Nicodemus. But Jesus said all his piety and goodness weren't enough. He said, "You must be born again."

In spite of all of his education and professional standing, Nicodemus saw something very special in Jesus Christ—something he couldn't understand. He saw in Jesus a new quality of living. He was honestly seeking to find out what this dimension of life was.

When Jesus told him that unless one is born again he cannot see the kingdom of God, he was explaining to Nicodemus that he didn't have to improve his moral standards or increase his educational credits, he needed to receive a new quality of life—eternal life—that begins in this world and carries into the next world.

On returning home from a trip one day I found my desk, as usual, piled high with letters to be answered. In this particular pile there happened to be two from two separate mental hospitals in different states. A glance at the handwriting and a reading of the letters made it clear that the writers needed to be in a mental institution. Yet each spoke of the Lord Jesus and the comfort He was.

I could not help thinking how kind and understanding and compassionate God has been in choosing to reveal Himself to man through simple childlike faith rather than the intellect. There would otherwise be no chance for little children or the mentally retarded or brain damaged. And yet the brilliant scientist, the true intellectual, the genius, must all come the same way. As Jesus said in Matthew 18:3, "Unless you are converted and become like children, you shall not enter the kingdom of heaven."

John Hunter, the English Bible scholar, tells the story about a young man who came up to him after he had been preaching on John 3. "He, like Nicodemus, was obviously very well educated, and he said: 'What you have been saying has really challenged me; in fact, if I could fully understand what you have told us, I would become a real Christian.' He was quite sincere in what he said, so

I questioned him and talked further with him. He was a graduate of a university, trained to think and evaluate facts.

"I asked, 'If you could really understand the full meaning of the gospel, you would become a Christian?'

"'Yes,' he replied, 'I would.'

"'Well, consider this,' I went on. 'I have a friend who is a missionary in the Congo. He works among the Pygmies, people with little capacity for understanding. If, in order to become a Christian, we had to understand the gospel message, how could these simple people ever be blessed?'

"His reply was quite honest: 'You know, I never thought of that!'

"'No,' I replied, 'but God did. The gospel message doesn't have to be understood by the seeking soul, only to be received in simple faith. It isn't fully understanding the gospel that gives me the blessing, but simply believing and receiving it.'

"Nicodemus began by 'knowing,' but he continued by believing and receiving."[6]

There are many people sitting in churches today who have never heard this message of the new birth. Some churches preach good works, social change, government legislation, and neglect the one thing that will help solve the problems of our world—changed men and women. Man's basic problem is first spiritual, then social. He needs a complete change from inside out.

Some time ago I attended a historic conference in Africa. Every country except one from the whole continent of Africa was represented by delegates. Never before had there been such a Christian gathering. Time after time I heard African leaders express appreciation for what Christian missions had done, especially in the fields of evangelism, medical aid, and education. One of the speakers said, "85 percent of all education south of the Sahara has been done by Christian missions."

An Anglican bishop from England told us, "Every social agency in England from the Society for the Prevention of Cruelty to Animals, on up, was founded as a result of a conversion to Christ and a spiritual awakening." We must be careful not to put the cart before the horse.

The Bible refers many times to this change Jesus talked about. Through the prophet Ezekiel, God said, "I will give you a new heart and put a new spirit within you" (Ezek. 36:26). In the book of Acts, Peter called it repenting and being converted. Paul speaks of it in Romans as being "alive from the dead" (Rom. 6:13). In Colossians Paul calls it "(a putting off of) the old self with its evil practices, and (a putting on of) the new self who is being renewed to a true knowledge according to the image of the One who created him" (Col. 3: 9, 10). In Titus he calls it "the washing of regeneration and renewing by the Holy Spirit" (Tit. 3:5). Peter said it was being "partakers of the divine nature" (2 Pet. 1:4). In the Church of England catechism it is called "a death unto sin and a new birth unto righteousness."

The context of John 3 teaches that the new birth is something that God does for man when man is willing to yield to God. We have seen that the Bible teaches that man is dead in trespasses and sins, and his great need is life. We do not have within ourselves the seed of the new life, this must come from God Himself.

One of the great Christian writers of this century, Oswald Chambers, said, "Our part as workers for God is to open men's eyes that they may turn themselves from darkness to light; but that is not salvation, that is conversion—the effort of a roused human being. I do not think it is too sweeping to say that the majority of nominal Christians are of this order; their eyes are opened, but they have received nothing. . . . When a man is born again, he knows that it is because he has received something as a gift from Almighty God and not because of his own decision."[7]

Conversion means "turning." The Bible is full of this concept and God pleads with man to turn to Him. He spoke through the prophet Ezekiel, "Repent . . . and *turn* your faces away from all your abominations" (Ezek. 14:6, emphasis mine). Another prophet, Isaiah, spoke, "*Turn* to Me, and be saved, all the ends of the earth; For I am God, and there is no other" (Isa. 45:22, emphasis mine).

The new birth is not just being reformed, it's being transformed. People are always making resolutions to do better, to change, and breaking those resolutions soon afterwards. But the Bible teaches us that through the new birth we can enter a new world.

The contrasts used in the Bible to express the change which comes over us when we are born again are very graphic; from lust to holiness; from darkness to light; from death to resurrection; from stranger to the kingdom of God to now being its citizen. The Bible teaches that the person who is born again has a changed will, changed affections, changed objectives for living, changed disposition, new purpose. He receives a new nature and a new heart. He becomes a new creation.

Before and After

The Bible is full of people from all walks of life who have been changed by an encounter with Jesus Christ. Christ met a woman in Samaria who was a prostitute and an outcast in her own town. To avoid meeting other women she went to a well during the heat of the day when she knew she wouldn't encounter other villagers. But there she met Christ. She was changed immediately into a new person. In fact, she became an instant missionary and rushed to her own city, where she was despised and scorned, to tell others about Jesus Christ. And we are told, "Many of the Samaritans believed in Him because of the word of the woman who testified, 'He told me all the things that I have done!'" (John 4:39).

Andrew was an ordinary fellow. He didn't seem to be the big personality man, but he was very quick to respond to Christ; in fact, he was on fire from the moment he met Jesus. The first thing he did was to go and find his brother to tell him the wonderful news about the Messiah. He may not have been a flaming evangelist, but wherever he appears in the biblical account, he is fruitful.

In these days of high taxes, the yearly or quarterly tax reports are not exactly greeted with enthusiasm. It wasn't any different in Jesus' time. Zacchaeus, a tax collector, and not a very honest one at that, was skillful in defrauding people, but when he met Jesus all that changed. He repented and wanted to make amends for his deceitful acts. "Behold, Lord, half of my possessions I will give to the poor, and if I have defrauded anyone of anything, I will give back four times as much" (Luke 19:8).

A young intellectual named Saul was on a journey along the road to Damascus, persecuting Christians, when he met Jesus Christ. To this day we speak about "Damascus Road experiences," because

Saul was never the same again. He became the great Apostle Paul. Many times he referred to that encounter, even recalling the very day and moment when he met Christ.

On the day of Pentecost a dramatic change occurred in three thousand people who were born again. In the morning they were lost, uncertain about the purpose of life, many of them guilty over the death of Christ. Others were afraid of either the secular or religious authorities. But at the end of the day they had been born into the kingdom of God. Each one had passed out of death into life. " 'Truly, truly, I say to you, he who hears My word, and believes Him who sent Me, has eternal life, and does not come into judgment, but has passed out of death into life' " (John 5:24).

Any person who is willing to trust Jesus Christ as his personal Savior and Lord can receive the new birth now. It's not something to be received at death or after death; it is for now. "Now is the accepted time; behold, now is the day of salvation" (2 Cor 6:2, KJV).

The New Birth Is for Now

The "before and after" advertisements for diet remedies or face-lifts cannot match the impact of the testimonies of those who have been born again. From corporate president to prison inmate, stories unfold of lives turned right side up.

A young woman wrote us: "Until last January I was a stranger to Jesus. I was a rebel, thief, a drunkard, a hard drug taker, an adulteress, a hippie, and a self-centered, confused young woman. Thinking I was going to stump everyone with my cynical questions, I went to a Bible study about a year ago out of curiosity. That night I became sincerely interested in the Bible. Finally after searching and studying the Scriptures for months, John 3:16 spoke to my heart and I gave my life to Christ. I never knew that this kind of happiness could exist. God shows you how to love and what it feels like to be loved. He was what I had been looking for since my early teens. He was 'the bag' I hadn't found. It seemed to me that drugs, liquor, free love, and bumming around the country would make me free, but they were all traps. Sin was the trap that led me to confusion, unhappiness, guilt, and near-suicide.

Christ has made me free. Being a Christian is exciting because there is always a new challenge, so much to learn. Now I wake up glad to see the day.

"He has made me new."

Johnny Cash says, "A few years ago I was hooked on drugs. I dreaded to wake up in the morning. There was no joy, peace, or happiness in my life. Then one day in my helplessness I turned my life completely over to God. Now I can't wait to get up in the morning to study my Bible. Sometimes the words out of the Scriptures leap into my heart. This does not mean that all my problems have been solved, or that I have reached any state of perfection. However, my life has been turned around. I have been born again!"

12

The New Birth Is
Not Just a "Feeling"

A MAN WHO was persuaded to go to a large evangelistic meeting recalled the following events:

"It was here, I believe for the first time in my life, that I heard the claims of Jesus Christ presented, simply and authoritatively.

"At the end of his talk the speaker invited those who wished to know more to come to the front of the auditorium. I went and was introduced to the speaker and we talked for a while. There were other people who wanted to ask questions, so I made my way to the exit, very interested in what he had said, but still in a deep fog.

"Just as I was about to go out the door I was confronted by a man who looked me in the eye and said:

"'Are you a Christian?'

"'Strange question,' I thought, putting on my best Sunday school smile and saying, 'Oh yes, I think so.'

"'Are you a Christian?' he insisted, a light in his eye.

"'Crank,' I thought, 'Humor him and then escape!'

"So I replied, 'Well, I'm trying to be.'

"'Ever try to be an elephant?'

"Grinning at my dumb astonishment, he took me by the arm, sat me down in a chair and explained that no amount of trying could ever transform me into a Christian (any more than it could turn me into an elephant). Then he began to explain what New Testament Christianity was all about. That Jesus Christ had died in *my* place. That HE had paid the full penalty which *my* sins demanded. As I was, I stood condemned before a holy God; I needed a Savior. Jesus alone could save me. Forgiveness for the past was possible in Him. Moreover, in His resurrection, He was offering me power to live the sort of life I had hitherto considered hopelessly out of reach.

"What a stupendous offer! If the living God were really asking to come into my wretched, tarnished life, to take over what I was only wasting and spoiling—how dare I refuse Him! He was promising, 'Behold I stand at the door and knock.'

"I flung open the door. He was as good as His word."

This man was born again. He had a turnabout. He thought he was a Christian, but he had never personally made a commitment to Jesus Christ.

Jesus made everything so simple and we have made it so complicated. He spoke to the people in short sentences and everyday words, illustrating his messages with parables and stories.

Paul told the Philippian jailer who asked what he must do to be saved, "Believe in the Lord Jesus, and you shall be saved" (Acts 16:31).

It's so simple that it's often overlooked. Although the gospel message is heard—especially in America—on radio stations, presented on television, sung on streetcorners, presented from pulpits, and explained in books, and tracts, millions overlook it. All you have to do to be born again is to repent of your sins and believe in the Lord Jesus as your personal Lord and Savior. You don't clean up, give up, or turn around yourself, you just come as you are. This is why we sing the hymn, "Just As I Am" at our Crusades.

Key Word: Repentance

In the New Testament Peter says, "Repent, therefore, and be *converted*, that your sins may be blotted out, [so that] the times of refreshing shall come from the presence of the Lord" (Acts 3:19, KJV, emphasis mine).

A person cannot turn to God to repent, or even to believe, without God's help. God must do the turning. Many times the Bible tells how men and women did that very thing, "Turn thou me, and I shall be turned; for thou art the Lord my God" (Jer. 31:18, KJV).

To many the word "repentance" is old-fashioned. It doesn't seem to have a proper place in a twentieth-century vocabulary. But repentance is one of the two vital elements in conversion and simply means recognition of what we are, and a willingness to change our minds toward sin, self, and God.

Repentance involves first of all an acknowledgment of our sin. When we repent we are saying that we recognize that we are sinners and that our sin involves us in personal guilt before God. This type of guilt does not mean incriminating self-contempt; it means seeing ourselves as God sees us, and saying, "God be merciful to me a sinner" (Luke 18:13, KJV). It is not just the corporate guilt of society we are acknowledging—it's so easy to blame the government, the school system, the church, the home, for our own personal guilt. The Bible teaches that when we reach the age of accountability—usually somewhere around ten or eleven years of age—God looks upon us as fullgrown adults, making moral and spiritual choices for which we will be held accountable at the judgment. Each of us has an individual guilt before God. From the moment we are conceived we have the tendency toward sin; then we become sinners by choice and, ultimately, sinners by practice. That is why the Bible says we have all sinned and come short of the glory of God.

Every person throughout the world, of whatever race, color, language, or culture, needs to be born again. We are guilty of "sin" (singular) which is expressed in "sins" (plural). We break God's laws and rebel against Him because we are sinners by nature. It is this disease of sin (singular) that Christ dealt with on the cross.

We have heard so much about "roots." The roots of man's individual and corporate problems lie deep in his own heart. We are a diseased human race. This disease can only be dealt with by the blood of Christ, just as in the Old Testament blood was shed on hundreds of altars, looking forward to the day when Jesus Christ would come and be "the Lamb of God who takes away the sin of the world" (John 1:29). He became the cosmic scapegoat for the entire world. All of our sins were laid on Him. This is why God can now forgive us. This is why He can infuse new life into us—which is called regeneration, or the new birth.

When we look at the attributes of God and realize how far short we fall of His perfection, there is no alternative to the recognition of our sinful nature. The Apostle Peter had been involved in sinful acts and harbored sinful thoughts, but far deeper than the physical or mental admission of wrongdoing, Peter realized that he had a twisted nature. He said, "Depart from me, for I am a sinful man, O Lord!" (Luke 5:8). Notice that he didn't say, "I sin," but "I am a sinful man."

Job saw how corrupt he was in relation to God's perfection, and said, "I have heard of thee by the hearing of the ear; but now mine eye seeth thee: Wherefore I abhor myself, and repent in dust and ashes" (Job 42:5,6, KJV). Job compared himself with God and repented; he recognized what he was before God.

Repentance also involves a genuine *sorrow* for sin. Sorrow is an emotion, and we are creatures who vary greatly in the degree of sorrow we may experience. Repentance without sorrow is hollow, however. The Apostle Paul said, "I now rejoice, not that you were made sorrowful, but that you were made sorrowful to the point of repentance; for you were made sorrowful according to the will of God, in order that you might not suffer loss in anything through us" (2 Cor. 7:9).

With repentance comes a change of purpose, a willing turnaround from sin. If we had to repent without God's help, then we would be almost helpless. The Scripture teaches that we are dead in trespasses and in sins. A dead man can do nothing; therefore we need God's help even in our repenting. Sometimes this involves "restitution." If we have stolen, lied, or cheated to the hurt of other people, we must go and make this right if at all possible.

I've had hundreds of letters from people who have told me that they have had money returned to them that had been stolen by people who claimed to be "born again." Many people, before their conversion, have been shoplifters. Many have felt that they must go back to the store, discuss their wrongdoing with the manager, and make restitution.

When my wife was counseling with Joe Medina after he was tempted and helped a friend rob a filling station, she told him that his repentance would never be real unless he confessed his crime. He did. He earned the money that summer and returned it in full. The filling station owner forgave him. Today that young man has finished four years at a Bible college and is now a minister.

When Jim Vaus, the underworld figure, came to Christ in 1949, he spent many weeks looking up people whom he had offended, injured, and stolen from. He returned everything he possibly could and apologized to all those whom he had offended.

This type of restitution is rare today, but it is most certainly taught in the Scriptures. It helps complete our repentance. It shows to those whom we have offended, and to the world, that we mean business with God.

When emotions are contrary to our willingness to turn from sin, hypocrisy enters the life of a believer, and doubts begin to grow. There are so many things in the Bible that seem so difficult to believe. When we become a new creature in Christ, we are propelled into an exhilarating, joyful, exciting experience which carries us emotionally for a time. Then doubts may enter our lives, quietly at first, but then more boldly as the questions begin to crowd out the trust. "How can I be willing to turn over my life to God when He might make me do something I don't want to do?"

When a wealthy, beautiful woman who was a leader in her community was converted, one of the first persons she told, a friend of many years, said, "Well, Dorothy, what are you going to do now—go to Africa as a missionary?"

Dorothy struggled with her emotions, but answered with her surrendered will, "If that's where God wants me, I'll go."

But it's not that easy for most to be willing to turn over the action and direction to God.

A wonderful old woman who wrote one of the classics in Christian books told a story about a young man of great intelligence who was having tremendous difficulties in his new Christian experience with this matter of will. He was a great doubter, and emotionally nothing seemed real to him. He was given this piece of advice: "'A man's will is really the man's self; . . . what his will does, he does. Your part then is simply to put your will . . . over on God's side, making up your mind that you will believe what He says [in the Bible], because He says it, and that you will not pay any regard to the feelings that make it seem so unreal. God will not fail to respond, sooner or later, with His revelation to such a faith.'

"The young man paused a moment, and then said solemnly, 'I understand, and will do what you say. I cannot control my emotions, but I can control my will; and the new life begins to look possible to me, if it is only my will that needs to be set straight in the matter. I can give my will to God, and I do.'"[1]

Biblical repentance is the fuel which is used to propel our life with God at the controls. Until we utilize that fuel, we are earthbound, tied down by our ego, our pride, our troubles and guilt. Young people are often chained in a prison of purposelessness, uncertainty, and even guilt. Many an older person faces old age and death with dread and fear. True repentance can release those chains.

Thus, repentance is *first*, and absolutely necessary, if we are to be born again. It involves simple recognition of what we are before God—sinners who fall short of His glory; *second*, it involves genuine sorrow for sin; *third*, it means our willingness to turn from sin.

Key Word: Faith

In considering conversion we have seen that it has a "turning-from" side called repentance. It also has a "turning-to" side, called faith.

Faith is first of all belief—belief that Christ was who He said He was. Second, faith is belief that He can do what He claimed He could do—He can forgive me, and come into my life. Third, faith is trust, an act of commitment, in which I open the door of my heart to Him. In the New Testament the words "faith," "belief," and "believe," are translations of similar Greek words so they are interchangeable.

Placing your faith in Christ means that first you must make a choice. The Scripture says, "Whoever believes in him [Jesus] is not condemned, but whoever does not believe stands condemned already because he has not believed in the name of God's one and only Son" (John 3:18, NIV). The person who believes is not condemned; the person who has not believed is condemned. In order not to be condemned you must make a choice—you must choose to believe.

So we can see how important belief is. The Bible says that without faith it is impossible to please God. But what does it mean to believe? It means to "commit" yourself to Christ, to "surrender" to Him. Believing is your response to God's offer of mercy, love, and forgiveness. God took the initiative and did everything that was needed to make the offer of salvation possible. When Christ bowed His head on the cross and said, "It is finished," He meant just that (John 19:30). God's plan for our reconciliation and redemption was complete in His Son. But only by believing in Jesus—committing yourself to Him, surrendering to Him—are you saved.

Belief is not just a feeling; it is the assurance of salvation. You may look at yourself in the mirror and say, "But I don't feel saved—I don't feel forgiven." But don't depend on feelings for your assurance. Christ has promised, and He cannot lie. Belief is a deliberate act of committing one's self to the person of Jesus Christ. It's not a "hanging on" to some vague idea. It is an act of trust in the God-Man, Jesus Christ.

The New Testament never used the words "belief" and "faith" in the plural. Christian faith does not mean accepting a long list of dos and don'ts. It means a single, individual relinquishment of mind and heart toward the one person, Jesus Christ. It does not mean believing everything or just anything. It is belief in a person, and that person is the Christ described in Scripture.

Faith is not anti-intellectual. Faith involves a very logical premise—that is, trusting that God's superior ability is able to save us.

Francis Schaeffer, a brilliant Christian living in Switzerland, explains that faith is not only logical, but that lack of faith is illogical. He writes: "Man is made in the image of God; therefore, on the side of the fact that God is a personal God the chasm stands not between God and man, but between man and all else. But on the side of God's infinity, man is as separated from God as the atom or any other finite [object] of the universe. So we have the answer to man's being finite and yet personal.

"It is not that this is the best answer to existence; it is the *only* answer. That is why we may hold our Christianity with intellectual integrity. The only answer for what exists is that he, the infinite-personal God, really is there."[2]

Faith in Christ is also voluntary. A person cannot be coerced, bribed, or tricked into trusting Jesus. God will not force His way into your life. The Holy Spirit will do everything possible to disturb you, draw you, love you—but finally it is your personal decision. God not only gave His Son on the cross where the plan of redemption was finished: He gave the law as expressed in the Ten Commandments and the Sermon on the Mount to show you your need of forgiveness; He gave the Holy Spirit to convict you of your need. He gives the Holy Spirit to draw you to the cross, but even after all of this, it is your decision whether to accept God's free pardon or to continue in your lost condition.

Faith also involves the whole person. In his book *Knowing God*, J. I. Packer says, "Knowing God is a matter of *personal involvement*, in mind, will, and feeling. It would not, indeed, be a fully personal relationship otherwise."[3]

So faith is not just an emotional reaction, an intellectual realization, or a willful decision; faith is all-inclusive. It involves the intellect, the emotion, and the will.

Steps Leading to Conversion

We have seen that conversion occurs when we repent and place our faith in Christ. But what is the process like as we approach the point of conversion? How long will it take? Will it be emotional or dramatic? My answer is, I don't know. If everyone had the same reaction we could apply a neat little chemical formula with predetermined results. The key word is *variety*.

We can see this clearly if we stop for a moment to reflect on God. First, the point we are heading for is a point where God Himself is going to do something; He is the one who converts us when we repent and believe in Christ. "Salvation is of the Lord." Second, His help starts coming long before that point. As we have already seen, during the time before conversion He is preparing us for repentance by the conviction of the Holy Spirit and by making us want to turn from our sins. Also He is preparing us for faith by showing us how forgiving and majestic Christ is.

Questions about length of time and amount of emotion in the conversion process, consequently, are very personal. God looks at each of us differently, because each of us is different. He will relate to you just as you are. He will relate to me just as I am. Of course, in His concern His goal for each of us will be the same—our new birth. But to help us to that point He will be just as personal as a shepherd who knows each of his sheep by name.

We could go to the experiences of people we know, or to your own experience. If you have not been born again, the very fact that you are reading this book right now may be the process God is using in your life to lead you toward a decision.

God knows the needs of your heart. When we look at the process He used with different people in the Bible prior to their conversion, we see that He understands their individuality. In John 1, for instance, He talked to several men who had not yet been converted. On being approached by Andrew and a friend, Jesus asked a question, "What do you seek?" (John 1:38) and then invited them to spend the day with Him where He was staying. Quiet conversation was Andrew's need if he was to gain a sense of his sin and a trust in Jesus.

Andrew brought along his erratic brother, Simon. Christ acted very differently toward him. Regarding him seriously, Jesus said, "You are Simon the son of John; you shall be called 'Cephas' (which translated means Peter)," the word for rock. Jesus revealed a flash of His majesty by telling this volatile young man that in trusting Him his character would be changed to a rocklike steadiness (John 1:42). To be converted Peter needed to see his sin of relying on himself, which made him such a changeable personality, and he needed to trust Christ as the one who had the power and concern to change him.

The next day Jesus found Philip and treated him in still another way. He simply said, "Follow Me" (John 1:43). Unlike Andrew or Peter, Philip needed a straightforward command. Philip then brought Nathanael, a very religious man of prayer who was seeking an experience with God. Jesus adapted to his special needs in John 1:51, saying, "Truly, truly, I say to you, you shall see the heavens open, and the angels of God ascending and descending upon the Son of Man.

Andrew, Peter, Philip, and Nathanael were all different. So Jesus treated them all differently. They all needed a personal relationship with Christ. This is essentially what the new birth is. To some of them the realization of what was happening came slowly. It took months of training by Jesus Himself. This is why I urge new converts to take plenty of time in Bible study and prayer before getting on a public platform to testify. The Scripture warns against "a novice." We have often unwittingly been guilty of this in our Crusades—putting up to give a testimony young converts who had really not grown in the grace and knowledge of Christ enough. Through long years of experience we have become far more careful.

After the conversion of the Apostle Paul he took three years of study in Arabia. It took God forty years to train Moses on the back side of a desert before he made his public appearance. In these days we often hear of a person who is in jail one day, and a few weeks later is on a public platform testifying concerning his conversion before a large crowd. Sometimes this is followed by a great tragedy—the so-called new convert had really not been born again; he had only professed Christ but had not been willing to pay the price of following Christ.

I know a young man who seemed to be gloriously converted in one of our Crusades, and I believe he was. He did have a rather long period of getting over his drug habit and growing in the knowledge of the Scriptures. We urged him to attend a Bible school, which he did for a year. His testimony was so thrilling that the invitations began to pour in from across America for him to give his witness. It wasn't long before this attention had caused him to backslide terribly, to the point of even leaving his wife and family. I am glad to report that he has been restored to fellowship with God, realizes his sins and mistakes, and is now going back to finish his studies.

What can we expect the process to be like as we approach the new birth? It will be tailored to our own environment, temperament, secret needs, and hopes. That is the way God works.

How Long Are the Steps?

The length of time and degree of emotion involved in the process which leads to our conversion is also varied. Some, but not all, will face an emotional crisis with symptoms similar to those accompanying mental conflict. They may experience deep feelings and even tears of repentance. The Holy Spirit is convicting them of sin. This is their way of responding to Him. Each of us may have a different emotional experience. The night I came to Christ there were several people around me weeping. I had no tears at all and wondered if my act of commitment was genuine.

I have learned since that many have had a much quieter conversion, with a shorter time in the process. Perhaps one person, reading the Scripture or singing a hymn, comes upon a simple statement and applies it to himself then and there. Another person hears a sermon and with no stress or conflict receives its message and believes in Christ. Conversion is no less real to these quiet people than to the more expressive or dramatic ones.

Acts 16 records two conversions which were striking contrasts. Lydia was a businesswoman in the city of Philippi. She had shown enough interest in God to be spending time and prayer by the side of a river, where she heard Paul preach. The Lord opened her heart to respond to the gospel message, and she was converted without fanfare or a strong emotional display.

Then there was the jailer in the city of Philippi where Paul was imprisoned. An earthquake came and the jailer panicked as he realized his prisoners could escape. He thought the only way out of his crisis was to kill himself. Just as he was drawing his sword he heard the Apostle Paul say, "Do yourself no harm, for we are all here!" (Acts 16:28).

The jailer couldn't believe what he heard! Why hadn't the prisoners escaped? He was shaking from head to foot, and called for a light. He took one look at Paul and Silas, his prisoners, and fell down at their feet, crying, "What must I do to be saved?" Paul told him to believe in the Lord Jesus Christ and he would be saved, and he was converted right there, in the rubble of the prison.

Jesus described the conversion experience like the movement of the wind. "The wind blows where it wishes and you hear the sound of it, but do not know where it comes from and where it is going; so is every one who is born of the Spirit" (John 3:8).

Wind can be quiet, gentle, or it can reach cyclone proportions. So it is with conversion, sometimes easy and tender, and other times a tornado which alters the entire landscape.

Is there one definite point in time, one hour of one day of one year when a person can say, "That was when I was born again"? I know many people who can point to that time and say with assurance, "That was my spiritual birthday." However, I know there are people who today are walking in fellowship with Jesus Christ, but have no memory of an exact time when they deliberately committed themselves to Him, and cannot remember when they did not love and trust Him. My wife is one of those great Christians in this category. However, it is my opinion that they may be the exception rather than the rule. Scripture teaches that belief is an act of the will, so whether they can remember the time or not, there was a moment when they crossed over the line from death to life.

Nevertheless, the issue for a person now is not so much "when" as "whether." When we were saved is not so important as whether we are now saved. We often cannot tell the exact moment when night becomes day, but we know when it is daylight. So the great question for a person to answer who has never by a conscious act of will committed himself to Christ as his Lord and Savior is this: "Are you now living in the day, in touch with Christ?"

How to Receive Christ

Just after I received Christ someone gave me a little tract entitled "Four Things God Wants You To Know," by an English writer. I often used those four points in my earlier preaching, and they were excellent. Years later, Bill Bright of Campus Crusade developed "The Four Spiritual Laws" which have been widely used throughout the world in helping people to understand how to be born again. Our own organization developed what we called "Four Steps to Peace with God," taken largely from one of my earlier books, *Peace With God.* I do not believe however, that there is a tidy little formula, or a recipe which has the Good Housekeeping seal of approval. However, I do believe these have provided little handles which help people to understand how to receive Christ.

Here are some guidelines from the Bible which will help you accept Christ as your Lord and Savior. You have seen the need, the direction, and the steps in previous chapters, and you may already have reached your own conclusions. Just the same, let me summarize what you must do.

First, you must recognize what God did: that He loved you so much He gave His Son to die on the cross. Substitute your own name for "the world" and "whoever" in this familiar verse: "For God so loved the world, that He gave His only begotten Son, that whoever believes in Him should not perish, but have eternal life" (John 3:16). "The Son of God . . . loved me, and delivered Himself up for me" (Galatians 2:20).

Second, you must repent for your sins. Jesus said, "Unless you repent, you will . . . perish" (Luke 13:3). He said, "Repent and believe" (Mark 1:15). It's not enough to be sorry; repentance is that turnabout from sin that is emphasized.

Third, you must receive Jesus Christ as Savior and Lord. "But as many as received Him, to them He gave the right to become children of God, even to those that believe in His name" (John 1:12). This means that you cease trying to save yourself and accept Christ as your only Lord and your only Savior. Trust Him completely, without reservation.

Fourth, you must confess Christ publicly. This confession is a sign that you have been converted. Jesus said, "Every one therefore who shall confess Me before men, I will also confess him before My Father who is in heaven" (Matt. 10:32). It is extremely important that when you receive Christ you tell someone else about it just as soon as possible. This gives you strength and courage to witness.

Make it happen *now*. "Now is the accepted time . . . now is the day of salvation" (2 Cor. 6:2, KJV). If you are willing to repent for your sins and to receive Jesus Christ as your Lord and Savior, you can do it now. At this moment you can either bow your head or get on your knees and say this little prayer which I have used with thousands of persons on every continent:

O God, I acknowledge that I have sinned against You. I am sorry for my sins. I am willing to turn from my sins. I openly receive and acknowledge Jesus Christ as my Savior. I confess Him as Lord. From this moment on I want to live for Him and serve Him. In Jesus' name. Amen.

These are the steps and the prayer which many years ago, in a book I wrote, were read by people just like yourselves who responded and wrote of their changed lives.

If you are willing to make this decision and have received Jesus Christ as your own Lord and Savior, then you have become a child of God in whom Jesus Christ dwells. You do not need to measure the certainty of your salvation by your feelings. Believe God. He keeps His word. You are born again. You are alive!

(If you would like more help and literature, please feel free to write me:

Billy Graham
Minneapolis, Minnesota

—that's all the address you need.)

13

Alive and Growing

"AFTER THINKING ABOUT it for three days, I realized I needed Jesus Christ, and I accepted Him. Now that my life has been turned over to Jesus Christ, I can function with an extra power bestowed by God."

Who made a statement like that? Someone down on the bottom of life's heap, struggling for worth and identity? No. A handsome, young University of Southern California athlete, John Naber, who gained international attention by earning four gold medals with his swimming achievements in the 1976 Olympics. John Naber said he was searching for something meaningful in his life and after attending one of our meetings he began to wake up to the realization of Jesus Christ. He was born again.

More and more celebrities, especially in the sports, entertainment, and political worlds, are telling of their new experiences of being made alive in Christ. While it is thrilling to hear about it, there are also dangers (as I have already expressed) in a "novice" who has very little grounding in the Word of God. Yet I cannot help rejoicing in every one of them and believe that God has been moving mightily in reaching out for people of extraordinary gifts and talents all over the world. Many of them He is greatly using to win others to Christ. A newspaper feature said that "evidence of a current religious revival is everywhere," and then related how famous personalities were "pinpointing the exact moment of spiritual turn-around" with their "often unbelievable accounts of being born again. Some say they have met Jesus Christ. Others experience a sensation similar to an electric shock. In all cases the new believers experience overwhelming feelings of love and joy."

Dean Jones, a Walt Disney film veteran, relates, "I was performing in summer stock at a New Jersey lodge and had gone to my room to be alone. Nothing was satisfying me. I looked out that window and felt fear and confusion. Impulsively, I knelt by the bed and spelled out my doubts to God; I don't know why I was moved to do this. I said to God, 'If you bring meaning to my life, I'll serve you.'"

There is nothing more exciting than a personal testimony from a person who has experienced a spiritual rebirth. This is more than an interesting story or fascinating experience. A new born man or woman has been given so many riches by God. We will outline them and then discuss how to draw from that wealthy potential.

Forgiven!

"Your sins are forgiven you for His name's sake" (1 John 2:12). What a stupendous promise! Throughout the New Testament we learn that the one who receives Christ as Lord and Savior also receives, immediately, the gift of forgiveness. The Bible says, "As far as the east is from the west, so far has He removed our transgressions from us" (Ps. 103:12).

"Forgive me." "I'm sorry." "I didn't mean it." How often we use those words and they echo back with a hollow sound. But God's forgiveness is not just a casual statement; it is the complete blotting out of all the dirt and degradation of our past, present, and future. The only reason our sins can be forgiven is because Jesus Christ paid their full penalty on the cross.

Guilt feelings provide the basis for many dramatic plots. Shakespeare's line from *Macbeth* is famous: "Out, damned spot! Out!" Guilt feelings are the focal point of much psychiatric counseling. Many feel like Judas, who, after he betrayed Christ, said, "I have betrayed innocent blood." So tremendous is the weight of our guilt that the great and glorious concept of forgiveness should be shouted by every believer in Jesus Christ.

God's goodness in forgiving us goes even farther when we realize that when we are converted we are also declared just—which means that in God's sight we are without guilt, clothed forever with Christ's righteousness.

As we saw in "The King's Courtroom," forgiveness and justification are God's free gifts.

Adopted by the King

When you were converted, God adopted you as His son or daughter. As an adopted child each of us can claim to be joint heir with Jesus Christ. "God sent forth His Son . . . that He might redeem those who were under the Law, that we might receive the adoption as sons" (Gal. 4:4,5).

I know a lawyer and his wife who have two adopted children, a boy and a girl. The little girl looks very much like her mother, and the young man could easily be the natural son of his father. The fact that they were chosen by their parents has given them a great sense of security and love.

To be the son or daughter of the Lord of the universe is a powerful realization.

The Indwelling Holy Spirit

When you were converted, the Spirit of God immediately came to live in you. Before He ascended into heaven, Jesus Christ said, "I will ask the Father, and He will give you another Helper, that He may be with you forever; that is the Spirit of truth . . . you know Him, because He abides with you, and will be in you" (John 14:16,17).

When Christ lived on this earth, He could be with only a small group of people at any one time. Now Christ dwells through the Holy Spirit in the hearts of all those who have received Him as Lord and Savior. Lloyd Ogilvie, pastor of the First Presbyterian Church in Hollywood, refers to the Holy Spirit as "the contemporary Christ." Paul wrote to the Romans, "He [God] will also give life to your mortal bodies through His Spirit who indwells you" (Rom. 8:11).

At the historic Congress on World Evangelization in Switzerland in 1974, the Holy Spirit was the subject of many addresses and discussions. The Reverend Gottfried Osei-Mensah of Nairobi, Kenya, said, "The Spirit is our Master. It is the work of the Holy Spirit, living in us, to free us from the rule of sin in our daily lives, and to help us live the new life we share with Christ."

How long does the Holy Spirit live in the heart of a believer? Forever. God does not give a gift as powerful as the Holy Spirit and then take it back. By faith you accept God's statements that you are indwelt by the Spirit of God, but you can watch Him at work, too. The Holy Spirit can rejuvenate a tired Christian, captivate an indifferent believer, and empower a dry church.

A clergyman from Buenos Aires, Argentina, said, "The Holy Spirit today is renewing the fruit of the Spirit—love, joy, peace. All those things are going to be the elements that show the world that we are his people."

The Holy Spirit is there to give you special power to work for Christ. He is there to give you strength in the moment of temptation.

Jesus promised that we would receive power from the Holy Spirit (Acts 1:8). Perhaps you have heard the story of the woodpecker who was pecking with his beak against the trunk of a tree. At that very moment, the lightning struck the tree, splitting it from top to bottom. When he'd recovered from the shock, the woodpecker flew away exclaiming, "I didn't know there was so much power in my beak!" I don't ask you, have you the Holy Spirit, but does the Holy Spirit have you?

Victory over Temptation

The Bible teaches that the new believer in Jesus Christ—the converted person—is to "abhor what is evil" (Rom. 12:9). Here is another strong admonishment, "in reference to your former manner of life, you lay aside the old self, which is being corrupted in accordance with the lusts of deceit" (Eph. 4:22).

Now wait a minute. How are we supposed to be able to stop doing some of the sinful things we have done for years, or get rid of some of the negative, suspicious, hateful, greedy attitudes which are ingrained in our personality? "I just can't do it myself," you might say.

You're right. However, the capacity to resist sin and obey God comes from the Holy Spirit, who lives in every true believer. It's not up to us to struggle against temptation alone. God lives in our hearts to help us resist sin. It is His job to work, and our job to yield.

What about the old bugaboo of temptation? The Bible doesn't say we won't be tempted; that would be foolish. We know that we live in a world full of temptations, most of them tied up in very attractive packages and offered as something we must try or buy—just once! But the converted man or woman has the offer of victory over temptation. "No temptation has overtaken you but such as is common to man; and God is faithful, who will not allow you to be tempted beyond what you are able; but with the temptation will provide the way of escape also, that you may be able to endure it" (1 Cor. 10:13).

To be tempted is not a sin; as a believer in Jesus Christ you do not need to blame yourself for an increase in the temptations that surround you. The indwelling Holy Spirit gives us strength to resist temptation.

Temptation is very powerful and will become even more so after you have been born again. The Scriptures tell us that we are in a spiritual warfare and that our enemies have more power and skill to tempt us than we have ever encountered before. Here is where many new believers make a big mistake. They think that when they are converted they will become perfect right away, that they will live on a continual high. Then they find themselves being tempted, in conflict, and even at times yielding to temptation. The new believer takes a look at himself and doesn't like what he sees. He is filled with discouragement and frustration. This is normal. The devil tempts you and God tests you. Often they are two sides to the same coin—God allows the devil to tempt you, and He uses it as a test, or as an experience to help deepen your faith and let you see how fragile you really are if you depend on yourself. He wants you to depend totally and completely on Him.

An old allegory illustrates this well: "Satan called together a council of his servants to consult how they might make a good

man sin. One evil spirit started up and said, 'I will make him sin.'—
'How will you do it?' asked Satan. 'I will set before him the pleasures of sin,' was the reply; 'I will tell him of its delights, and the
rich rewards it brings.'—'Ah,' said Satan, 'that will not do; he has
tried it, and knows better than that.' Then another imp started up
and said, 'I will make him sin.'—'What will you do?' asked Satan.
'I will tell him of the pains and sorrows of virtue. I will show him
that virtue has no delights, and brings no rewards.'—'Ah, no!'
exclaimed Satan, 'that will not do at all; for he has tried it, and
knows that "Wisdom's ways *are* ways of pleasantness, and all her
paths are peace."'—'Well,' said another imp, starting up, 'I will
undertake to make him sin.'—'And what will you do?' asked Satan,
again. 'I will discourage his soul,' was the short reply. 'Ah, that
will do!" cried Satan; 'that will do! We shall conquer him now.'"[1]

Spiritual conflict is at work in the heart of every believer. It is
true that the Christian possesses a new nature, but the old sin
nature is still there. It is now up to us, day by day, to yield to the
new nature which Christ dominates.

There is the story of a housewife who found a mouse in her
kitchen and took a broom to it. The mouse didn't waste its time
contemplating either the housewife or the broom, but got busy
looking for the hole. And so it is with us when we are caught by
temptation. We don't spend time contemplating the temptation
but get busy looking for a way out. The Scripture says, "God . . .
will not allow you to be tempted beyond what you are able; but
with the temptation will provide the way of escape also" (1 Cor.
10:13).

When the Christian sins he is miserable. Sometimes he avoids
other Christians, stops going to church, believes that he is misunderstood. However, every Christian has access to God through
prayer and when he confesses his sin God restores fellowship with
him. This is the difference between the believer and the unbeliever.
The unbeliever makes sin a practice; the believer does not.

A word about how believers should treat a "fallen" brother:
Some years ago we knew a young college student recently converted from a life of drugs. Shortly after his conversion he agreed
to turn informer for a narcotics agent in order to try and catch the
pushers in that area. Fellow Christians warned him against doing

this, but he had already committed himself and the inevitable happened. He blew his Christian witness when he had to pretend to be a drug-user himself in order to convince the pusher that he was for real, at one point having to take two shots of heroin. (Incidentally, the shots had an effect on him opposite to that before his conversion—instead of getting high he had violent withdrawals.) The Sunday before he left the school to return to his home, he stood up before the Sunday school class to tell them what had happened. The pusher had been caught, and although this young man had blown his Christian witness, he wanted the students to know that he was still a believer and a follower of the Lord. He stood up before the class, holding two fingers together to explain, "Me and Jesus are just like this." This gave the teacher an opportunity to talk to the students on how a brother should be treated when he has apparently fallen. During the time when he was trying to assist the narcotics agent, all the Christians on campus thought he had backslidden and gave him the cold shoulder. Actually, when we see a brother fall (or one whom we think has fallen) we should, like the Good Samaritan, get down and help him up again and do what we can to encourage him, pray for him, and let him know that we love him and believe in him.

The believer hates sin and wants to abide by God's commands. Paul says believers "do not walk according to the flesh, but according to the Spirit" (Rom. 8:4). The Holy Spirit who indwells us convicts us in various ways. A believer will begin to realize that the dirty jokes which were once a part of his office repertoire are sticking in his throat. The cocktail parties which were once so interesting and funny have become dull and boring. Ruth and I have sometimes gone to cocktail parties in various parts of the world. Always we have taken a soft drink and tried to be a witness. The first convert of the New York Crusade was a direct result of my going to a cocktail party like this on board a ship coming from Japan in the early 1950s. Such occasions may afford a great opportunity for Christian witness. We have often had a whole group of people gather around us and ask spiritual questions. In this same way Jesus talked with publicans and sinners, and for a clear purpose. On the other hand, going to cocktail parties just to be one of the gang not only often becomes boring, but carries the painful risk of hearing someone swear and take the name of the Lord in vain.

The choices of a new believer are made from a new perspective. He may hand himself over to sin (and feel miserable in it) or give himself over to God. Paul's advice is excellent: "I urge you therefore, brethren, by the mercies of God, to present your bodies a living and holy sacrifice, acceptable to God, which is your spiritual service of worship. And do not be conformed to this world, but be transformed by the renewing of your mind, that you may prove what the will of God is, that which is good and acceptable and perfect" (Rom. 12:1,2).

The transformation by "renewing of your mind" may happen quickly and dramatically, as the addict who experiences instant withdrawal, or it may permeate into your lifestyle more gradually.

Growing Slowly, Almost Imperceptibly —but Growing!

Many people grow into Christian maturity very rapidly; others much more slowly, almost imperceptibly. I once saw a picture on television of flowers growing, budding, and opening. This was done by slow-motion photography over a long period of time. If you had watched the same process with your naked eye in your garden it would have taken days. In the same way, we watch our lives from day to day and often get discouraged at the slow growth. But if you wait for a year or two and then look back over your life you will see how much you have grown. You've become kinder, more gracious, more loving. You love the Scriptures more. You love to pray more. You are a more faithful witness. You never will reach that point of full maturity in Christ until you see Him face to face in heaven.

Abrupt or gradual, the changes in a converted person are a part of his growth. He is not reborn full-grown; rather he is reborn with the energies of new life that will mature him as time passes. This growth is spiritual and moral. It's just like a baby learning to crawl, then toddle, then walk, then run. It takes time, study, patience, and discipline.

A person can attempt to imitate Christian growth by religious effort, but the result is like a plaster of Paris model of Michelangelo's David. It's phoney and easily broken.

A Christian grows as the life of God exerts its new power from deep in the center of his personality. The unconverted person cannot duplicate that life, no matter how religious he tries to act. He lacks the sources for growth because he has not been reborn.

A group of students at Harvard once tried to fool the famous professor of zoology Agassiz. They took parts from a number of different bugs and with great skill attached them together to make a creation they were sure would baffle their teacher. On the chosen day they brought it to him and asked that he identify it. As he inspected it with great care, the students grew more and more sure they had tricked this genius.

Finally, Professor Agassiz straightened up and said, "I have identified it." Scarcely able to control their amusement, they asked its name. Agassiz replied, "It is a humbug."

A person with genuine life from God will detect the counterfeit and think, "Humbug."

The new convert is a babe in Christ. A babe must be nourished in order to grow. He must be protected because he has been born into a world of many enemies. His primary battle will be with "the world," "the flesh," and "the devil." This is why he needs the encouragement of his family, Christian friends, and especially the Church. At the time of birth the child of God is born into great riches, and has a marvelous inheritance, but it takes some time to find out about all his wealth.

The most important thing in the beginning of new life is to be nourished and strengthened. Here are the important nutrients to use.

Get a Bible

If you have a Bible, fine. If the Scriptures are a whole new world to you, however, I would advise that you get one of the newer translations which may be easier for you to understand. It is important for you to begin reading the New Testament, and the Gospel of John is a good place to start.

Saturate yourself in the Word of God. Don't worry about understanding everything you read, because you won't. Pray before you read and ask the Holy Spirit to clarify what you are reading. The Scriptures are the greatest source of hope you will find in this hopeless world. "For whatever was written in earlier times was written for our instruction, that through perseverance and the encouragement of the Scriptures we might have hope" (Rom. 15:4).

Memorize portions of the Word of God. "Thy word have I hid in mine heart, that I might not sin against thee" (Ps. 119:11, KJV). Try taking a Bible verse that speaks to your needs and typing it on a file card. Put it in your pocket or purse and refer to it frequently. Review it daily, and by the end of the week you will have a verse memorized.

Satan is the great discourager. He doesn't want you to read the Bible or memorize Scripture. In the past you may not have been attacked by Satan, but now you've done something which makes him very angry. You've left his camp and joined the army of God. You're a Christian soldier and Satan will unleash all of his secret weapons. From now on it's upstream all the way against the current of the evils of this world.

But you can overcome everything he hurls at you with the weapon God has provided—"the sword of the Spirit, which is the word of God" (Eph. 6:17). Not only is the Word of God a sword to be used in offense, but you also have a shield to be used in defense. You have "the shield of faith with which ye shall be able to quench all the fiery darts of the wicked" (Eph. 6:16, KJV).

When Christ was in the wilderness He was tempted by Satan, and every time he met temptation with Scripture, saying, "It is written" (Matt. 4).

Christ needed this mighty weapon, and so do we.

Learn to Pray

There are complete books written about prayer, seminars held which deal in prayer, and hundreds of sermons on the power of prayer. The new believer is sometimes baffled by what and how to pray.

Jesus said, "Men ought always to pray" (Luke 18:1, KJV). The Apostle Paul said, "Pray without ceasing" (1 Thess. 5:17).

A prayer does not have to be eloquent or contain the language and terms of a theologian. When you made your decision for Christ, you were given the privilege of addressing God as Father. You pray to Him as a child talking to his loving and gracious father. In the beginning you may not be fluent, but it's important to begin. My wife has a notebook she has kept of our children as they were beginning to talk with us. She treasures these first attempts, mistakes and all. She said, "I wouldn't take anything for that book."

When Paul said we should pray without "ceasing," he chose a term used in his day to describe a persistent cough. Off and on, throughout our day we should be turning quickly to God to praise and thank Him, and to ask for His help. Prayers should be specific. God is interested in everything you do and nothing is too great or too insignificant to share with Him.

Find Christian Fellowship

God doesn't intend for you to live the Christian life alone. This is why he has brought other believers together to form fellowships. A church where the Bible is taught and believed is the first place a reborn man or woman must seek. I do not advise that just any church will do. Is the pastor teaching the Word of God or expounding his own or some other philosophy of living? You'll know. Does the church have Bible classes for all ages?

Without the fellowship of believers, a newly born Christian has a tendency to wither. The writer of the book of Hebrews says, "Let us consider how to stimulate one another to love and good deeds, not forsaking our own assembling together, as is the habit of some but encouraging one another" (Heb. 10: 24,25).

Perhaps there's a Bible class or prayer group in your community. It's exciting to find a whole new set of friends, people who are in various stages of their own Christian growth, growth, to share with and strengthen your faith.

One of my daughters lives in a high middle-class neighborhood. Some of the social leaders of the city are her neighbors. After a great deal of prayer she decided that she would go to her neighbors' houses and ask them if they would like to have a Bible study. She knocked on the door of house after house, and in almost every instance the women not only said "yes," but some of them burst into tears and said, "I've been waiting for someone to ask me to a Bible class so I could learn the Bible." Today, my daughter teaches a weekly Bible class of three hundred women, with many on the waiting list to get in. If there's not a Bible class in your community, perhaps you could start one. You will find your neighbors "hungrier" and "thirstier" than you had ever dreamed. They are just waiting for someone to take the initiative. At first it may be that only two or three of you will meet, read a passage in the Bible, discuss it, have prayer over a cup of coffee. There are tens of thousands of such Bible classes springing up throughout the world in homes, in offices, in professional football teams. Even the touring golf professionals have a weekly Bible class that attracts anywhere from ten to fifty of the golfers and their wives.

You are no longer alone. The fatherhood of God forms the true brotherhood of man, an ideal which the philosophers and moralists have sought from the beginning of time. This brotherhood erases barriers of language, cultural background, and race. One of the greatest joys a Christian experiences is that of meeting a fellow believer in an unexpected place. The waitress in the restaurant finds a common bond with her customer. The passenger on an airplane discovers that the stewardess is a believer. You are in a foreign country and immediately feel at home when you encounter another Christian. No lengthy introductions are necessary. You share the greatest bond on earth. There is no fellowship on earth to compare with it.

At the beginning of this book I said that I believed the most important subject in the entire world is that of the new birth. It is the most important event which can happen to any man, woman, or child.

It is only when you are born again that you can experience all the riches God has in store for you. You are not just a living person, you are truly ALIVE!

NOTES

Preface

1. Corrie ten Boom, *In My Father's House* (Old Tappan, N.J.: Fleming Revell Publishing Co., 1976), p. 24.
2. *Los Angeles Times*, September 23, 1976, pp. 3, 30.
3. *Time*, September 27, 1976, p. 86.

Chapter One

1. Charles Colson, *Born Again* (Old Tappan, N.J.: Chosen Books, 1976), p. 110.
2. Bertrand Russell, *Power: A New Social Analysis* (New York: Norton, 1938), p. 11.
3. H. R. Rookmaaker, *Modern Art and the Death of a Culture* (London: Inter-Varsity Press, 1970), p. 196.
4. Ibid., p. 202.
5. Os Guinness, *Dust of Death* (Downers Grove, Ill.: Inter-Varsity Press, 1973), p. 233.
6. Hal Lindsey, *The Terminal Generation* (Old Tappan, N.J.: Fleming H. Revell Co., 1976), p. 83.
7. Rookmaaker, *Modern Art*, p. 233.
8. Guinness, *Dust of Death*, p. 392.

Chapter Three

1. Josh McDowell, *Evidence That Demands a Verdict* (Campus Crusade for Christ, 1972), p. 17 ff.

Chapter Four

1. Sir James Frazer, *The Golden Bough* (New York: Macmillan Co., 1960), p. 194.
2. Ibid., p. 196.
3. Walter Kaufmann, *Critique of Religion and Philosophy* (New York: Harper and Row, 1958), p. 74.
4. Ibid., p. 88.
5. Tw. W. Doane, *Bible Myths* (New York: University Books, 1971), p. 252.

6. *Time*, December 30, 1974, p. 38.
7. Ibid., p. 40.

Chapter Five

1. *Time*, June 30, 1975, p. 10.
2. *Time*, February 2, 1976, p. 62.
3. William Barclay, *Letters to Timothy* (Philadelphia: Westminster Press, 1960), p. 44.

Chapter Six

1. *Time*, February 7, 1977, p. 37.

Chapter Seven

1. Josh McDowell, *Evidence That Demands A Verdict* (Campus Crusade, 1972), p. 89.
2. Harry Rimmer, *The Magnificence of Jesus* (Grand Rapids, Mich.: Wm. B. Eerdmans Publishing Co., 1943), p. 112.
3. C. S. Lewis, *Surprised By Joy* (New York: Harcourt, Brace & World, 1955), pp. 228 ff.

Chapter Nine

1. Nicolaus von Zinzendorf, 1739, tr. John Wesley, 1940.
2. *Saturday Evening Post*, September 1, 1951, p. 19.

Chapter Ten

1. Josh McDowell, *Evidence That Demands a Verdict* (Campus Crusade, 1972), p. 193.
2. Ibid., p. 233.

Chapter Eleven

1. *Time*, December 13, 1976, p. 93.
2. Ibid., E-3, p. 94.

3. Thomas Harris, *I'm OK—You're OK* (New York: Harper & Row, 1967), p. 229.
4. Sergiu Grossu, *The Church in Today's Catacombs* (New Rochelle, N.Y.: Arlington House Publishers, 1975), p. 43.
5. Ostrander and Schroeder, *Psychic Discoveries Behind the Iron Curtain* (Englewood Cliffs, N.J.: Prentice-Hall, 1970), pp. 151 ff.
6. John Hunter, *Impact* (Glendale, Calif.: Regal Books, 1966), pp. 45, 46.
7. Oswald Chambers, *My Utmost for His Highest* (New York: Dodd Mead & Company, 1946), p. 10.

Chapter Twelve

1. Hannah Pearsall Smith, *The Christian's Secret of a Happy Life* (London: Nisbet and Co. Ltd., 1945), p. 88.
2. Francis A. Schaeffer, *He is There and He is Not Silent,* (Wheaton, Ill.: Tyndale House, 1972), p. 15.
3. J. I. Packer, *Knowing God* (Downers Grove, Ill.: Inter-varsity Press, 1973), p. 35.

Chapter Thirteen

1. Hannah Pearsall Smith, *The Christian's Secret of a Happy Life*, p. 133.

The Holy Spirit

CONTENTS

PREFACE

AN OLD AMERICAN Indian legend tells of an Indian who came down from the mountains and saw the ocean for the first time. Awed by the scene, he requested a quart jar. As he waded into the ocean and filled the jar he was asked what he intended to do with it. "Back in the mountains," he replied, "my people have never seen the Great Water. I will carry this jar to them so they can see what it is like."

Before he died, Pope John was asked what church doctrine most needed reemphasis today. He replied, "The doctrine of the Holy Spirit."

A number of years ago, my wife and I had the privilege of spending a brief vacation in Switzerland as the guests of Dr. Karl Barth, the noted Swiss theologian. During the course of our conversations I asked him what he thought the next emphasis on theology would be. He replied without hesitation, "The Holy Spirit."

Attempting to write a book on so vast a subject as the Holy Spirit is like trying to capture the ocean in a quart jar. The subject is so infinite—and our minds are so finite.

This book really began as part of my personal spiritual pilgrimage. Throughout my ministry as an evangelist I have had a growing understanding of the ministry of the Holy Spirit. In recent years my attention has been drawn in a fresh way to the ministry of the Holy Spirit because of the renewed interest in His work in many parts of the world. Sensing my own need for further understanding, I began a systematic study of what the Bible teaches about the person and work of the Holy Spirit. It was not my original intention to write a book, but as I began to examine the subject in more depth I became concerned over the misunderstanding and even ignorance in some Christian circles concerning the Third Person of the Trinity.

In some ways I have been hesitant to write this book. But writing it has given me new insight into the ministry of the Holy Spirit; it has also helped me understand some of the movements of the Holy Spirit in our world today. My hope and prayer is that this book will be informative and clarifying for many Christians. I also pray it will be a unifying book. The Holy Spirit did not come to divide Christians but, among other reasons, He came to unite us.

My sole concern has been to see what the Bible has to say about the Holy Spirit. The Bible—which I believe the Holy Spirit inspired—is our only trustworthy source, and any reliable analysis of the person and work of the Holy Spirit must be biblically-based. As never before I have realized that there are some things we cannot know completely, and some issues are open to differences of interpretation by sincere Christians. About areas where there are honest differences among Christians I have tried not to be dogmatic.

I am thankful the Holy Spirit is at work in our generation, both in awakening the Church and in evangelism. May God use this book to bring renewal and challenge to many.

I owe a great debt to many people who have helped me during the writing of this book. I am grateful for my colleague Roy Gustafson who first suggested writing on this subject. Several people have been especially helpful in reading early drafts of the manuscript, either in part or the whole, and making constructive suggestions—including Dr. Harold Lindsell (former editor of *Christianity Today*), Mr. Paul Fromer (Wheaton College), Canon Houghton (former chairman of British Keswick), Dr. Thomas Zimmerman (General Superintendent of the Assemblies of God), Dr. Merrill C. Tenney (Dean Emeritus, Wheaton Graduate School), and Dr. Donald Hoke (Secretary, Lausanne Committee for World Evangelization). I am also thankful for the graciousness of Mr. and Mrs. Bill Mead, whose generosity enabled my wife, Ruth, and me to join them for several periods of work on the book. I will never forget those days of sitting around in a circle with the Meads and my longtime colleagues, the Cliff Barrows, the Fred Dienerts, and the Grady Wilsons, discussing various chapters of the book. I am also thankful for the suggestions of my colleague, Dr. John Akers, the help of the Reverend Ralph Williams of our Minneapolis office, and of Sally Wilson in Montreat who suggested illustrations and Scriptures to add to my original notes. My secretary, Stephanie Wills, has patiently typed and retyped the manuscript through its various drafts.

Introduction:
Man's Cry—God's Gift

MAN HAS TWO great spiritual needs. One is for forgiveness. The other is for goodness. Consciously or unconsciously, his inner being longs for both. There are times when man actually cries for them, even though in his restlessness, confusion, loneliness, fear, and pressures he may not know what he is crying for.

God heard that first cry for help, that cry for forgiveness, and answered it at Calvary. God sent His only Son into the world to die for our sins, so that we might be forgiven. This is a gift for us— God's gift of salvation. This gift is a permanent legacy for everyone who truly admits he has "fallen short" and sinned. It is for everyone who reaches out and accepts God's gift by receiving Jesus Christ as his Lord and Savior. Paul calls it God's "indescribable" gift (2 Cor. 9:15).

But God also heard our second cry, that cry for goodness, and answered it at Pentecost. God does not want us to come to Christ by faith, and then lead a life of defeat, discouragement, and dissension. Rather, He wants to "fulfill every desire for *goodness* and the work of faith with power; in order that the name of our Lord Jesus Christ may be glorified in you" (2 Thess. 1:11, 12). *To the great gift of forgiveness God adds also the great gift of the Holy Spirit.* He is the source of power who meets our need to escape from the miserable weakness that grips us. He gives us the power to be truly good.

If we are to live a life of sanity in our modern world, if we wish to be men and women who can live victoriously, we need this two-sided gift God has offered us: first, the work of the Son of God *for* us; second, the work of the Spirit of God *in* us. In this way God has answered mankind's two great cries: the cry for forgiveness and the cry for goodness.

As a friend of mine has said, "I need Jesus Christ for my eternal life, and the Holy Spirit of God for my internal life."

If you believe in Jesus Christ, a power is available to you that can change your life, even in such intimate areas as your marriage, your family relationships, and every other relationship. Also, God offers power that can change a tired church into a vital, growing body, power that can revitalize Christendom.

Unfortunately, this power has been ignored, misunderstood, and misused. By our ignorance we have short-circuited the power of the Holy Spirit.

Many books are written about this power, many prayers are said pleading for this power. Scores of Christians would like to have it, but they aren't sure what it is.

When the world looks at a Christian, certain mental clichés come to mind: it sees the believer as a stiff-necked, sober-faced person without a sense of humor; a person who can't make it himself so he uses "God as a crutch"; one who has left his brains in kindergarten.

Now, if this cold stereotype applies in any way to us or the Church, then we need to know about the exciting, revolutionary power available exclusively to Christian believers. No one can buy it, claim it, or use it without first knowing its source.

The Holy Spirit Was Promised

When Jesus was teaching His disciples, preparing them for what He knew was the end, His heart ached for them because He knew they were confused and sad. I can imagine that He moved from one to another, putting His arms around them. To each He explained in simple fashion, as we do to our children, the important truths He wanted them to understand. At one point He said,

"But now I am going to Him who sent Me; and none of you asks Me, 'Where are You going?' But because I have said these things to you, sorrow has filled your heart. But I tell you the truth, it is to your advantage that I go away; for if I do not go away, the Helper shall not come to you; but if I go, I will send Him to you" (John 16:5–7).

There was a promise! The coming of the Spirit was based upon the word of the Lord Jesus Christ. No conditions were attached. Jesus didn't say that He would send the Helper (or "Comforter") to some believers and not to others. Nor did He say that we had to belong to some special organization or be higher on the scale of spiritual performance than someone else. He simply said, "If I go, I will send Him to you."

When Jesus Christ makes a promise, He does not break or forget it. We may doubt the promises of friends or family; we may even doubt our own promises to others. But we have never been given a promise by Jesus that has not been a certainty.

Some people dismiss Jesus Christ as a "great teacher" or one of the outstanding religious leaders of the world. However, when it comes to promises, it's interesting to contrast His words with other great religious and philosophical leaders. For example, as the founder of Buddhism was bidding his followers farewell he said, "You must be your own light." Or when Socrates was about to take that fatal cup, one of his disciples mourned that he was leaving them orphans. The leaders of the world's religions and philosophies were unable to promise that they would never leave their followers.

The disciples of Jesus Christ, however, were not left alone. He said, "I will not leave you as orphans; I will come to you" (John 14:18). It is interesting that the Greek word for "orphans" is the same as the word used by the disciple of Socrates when he realized that his master was going to leave him alone.

The Promise Fulfilled

Jesus said He would leave His disciples for a while, and He did. During the dreadful hours of the crucifixion, death, and burial, agonizing doubt gripped the minds of those who loved Him. He had not yet been "glorified," so the promise of His Spirit was not yet a fact.

But we know what happened. God raised Him from the dead and gave Him glory. Addressing Christians, the Scriptures say that Christ came "for the sake of you who through Him are believers in God, who raised Him from the dead and gave Him glory, so that your faith and hope are in God" (1 Peter 1:20, 21).

God had said to "wait" for the Spirit to come. Jesus rose from the dead and was seen by His disciples. Unable to grasp what was happening, they failed to recognize Him at first, and were frightened because they thought they were seeing a ghost. To confirm His physical reality, Jesus told them to touch Him, and even asked for something to eat. A spirit didn't have flesh, did it? A ghost couldn't eat, could it?

So this was truly Jesus, not the Spirit He had promised. However, He told them still to wait! The time was not yet.

Fifty days later the promise was fulfilled at Pentecost. What a day it was! It is difficult for us to imagine, with our practical, earthbound, scientific mentality, the amazing happening of that day.

"And when the day of Pentecost had come, they were all together in one place. And suddenly there came from heaven a noise like a violent, rushing wind, and it filled the whole house where they were sitting. And there appeared to them tongues as of fire distributing themselves, and they rested on each one of them. And they were all filled with the Holy Spirit and began to speak with other tongues, as the Spirit was giving them utterance" (Acts 2:1–4).

The one for whom they were asked to "wait" had come!

What a difference the emphasis of one word makes in the description of a happening of such world-shaking importance! Before the day of Pentecost the emphasis was on the word "ask." "If you then, being evil, know how to give good gifts to your children, how much more shall your Heavenly Father give the Holy Spirit to those who *ask* Him?" (Luke 11:13, italics mine).

After Pentecost the emphasis was on the word "receive." In his powerful sermon that day, Peter said, "Repent, and let each of you be baptized in the name of Jesus Christ for the forgiveness of your sins; and you shall *receive* the gift of the Holy Spirit" (Acts 2:38, italics mine).

This is the good news: we are no longer waiting for the Holy Spirit—He is waiting for us. We are no longer living in a time of promise, but in the days of fulfillment.

The members of the early Church, those men, women, and children who knew the reality of the Holy Spirit as a force, were totally transformed. The rush of power they experienced on the day of Pentecost is characteristic of the age that gave us the New Testament. The Holy Spirit was promised, the promise was fulfilled, the disciples were changed, and the glory of it for us is that He is present in every true believer today. And so His power is available today.

Who is this Person whom Christ promised to send to earth in His place? Who is this Person whom He uses to transform human nature? Who is this Person who can give you supernatural power to face any crisis? And how can you and I know His power in our lives day by day?

We will find out.

1

Who Is the Holy Spirit?

SOME YEARS AGO a teacher in a fifth-grade class asked his students if anyone could explain electricity. One boy raised his hand. The teacher asked, "How would you explain it, Jimmy?" Jimmy scratched his head a moment and then replied, "Last night I knew it, but this morning I've forgotten." The teacher shook his head sadly and said to the class, "What a tragedy. The only person in the world ever to understand electricity, and he's forgotten!"

That teacher's position may describe you and me when we study the doctrine of the Trinity. We accept the fact that the Holy Spirit is God, just as much God as God the Father and God the Son. But when it comes to explaining it, we are at a loss.

In recent years people have talked more about the Holy Spirit and written more books about Him than possibly any religious theme other than the occult. This has come about largely because of the influence of the charismatic movement, which has been called Christendom's "third force" alongside Catholicism and Protestantism. The more recent charismatic movement, which has some of its roots in historic Pentecostalism and stresses the Holy Spirit, is now deeply entrenched in most of the mainline denominations and in Catholicism. We may feel that it is such a vast subject and we know so little about it. Nevertheless, God in His Word has revealed all we should know.

Many questions will arise in this book for which answers are being sought by puzzled and at times untaught believers. In fact, millions of Christians on every continent are now asking these questions. They are seeking and deserve biblical answers.

For example: What is the baptism of the Holy Spirit? When does it take place? Is speaking in tongues *possible* or necessary today? Is there an experience called a "second blessing"?

To start our study, we need to ask a critical question at the very beginning: Who is the Holy Spirit?

The Holy Spirit Is a Person

The Bible teaches that the Holy Spirit is a *person.* Jesus never referred to "it" when He was talking about the Holy Spirit. In John 14, 15 and 16, for example, He spoke of the Holy Spirit as "He" because He is not a force or thing but a person. Whoever speaks of the Holy Spirit as "it" is uninstructed, or perhaps even undiscerning. In Romans 8:16 the King James Version refers to the Holy Spirit as "itself." This is a mistranslation. Nearly all of the newer translations have changed "itself" to "himself."

We see from the Bible that the Holy Spirit has intellect, emotions, and will. In addition to this, the Bible also ascribes to Him the acts we would expect of someone who was not just a force, but a real person.

He speaks: "He who has an ear, let him hear what the Spirit says to the churches. To him who overcomes, I will grant to eat of the tree of life, which is in the Paradise of God" (Rev. 2:7).

"And while they were ministering to the Lord and fasting, the Holy Spirit said, 'Set apart for Me Barnabas and Saul for the work to which I have called them'" (Acts 13:2).

He intercedes: "And in the same way the Spirit also helps our weakness; for we do not know how to pray as we should, but the Spirit Himself intercedes for us with groanings too deep for words" (Rom. 8:26).

He testifies: "When the Helper comes, whom I will send to you from the Father, that is the Spirit of truth, who proceeds from the Father, He will bear witness of Me" (John 15:26).

He leads: "And the Spirit said to Philip, 'Go up and join this chariot'" (Acts 8:29).

"For all who are being led by the Spirit of God, these are sons of God" (Rom. 8:14).

He commands: "And they passed through the Phrygian and Galatian region, having been forbidden by the Holy Spirit to speak the word in Asia; and when they had come to Mysia, they were trying to go into Bithynia, and the Spirit of Jesus did not permit them" (Acts 16:6, 7).

He guides: "When the Spirit of truth comes, he will guide you into all the truth; for he will not speak on his own authority, but whatever he hears he will speak, and he will declare to you the things that are to come" (John 16:13 rsv).

He appoints: "Be on guard for yourselves and for all the flock, among which the Holy Spirit has made you overseers, to shepherd the church of God which He purchased with His own blood" (Acts 20:28).

He can be lied to: "But Peter said, 'Ananias, why has Satan filled your heart to lie to the Holy Spirit, and to keep back some of the price of the land? While it remained unsold, did it not remain your own? And after it was sold, was it not under your control? Why is it that you have conceived this deed in your heart? You have not lied to men, but to God'" (Acts 5:3, 4).

He can be insulted: "How much severer punishment do you think he will deserve who has trampled under foot the Son of God, and has regarded as unclean the blood of the covenant by which he was sanctified, and has insulted the Spirit of grace?" (Heb 10:29).

He can be blasphemed: "Therefore I say to you, any sin and blasphemy shall be forgiven men, but blasphemy against the Spirit shall not be forgiven. And whoever shall speak a word against the Son of Man, it shall be forgiven him; but whoever shall speak against the Holy Spirit, it shall not be forgiven him, either in this age, or in the age to come" (Matt. 12:31, 32).

He can be grieved: "And do not grieve the Holy Spirit of God, by whom you were sealed for the day of redemption" (Eph. 4:30)

Each of the emotions and acts we have listed are characteristics of a person. The Holy Spirit is not an impersonal force, like gravity or magnetism. He is a Person, with all the attributes of personality. But not only is He a Person; He is divine as well.

The Holy Spirit Is a Divine Person: He Is God

Throughout the Bible it is clear that the Holy Spirit is God Himself. This is seen in the attributes which are given to the Holy Spirit in Scripture, for example. Without exception these attributes are those of God Himself.

He is eternal: This means that there never was a time when He was not. "How much more will the blood of Christ, who through the eternal Spirit offered Himself without blemish to God, cleanse your conscience from dead works to serve the living God?" (Heb. 9:14).

He is all-powerful: "And the angel answered and said to her, 'The Holy Spirit will come upon you, and the power of the Most High will overshadow you; and for that reason the holy offspring shall be called the Son of God'" (Luke 1:35).

He is everywhere present (that is, omnipresent) at the same time: "Where can I go from Thy Spirit? Or where can I flee from Thy presence?" (Ps. 139:7).

He is all-knowing (that is, omniscient): "For to us God revealed them through the Spirit; for the Spirit searches all things, even the depths of God. For who among men knows the thoughts of a man except the spirit of the man, which is in him? Even so the thoughts of God no one knows except the Spirit of God" (1 Cor. 2:10, 11).

The Holy Spirit is called God: "But Peter said, 'Ananias, why has Satan filled your heart to lie to the Holy Spirit, and to keep back some of the price of the land? While it remained unsold, did it not remain your own? And after it was sold, was it not under your control? Why is it that you have conceived this deed in your heart? *You have not lied to men, but to God*'" (Acts 5:3, 4, italics mine).

"And we all, with unveiled face, beholding the glory of the Lord, are being changed into his likeness from one degree of glory to another; for this comes from the Lord who is the Spirit" (2 Cor. 3:18 RSV).

He is the Creator: The first biblical reference to the Holy Spirit is Genesis 1:2 (Moffatt) where we are told "the spirit of God was hovering over the waters." Yet Genesis 1:1 says, "In the beginning God created the heavens and the earth." And in Colossians 1 where

Paul is writing to the Church at Colossae about the Lord Jesus Christ, among other tremendous truths he tells us, "For in Him all things were created, both in the heavens and on earth, visible and invisible, whether thrones or dominions or rulers or authorities—all things have been created through Him and for Him. And He is before all things, and in Him all things hold together" [cohere] (Col. 1:16, 17).

Thus, God the Father, God the Son, and God the Holy Spirit were together creating the world. To understand and accept these facts is of the greatest importance to every Christian, both theologically and practically.

One day I made a few of these assertions about the Holy Spirit to some seminary students. One asked, "But He is usually mentioned last. Doesn't that imply inferiority?" Yet in Romans 15:30 He is not mentioned last: "Now I urge you, brethren, by our Lord Jesus Christ and by the love of the Spirit, to strive together with me in your prayers to God for me." And in Ephesians 4:4 Paul says, "There is one body and one Spirit, just as also you were called in one hope of your calling."

But more than this, the usual placement of the three persons of the Trinity in the New Testament has to do with their order and function. Thus we say that we pray to the Father through the Son and in the power of the Holy Spirit. Moreover, I have already shown that *functionally* the Father came first, then the Son became incarnate, died and rose again. Now the Spirit does His work in this age of the Spirit. The order has nothing to do with equality, but only with function and chronology.

The Trinity

When I first began to study the Bible years ago, the doctrine of the Trinity was one of the most complex problems I had to encounter. I have never fully resolved it, for it contains an aspect of mystery. Though I do not totally understand it to this day, I accept it as a revelation of God.

The Bible teaches us that the Holy Spirit is a living being. He is one of the three persons of the Holy Trinity. To explain and illustrate the Trinity is one of the most difficult assignments to a

Christian. Dr. David McKenna once told me that he was asked by his small son, Doug, "Is God the Father God?" He answered, "Yes." "Is Jesus Christ God?" "Yes." "Is the Holy Spirit God?" "Yes." "Then how can Jesus be His own Father?" David thought quickly. They were sitting in their old 1958 Chevrolet at the time. "Listen, son," he replied, "under the hood is one battery. Yet I can use it to turn on the lights, blow the horn, and start the car." He said, "How this happens is a mystery—but it happens!"

The Bible *does* teach us the reality of the Trinity, both in the Old and New Testaments. Let us look at some of the major passages.

God unfolds His revelation of Himself in the Bible progressively. But there are indications from the very beginning of the Book of Genesis that God subsists in three persons—the Father, the Son, and the Holy Spirit—and that these three persons constitute the one God. Christianity is trinitarian, not unitarian. There is only one God, not three, so it is clear that the Christian faith is not polytheistic.

The Bible begins with the majestic statement: "In the beginning God created the heavens and the earth" (Gen. 1:1).

Hebrew scholars have told me there are three numbers in the Hebrew language: Singular, one; dual, two; plural, more than two. The word translated "God" in Genesis 1:1 is plural, indicating more than two. The Hebrew word used here is *Elohim.* Matthew Henry says it signifies "the plurality of persons in the Godhead, Father, Son, and Holy Ghost. This plural name of God . . . [confirms] our faith in the doctrine of the Trinity, which, though but darkly intimated in the Old Testament, is clearly revealed in the New."[1]

As we have seen concerning creation, even from the beginning God gives us glimpses of the truth that the Godhead consists of more than one person. I have italicized some of the key words. In Genesis 1:26, God said, "Let *us* make man in *our* image, according to *our* likeness; and let them rule over the fish of the sea and over the birds of the sky and over the cattle and over all the earth, and over every creeping thing that creeps on the earth." Further, in Genesis 3:22 the Lord God said, "Behold, the man has become like one of *Us,* knowing good and evil." And in Genesis 11: 6, 7, the

Lord said, "Behold, they are one people, and they all have the same language. And this is what they began to do, and now nothing which they purpose to do will be impossible for them. Come, let *Us* go down and there confuse their language, that they may not understand one another's speech." When Isaiah heard the voice of the Lord saying, "Whom shall I send, and who will go for *us?*" he answered, "Here am I. Send me!" (Isa. 6:8).

The New Testament's doctrine of the Trinity is much more fully developed than that of the Old Testament. Since revelation is progressive, more light is thrown on this subject as God more fully disclosed Himself at the time of Christ and the apostles.

The last command of Jesus before His ascension is recorded in Matthew 28:18–20. In it He ordered His followers to "make disciples of all the nations," baptizing converts "in the name of the Father and the Son and the Holy Spirit, teaching them to observe all that I commanded you; and lo, I am with you always, even to the end of the age." Here Jesus taught that after He left this earth, His followers were to carry His gospel message to all nations. The Holy Spirit was to use them to call out a people for His name. This trinitarian commission to baptize associates the Holy Spirit with God the Father and God the Son as their equal. He is God the Holy Spirit.

It is thrilling to note that Jesus says believers will not be left alone. Through the Holy Spirit whom He and the Father sent, He will never leave us nor forsake us (Heb. 13:5). He will remain with every believer right to the end. This thought has encouraged me a thousand times in these dark days when satanic forces are at work in so many parts of the world.

Along this line the apostle Paul also said, "The grace of the Lord Jesus Christ, and the love of God, and the fellowship of the Holy Spirit, be with you all" (2 Cor. 13:14). This benediction clearly indicates that the Holy Spirit is one with the Father and one with the Son in the Godhead. *It is not one plus one plus one equals three. It is one times one times one equals one.* The Holy Spirit is one with the Father and the Son. If the Father is God, and Jesus is God, then the Holy Spirit is also God.

The chief problem connected with the doctrine of the Trinity concerns Christianity's claim to be also monotheistic. It rejects polytheism, the belief in more than one God. The answer is that trinitarianism preserves the unity of the Godhead, and at the same time it acknowledges that there are three persons in that Godhead which is still of one essence. God is one, but that oneness is not simple—it is complex.

This is a terribly difficult subject—far beyond the ability of our limited minds to grasp fully. Nevertheless, it is extremely important to declare what the Bible holds, and be silent where the Bible is silent. God the Father is fully God. God the Son is fully God. God the Holy Spirit is fully God. The Bible presents this as fact. It does not explain it. Nevertheless, many explanations have been suggested, some of which sound logical, but they do not preserve the truth of Scriptural teaching.

One Christian heresy in the early church was called "modalism." It taught that God appeared at different times in three different modes or forms—as Father, then as Son, and finally as Holy Spirit. Those who held this view thought it preserved the unity of monotheism. But it also meant that when Jesus prayed, He had to be talking to Himself. Further, to say, as Acts 2 does, that the Father and the Son sent the Holy Spirit, makes little sense if we accept modalism. Moreover, it violated the clearest presentation of the Trinity-in-unity as expressed in Matthew's statement by Jesus in the Great Commission. It was Jesus who said that His disciples were to baptize their converts "in the name of the Father and the Son and the Holy Spirit." The Greek construction makes it clear that Jesus is referring to three separate persons. He clearly taught the doctrine of the Trinity.

We have seen that the Holy Spirit is a person, and is God, and is a member of the Trinity. Anyone who fails to recognize this is robbed of his joy and power. Of course a defective view of any member of the Trinity will bring about this result because God is all important. But this is especially true for the Holy Spirit, for although the Father is the source of all blessing, and the Son is the channel of all blessing, it is through the Holy Spirit at work in us that all truth becomes living and operative in our lives.

The most important point I can make in summary is this: there is nothing that God is that the Holy Spirit is not. All of the essential aspects of deity belong to the Holy Spirit. We can say of Him exactly what was said of Jesus Christ in the ancient Nicene Creed: He is very God of very God! So we bow before Him, we worship Him, we accord Him every response Scripture requires of our relationship to Almighty God.

Who is the Holy Spirit? He is God!

2

When the Holy Spirit Has Come

As I was writing this chapter, my wife and I sat on the porch in the hot spring sun, and we talked about the refreshment of the wind as evening came. We especially discussed the power and the mystery of the wind.

It is interesting that in Scripture, in both the original Hebrew and Greek languages, the word used in speaking of the Spirit is the word that can also mean "wind." In like-manner, the Holy Spirit works in different ways in our lives, and in different times in history.

I have seen tornadoes in Texas and Oklahoma, and even in my home state of North Carolina when I was a boy. Yes, I have seen the power of the wind. I have seen the air-brakes that use the wind, or the air, to stop the giant truck going down the highway. That same force can lift a giant airplane.

"The manager of a granite quarry in North Carolina said: 'We supplied the granite for the municipal building in New York City. We can lift an acre of solid granite ten feet thick to almost any height we desire for the purpose of moving it. We do it with air. We can do it as easily as I can lift a piece of paper.'

"Air! Air—this invisible envelopment in which we live and move, this substance so immaterial that we can move our hands through it as though it had no reality at all. But the power it possesses! How great, how terrible!"[1]

We have seen something of the nature and personality of the Holy Spirit. Now we must catch a vision of His distinctive work in each of the great ages of time. But first, to place it in perspective, we must see how the Triune God is at work in every age.

The elements of mystery in this make it difficult for the human mind to comprehend fully. Simultaneously the Father, the Son, and the Holy Spirit have different functions to perform that are distinctive to each. For instance, it was not the Father or the Holy Spirit who died on the cross of Calvary. It was God the Son. We need to understand such facts, especially when we think of this present age and the work of God in it.

As we study the Bible, the work of God the Father is especially emphasized in the Old Testament. The work of God the Son is emphasized in the Gospels. From the day of Pentecost until the present, however, the emphasis is on the work of God the Holy Spirit. And yet the Bible also tells us God the Holy Spirit has been at work throughout history, from the beginning of the world. Therefore, we begin our study of the work of the Holy Spirit by examining briefly His activities in the eras before Pentecost, before concentrating on His unique ministry since then.

The Spirit's Work from Creation to Bethlehem

As we have seen in the previous chapter, the Holy Spirit was at work in creation. According to Genesis 1:2, "The earth was formless and void, and darkness was over the surface of the deep." Immediately, we are told that "the Spirit of God was moving over the surface of the waters." The Hebrew word for "moving" means "brooding" or "hovering." Just as a hen broods over her eggs for the purpose of hatching them and bringing forth new life, so the Holy Spirit brooded over the original creation of God for the purpose of filling its void with life in various forms. The creation recorded in the rest of Genesis 1, together with Genesis 2, resulted. Thus, from the beginning the Holy Spirit was active in creation along with the Father and the Son.

When God "formed man of dust from the ground" (Gen. 2:7), the Holy Spirit was involved. We learn this indirectly in Job 33:4, "The Spirit of God has made me, And the breath of the Almighty gives me life." A play on words here shows how intimately God's Spirit and our breath are related: both "Spirit" and "breath" are from the same Hebrew word.

Genesis 2:7 also says that the Lord God "breathed into his nostrils the breath of life; and man became a living being." While the Hebrew word translated "breath" here is not the one also meaning spirit, clearly man owes his very life to God according to this passage. And the breath of God that started man on his earthly journey was, in fact, the Holy Spirit, as Job 33:4 tells us.

Psalm 104:30 carries our understanding of the Spirit in creation a step further. Not only was the Spirit at work in the formation of the earth and the first man, but the Spirit is always the creator of life. "Thou [God] dost send forth Thy Spirit, they are created; And Thou dost renew the face of the ground." Who are the "they" whom the Spirit creates? The entire psalm clarifies this, but just in verses 18–26 we learn that included are wild goats and rock badgers (18), beasts of the forest such as young lions (20, 21), man (23), and whatever lives on the earth or in the sea (24, 25).

Understanding that the Spirit gives life, a married woman in the Old Testament who was unable to bear a child would go to the tabernacle or temple. There either she prayed or the priest petitioned God to open her womb. Now, such a woman knew the basic facts of life just as we do, although she did not possess as much scientific knowledge about the birth process as we do today. Yet even to us it is still one of the mysteries of nature and one of nature's miracles that sperm can penetrate an ovum and initiate a new life. This is simply a medical or biological way of describing the touch of God's hand in the creation of life.

Hannah is a classic illustration of this. She went to the tabernacle to pray for a son. Eli, the high priest, thought at first that she was drunk, but she informed him she was a woman in sorrow who had poured out her soul to the Lord. Eli responded, "Go in peace; and may the God of Israel grant your petition that you have asked of Him" (1 Sam. 1:17). She later conceived and Samuel the prophet was born. While in the story itself God's spirit is not mentioned, our understanding of His place according to Psalm 104:30 (and Job 33:4) shows us that the life-giving function distinctively belonged to God's Spirit.

Yet Psalm 104:30 says more than just that we owe our creation to the Spirit. The face of the ground is also renewed by Him. God feeds what He creates.

So believers in the Old Testament were rightly convinced that God had something to do with the growing of crops. They attributed a good harvest to Him: "He causes the grass to grow for the cattle, And vegetation for the labor of man, So that he may bring forth food from the earth" (Ps. 104:14). In Deuteronomy 28 the conditions for blessing or cursing in the promised land were enunciated. If Israel obeyed God there was the promise: "Blessed shall be the offspring of your body and the produce of your ground," and "The Lord will make you abound . . . in the produce of your ground" (Deut. 28:4, 11). Israel's Feast of Firstfruits formally recognized that God was responsible for abundance. Today as we bow our heads before meals to thank God for the food we continue to acknowledge God as the One who sustains us.

However, God both blesses and curses, delivers and punishes. The Old Testament often attributes the salvation of Israel to the Spirit of God. He strove with people before the flood (Gen. 6:3). I believe that He is striving with people today exactly as He did before the flood. Jesus said, "And just as it happened in the days of Noah, so it shall be also in the days of the Son of Man" (Luke 17:26). The same sick perversions, moral decay, and erosions are prevalent today. The Holy Spirit is mightily striving but the vast majority of the human race will not listen.

Then from time to time the Holy Spirit took possession of certain men in order to deliver God's people. For instance, in the Book of Judges alone, He came upon Othniel (3:10), Gideon (6:34), Jephthah (11:29), and Samson (13:25).

The three main expressions used in the Old Testament for the work of the Holy Spirit on human beings are:

(1) He *came* upon men: "Then the Spirit of God came on Zechariah" (2 Chron. 24:20). (2) He *rested* on men: "the Spirit rested upon them" (Num. 11:25). (3) He *filled* men: "I have filled him with the Spirit of God" (Exod. 31:3).

The Spirit used not only judges and prophets to deliver Israel, but also kings. They were anointed with oil, a symbol that they were empowered with the Holy Spirit. So when Samuel anointed David in 1 Samuel 16:13, "the Spirit of the Lord came mightily upon David from that day forward."

Yet the next verse sounds a note of solemnity. While in Judges the Spirit often departed when the select person's task was done, He also might withdraw when the chosen one disobeyed. This occurred to Saul according to 1 Samuel 16:14, and also to Samson, as we see by comparing Judges 14:19 with 16:20. David's concern that the Spirit might withdraw from him occasioned his prayer, "Do not take Thy Holy Spirit from me" (Ps. 51:11).

God's great deliverance, of course, came not with a human anointed king, but with the Messiah, a title that means "Anointed." Isaiah had recorded prophetically that the Messiah would say, "The Spirit of the Lord God is upon me, Because the Lord has anointed me" (Isa. 61:1). And Jesus, reading this in the synagogue 800 years later, said, "Today this Scripture has been fulfilled in your hearing" (Luke 4:21).

It is not always easy to separate the roles of the Father, the Son, and the Holy Spirit in the Old Testament. But we do know that Jesus appeared from time to time in "theophanies" which are simply appearances of our Lord before the Incarnation. We also know that the use of the name of God in the Old Testament can refer to different members of the Trinity.

In summary, we have seen that the Holy Spirit was at work before the world began. Then He renewed and fed His creation. He was active throughout the Old Testament, both in the world of nature and among His people, guiding and delivering them through the judges, prophets, kings, and others. And He told of a coming day when the Anointed One would come.

The Spirit's Work from Bethlehem to Pentecost

During the period of time covered by the four Gospels, the work of the Holy Spirit centered around the person of Jesus Christ. The God-man was begotten of the Spirit (Luke 1:35), baptized by the Spirit (John 1:32, 33), led by the Spirit (Luke 4:1), anointed by the Spirit (Luke 4:18; Acts 10:38), and empowered by the Spirit (Matt.

12:27, 28). He offered Himself as an atonement for sin by the Spirit (Heb. 9:14), was raised by the Spirit (Rom. 8:11), and gave commandments by the Spirit (Acts 1:2).

Without a doubt one of the most awe-inspiring passages in Scripture relates what the angel said to Mary: "The Holy Spirit will come upon you, and the power of the Most High will overshadow you; and for that reason the holy offspring shall be called the Son of God" (Luke 1:35). Overly skeptical people, and others with too limited a view of science, may scoff in utter disbelief, but the angel dispelled all doubt when he said, "For nothing will be impossible with God" (Luke 1:37).

For Christians, any suggestion that God the Holy Spirit was not capable of bringing the virgin birth to pass is nonsense. If we believe that God is God—and that He rules His universe—nothing is too great for His limitless power. At all times God does whatever He chooses. When He planned the Messiah's birth, He performed a miracle. He bypassed one link in the normal physiological chain of birth: no human male participated. The life that was formed in the womb of the virgin was none other than the incarnate life of God the Son in human flesh. The virgin birth was a sign so extraordinary that it was obviously God and not man at work in the Incarnation. There are some so-called theologians today who deny the Incarnation—they reject the deity of Jesus Christ. In so doing they come very close to blaspheming the Holy Spirit!

The Holy Spirit was also at work among the disciples of Jesus before Pentecost. We know this because Jesus said of them, "He [the Holy Spirit] abides with you" (John 14:17). Jesus also said to Nicodemus, "Unless one is born of water and the Spirit, he cannot enter into the kingdom of God" (John 3:5). Again, He said, "You must be born again" (John 3:7).

Yet the operation of the Spirit among men in Jesus' day differed from His work today. For in John 7:39 we are told by the apostle John concerning the word of Jesus: "But this He [Jesus] spoke of the Spirit, whom those who believed in Him were to receive; for the Spirit was not yet given, because Jesus was not yet glorified."

Exactly what the difference was the Bible does not reveal completely. However, we know that the coming of the Spirit at Pentecost was in a far greater measure than anything they had ever experienced before. At any rate, we have seen that the Holy Spirit was at work in various ways in the birth and life of our Lord Jesus Christ and in the lives and ministries of His disciples.

The Spirit's Work from Pentecost till Now

In Acts, Luke records the ascension of Jesus into heaven (Acts 1:9–11). In chapter 2 he depicts the descent of the Holy Spirit to earth (Acts 2:1–4). Jesus had said, "If I do not go away, the Helper [Holy Spirit] shall not come to you; but if I go, I will send Him to you" (John 16:7). It was in fulfillment of this promise that Peter, speaking of the glorified Christ, said, "Therefore having been exalted to the right hand of God, and having received from the Father the promise of the Holy Spirit, He has poured forth this which you both see and hear" (Acts 2:33).

Many years ago a great Arctic explorer started on an expedition to the North Pole. After two long years in the lonely northland he wrote a short message, tied it under the wing of a carrier pigeon, and prepared to turn it loose to make the two thousand mile journey to Norway. The explorer gazed around him at the desolation. Not a creature to be seen. There was nothing but ice, snow, and never-ending bitter cold. He held the trembling little bird in his hand for a moment and then released her into the icy atmosphere. The bird circled three times, and then started her southward flight for multiplied hundreds of miles over ice and frozen ocean wastes until at last she dropped into the lap of the explorer's wife. By the arrival of the bird, his wife knew that all was well with her husband in the dark night of the arctic North.

Likewise the coming of the Holy Spirit, the Heavenly Dove, proved to the disciples that Christ had entered the heavenly sanctuary. He was seated at the right hand of God the Father, for His atoning work was finished. The advent of the Holy Spirit fulfilled Christ's promise; and it also testified that God's righteousness had been vindicated. The age of the Holy Spirit, which could not commence until Jesus was glorified, had now begun.

Unquestionably the coming of the Holy Spirit on the day of Pentecost marked a crucial turning point in the history of God's dealings with the human race. It is one of five past events, all of which are essential components of the Christian gospel: the Incarnation, the Atonement, the Resurrection, the Ascension, and Pentecost. A sixth component is still future: the Second Coming of Jesus.

The Incarnation as the first event marked the redemptive entrance of God into human life as true man. The second event in the series was the means by which God could remain just and yet justify guilty men—the Atonement. The third, the Resurrection, demonstrated that man's three great enemies—death, Satan, and hell—had been dealt their death blow. The fourth—the Ascension—showed that the Father had accepted the atoning work of the Son and that His righteous demands had been met. Pentecost, the fifth, assures us that the Spirit of God has come to achieve His certain purposes in the world, in the church, and in the individual believer!

The Jewish religious calendar centered in a number of annual feasts. However, the three most important were those in which all males were required to appear before the Lord (Deut. 16:16). These were the feasts of Passover, Tabernacles, and Pentecost.

"The Feast of Passover" commemorated the time when the Israelites were miraculously freed from a long period of slavery in Egypt. After killing an "unblemished" lamb (Exod. 12:5), the Israelites placed the blood over the door of each Israelite house and the lamb was roasted and eaten. The blood of the lamb brought about deliverance from God's judgment. The Old Testament passover found its final fulfillment in the death of Christ on Calvary, "For Christ our Passover also has been sacrificed" (1 Cor. 5:7). The Book of Hebrews teaches us that there is therefore no more need for the offering of the blood of bulls and goats. Jesus Christ, once and forever, offered Himself for the salvation of men by shedding His blood.

"The Feast of Tabernacles" (the present-day word for tabernacle is "booths" or "tents") reminded Israel of the days during the exodus from Egypt when the people lived not in houses, but in booths made of cut branches. The celebration came when the harvests were in, so it is called the "Feast of Ingathering" in Exodus 23:16. Perhaps celebration of deliverance from Egypt was fulfilled in the greater deliverance and blessing that came with redemption in Christ. John 7:38 may suggest that the coming of the Holy Spirit quenches thirst as neither the water of the desert nor the rain needed for harvest could do.

Pentecost was known as the "Feast of Weeks" because it was celebrated on the day following the passage of seven sabbaths—a Week of Weeks—from Passover. Because it fell on the fiftieth day, it gained the name "Pentecost," from the Greek word for "fiftieth." The Feast of Pentecost celebrated the beginning of the harvest; in Numbers 28:26 it was called "the day of the first fruits." In a real sense, the Day of Pentecost in the New Testament on which the Holy Spirit came was "a day of first fruits"—the beginning of God's harvest in this world, to be completed when Christ comes again. Pentecost in the New Testament marked the commencement of the present age of the Holy Spirit. Believers are under His guidance even as the disciples of Jesus were under Him. From heaven Jesus still exercises lordship over us, but, not being physically with us now, He transmits His directions by means of the Holy Spirit who makes Christ real to us. Since Pentecost the Holy Spirit is the link between the first and second advents of Jesus. He applies the work of Jesus Christ to men in this age, as we will see in the pages that follow.

When I began studying about the Holy Spirit shortly after I became a Christian, one of the first questions I asked myself was: Why did the Holy Spirit have to come? I soon found the answer in my Bible study. He came because He had a work to do in the *world*, in the *Church*, and in the individual *Christian*, as we will now discover.

The Holy Spirit's Present Work in the World

In regard to the world, the Spirit's work is twofold. First, He has come to reprove it of sin, righteousness, and judgment (John 16:7–11). The Bible teaches us, and we know from experience, that all have sinned and are coming short of the glory of God (Rom. 3:23). Sinful man cannot inherit eternal life. Everyone who has ever been born recapitulates Adam's fall. Everyone is born with the seed of sin within him which, with the coming of the age of accountability, culminates in a multitude of sins. There is a difference between sin and sins. Sin is the root, sins are the fruit.

However, a person may not be consciously aware that his deepest problem is sin, or that his sin has separated him from fellowship with God. Therefore, it is the work of the Holy Spirit to disturb and convict him in his sin. Until this takes place he cannot experience salvation. In our crusade meetings I have seen people walk out shaking their fists at me as I was preaching. They are not actually hostile toward me, I know, but they have been brought under conviction by the Holy Spirit. Often people like this later return to find Christ.

But the Holy Spirit not only convicts of sin, He convinces men that Jesus is the righteousness of God. He shows sinners that Jesus is the way, the truth, and the life, and that no one comes to the Father but by Him.

The Holy Spirit also convicts the world of judgment, because the prince of this world is judged, and all will be judged if they refuse God's offer of everlasting life. When the apostle Paul testified before Agrippa, he said that on the Damascus road at the time of his conversion God had told him the nature of his ministry. It would concern Gentiles and be "to open their eyes so that they may turn from darkness to light and from the dominion of Satan to God, in order that they may receive forgiveness of sins . . ." (Acts 26:18).

At the moment Jesus Christ died on the cross, Satan suffered an overwhelming defeat. That defeat may not be apparent as we read our newspapers and watch the television screens, but Satan is a defeated enemy in principle. He still wages his wicked warfare, and his total destruction and removal from the earth are near at hand. But until then, he will intensify his activities. It is quite apparent to Christians all over the world that new demons are abroad. Perversions, permissiveness, violence, and a hundred other sinister trends are now rampant on a world-wide scale perhaps unknown since the days of Noah. The Holy Spirit has come to show us these things, for He is deeply involved in biblical prophecy, as we will see later.

The Holy Spirit's work in the world is not confined to the ministry of conviction concerning sin, righteousness, and judgment, however. His *second work* in the world is to hinder the growth of lawlessness, that is, to engage in the ministry of preservation. The apostle Paul said, "For the mystery of lawlessness is already at work; only he who now restrains will do so until he is taken out of the way" (2 Thess. 2:7).

The Scripture makes it clear that this planet would already be a literal hell on earth were it not for the presence of the Holy Spirit in the world. The unbelieving world little knows what it owes to the restraining power of the Holy Spirit.

Several theologians to whom I have talked recently, both in Europe and America, hold the view that the Holy Spirit is gradually being withdrawn from the world as we enter what may be the climactic moments of the end of the present age. When He is totally withdrawn "all hell will break loose." The world will experience wars, violence, eruptions, perversions, hatred, fear—of which we are only seeing glimpses today. The human race will be in a hell of its own making. Free from the restraints of the Holy Spirit the Antichrist will reign supreme for a short period until he is crushed by the coming of the Lord Jesus Christ and the armies of heaven!

The Holy Spirit also *acts through* the people of God, who are called the salt of the earth and the light of the world by Jesus in His Sermon on the Mount (Matt. 5:13, 14). These are apt metaphors because salt and light are forces that operate silently and unobtrusively, yet with great effect. Salt and light speak of the influence Christians can exercise for good in society. We who are believers sometimes find it difficult to understand what influence we can have when we are such a minority, are so often divided, and are disobedient from time to time. By the power of the Spirit, however, we can restrain evil and do good!

To spell out the metaphors further, salt and light are essential in our homes: light dissipates the darkness, and salt prevents decay. The Bible tells us that the state of the world will grow darker as we near the end of the age. The world has no light of its own—and it is marked by a process of accelerating decay. However, Jesus taught us that we who are His followers, though weak and small in number, act as salt so that we can hinder the process of decline. Christians at work in the world are the only real spiritual light in the midst of great spiritual darkness. In studying the Old Testament prophets we discover that a part of the judgment on the wicked is the destruction of the righteous.

This places a tremendous responsibility on all of us. Only as the world sees our good works do they know that a light is shining. Only as the world senses our moral presence are they conscious of the salt. This is why Christ warned against the salt losing its saltness, and the light dimming. He said, "Let your light shine" (Matt. 5:16). If you and I filled this role faithfully, there would be a dramatic but peaceful revolution in the world almost overnight. We Christians are *not* powerless. We have the mighty power of God available through God the Holy Spirit, even in this world.

The Holy Spirit's Work in the Church

The Spirit is active not only in the world, but also in the Church. When speaking of the Church, I am not talking about the Presbyterian, Baptist, Methodist, Anglican, Lutheran, Pentecostal, or Catholic churches, but the whole body of believers. The word "Church" comes from the Greek word that means "called together ones."

Although the Church was veiled in mystery in the Old Testament, yet Isaiah proclaimed, "Therefore thus says the Lord God, 'Behold, I am laying in Zion for a foundation a stone, a tested stone, a precious cornerstone, of a sure foundation'" (Isa. 28:16 RSV). The New Testament speaks of Christ as that "sure foundation" of His Church, and all believers are little building stones built into a holy temple in the Lord (1 Peter 2:5). Christ is also the head of His body, the universal Church. And He is the head of every local congregation of believers. Every person who has repented of his sin and received Jesus Christ as Savior and Lord is a member of this body called the Church. So the Church is more than a religious organization. It is an organism with Christ as its living head. It is alive, with the life of Christ made living in each member.

What part does the Holy Spirit play in this? *First*, the Bible beautifully tells us that the Church was brought into being by Him: "For by one Spirit we were all baptized into one body, whether Jews or Greeks, whether slaves or free, and we were all made to drink of one Spirit. For the body is not one member, but many" (1 Cor. 12:13, 14).

Second, by the Spirit God lives in the Church: "And in him [Christ] you too are being built together to become a dwelling in which God lives by his Spirit" (Eph. 2:22 NIV). God does not dwell today in temples made with hands. But if we recognize that in our church gatherings God is really in our midst personally, it will deepen our worship.

One point about the relation of the Holy Spirit and Jesus Christ needs clarification. The Scriptures speak of "Christ in you," and some Christians do not fully understand what this means. As the God-man, Jesus is in a glorified body. And wherever Jesus is, His body must be also. In that sense, in His work as the second person of the Trinity, Jesus is now at the right hand of the Father in heaven.

For example, consider Romans 8:10 (KJV), which says, "If Christ is in you, the body is dead because of sin." Or consider Galatians 2:20, "Christ lives in me." It is clear in these verses that if the Spirit is in us, then Christ is in us. Christ dwells in our hearts by faith. But the Holy Spirit is the person of the Trinity who actually dwells in us, having been sent by the Son who has gone away but who will come again in person when we shall literally see Him.

Believers are indeed the dwelling place of the Spirit. But, unfortunately, they are often lacking in the fruit of the Spirit. They need to be quickened and given new life. This was brought home to me forcefully by Bishop Festo Kivengere. In an article on the remarkable revivals that have swept East Africa, he said: "I want to share with you . . . the glorious work of the Holy Spirit in bringing new life to a dead church. . . . You can call it renewal, coming to life or whatever you choose. . . . The Lord Jesus in his risen power through the power of the Holy Spirit began to visit a church which was scattered like bones. . . . It may surprise some of you . . . that you can be evangelical and dry, but you can. And then Jesus Christ came. . . . The attraction, the growing power came through a simple presentation of the New Testament and the Holy Spirit took men and women, including myself, from our isolation and drew us to the center, the Cross. The theme of East African revival was the Cross and we needed it. . . . The Holy Spirit drew men and women from their isolation, and changed us—sins were sins in the glare of God's love and hearts were melted."[2]

For example, I have a pastor friend in Florida. His various degrees came from one of America's most prestigious eastern universities. He pastored a church in New England. Through his much learning, he had become almost an "agnostic," though deep in his heart he still believed. He said he watched his church in New England dwindle around him. There was no authority or power in his ministry. Then through a series of events he came to accept the Bible as the infallible Word of God. He began to live and speak with power. The fruit of the Spirit was evident in his life and spiritual power was evident in his ministry. He saw his church blossom like a rose. People began to come from all around to hear him preach.

Third, the Holy Spirit gives gifts to specific people in the Church "for the equipping of the saints for the work of service, to the building up of the body of Christ" (Eph. 4:12). Since we will examine these gifts more closely in later chapters, it is enough to say here that the Holy Spirit gives every Christian some gift the moment he receives Christ. No Christian can say, "I have no gift." Every believer has at least one gift from the Holy Spirit. A weakness in today's churches is the failure to recognize, cultivate, and use fully the gifts God has given people in the pews.

I have a pastor friend on the west coast of the United States. One Sunday he passed out blank slips of paper to his congregation. He said, "I want you to spend a week studying, thinking, and praying about what gift you have from the Holy Spirit. Write it on this slip of paper. Then we will collect the slips next Sunday morning." More than 400 slips of paper were turned in the following Sunday. Some listed only one gift—some listed two or three—and some said they were not certain about their gift. However, as a result the entire congregation was mobilized. All the gifts began to be used. It transformed the church into a "growth" church and a spiritually revitalized membership. Until then the people were expecting the pastor to have all the gifts and to do all the work. They were simply spectators. Now they realized that they had as great a responsibility to use their gifts as the pastor has to use his gifts.

The Holy Spirit's Work in the Believer's Life

Having considered the Holy Spirit's work in the world and the Church, we must now consider each believer. *First*, the Holy Spirit illumines (enlightens) the Christian's mind: "For to us God revealed them through the Spirit; for the Spirit searches all things, even the depths of God" (1 Cor. 2:10); "And do not be conformed to this world, but be transformed by the renewing of your mind" (Rom. 12:2); "And that you be renewed in the spirit of your mind" (Eph. 4:23).

In a small book stressing the importance of allowing God to develop and use our converted minds, John R. W. Stott says: "Nobody wants a cold, joyless, intellectual Christianity. But does this mean we should avoid 'intellectualism' at all costs?. . . Heaven forbid that knowledge without zeal should replace zeal without knowledge! God's purpose is both, zeal directed by knowledge, knowledge fired with zeal. As I once heard Dr. John Mackay say, when he was President of Princeton Seminary, 'Commitment without reflection is fanaticism in action. But reflection without commitment is the paralysis of all action.'"[3]

Dr. Stott stresses how mistaken are those who say that what matters in the end is "not doctrine but experience." In rebuttal he says, "This is tantamount to putting our subjective experience above the revealed truth of God."[4] It is the business of the Holy Spirit to lift the veil Satan has put over our minds, and to illuminate them so that we can understand the things of God. He does this especially as we read and study the Word of God, which the Holy Spirit has inspired.

Second, the Holy Spirit not only illumines the Christian's mind, but also indwells his body. "Do you not know that your body is a temple of the Holy Spirit who is in you, whom you have from God, and that you are not your own?" (1 Cor. 6:19).

If we Christians realized that God Himself in the person of the Holy Spirit really dwells within our bodies, we would be far more careful about what we eat, drink, look at, or read. No wonder Paul said, "But I buffet my body and make it my slave, lest possibly, after I have preached to others, I myself should be disqualified"

(1 Cor. 9:27). Paul disciplined his body for fear of God's disapproval. This should drive us to our knees in confession.

In other ways I need not enlarge upon now the Holy Spirit works in the lives of believers. For example, He comforts them (Acts 9:31); He guides them (John 16:13); He sanctifies them (Rom. 15:16); He tells His servants what to preach (1 Cor. 2:13); He directs missionaries where to go (Acts 13:2); He helps us in our infirmities (Rom. 8:26); and He even tells believers where they are not to go (Acts 16:6,7).

In summation, broadly speaking, the operations of the Holy Spirit among men in the three periods of human history may be defined by three words: "upon," "with," "in." In the Old Testament He came *upon* selected persons and remained for a season (Judg. 14:19). In the Gospels He is represented as dwelling *with* the disciples in the person of Christ (John 14:17). From the second chapter of Acts onward He is spoken of as being *in* the people of God (I Cor. 6:19).

3

The Holy Spirit
and the Bible

"SOME TIME AGO a man took his worn New Testament to a bookbinder to bind it with a fine Morocco leather cover and to print *The New Testament* on the edge in gold leaf letters.

"At the appointed time he returned to find his New Testament beautifully bound. The bookbinder had one apology, however: 'I did not have small enough type in my shop to print out fully the words on the edge so I abbreviated them.' Looking on the edge of his Book, the man saw—T.N.T.

"This is true! It is God's dynamite."[1]

In the New Testament Paul declares that all Scripture comes from God. In fact, he says: "All Scripture is inspired by God and profitable for teaching, for reproof, for correction, for training in righteousness" (2 Tim. 3:16). He used a Greek word for "inspired" that literally means "God-breathed." Somewhat as God breathed life into man and made him a living soul, so also He breathed life and wisdom into the written Word of God. This makes the Bible the world's most important book, especially to everyone who believes in Christ. The Bible is the constant fountain for faith, conduct, and inspiration from which we drink daily.

The Holy Spirit Was the Inspirer of Scripture

Hundreds of passages indicate—either directly or indirectly—that God the Holy Spirit inspired the men who wrote the Bible.

We do not know exactly how He imprinted His message on the minds of those He chose to write His Word, but we know He did lead them to write what He wanted. "For no prophecy was ever made by an act of human will, but men moved by the Holy Spirit spoke from God" (2 Peter 1:21).

It seems that each book of the Bible came into being because of a special need at that time. Yet even as God was meeting a particular need, He was looking into the distant future too. He designed the Bible to meet the needs of all people in all ages. For this reason, biblical writers sometimes wrote about future events they did not understand fully but saw only dimly. Isaiah may not have fully understood the fifty-third chapter of his book as he detailed the suffering of Jesus Christ more than 700 years before it took place. "As to this salvation, the prophets who prophesied of the grace that would come to you made careful search and inquiry, seeking to know what person or time the Spirit of Christ within them was indicating as He predicted the sufferings of Christ and the glories to follow" (1 Peter 1:10, 11).

Throughout both the Old and New Testaments we find constant references to the Spirit of God inspiring the men of God who would write the Scriptures. For example, the Bible teaches that the Spirit spoke through David, who wrote many of the Psalms: "The Spirit of the Lord spoke by me, and His word was on my tongue" (2 Sam. 23:2).

He also spoke through the great prophet Jeremiah: "I will put My law within them, and on their heart I will write it; and I will be their God, and they shall be My people. And they shall not teach again, each man his neighbor and each man his brother, saying, 'Know the Lord,' for they shall all know Me, from the least of them to the greatest of them," declares the Lord, "for I will forgive their iniquity, and their sin I will remember no more" (Jer. 31:33, 34).

Ezekiel said: "The Spirit then entered me and made me stand on my feet, and He spoke with me and said to me, 'Go, shut yourself up in your house'" (Ezek. 3:24).

The apostle Peter spoke of "all things, about which God spoke by the mouth of His holy prophets from ancient time" (Acts 3:21).

The Book of Hebrews quotes from the Law (Heb. 9:6–8), the prophets (Heb. 10:15–17), and the Psalms (Heb. 3:7–10), in each case attributing authorship to the Holy Spirit.

Jesus assured the disciples in advance that the Holy Spirit would inspire the writers of the New Testament: "The Holy Spirit . . . will teach you all things, and bring to your remembrance all that I said to you" (John 14:26). This embraces the four Gospels, Matthew to John. Jesus' statement, "He will guide you into all the truth" (John 16:13), takes in the books from Acts to Jude. "He will disclose to you what is to come" (John 16:13), covers the Book of Revelation as well as many other passages throughout the New Testament. Thus, as someone has said, Scripture is literature indwelt by the Spirit of God.

Just as God the Holy Spirit inspired the writing of the Scriptures, so He was instrumental in the selection of the sixty-six books that comprise the canon of the Bible. Contrary to the opinion of many, the question of what books were included in the Bible was not settled simply by the human choice of any church council. The Holy Spirit was at work in Spirit-filled believers who selected the sixty-six books we have in our Bibles. And at last, after years and even centuries of discussion, prayer, and heartsearching, the canon of Scripture was closed. The Holy Spirit in His work did not bypass the human processes, but instead, He worked through them.

"Inspiration by the Spirit" Defined

When discussing the inspiration of the Bible, we immediately touch one of the most controversial questions of the ages. Ever since Satan questioned Eve in the Garden of Eden, "Indeed, has God said . . . ?" men have attacked the Word of God. But every time in history they have doubted it, dire consequences have resulted—whether in the life of an individual, a nation (ancient Israel), or the Church. Without exception the individual, the nation, or the Church went into a period of spiritual decline. Often idolatry and immorality followed.

Competent scholars agree that the Holy Spirit did not merely use the biblical writers as secretaries to whom He dictated the

Scriptures, although some sincere Christians think He did this. The Bible itself does not state in detail just *how* the Holy Spirit accomplished His purpose in getting the Scripture written. However, we do know that He used living human minds and guided their thoughts according to His divine purposes. Moreover, it has always been clear to me that we cannot have inspired ideas without inspired words.

It would be helpful if we define the important words associated with God-breathed Scripture. The first is *inspiration.*

When we speak of the *total* (or *plenary) inspiration* of the Bible, we mean that all of the Bible, not just some parts of it, are inspired. Dr. B. H. Carroll, founder of the largest theological seminary in the world (Southwestern Baptist Theological Seminary of Fort Worth, Texas), spoke and wrote at length on this subject:

... the Bible is called holy because it is that infallible, *theopneustos* [God-breathed-out], product of the Holy Spirit. . . .

A great many people say, "I think the Word of God is in the Bible, but I don't believe that all of the Bible is the Word of God; it contains the Word of God, but it is not the Word of God."

My objection to this is that it would require inspiration to tell the spots in it that were inspired. It would call for an inspiration more difficult than the kind that I talk about, in order to turn the pages of the Bible and find out which part is the Word of God. . . .

In other words, with reference to the Scriptures, inspiration is plenary, which means full and complete, hence my question is, "Do you believe in the plenary inspiration of the Bible?" If the inspiration is complete, it must be plenary.

My next question is this: "Do you believe in plenary verbal inspiration?"

I do, for the simple reason that the words are mere signs of ideas, and I don't know how to get at the idea except through the words. If the words don't tell me, how shall I know? Sometimes the word is a very small one, maybe only one letter or a mere element. The word with one letter—the smallest letter—shows the inspiration of the Old Testament. The man that put that there was inspired.

Take the words of Jesus. He says, "Not one jot or tittle of that law shall ever fail."

The "jot" is the smallest letter in the Hebrew alphabet and the "tittle" is a small turn or projection of a Hebrew letter. He says the heavens may fall, but not one jot or tittle of that law shall fail. Then He says that the Scriptures cannot be broken.

What is it that cannot be broken? Whatever is written cannot be broken if it is *theopneustos*. But the word is not inspired if it is not *theopneustos*, which means God-breathed, or God-inspired."[2]

We could say much more about the complete trustworthiness of the Bible. By way of illustration, hundreds of times the Bible uses phrases like "God said," or "The word of the Lord came unto me saying." It is also interesting that Jesus never once told us to doubt the difficult passages of the Old Testament Scriptures. For example, He accepted as fact, not fiction, the stories of Jonah and the fish, Noah and the ark, and the creation of Adam and Eve. If these stories had not been literally true, He surely would have told us so. But time after time Jesus (and the New Testament writers) quoted the Scriptures as authoritative and as the very Word of God.

Of course, inspiration by the Holy Spirit does not refer to the many English translations, but to the original languages. No modern language, whether English, French, or Spanish, has in it the exact equivalent for every Greek or Hebrew word. However, numerous scholars agree that most of the translations, even with their variations, do not alter or misrepresent the basic theological teachings of the Scriptures—especially those dealing with salvation and Christian living.

My wife has more than twenty different translations available at all times. By the time she has compared the various wordings of all these, she can be reasonably sure that she has a good idea of the meaning the Holy Spirit intended to convey in any passage of Scripture.

It is also interesting that some words could not be translated into other languages so it was necessary to lift them from the original tongue. The Greek word for "baptism" had no English equivalent, so it came to *be* the English word. The Holy Spirit has seen to it that the Bible is not a dead book but a living vehicle for Him to use as He wishes.

There is a second word we should discuss when we talk about the Bible. Not only is the Bible inspired, but it is also *authoritative*. When we say the Bible is authoritative, we mean that it is God's binding revelation to us. We submit to it because it has come from God. Suppose we ask: What is the source of our religious knowledge? The answer is, the Bible, and it is authoritative for us. As Dr. John R. W. Stott has written,

"To reject the authority of either the Old Testament or the New Testament is to reject the authority of Christ. It is supremely because we are determined to submit to the authority of Jesus Christ as Lord that we submit to the authority of Scripture. . . . submission to Scripture is fundamental to everyday Christian living, for without it Christian discipleship, Christian integrity, Christian freedom and Christian witness are all seriously damaged if not actually destroyed."[3]

Yes, every area of our lives is to be under the Lordship of Jesus Christ. And that means the searchlight of God's Word must penetrate every corner of our lives. We are not free to pick and choose the parts of the Bible we want to believe or obey. God has given us all of it, and we should be obedient to all of it.

Having declared what I believe about the authority, inspiration, and infallibility of the Bible, I must still answer one further question. On what basis have I come to believe all of this about the Bible? There are various reasons for having confidence in the Bible as God's Word, but it is at this point that the work of the Holy Spirit is most plainly manifested. The truth of the matter is that the same Holy Spirit who was the author of the Scriptures through the use of human personalities also works in each of us to convince us the Bible is the Word of God to be trusted in all its parts.

In his *Institutes of the Christian Religion*, John Calvin has a word about the testimony of the Holy Spirit that I like:

"The same Spirit, therefore, who has spoken through the mouths of the prophets must penetrate into our hearts to persuade us that they faithfully proclaimed what had been divinely commanded. . . . Until he illumines their minds, they ever waver among many doubts! . . . Let this point therefore stand: that those whom the Holy Spirit has inwardly taught truly rest upon Scripture, and that Scripture indeed is self-authenticated; hence, it is not right to subject it to proof and reasoning. And the certainty it deserves with us, it attains by the testimony of the Spirit. For even if it wins reverence for itself by its own majesty, it seriously affects us only when it is sealed upon our hearts through the Spirit."

Calvin continues, "Therefore, illumined by his power, we believe neither by our own nor by anyone else's judgment that Scripture is from God; but above human judgment we affirm with utter certainty (just as if we were gazing upon the majesty of God himself) that it has flowed to us from the very mouth of God by the ministry of men. We seek no proofs, no marks of genuineness upon which our judgment may lean; but we subject our judgment and wit to it as to a thing far beyond any guesswork! This we do, not as persons accustomed to seize upon some unknown thing, which, under closer scrutiny, displeases them, but fully conscious that we hold the unassailable truth![4]

The Illumination of the Spirit

That the writers of the Old and New Testaments were inspired by the Holy Spirit is one part of the story. In addition, He illumines the minds and opens the hearts of its readers. We find spiritual response to the Word of God described in scores of ways. Jeremiah said, "Thy words were found and I ate them, And Thy words became for me a joy and the delight of my heart; For I have been called by Thy name, O Lord God of hosts" (Jer. 15:16). Furthermore, Isaiah said, "The grass withers, the flower fades, But the word of our God stands forever" (Isa. 40:8).

Jesus warned the Sadducees of His day that they entertained many errors in their teachings because they did not know the Scriptures or the power of God (Matt. 22:29). This links the Scriptures to the power of the Holy Spirit, who effects change through the Bible. Moreover, John records Jesus' words, "the Scripture cannot be broken" (John 10:35). Jesus also said, "You are already clean because of the word which I have spoken to you" (John 15:3).

So through the Bible the Holy Spirit not only gives us doctrinal and historical truth; He also uses it as the vehicle for speaking to our hearts. This is why I constantly urge people to study the Scriptures—whether they fully understand what they are reading or not. The reading of Scripture itself enables the Holy Spirit to enlighten us and to do His work in us. While we read the Word, its message saturates our hearts, whether we are conscious of what is happening or not. The Word with all its mysterious power touches our lives and gives us its power.

This is seen, for example, in a statement Paul made: "Eye hath not seen, nor ear heard, neither have entered into the heart of man, the things which God hath prepared for them that love him. But God hath revealed them unto us by his Spirit . . ." (1 Cor. 2:9, 10 KJV).

Note that Paul does not say God reveals these wonderful things to us by His *Word* (although it is there that we find them), but rather He does it by His *Spirit* through His Word. "We have received, not the spirit of the world, but the Spirit who is from God, that we might know the things freely given to us by God" (1 Cor. 2:12).

As the Reverend Gottfried Osei-Mensah of Kenya said at the Lausanne Congress on Evangelization in 1974: "It is the work of the Holy Spirit to reveal truths previously hidden from human search and understanding, and to enlighten men's minds to know and understand them (1 Cor. 2:9, 10). . . . If the role of the Holy Spirit is to teach, ours is to be diligent students of the Word."[5]

This has been my experience as I have studied the Scriptures. Things I may have known intellectually for years have come alive to me in their fuller spiritual significance almost miraculously. As I have studied the Scriptures, I have also learned that the Spirit always lets more light shine from the Word. Almost every time I read an old, familiar passage I see something new. This happens because the written Word of God is a living Word. I always come to the Scriptures with the Psalmist's prayer, "Open my eyes, that I may behold wonderful things from Thy law" (Ps. 119:18).

The Unity of the Spirit and the Word

A glorious unity exists between the Holy Spirit and the Word of God. On the day of Pentecost Peter illustrated this in quoting from the Old Testament, "This is that which was spoken by the prophet Joel" (Acts 2:16 KJV). "This" refers to the promised Spirit. "That" refers to the written Word. "This is that" shows the wonderful unity that exists between the Spirit and the Word.

"Where the word of a king is, there is power" (Eccl. 8:4 KJV), and "where the Spirit of the Lord is, there is liberty" (2 Cor. 3:17). These two things—power and liberty—will characterize the utterances of that man who, filled with the Spirit, proclaims the Word of God. James Hervey describes the change that took place in Wesley when he was controlled by the Spirit. "Wesley's preaching," he says, "once was like the firing of an arrow—all the speed and force depended on the strength of his arm in bending the bow; now it was like the fire of a rifle ball—the force depending upon the power, needing only a finger touch to let it off."

I believe effective preaching must be biblical preaching, whether it is the exposition of a single word in the Bible, a text, or a chapter. The Word is what the Spirit uses. So the important element is that the Word of God be proclaimed. Thousands of pastors, Sunday school teachers and Christian workers are powerless because they do not make the Word the source of their preaching or teaching. When we preach or teach the Scriptures, we open the door for the Holy Spirit to do His work. God has not promised to bless oratory or clever preaching. He has promised to bless His Word. He has said that it will not return to Him "empty" (Isa. 55:11).

It is the Word of God which changes our lives also. Remember, God has given us His Word "for teaching, for reproof, for correction, for training in righteousness; that the man of God may be adequate, equipped for every good work" (2 Tim. 3:16, 17). Are these things happening in our lives? Are we learning God's truth? Jesus said, "Thy word is truth" (John 17:17). Are we being convicted of sin in our lives, and our need of God's correction and God's righteousness, as we read the Word of God? The Bible says, "For the word of God is living and active and sharper than any two-edged sword, and piercing as far as the division of soul and spirit, of both joints and marrow, and able to judge the thoughts and intentions of the heart. And there is no creature hidden from His sight, but all things are open and laid bare to the eyes of Him with whom we have to do." (Heb. 4:12, 13). Let the study of the Bible become central in your life—not just so you will know it, but that you will obey it. Let Job's statement be yours: "I have not departed from the command of His lips; I have treasured the words of His mouth more than my necessary food" (Job 23:12).

George Muller (the great founder of the Bristol Orphanage in the last century) once said, "The vigor of our Spiritual Life will be in exact proportion to the place held by the Bible in our life and thoughts. . . . I have read the Bible through one hundred times, and always with increasing delight. Each time it seems like a new book to me. Great has been the blessing from consecutive, diligent, daily study. I look upon it as a lost day when I have not had a good time over the Word of God."[6]

The Spirit Is Using the Word Today

The Spirit has the power to transform and inspire lives today through the Bible. Here are some situations where He has recently touched people:

A former surgeon-general of Portugal was out walking one rainy day. When he returned to his home, he found a piece of paper sticking to his shoe. When he pulled it off, he discovered it to be a tract that presented the Gospel by using Scripture. On reading it, he was soundly converted to Jesus Christ.

Dr. J. B. Phillips writes in the preface to his *Letters to Young Churches* that he was "continually struck by the living quality of the material" on which he worked; often he "felt rather like 'an electrician rewiring an ancient house without being able to turn the mains off'."[7]

Many prisoners in the "Hanoi Hilton" during the Vietnam war were gloriously sustained by the Spirit through the Word of God. These men testified to the strength they received from the Word of God. Howard Rutledge, in his book *In the Presence of Mine Enemies*, tells how the prisoners developed a code system that the enemy was never able to break. By it they communicated with one another, sharing names and serial numbers of every prisoner. They also passed along other messages as well, including Scripture verses that they knew.

Geoffrey Bull, a missionary on the borders of Tibet, said in his book, *When Iron Gates Yield*, that during his three years of imprisonment he was relentlessly brainwashed and would have succumbed had it not been for Scriptures he had committed to memory. He repeated them over and over to himself when he was in solitary confinement. Through them God strengthened him to face the torture designed to break him down.

I have written here mainly of those who were imprisoned or in desperate circumstances. Yet much could be said about the daily nourishment and reinforcement of faith we all receive from studying the Word of God, and the wisdom it provides us for day-to-day living. It reminds me of Hebrews 11:32, "And what more shall I say? For time would fail me to tell of Gideon, Barak, Samson, Jephthah . . ." (RSV). Tens of thousands of God's saints and sufferers through the ages have found their dark nights lightened and tortured souls strengthened because they found help from the Spirit in the Word of God.

As we approach the end of the age, persecution is going to be intensified. We are already seeing evidences in many parts of the world. The Scriptures you memorize now and the teachings of the Word of God you learn now will sustain you in that hour!—if you are called on to suffer physically and mentally for the name of Christ!

4

The Holy Spirit
and Salvation

DURING ONE OF our London Crusades, a Russian nobleman came one evening. He spoke no English. Yet when the invitation was given to receive Christ he responded. The trained Russian-speaking counselor asked him how, knowing no English, he had understood enough of the message to respond so intelligently. "When I entered this place," the nobleman replied, "I was over-whelmed with a longing for God. Tell me, how can I find Him?"

This is but one of hundreds of similar stories that have come to my attention during my years of ministry. In our Crusades we have counselors who speak various languages. For example, in our recent Crusade in Toronto, trained counselors were available to help in twenty-eight languages. It is amazing that in almost every service people respond to the "invitation" who understand little or no English. To me, this is clearly the work of the Holy Spirit drawing people to the Savior in spite of the language barrier.

When a person comes to Christ, the Bible tells us the Holy Spirit has been at work in a number of ways. Some of these we may not fully understand, and yet this does not alter the fact that the Holy Spirit is deeply involved in our salvation. In this chapter we will look at some of the ways the Spirit works to bring us to Christ.

The Need for Spiritual Rebirth

We live in a revolutionary, changing world. Man's moral capacities lag far behind his technological skills and discoveries.

This could mean disaster for the human race. In light of this, the greatest need in the world is to bring about the transformation of human nature. Many of our technologists are saying there is a great need for a new breed of man. Even the political radicals and the humanists talk about the "new man." From this it is clear that they acknowledge that man, as he is, is not good enough. So they also look for the arrival of the new man who, they say, will come into being when society has been changed so that a new environment can produce him.

There are also the technocrats who believe that technology is now advancing so rapidly that we will soon be able to create an entirely new human race. We have genetic engineers who believe that by the end of this century they will be able to create any type of person they want.

But there is only one ultimate answer to the need of man to be changed. Science and technology cannot change man's basic nature. Economic restructuring cannot change man's basic nature. No amount of self-improvement or wishful thinking can change man's basic nature. Only God—the One who created us—can recreate us. And that is precisely what He does when we give ourselves to Jesus Christ. The Bible says, "Therefore if any man is in Christ, he is a new creature; the old things passed away; behold, new things have come" (2 Cor. 5:17). What a tremendous statement!

The Bible speaks of this change in various ways. One of the most vivid is the term "born again." Just as we have been born physically, so we can be born again—spiritually. "For you have been born again not of seed which is perishable but imperishable, that is, through the living and abiding word of God" (1 Peter 1:23).

Certainly few passages in the New Testament speak as directly about the Holy Spirit's role in our salvation as the third chapter of John. In it, John recounts for us an interview Jesus had with a very influential religious leader named Nicodemus. Nicodemus was wealthy, and a member of the Sanhedrin, the ruling council of the Jewish nation. He probably fasted several times a week, and spent time each day in the Temple in prayer. He tithed his income, and was apparently a noted religious teacher. He would have been considered a model Christian in some circles today. But Jesus said all his goodness was not enough. Instead, Jesus said, "You must be born again" (John 3:7).

Jesus went on to explain that this new birth—this spiritual regeneration—is accomplished by the Holy Spirit. "The wind blows where it wishes and you hear the sound of it, but do not know where it comes from and where it is going; so is every one who is born of the Spirit" (John 3:8). There is something mysterious about this; we cannot fully understand how the new birth comes to us. It is from above, not from the earth or from within our human nature. It comes because of the love and grace of God. It comes because of the death and resurrection of Jesus Christ. It comes because of the action of the Holy Spirit.

In its notes on John 3 the *Open Bible* describes the encounter between Jesus and Nicodemus this way: "What a shock it must have been [to Nicodemus] to learn that his religion was not enough! It never is. He came to Jesus, addressing Him as 'a teacher come from God.' Jesus knew Nicodemus, as He knows all men [John 2:24, 25], and Jesus knew that he needed more than a teacher—he needed a Saviour. He needed more than religion—he needed regeneration. He needed more than law—he needed life. Jesus began by going right to the point when He said, 'Ye must be born again.' Nicodemus asked, 'How can a man be born when he is old?' [This was a very natural question for Nicodemus to ask.] Then Jesus pointed out the dissimilarity in the two births: 'That which is born of flesh is flesh' (the flesh will never change); and 'that which is born of the Spirit is spirit' (the Spirit will never change). [John 3:6]"[1]

Jesus knew what lies in the hearts of all men—the fatal disease that causes lying, cheating, hate, prejudice, greed, and lust. He said, "For out of the heart come evil thoughts, murders, adulteries, fornications, thefts, false witness, slanders. These are the things which defile the man" (Matt. 15:19, 20). Psychologists realize something is wrong with the human race, but they disagree as to the problem. The Bible says man's problem is the direct result of his decision as an intelligent, moral, responsible being to revolt against the will of his Maker. Man's disease is called S-I-N in the Bible.

Sin is a transgression of the law (1 John 3:4). It is falling short of doing one's duty, a failure to do what one knows he ought to do in God's sight. It is iniquity—a turning aside from a straight path. Isaiah said, "All of us like sheep have gone astray, each of us has turned to his own way" (Isa. 53:6). The Bible teaches that the sinner is "dead" before God when it says that "through one man sin entered into the world, and death through sin, and so death spread to all men, because all sinned" (Rom. 5:12). Thus a radical change is needed in the inner being of every man. This is a change man cannot earn, nor is it something he can do for himself. It is a change science cannot accomplish for him; it is something God alone can and must do.

The Holy Spirit Convicts Us and Calls Us

One of the most devastating effects of sin is that it has blinded us to our own sin. "The god of this world has blinded the minds of the unbelieving, that they might not see the light of the gospel of the glory of Christ, who is the image of God" (2 Cor. 4:4). Only the Holy Spirit can open our eyes. Only He can convict us of the depth of our sin, and only He can convince us of the truth of the gospel. That is one reason the Holy Spirit is called "the Spirit of truth" in John 14:17. In speaking of the Holy Spirit, Jesus said, "And He, when He comes, will convict the world concerning sin, and righteousness, and judgment; concerning sin, because they do not believe in Me; and concerning righteousness, because I go to the Father, and you no longer behold Me; and concerning judgment, because the ruler of this world has been judged" (John 16: 8-11).

J. Gresham Machen wrote: "There must be the mysterious work of the Spirit of God in the new birth. Without that, all our arguments are quite useless. . . . What the Holy Spirit does in the new birth is not to make a man a Christian regardless of the evidence, but on the contrary to clear away the mists from his eyes and enable him to attend to the evidence."[2]

We should also remember that it is the truth of the Word of God which is used by the Holy Spirit to bring conviction to our hearts. The Bible tells us, "So faith comes from hearing, and hearing by the word of Christ" (Rom. 10:17). Or again we read that, "The word of God is living and active and sharper than any two-edged sword, and piercing as far as the division of soul and spirit, of both joints and marrow, and able to judge the thoughts and intentions of the heart" (Heb. 4:12). God the Holy Spirit can take the humblest preaching or the feeblest words of our witness to Christ, and transform them by His power into a convicting word in the lives of others.

Apart from the ministry of the Holy Spirit we would never clearly see the truth of God concerning our sin, or the truth of God about our Savior. I believe this is what Jesus meant in John 6:44: "No one can come to Me, unless the Father who sent Me draws him; and I will raise him up on the last day."

However, the Bible also gives us a solemn warning about resisting the calling of the Holy Spirit. In Genesis 6:3 we read: "My Spirit shall not strive with man forever." Without the "striving" of the Spirit it would be impossible for a person to come to Christ. Yet, there is also the danger that we will pass the point of no return, and that our hearts will be so calloused and hardened by sin that we will no longer hear the voice of the Spirit.

Again, there is much we may not understand fully about this, and it is not our place to say when that point has been reached in another person's life. No man could have been more hardened, seemingly, than King Manasseh in the Old Testament, and yet he eventually repented of his sin and was forgiven by God in His grace (2 Chron. 33). But we dare not neglect the warning of the Bible that tells us, "Now is the time of God's favor, now is the day of salvation" (2 Cor. 6:2 NIV). The writer of Proverbs said, "A man who hardens his neck after much reproof will suddenly be broken beyond remedy" (Prov. 29:1).

The Holy Spirit Regenerates Us

Along with repentance and faith, one of the works of the Spirit of God in the heart of man is regeneration. "Regeneration" is another term for renewal or rebirth. "He saved us, not on the basis of deeds which we have done in righteousness, but according to His mercy, by the washing of regeneration and renewing by the Holy Spirit" (Titus 3:5). Actually the Greek word translated "regeneration" here is a compound of two Greek words; it literally means "birth again" or new birth.

This is a once-for-all change, though it has continuing effects. In John 3:3 the Bible speaks of one being "born again," and the Amplified Version suggests "born anew" or "born from above" to clarify the meaning. The sinner in his natural state is spiritually dead in trespasses and sins. In regeneration that which is dead is made alive. He is justified by God from the guilt of a broken law, and he is forgiven of every sin. Further, by the new birth the justified sinner becomes a new creation—a new creature (2 Cor. 5:17; Gal. 6:15 RSV). Moreover, regeneration, like justification, is immediate and constitutes a one-time act of the Holy Spirit, though the person who is "born again" might, or might not, be conscious of the exact time. Theologians have long debated exactly when regeneration actually takes place in a person's life. In spite of some disagreements, the central issue is clear: it is the Holy Spirit who regenerates us within.

The gift of new or divine life to the regenerated person comes to the soul from Christ through the Holy Spirit. Jesus said that the new birth is "a mystery." He uses the illustration of the wind blowing: we sense its effects but we cannot see where it comes from or where it is going. Thus regeneration is a hidden transaction in the same sense that it is something which takes place within the individual heart and may or may not be known to the one who receives it—and often it is not immediately visible to people around him. The results that flow from the new birth are so incalculably significant that they deserve to be called "a miracle"— the greatest of all miracles! Even as unbelieving men did not know Jesus on earth, and failed to realize that God incarnate was standing before them, so it is possible for "the new man" in Christ to go unrecognized for at least a while. Yet, known or unknown to the world, the new man exists within. Sooner or later the new birth will manifest itself in godly living. But the divine life, which will abide forever, is there, and the "new man" who possesses the kingdom of God is there (2 Cor. 5:17)—a new creature.

This is not to deny the importance of personal faith and decision. We do not passively sit back and wait for the Spirit to do His work before we come to Christ. We are commanded to "Ask, and it shall be given to you; seek, and you shall find; knock, and it shall be opened to you" (Matt. 7:7). We have the promise of God: "And you will seek Me and find Me, when you search for Me with all your heart" (Jer. 29:13). Furthermore, the Scripture tells us that even faith itself is a gift of God's grace. "Because of his kindness you have been saved through trusting Christ. And even trusting is not of yourselves; it too is a gift from God" (Eph. 2:8 LB). We therefore have everything we need to decide for Christ, but we still have a responsibility to respond to the call and conviction of the Holy Spirit.

When a person is born again, the process is uncomplicated from the divine perspective. The Spirit of God takes the Word of God and makes the child of God. We are born again through the operation of the Holy Spirit, who in turn uses the divinely inspired Word of God. God's Spirit brings life to men. At this point the Holy Spirit indwells a person for life. He receives *eternal* life.

As an evangelist for over thirty-five years, I have watched hundreds of thousands of people come down aisles in auditoriums, stadiums, churches, tents, and brush arbors, to make what has often been referred to as a "decision" for Christ. Years ago I tried to change the terminology to "inquirers." Walking down an aisle in an evangelistic meeting does not necessarily mean a person has been or will be regenerated. Going forward to make some kind of public commitment to Christ is only a visible, though an important, act. It may or may not reflect what is going on or has already taken place in the human heart. Regeneration is *not* the work of the evangelist; it is the work of God's Spirit. The indispensable condition of the new birth is repentance and faith, but repentance and faith itself does not save. Genuine faith is God's gift to a person—as I have said, even helping us to repent. When a person displays that kind of repentance and faith, we may be sure that God the Holy Spirit accompanies it with regeneration. In this we see the love and grace of God shed abroad toward judgment-bound sinners through Jesus Christ.

Thus, to be born again means that "as the Father raises the dead and gives them life, even so the Son also gives life to whom He wishes" (John 5:21). In Acts, Peter called it "repenting" or "being converted." In Romans 6:13, Paul spoke of it as being "alive from the dead." To the Colossians, Paul said, ". . . you laid aside the old self with its evil practices, and have put on the new self who is being renewed to a true knowledge according to the image of the One who created him" (Col. 3:9, 10).

You and I cannot inherit regeneration: Rather, "as many as received Him [Jesus], to them He gave the right to become children of God, even to those who believe in His name" (John 1:12). A person may have been baptized, as Hitler and Stalin were, but that is no guarantee that he has been regenerated. Simon the Sorcerer was baptized by Philip after having "believed" in some fuzzy mental sense, but Peter told him, "Your heart is not right before God" (Acts 8:21).

A person may be confirmed in one of the more liturgical churches, but that does not necessarily mean he has been regenerated. In the Book of Acts we read, "The Lord was adding to their number day by day those who were being saved" (Acts 2:47). The one indispensable condition for admission to the fellowship of the early church was that each one first had to have been regenerated.

Nor can one be regenerated by doing good works: "He saved us, not on the basis of deeds which we have done in righteousness, but according to His mercy, by the washing of regeneration and renewing by the Holy Spirit" (Titus 3:5). A man can join every club in town and become involved in every charitable event and be a "good," "moral" person all his life, and still not know what it means to be regenerated.

Others try to be regenerated by reformation. They do their best to reform by making new resolutions. But the Bible says, "All our righteous deeds are like a filthy garment" in the sight of God (Isa. 64:6).

Some well-meaning people even try to find salvation through imitating Christ in their lives. But this is not acceptable to God, because no one can really imitate Christ. Christ was pure. Men are sinners, *dead* in sin. What they need is life, and this can be supplied only by the Holy Spirit through regeneration.

Have you been regenerated by the power of the Spirit of God? Nothing less can bring true spiritual rebirth to your life. But God sent His Son into the world to give us new life. God has given us His Word, and the power of the Holy Spirit can take it and bring regeneration—spiritual rebirth—to us.

The new birth will bring about a change in your relationship with God, a change in your relationship with your family, a change in your relationship with yourself, a change in your relationship with your neighbors. Gradually, if you are an obedient believer, it will bring about a change in disposition, affection, aims, principles, and dimensions.

The Holy Spirit Assures Us

After we receive Christ as Savior we may be confused sometimes because many of the old temptations have not disappeared. We still sin. Sometimes we lose our tempers. Pride and jealousy may still crop up from time to time. This is not only confusing, it is discouraging and sometimes leads to spiritual depression. We may even have some particular "besetting sin" which plagues us, and which we do not seem to be able to conquer.

But the moment you and I received Christ and were regenerated by the Holy Spirit we were given a new nature. Thus, those of us who are born again have two natures. The old nature is from our first birth; the new is from our new birth. By the old birth we are children of the flesh; by the new birth we are children of God. This is why Jesus told Nicodemus that he "must be born again."

Whatever the problem, whenever the old nature within us asserts itself, a new believer may begin to doubt whether or not he has really been born again. Satan would want us to doubt the reality of our salvation—which is really doubting God's Word to us. We will write more fully about the assurance of our salvation in a later chapter, but at this point we need to remind ourselves that the Holy Spirit also gives us assurance that we have been born again and have become members of the family of God. "And the Holy Spirit also bears witness to us" (Heb. 10:15). By the written Word of God, and by the quiet work of the Spirit in our hearts, we know we have been born again—regardless of the accusations of Satan. "The Spirit Himself bears witness with our spirit that we are children of God" (Rom. 8:16).

How to Become Born Again

First, realize that you are a sinner in God's eyes. You may not consider yourself a bad person, because you know you have lived a fairly decent life. On the other hand, you may be carrying a burden of guilt over some sins committed in the past. Whatever your background, the Bible tells us "there is none righteous, no, not one" (Rom. 3:10 KJV). We have all broken the Law of God, and we all deserve nothing but God's judgment and wrath.

Second, realize that God loves you and sent His Son to die for you. You deserve to die for your sins, but Christ died in your place. "For Christ also died for sins once for all, the just for the unjust, in order that He might bring us to God" (1 Peter 3:18). That is the wonder of the gospel—that God loves us! He loves you, in spite of the fact you are a sinner.

Third, repent of your sins. Repentance comes from a Greek word meaning "a change of mind." It means that I admit I am a sinner, and that I feel sorry for the fact I have sinned. But repentance also means I actually turn my back on my sins—I reject them—and determine by God's grace to live as He wants me to live. Jesus said, "unless you repent, you will all likewise perish" (Luke 13:3). Repentance involves a willingness to leave sin behind, and turn my life over to Jesus Christ as Lord of my life. We see ourselves as God sees us and we pray, "God, be merciful to me, the sinner!" (Luke 18:13).

Fourth, come by faith and trust to Christ. Salvation, the Bible tells us, is a free gift. God has done everything possible to make salvation available to us, but we must respond and make that gift our own. "For the wages of sin is death, but the free gift of God is eternal life in Christ Jesus our Lord" (Rom. 6:23).

How do you accept this gift? By a simple act of faith in which you say "yes" to Christ. If you have never accepted Christ into your life, I invite you to do it right now before another minute passes. Simply tell God you know you are a sinner, and you are sorry for your sins. Tell Him you believe Jesus Christ died for you, and that you want to give your life to Him right now, to follow Him as Lord the rest of your life. "For God so loved the world, that He gave His only begotten Son, that whoever believes in Him should not perish, but have eternal life" (John 3:16).

If you have done that, God has forgiven all your sins. What a wonderful thing to know that every sin you ever committed—even the things you did not realize were sins—are all washed away by the blood of Jesus Christ, "in whom we have redemption, the forgiveness of sins" (Col. 1:14). More than that—you can accept by faith now that you are a new creation in Christ.

In their conversation Jesus reminded Nicodemus of an incident in the wilderness journey of the ancient Israelites. God had judged His sinning people by sending among them serpents whose bites were fatal. Many Israelites were suffering and dying. Then God told Moses to fashion a serpent of brass and lift it high on a pole. All who looked upon that serpent by faith after they had been bitten would be saved. That sounded like an insult to their intelligence. There was no healing quality in brass. And they knew that rubbing medicine on their bites would not heal them. Fighting the serpents was of no avail. Making an offering to the serpent on the pole wouldn't help. Prayer to the serpent would not save them from death. Even Moses the prophet of God could not help them.

Rather, *all* they had to do was look at the serpent of brass in childlike faith that God would save them totally by His grace. When they looked at the serpent of brass, they were looking beyond the serpent to God Himself. So it is as if Jesus said, "I am going to be lifted up—look unto me and be saved." Of course, His "lifting up" was to take place at His forthcoming death on the cross. No one can come to Christ unless the Holy Spirit draws him to the cross, where Jesus by His blood cleanses away the sin of each person who places his faith in Him.

As with the Israelites in the wilderness, God does not mean to insult our intelligence. But if you have not believed in Christ, your mind has been blinded spiritually by the devil and affected by sin. That is why the apostle Paul said, "For since in the wisdom of God the world through its wisdom did not come to know God, God was well-pleased through the foolishness of the message preached to save those who believe" (1 Cor. 1:21).

At first it looks foolish to believe that Jesus Christ, who died on a cross and rose again 2,000 years ago, can transform your life radically today by the Holy Spirit. Yet millions of Christians on every continent would rise at this moment to testify that He has transformed their lives. It happened to me many years ago. It could happen to you—today!

5

Baptism with the Spirit

MANY YEARS AGO when I was attending a small Bible school in Florida, I visited what was called a "brush arbor revival meeting." The speaker was an old-fashioned Southern revival preacher. The little place seated about two hundred people and was filled. The speaker made up in thunder what he lacked in logic, and the people loved it.

"Have you been baptized with the Holy Spirit?" he asked the audience during the sermon.

Apparently he knew a great many in the audience because he would point to someone and ask, "Brother, have you been baptized with the Spirit?" And the man would answer, "Yes, bless God."

"Young man," he said, spotting me, "have you been baptized with the Holy Spirit?" "Yes, sir," I replied.

"When were you baptized with the Holy Spirit?" he asked. He had not questioned the others on this.

"The moment I received Jesus Christ as my Savior," I replied. He looked at me with a puzzled expression, but before going to the next person he said, "That couldn't be."

But it could! It was.

I do not doubt the sincerity of this preacher. However, in my own study of the Scriptures through the years I have become convinced that there is only one baptism with the Holy Spirit in the life of every believer, and that takes place at the moment of conversion. This baptism with the Holy Spirit was initiated at Pentecost, and all who come to know Jesus Christ as Savior share in that experience and are baptized with the Spirit the moment they are regenerated. In addition, they may be filled with the Holy Spirit; if not, they need to be.

The scriptural usage of the word *baptism* shows that it is something initiatory both in the case of water baptism and Spirit baptism, and that it is *not repeated.* I can find no biblical data to show that the baptism with the Spirit would ever be repeated.

"For by one Spirit we were all baptized into one body" (1 Cor. 12:13). The original Greek of this passage makes it clear that this baptism of the Spirit is a completed past action. (The King James Version incorrectly translates it into the present tense rather than the past.)

Two things stand out in that verse: first, the baptism with the Spirit is a collective operation of the Spirit of God; second, it includes every believer. Dr. W. Graham Scroggie once said at Keswick, "Observe carefully to whom the Apostle is writing and of whom he is speaking." He uses the word *"all"*—"It is not to the faithful Thessalonians, nor to the liberal Philippians, nor to the spiritual Ephesians, but to the carnal Corinthians (1 Cor. 3:1)," Scroggie went on. The clear indication is that baptism with the Spirit is connected with our *standing* before God, not our current subjective *state;* with our *position* and not our *experience.*

This becomes still clearer if we examine the experiences of the Israelites described in 1 Corinthians 10:1–5. In these verses there are five *alls.* "All under the cloud," "all passed through the sea," "all were baptized," "all ate," "all drank." It was after all these things happened to all the people that the differences came: "Nevertheless, with most of them God was not well-pleased" (1 Cor. 10:5).

In other words, they were all part of the people of God. This did not mean, however, that all lived up to their calling as God's holy people. In like manner, all believers are baptized with the Holy Spirit. This does not mean, however, that they are filled or controlled by the Spirit. The important thing is the great central truth—when I come to Christ, God gives His Spirit to me.

Differences That Divide Us

I realize that baptism with the Holy Spirit has been differently understood by some of my fellow believers. We should not shrink from stating specific differences of opinion. But we should also try to understand each other, pray for each other, and be willing to learn from each other as we seek to know what the Bible teaches. The differences of opinion on this matter are somewhat similar to differences of opinion about water baptism and church government. Some baptize babies; others do not. Some sprinkle or pour; others only immerse. Some have congregational church polity; others have presbyterian or representative democracy; still others have the episcopal form. In no way should these differences be divisive. I can have wonderful Christian fellowship, especially in the work of evangelism, with those who hold various views.

On the other hand, the question of the baptism with the Holy Spirit, in my judgment, is often more important than these other issues, especially when the doctrine of the baptism with the Spirit is distorted. For example, some Christians hold that the Spirit's baptism only comes at some time subsequent to conversion. Others say that this later Spirit baptism is necessary before a person can be fully used of God. Still others contend that the baptism with the Spirit is always accompanied with the outward sign of a particular gift, and that unless this sign is present the person has not been baptized with the Spirit.

I must admit that at times I have really wanted to believe this distinctive teaching. I, too, have wanted an "experience." But I want every experience to be biblically based. The biblical truth, it seems to me, is that we are baptized into the body of Christ by the Spirit at conversion. This is the only Spirit baptism. At this time we can and should be filled with the Holy Spirit, and afterward, be refilled, and even filled unto all fullness. As has often been said, "One baptism, but many fillings." I do not see from Scripture that this filling by the Holy Spirit constitutes a second baptism, nor do I see that speaking in tongues is a necessary accompaniment of being filled with the Spirit.

Sometimes these different opinions are really only differences in semantics. As we shall see in the next chapter, what some people call the baptism of the Spirit may really be what the Scripture calls the filling of the Spirit, which may take place many times in our lives after our conversion.

There are, incidentally, only seven passages in the New Testament which speak directly of the baptism with the Spirit. Five of these passages refer to the baptism with the Spirit as a future event; four were spoken by John the Baptist (Matt. 3:11; Mark 1:7, 8; Luke 3:16; and John 1:33) and one was spoken by Jesus after His resurrection (Acts 1:4, 5). A sixth passage looks back to the events and experiences of the day of Pentecost (Acts 11:15–17) as fulfilling the promises spoken by John the Baptist and Jesus. Only one passage— 1 Corinthians 12:13—speaks about the wider experience of all believers.

During my ministry I have known many Christians who agonized, labored, struggled, and prayed to "get the Spirit." I used to wonder if I had been wrong in thinking that having been baptized by the Spirit into the body of Christ on the day of my conversion I needed no other baptism. But the longer I have studied the Scriptures the more I have become convinced that I was right. Let's trace out what God did in Christ's passion week, and fifty days later at Pentecost, to see that we need not seek what God has already given every believer.

Calvary and Pentecost

When Jesus died on the cross, He bore our sins: "God sending his own Son in the likeness of sinful flesh, and for sin, condemned sin in the flesh" (Rom. 8:3 KJV).

Isaiah prophesied, "The Lord hath laid on him the iniquity of us all" (Isa. 53:6 KJV). Paul said, "He hath made him to be sin for us, who knew no sin" (2 Cor. 5:21 KJV). This made the holy Jesus represent sin for the whole world.

Quite clearly Jesus did not say that His death on the cross would mark the cessation of His ministry. The night before His death He repeatedly told the disciples that He would send the Holy Spirit.

The night before He was to die, He told His disciples, "It is expedient for you that I go away: for if I go not away, the Comforter will not come unto you; but if I depart, I will send him unto you" (John 16:7 KJV). Before He could send the Holy Spirit, who is the Comforter, Jesus had to go away: first, to the death of the cross; then to the resurrection; then, to the ascension into heaven. Only then could He send the Holy Spirit on the day of Pentecost. And after His death and resurrection He commanded them to remain in Jerusalem to await the gift of the Spirit, "Tarry ye in the city . . . until ye be endued with power from on high" (Luke 24:49 KJV). Before He ascended He told them to stay in Jerusalem until they were "baptized with the Holy Spirit not many days hence" (Acts 1:5 KJV).

That's why John the Baptist proclaimed the twofold mission of Christ: first, he proclaimed the ministry of Christ as "the Lamb of God, which taketh away the sin of the world" (John 1:29 KJV); second, he predicted that Christ's ministry at Calvary would be followed by His ministry through baptism with the Holy Spirit (John 1:33).

When Christ rose from the dead this baptism with the Spirit that was to signify the new age still lay in the future; but it was to occur fifty days after the resurrection.

Ten days after the ascension, Pentecost dawned. The promise was fulfilled. The Holy Spirit came on 120 disciples. A little later when Peter was explaining it to a much larger crowd, he referred to the gift as "the gift of the Holy Spirit." He urged his audience, "Repent, and be baptized . . . and ye shall receive the gift of the Holy Spirit" (Acts 2:38 KJV).

John Stott reminds us, "The 3,000 do not seem to have experienced the same miraculous phenomena (the rushing mighty wind, the tongues of flame, or the speech in foreign languages). At least nothing is said about these things. Yet because of God's assurance through Peter they must have inherited the same promise and received the same gift (verses 33, 39). Nevertheless, there was this difference between them: the 120 were regenerate already, and received the baptism of the Spirit only after waiting upon God for ten days. The 3,000 on the other hand were unbelievers, and received the forgiveness of their sins and the gift of the Spirit simultaneously—and it happened immediately they repented and believed, without any need to wait.

"This distinction between the two companies, the 120 and the 3,000, is of great importance, because the *norm* for today must surely be the second group, the 3,000, and not (as is often supposed) the first. The fact that the experience of the 120 was in two distinct stages was due simply to historical circumstances. They could not have received the Pentecostal gift before Pentecost. But those historical circumstances have long since ceased to exist. We live after the event of Pentecost, like the 3,000. With us, therefore, as with them, the forgiveness of sins and the 'gift' or 'baptism' of the Spirit are received together."[1]

From that day onward, the Holy Spirit has lived in the hearts of all true believers, beginning with the 120 disciples who received Him at Pentecost. When they received the Holy Spirit, He united them by His indwelling presence into one body—the mystical body of Christ, which is the Church. That is why when I hear terms like "ecumenicity," or "ecumenical movement," I say to myself: an ecumenicity already exists if we have been born again. We are all united by the Holy Spirit who dwells within our hearts whether we are Presbyterian, Methodist, Baptist, Pentecostal, Catholic, Lutheran, or Anglican.

There were, it is true, several other occasions recorded in the Book of Acts which were similar to Pentecost, such as the so-called "Samaritan Pentecost" (Acts 8:14–17) and the conversion of Cornelius (Acts 10:44–48). Each of these, however, marked a new stage in the expansion of the Church. Samaritans were a mixed race, scorned by many as unworthy of the love of God. Their baptism by the Spirit was a clear sign that they too could be part of God's people by faith in Jesus Christ. Cornelius was a Gentile, and his conversion marked still another step in the spread of the Gospel. The baptism of the Spirit which came to him and his household showed conclusively that God's love extended to the Gentiles as well.

In view of all this, no Christian need strive, wait, or "pray through to get the Spirit." He has received Him already, not as a result of struggle and work, agonizing and prayer, but as an unmerited and unearned gift of grace.

W. Graham Scroggie once said something like this at Keswick, "On the day of Pentecost all believers were, by the baptism of the

Spirit, constituted the body of Christ, and since then every separate believer, every soul accepting Christ in simple faith, has in that moment and by that act been made partaker of the blessing of the baptism. It is not therefore a blessing which the believer is to seek and receive subsequent to the hour of his conversion."

Three Possible Exceptions Explained

I have just suggested that all believers have the Holy Spirit, who comes to dwell within them at the time of their regeneration or conversion. However, some have urged that the Book of Acts gives us several examples of people who did not receive the Holy Spirit when they first believed. Instead, some contend, these incidents indicate that a baptism with the Spirit occurs subsequent to our incorporation into the body of Christ. Three passages are of particular interest at this point. Personally I found these passages difficult to understand when I was a young Christian (and to some extent I still do) and I know many people have had the same experience. I would not pretend to have all the answers to the questions raised by these passages, but my own study has led me to some observations which might be helpful.

The first passage is found in Acts 8 where Philip's trip to Samaria is recounted. He preached Christ and performed a number of miracles. The Samaritans were emotionally stirred. Many of them professed faith and were baptized. The apostles in Jerusalem were so concerned about what was happening in Samaria that they sent two of their leaders, Peter and John, to investigate. They found a great stir and a readiness to receive the Holy Spirit. "Then they began laying their hands on them, and they were receiving the Holy Spirit" (Acts 8:17).

As we compare Scripture with Scripture, we immediately discover one extraordinary feature in this passage: When Philip preached in Samaria, it was the first time the gospel had been proclaimed outside Jerusalem, evidently because Samaritans and Jews had always been bitter enemies. This gives us the clue to the reason the Spirit was withheld till Peter and John came: It was so they might see for themselves that God received even hated Samaritans who believed in Christ. There could now be no question of it.

Notice too what happened when the Spirit of the Lord suddenly removed Philip, taking him down to Gaza where he witnessed to the Ethiopian eunuch. When the Ethiopian believed and received Christ, he was baptized with water. But at no time did Philip lay hands on him and pray for him to receive the Holy Spirit, nor was anything said about a second baptism. Thus the situation in Samaria as recounted in Acts 8 was unique and does not fit with other passages of Scripture as we compare Scripture with Scripture.

A second passage that gives some people difficulty deals with the conversion of Saul on the road to Damascus as recorded in Acts 9. Some say that when he was later filled with the Spirit in the presence of Ananias (v. 17), he experienced a second baptism of the Spirit.

Here again the situation is unique. God had chosen this persecutor of the Christians "to bear My name before the Gentiles and kings and the sons of Israel" (v. 15). When Saul called Jesus "Lord," he used a term that can mean "my very own lord," signifying his conversion, or simply "Sir," a title of respect rather than a confession of faith. We do know that later Ananias called Paul "brother," as most of our English translations phrase it (v. 17). But here again, most of the Jews of that day called each other "brother." He might have been calling Saul a brother in the sense that American black people often refer to each other as "brother."

In other words, when did Saul's regeneration take place? Was it on the Damascus road, or could it have been over a period of three days of witnessing by Ananias (which would cover the period of Saul's blindness)? I am convinced that the new birth is often like natural birth: the moment of conception, nine months of gestation, and then birth. Sometimes it takes weeks of conviction by the Holy Spirit. I've seen people in our crusades come forward more than once, and not experience the assurance of their salvation until the third or fourth time. When were they regenerated? Only God the Holy Spirit knows; it might have been at baptism or confirmation and they came forward for assurance. It may be that some are coming (as I sometimes have said) to "re-confirm their confirmation."

Furthermore, Acts 9:17 says Paul is to be filled with the Holy Spirit. The verse does not use the word baptism, and when he was filled it does not say he spoke in other tongues. My point is that even if Paul was regenerated on the Damascus road, his later filling is not presented as a second baptism. And possibly his regeneration did not occur until Ananias came to him. So the passage does not teach that Paul was baptized twice with the Spirit.

A third text that has given rise to some controversy is Acts 19: 1–7. Paul visited Ephesus and found twelve professing disciples who had not received the Holy Spirit. On reading this passage the question immediately arises: Were these twelve people true Christians before their meeting with Paul? They seemed to be ignorant about the Holy Spirit and Jesus. Also they talked about John's baptism. Certainly, Paul did not reckon their earlier baptism sufficient grounds for calling them believers. He had them undergo water baptism in the name of Christ.

Probably thousands of people had heard John or Jesus during the previous few years. John's baptism had made a deep impression on them, but during the intervening period of time they probably had lost all contact with the teachings of both John and Jesus. Thus, again we have a unique situation. The very fact that the apostle asked such searching questions would indicate that he doubted the genuineness of their conversion experience.

However, we must still deal with Acts 19:6: "And when Paul had laid his hands upon them, the Holy Spirit came on them; and they began speaking with tongues and prophesying." Dr. Merrill Tenney calls them "belated believers." The interesting thing is that all these events took place simultaneously. Whether the tongues spoken of here were the tongues to which Paul refers in 1 Corinthians 14, or Luke speaks about at Pentecost, we are not told. The word "prophesying" here carries with it the idea of testimony or proclamation. Apparently they went about telling their friends how they had come to believe in Jesus Christ. In my thinking, this does not suggest a second baptism with the Spirit subsequent to a baptism with the Spirit at regeneration. Rather, it appears that they were regenerated and baptized with the Spirit at the same time.

To summarize, it is my belief that Pentecost instituted the Church. Then all that remained was for Samaritans, Gentiles and "belated believers" to be brought into the Church representatively. This occurred in Acts 8 for Samaritans, Acts 10 for Gentiles (according to Acts 11:15), and Acts 19 for belated believers from

John's baptism. Once this representative baptism with the Spirit had occurred, the normal pattern applied—baptism with the Spirit at the time each person (of whatever background) believed on Jesus Christ.

Our Share in Pentecost

Pentecost was an event then which included not only those who participated at that moment but also those who would participate in the centuries ahead. Perhaps we can use the atonement here by way of analogy. Christ died once for all; He died for members of His body who were not yet born or regenerated. Thus, you and I became members of His body by regeneration through the one-time shedding of His blood. So also you and I in similar fashion now participate in the new reality, the Church. What was formed by the baptism with the Spirit at Pentecost is, on our part, entered into when we were made to "drink of one Spirit" (1 Cor. 12:13) so that each believer comes into the benefits of it at the moment of his regeneration even as, at the same time, he comes into the benefits of the shed blood of Jesus for justification. So the Lord adds to the Church those who are being saved (Acts 2:47).

It may sound strange to speak of present-day believers as sharing in an event that took place 2,000 years ago. However, the Bible offers many examples similar to those of the atonement and the baptism with the Spirit. In Amos 2:10 (KJV), God said to His erring people, "I brought *you* up from the land of Egypt, and led you forty years through the wilderness" (italics mine), although the people whom the prophet addressed lived hundreds of years after the Exodus. The fact is that the nation was regarded as one and continuous; and so it is with the Church.

One Baptism and Regeneration

Since the baptism with the Spirit occurs at the time of regeneration, Christians are never told in Scripture to seek it. I am convinced that many of the things some teachers have joined to baptism with the Holy Spirit really belong to the fullness of the Spirit. Thus, the purpose of the baptism with the Holy Spirit is to bring the new Christian into the body of Christ. No interval of time falls between regeneration and baptism with the Spirit. The moment we received Jesus Christ as Lord and Savior we received the Holy Spirit. He came to live in our hearts. "Any one who does not have the Spirit of Christ does not belong to him," said Paul in Romans 8:9 (RSV). It is not a second blessing, or third, or fourth. There are and will be and should be *new fillings*—but not *new baptisms.*

Nowhere in the New Testament is there a command to be baptized with the Holy Spirit. Surely if baptism with the Spirit were a necessary step in our Christian lives, the New Testament would be full of it. Christ Himself would have commanded it. But we are not commanded as Christians to seek something that has already taken place. Thus, when I was asked as a young Bible school student in Florida if I had received the baptism of the Spirit, it was correct for me to respond that I had already received it at the moment of my conversion.

The Unity of the Spirit

In 1 Corinthians 12:13, the apostle Paul writes, "For by one Spirit we were all baptized into one body—Jews or Greeks, slaves or free—and all were made to drink of one Spirit" (RSV). Paul has been talking about the need for *unity* in the disobedient and carnal Corinthian church. David Howard says: "Notice the emphasis in these phrases: 'the same Spirit' (vv. 4, 8, 9); 'one Spirit' (vv. 9, 13. . .); 'one and the same Spirit' (v. 11); 'the same Lord' (v. 5);. . . 'the body is one' (v. 12); 'one body' (v. 12, 13); 'there are many parts, yet one body' (v. 20); 'that there may be no discord in the body' (v. 25)."[2]

Howard later continues, "In this context of unity Paul says, 'For by one Spirit we were all baptized into one body—Jews or Greeks, slaves or free—and all were made to drink of one Spirit.' John R. W. Stott [*The Baptism and Fullness of the Holy Spirit*, p. 22] points out in this connection, 'So the baptism of the Spirit in this verse, far from being a dividing factor . . . is the great uniting factor.'"[3]

The Conclusion of the Matter

This much all Christians are agreed upon: Every true believer must be baptized by the Spirit into the body of Christ. Beyond that opinions differ significantly, however. But even here we should never forget a crucial area of agreement.

To see it, we must first recall that we all believe salvation is past, present, and future: We *have been saved* (justification), we *are being saved* (sanctification), and we *will be saved* (glorification). Between the time we are justified and the time when we shall be glorified falls that period in our pilgrim journey we call sanctification.

This has to do with holiness. And holiness proceeds from the work of the Spirit in our hearts. Whatever may be our differences about a second Spirit baptism, tongues, and Spirit-filling, all Christians are agreed that we should seek after *holiness*—without which no man shall see the Lord. Let us, therefore, seek ardently the kind of life that reflects the beauty of Jesus and marks us as being what saints (in the best sense of that word) ought to be!

How does this kind of life come? It comes as we are filled with the Holy Spirit—as He works in and through us as we are yielded to God and His will. It is to this subject of the filling of the Spirit that we must now turn in the next chapter.

6

The Seal, the Pledge,
and the Witness
of the Holy Spirit

AN ENGLISH MISSIONARY died in India in the early part of this century. Immediately after his death his former neighbors broke into his house and started carrying away his possessions. The English Consul was notified, and since there was no lock on the door of the missionary's house, he pasted a piece of paper across it and affixed the seal of England on it. The looters did not dare break the seal because the world's most powerful nation stood behind it.

The sealing of the Holy Spirit is one of a series of events that take place simultaneously, of which we may not even be aware, the moment we repent of our sins and receive Christ as Savior. First, of course, God regenerated and justified us. Second, the Holy Spirit baptized us into the body of Christ. Third, the Holy Spirit took up His abode in our hearts immediately. Several other events accompanying our salvation, together with His continuing work in us, are the focus of this and the next chapters.

The Seal

The fourth event is what the Bible calls "the Seal." It translates a Greek word that means to confirm or to impress. This word is used three times in the New Testament in connection with believers. It is also mentioned in the life of Jesus. John says that "on Him [Jesus] the Father, even God, has set His seal" (John 6:27). Here we see that the Father sealed the Son.

At the moment of conversion, however, believers are sealed with the Spirit for the day of redemption: "Having also believed, you were sealed in Him with the Holy Spirit of promise" (Eph. 1:13; cf. 4:30).

It seems to me that Paul had two main thoughts in mind concerning our sealing by the Holy Spirit. One concerns security, and the other, ownership. Sealing in the sense of security is illustrated in the Old Testament when the king sealed Daniel into the lion's den so that he could not get out. Also, in ancient times, as when Esther was queen (Esth. 8:8), the king often used his own ring to affix his mark or seal to letters and documents written in his name. Once he had done this, no one could reverse or countermand what he had written.

Pilate did much the same when he ordered the soldiers to secure the tomb of Jesus. He said, "'You have a guard; go, make it as secure as you know how.' And they went and made the grave secure, and along with the guard they set a seal on the stone" (Matt. 27:65, 66). "Seal" in this passage is the same Greek word used in passages which speak of the sealing of the Holy Spirit. A. T. Robertson says that the sealing of the stone was "probably by a cord stretched across the stone and sealed at each end as in Dan. 6:17. The sealing was done in the presence of the Roman guard who were left in charge to protect this stamp of Roman authority and power."[1] In an even more meaningful way, when the Holy Spirit seals us or puts His mark on us, we are secure in Christ.

One of the most thrilling thoughts that has ever crossed my mind is that the Holy Spirit sealed me. And He has sealed you— if you are a believer.

Nothing can touch you. "For I am convinced that neither death, nor life, nor angels, nor principalities, nor things present, nor things to come, nor powers, nor height, nor depth, nor any other created thing, shall be able to separate us from the love of God, which is in Christ Jesus our Lord" (Rom. 8:38, 39).

Yet this sealing with the Holy Spirit signifies more than security. It also means ownership. In the Old Testament we read that Jeremiah bought a piece of property, paid for it in front of witnesses, and sealed the purchase according to the Law and custom (Jer. 32:10). He was now the owner.

The allusion to the seal as the proof of purchase would have been especially significant to the Ephesians. The city of Ephesus was a seaport, and the shipmasters of the neighboring ports carried on an extensive trade in timber. The method of purchase was this: the merchant, after selecting his timber, stamped it with his own signet—an acknowledged sign of ownership. In due time the merchant would send a trusted agent with the signet; he would locate all the timbers that bore the corresponding impress, and claim them. Matthew Henry sums it up: "By him [the Holy Spirit] believers are sealed; that is, separated and set apart for God, and distinguished and marked as belonging to him."[2] You and I are God's property forever!

The Pledge

As we trust in Christ, God gives us the Spirit not only as a seal, however. He is also our pledge, or, as some translations read, "earnest," according to such passages as 2 Corinthians 1:22 and Ephesians 1:14.

"Now He who establishes us with you in Christ and anointed us is God, who also sealed us and gave us the Spirit in our hearts as a pledge" (2 Cor. 1:21, 22).

In the apostle Paul's day, businessmen considered a pledge to do three things: it was a down payment that sealed a bargain, it represented an obligation to buy, and it was a sample of what was to come.

Suppose you were to decide to buy a car. The pledge would first be a down payment sealing the transaction. It would also represent an obligation to buy the car. And it would be a sample of what was to come—the remaining portion of the selling price.

The Holy Spirit likewise seals God's purchase of us. And His presence shows God's sense of obligation to redeem us completely. Perhaps best of all, the presence of the Holy Spirit, living in fellowship with us, provides us with a foretaste, a sample, of our coming life and inheritance in God's presence.

In Numbers 13 when the spies of Israel set out to scout the land of Canaan, they reached it at the time of the first ripe grapes. They came to "the valley of Eshcol and from there cut down a branch with a single cluster of grapes" (Num. 13:23). This they brought back with them for the people of Israel to see. The cluster of grapes was the pledge of their inheritance. It was a small foretaste of what lay before them in the Promised Land. This was God's pledge that as they moved forward in faith, they would receive in full what they now had only in part.

Recently, one of New York's leading grocery stores exhibited a basket of choice and beautiful grapes in the window. A notice appeared above the basket announcing: "A whole carload like this sample basket is expected in a few days." The grapes were a "pledge" of what was to come. The firstfruits are but a handful compared with the whole harvest; so, reasoning from the known to the unknown, we ask with the hymnwriter:

> "What will Thy presence be,
> If such a life of joy can crown
> Our walk on earth with Thee?"

The New Testament refers to the pledge of the Spirit three times:

1. "[God] also sealed us and gave us the Spirit in our hearts as a pledge" (2 Cor. 1:22). Here the Spirit's presence in our lives is God's pledge that He will fulfill His promise.

2. "Now He who prepared us for this very purpose is God, who gave to us the Spirit as a pledge" (2 Cor. 5:5). The context here suggests that the Spirit in our lives is God's pledge that we shall receive spiritual bodies at Christ's coming.

3. "[The Holy Spirit] is given as a pledge of our inheritance, with a view to the redemption of God's own possession, to the praise of His glory" (Eph. 1:14). Here the Spirit is God's pledge guaranteeing our inheritance until the future brings the total redemption of those who are God's possession.

In summary, we can say that when we are baptized into the body of Christ, the Spirit enters our lives and by His presence seals us. He is God's pledge assuring us of our inheritance to come.

The conclusion of the matter has been graphically expressed by Matthew Henry: "The earnest [this is the King James version's word for 'pledge'] is part of payment, and it secures the full sum: so is the gift of the Holy Ghost; all his influences and operations, both as a sanctifier and a comforter, are heaven begun, glory in the seed and bud. The Spirit's illumination is an earnest [pledge] of everlasting light; sanctification is an earnest of perfect holiness; and his comforts are earnests of everlasting joys. He is said to be the earnest, *until the redemption of the purchased possession.* It may be called here the possession, because this earnest makes it as sure to the heirs as though they were already possessed of it; and it is purchased for them by the blood of Christ. The redemption of it is mentioned because it was mortgaged and forfeited by sin; and Christ restores it to us, and so is said to redeem it, in allusion to the law of redemption."[3]

The Witness of the Spirit

Not only is the Holy Spirit our seal and our pledge, but He is also our witness within, assuring us of the reality of our salvation in Jesus Christ.

Jesus personally spoke to His disciples and provided them with assurance when He was with them. In like manner the Holy Spirit witnesses to and in the hearts of all true believers. Several passages in the New Testament touch on this subject.

First, the Scripture teaches us the Holy Spirit is a witness to the finality and sufficiency of Jesus Christ's atonement for us. We find this in Hebrews 10:15–17, where the writer contrasts the ineffectiveness of the oft-repeated Levitical sacrifices with the sacrifice of Christ, which was offered *one* for all and *once* for all. Our conscience could never be finally relieved of its burden of sin by the continual animal sacrifices. But on the other hand, "by one offering He [Jesus Christ] has perfected for all time those who are sanctified. And the Holy Spirit also bears witness to us" (Heb. 10:14, 15). It is a witness linked to Jeremiah 31, "I will forgive their iniquity, and their sin I will remember no more" (v. 34). Since this witness to us is engraved in the written Word of God that never varies, its comfort relieves us of our fears through all the changing scenes of time.

Second, the Scripture also teaches us the Holy Spirit witnesses that we have become, by faith in Jesus Christ and His work on the cross, the children of God. "The Spirit Himself bears witness with our spirit that we are children of God" (Rom. 8:16). We have not only been saved and baptized into the body of Christ, but we have been adopted into the family of God. "And because you are sons, God has sent forth the Spirit of His Son into our hearts, crying, 'Abba! Father!' Therefore you are no longer a slave, but a son; and if a son, then an heir through God" (Gal. 4:6, 7). Because we are declared sons of God by the Spirit's witness we can cry out from our hearts, "Abba, Father." This is the Magna Charta of the Christian's liberation from the power of sin to the privileges and wealth of Christ. The fact of our sonship is repeatedly declared. Each day you and I should sing, "I am a child of the King."

C. S. Lewis wrote this about the Christian's personal relationship with God: "To put ourselves thus on a personal footing with God could, in itself and without warrant, be nothing but presumption and illusion. But we are taught that it is not; that it is God who gives us that footing. For it is by the Holy Spirit that we cry 'Father.' By unveiling, by confessing our sins and 'making known' our requests, we assume the high rank of persons before Him. And He, descending, becomes a Person to us.'"

Thus, by the Holy Spirit the Christian has a witness within himself. "The one who believes in the Son of God has the witness in himself" (1 John 5:10). Our sins and iniquities are remembered against us no more. We have been adopted into the heavenly family. The Spirit bears witness that as believers in the Lord Jesus Christ we have eternal life.

Finally, the Scripture teaches us the Holy Spirit witnesses to the truth of every promise God has given us in His Word. The Spirit, who inspired the written Word of God, also works in our hearts to assure us that its promises are true, and that they are for us. We know Christ is our Savior, because the Bible tells us this and the Spirit assures us it is true. We know we have become children of God because the Bible tells us this and the Spirit again assures us it is true. "But when He, the Spirit of truth, comes, He will guide you into all the truth" (John 16:13). "Thy word is truth" (John 17:17). Sometimes I speak with people who tell me they are lacking the assurance of their salvation. When I inquire further, I often find they have been neglecting the Word of God. "And the witness is this, that God has given us eternal life, and this life is in His Son. He who has the Son has the life; he who does not have the Son of God does not have the life. These things I have *written* to you who believe in the name of the Son of God, in order *that you may know that you have eternal life*" (1 John 5:11–13, italics mine).

The Spirit therefore witnesses in our hearts, convincing us of the truth of God's presence and assurance. This is something often difficult to explain to an unbeliever, but countless believers know of the Spirit's assurance in their hearts.

John Wesley, the founder of the Methodist church, once observed, "It is hard to find words in the language of men, to explain the deep things of God. Indeed, there are none that will adequately express what the Spirit of God works in His children. But . . . by the testimony of the Spirit, I mean, an inward impression on the soul, whereby the Spirit of God immediately and directly witnesses to my spirit, that I am a child of God; that Jesus Christ hath loved me, and given Himself for me; that all my sins are blotted out, and I, even I, am reconciled to God."[5]

We can see then that God places a *seal* on us when we receive Christ. And that seal is a person—the Holy Spirit. By the Spirit's presence God gives us security and establishes His ownership over us.

Further, the Spirit is God's *pledge.* He not only seals the arrangement, but He represents God's voluntary obligation to see us through. And fellowship with the Spirit is a sample of what we can expect when we come into our inheritance in heaven.

Finally, the Spirit *witnesses* to us by His Word and within our hearts that Christ died for us, and by faith in Him we have become God's children. What a wonderful thing to know the Holy Spirit has been given to us as a seal—a pledge—and a witness! May each of these give us new assurance of God's love for us, and give us confidence as we seek to live for Christ. And with the apostle Paul may we say, "Thanks be to God for His indescribable gift!" (2 Cor. 9:15).

7

The Christian's Inner Struggle

AN ESKIMO FISHERMAN came to town every Saturday afternoon. He always brought his two dogs with him. One was white and the other was black. He had taught them to fight on command. Every Saturday afternoon in the town square the people would gather and these two dogs would fight and the fisherman would take bets. On one Saturday the black dog would win; another Saturday, the white dog would win—but the fisherman always won! His friends began to ask him how he did it. He said, "I starve one and feed the other. The one I feed always wins because he is stronger."

One or Two Natures?

This story about the two dogs is apt because it tells us something about the inner warfare that comes into the life of a person who is born again.

We have two natures within us, both struggling for mastery. Which one will dominate us? It depends on which one we feed. If we feed our spiritual lives and allow the Holy Spirit to empower us, He will have rule over us. If we starve our spiritual natures and instead feed the old, sinful nature, the flesh will dominate.

Every Christian can identify with the apostle Paul when he said, "For that which I am doing, I do not understand; for I am not practicing what I would like to do, but I am doing the very thing I hate. . . . I find then the principle that evil is present in me . . . but I see a different law in the members of my body, waging war against the law of my mind, and making me a prisoner of the law of sin which is in my members" (Rom. 7:15, 21, 23).

Many young Christians have said things like this to me from time to time: "Since I became a Christian, I have had struggles within that I never had before. I didn't know I was such a sinner! I never wanted to sin like this before. I thought God had saved me from my sins!"

Actually, strange as it may seem, this condition is something to be thankful for. It is an evidence that the Holy Spirit has come into your life, illuminating the darkness of sin, sensitizing your conscience to sin, awakening in you a new desire to be clean and free from sin before God. Those old sins were there before. Those old temptations were there strongly before, but they didn't appear evil to you then. But now the Holy Spirit has come into your life. You are a new person, born again by this same Spirit. And everything looks different now.

The Struggle within

Now you have become keenly aware of the basic problem in a Christian's life, the struggle with sin. In the New Testament the apostle Paul talks of every Christian being in an intense spiritual battle: "For our struggle is not against flesh and blood, but against the rulers, against the powers, against the world forces of this darkness, against the spiritual forces of wickedness in the heavenly places" (Eph. 6:12). So there are external spiritual forces which are at work in this world, seeking to keep us from God and His will. But we must not always blame Satan for everything that goes wrong or every sin we commit. Often it is our own sinful nature which is at work within us. "For the flesh sets its desire against the Spirit, and the Spirit against the flesh; for these are in opposition to one another, so that you may not do the things that you please" (Gal. 5:17).

And this is not just external to us. This battle goes on inside of us. And that's the theme of Romans 7, especially verses 7 through

25. Look at Romans 7:7 and 8, for example. (Read it in a good modern translation of the Bible.) Let me paraphrase what Paul is saying:

Before I heard the law of God and the good news of salvation, I didn't know covetousness was sin, but then I heard the tenth commandment, "Thou shalt not covet." God's law showed me this sin in my heart, and I suddenly became keenly aware how much covetousness was a live, writhing evil within me. And I realized how great a sinner I was, doomed to die—but for Christ! As a Christian I began to fight this evil desire in me. And what a struggle! I tried to stop coveting and envying, but I couldn't.

That's the picture, and I'm sure you have often felt just as Paul did. Maybe your sin is wrong sexual desires, pride, gluttony, laziness, or anger, or some other besetting sin (Heb. 12:1 KJV). But you feel the same inner struggle. Sometimes you conclude just as Paul did in Romans 7:22–24 which I quoted above.

But don't stop there! Note Paul's glorious conclusion in verse 25 and 8:2 (there were no chapter divisions in Paul's original letter!): "Thanks be to God through Jesus Christ our Lord! . . . For the law of the Spirit of life in Christ Jesus has set you free from the law of sin and of death." As a great saint said many years ago, "Sin no longer reigns, but it still fights!"

Horatius Bonar was a brilliant theologian, a great saint, and a compassionate pastor. He died at the age of 33, but not before a great revival had taken place in his church in Scotland. His sermons and books have blessed God's people for the last 150 years. He spoke honestly for all of us when he said: "While conversion calms one kind of storm it raises another, which is to be lifelong."[1] Efforts to explain this struggle by theologians have gone on for centuries. Some have taken Paul's words and spoken of the "two natures" in the Christian—the "old man" and the "new man." This terminology comes from such passages as Ephesians 4:22–24 where Paul says, "That, in reference to your former manner of life, you lay aside the *old self*, which is being corrupted in accordance with the lusts of deceit . . . and put on the *new self*, which in the likeness of God has been created in righteousness and holiness of the truth" (italics mine).

Speaking of this in the footnote on that passage, *The New Scofield Reference Bible* says, "The 'new man' is the regenerate man as distinguished from the old man . . . and is a new man as having become a partaker of the divine nature and life . . . in no sense the old man made over, or improved."[2] In a footnote on Romans 7:15, Scofield continues, "The apostle personifies the struggle of the two natures within the believer—the old or Adamic nature, and the divine nature received through the new birth."[3]

How can we visualize and understand what is going on inside of us? I think Romans 8:1–13 describes it best. Let me try to paraphrase what Paul is saying here, and let me put it in the first person—this is how it applies to me:

I was born in sin. For years I was controlled by sin and didn't know it. I was literally "dead in trespasses and sin" (Eph. 2:1). Then I heard the Word of God, the law and the Gospel. I was convicted. I saw my sins for the first time. I accepted Christ. And now the law of God is speaking to me every day through the Word of God.

Now I have become conscious of sins I didn't know I had. Sometimes I despair (like Paul in Romans 7:24: "Wretched man that I am!"), but, praise the Lord, I know now there is no condemnation anybody can bring against me because I am in Christ (Rom. 8:1). Christ has set me free from the law of sin and death (Rom. 8:2). I am still me—with my old sinful personality and nature, sinful habits that have grown strong in the many years before I was a Christian. But now the Holy Spirit has come into my life. He shows me my sin. He actually condemns the sin in me (Rom. 8:3). And by His power He helps me to meet the requirements of God's law (Rom. 8:4).

If I keep thinking about my old life and my sins, I will go back to that life. The old "me" will continue to sin. But if I put my mind on Christ and try to listen and obey the Holy Spirit (Rom. 8:5), the Holy Spirit will give me life and peace (Rom. 8:6). If a man is a Christian, he has the Holy Spirit (Rom. 8:9). His spirit has been made alive (Rom. 8:10). The Holy Spirit is giving life to his body, bringing it back from the deadness of sin (Rom. 8:11) and bringing abundant new life in Christ.

The Two Natures

God uses many strong figures of speech to describe what the Holy Spirit does for us throughout the Bible. We have already noticed this in John 3. He says we are "born again" by the Holy

Spirit. This is clearly an illustration to describe, in physical terms, a great spiritual truth. And here in regard to our Christian life in Romans 7 and 8 and in Ephesians 4, God uses psychological terms—"new nature . . . old nature" or "new man and old man"— to try to make us understand the radical change that takes place in our Christian life when we are controlled by the Holy Spirit.

We consciously feel that we are just one person. When I have sinned, deep down I know that I did it. I felt the pull of temptation. I responded and at some point willed to sin. At some point I said "Yes" to the devil as he tempted me through my old habits, my old desires, my old motives, or appealed to my old goals in life. This is what Paul means in talking about the "old nature" or the sin principle. But it is really me. I am one person before God. I am responsible for my sins. I can't blame the sin principle that still lives within. I have a choice either to yield to the Spirit—the new impetus in my life—or the old force of sin.

But now the Holy Spirit has come into my heart. He has given me new life—God's quality of eternal life. And He Himself is in me to break the old habits, to purify my motives, to set my eyes on new goals, especially the goal of becoming like the Lord Jesus Christ (Rom. 8:29).

So for the rest of my Christian life until Christ comes and calls me home, I am being sanctified (growing more and more into spiritual maturity) by the Holy Spirit through the Word of God. Best of all, the Holy Spirit is daily, quietly making me to be conformed more and more to the Lord Jesus Christ if I am cooperating with Him: "But we all, with unveiled face beholding as in a mirror the glory of the Lord, are being transformed into the same image from glory to glory, just as from the Lord, the Spirit" (2 Cor. 3:18).

But never forget there will always be a struggle, both without and within. The devil is an implacable enemy. He never gives up. Through "the world" and the flesh, he appeals to the old force within me to reassert itself. He appeals to my lusts, my covetousness, and my pride, just as he did to Eve and Adam (Gen. 3). I will always feel the pull of temptation. My old tendencies will be awakened and will want to sin. *But* I have the Holy Spirit within me, a more powerful principle or force: "Greater is He who is in you than he who is in the world" (1 John 4:4). If I cooperate with

Him and turn to Him for help, He will give me the power to resist temptation. He will make me stronger as a result of every test.

Perhaps the next time the devil will appeal to a different weakness in *"the flesh."* I have a different set of temptations. But the Holy Spirit is always in my heart to give me victory over this new struggle, and as I win victory after victory I get stronger. Dr. Bonar says that God recognizes the saint's inner conflict "as an indispensable process of discipline, as a development of the contrast between light and darkness, as an exhibition of the way in which God is glorified in the infirmities of His saints, and in their contests with the powers of evil."[4]

In Romans 7 Paul is not saying he cannot help but sin because of his old nature which he can't control. Rather, Paul is describing the struggle all of us are going to have and telling us we can have victory in Christ by the power of His Holy Spirit that lives within us (Rom. 8:4).

Sanctification

The word sanctification comes from the Greek word which means "to be separate" or "set apart for a purpose." Paul speaks of the believer as having been "sanctified by the Holy Spirit" (Rom. 15:16). He wrote to the Corinthians saying that they, *having been sanctified*, are called to be saints (1 Cor. 1: 2). We Christians are to be "progressively sanctified" or "made righteous" in holiness as we daily abide in Christ—and obey His Word. Abiding and obedience are the keys to a successful Spirit-dominated life. We are as much sanctified as we are possessed by the Holy Spirit. It is never a question of how much you and I have of the Spirit, but how much He has of us.

The Scriptures teach that "sanctification" has *three parts* to it. *First*, the moment you receive Christ there is an immediate sanctification. *Second*, as we progress in the Christian life there is a "progressive sanctification." *Third*, when we go to heaven there will be total and "complete" sanctification, which is called "glorification."

We have a friend on one of the Caribbean islands who purchased the ruins of an old mansion. In his eyes he sees it as it will someday be, beautiful, restored, perfect. It is "sanctified." In the mean-time, he is working on it with his limited resources, his ingenuity, and his love. To the average beholder it may look like something out of a horror movie, with its scraps of lumber, patched tin roof, fabulous tile floor. But to our friend it is special. Loved. He sees it as it will be someday. Perhaps the world sees the body of Christ (the true Church) as others see this mansion. But God sees it as it will eventually be. Perfect, complete. It is being sanctified. In our friend's eyes, the mansion is already beautiful, because he sees in his mind's eye the finished product. When he begins work on it, it will be in the process of being restored. And someday our friend will complete his work, and the mansion will be in reality what he always hoped it would be.

In a far greater way, God looks on us in Jesus Christ. He sees us now as fully sanctified, because He knows what we will be some day. Also He is at work in us restoring us—we are being sanctified. And some day that process will be complete when we go to be with Him throughout all eternity. We will be fully sanctified.

J. B. Phillips says that God predestinates us "to bear the family likeness of his Son" (Rom. 8:29). That is what is happening to us now as believers. We are being progressively sanctified—to spiritual maturity—to bear the family likeness of His Son. Remember that Jesus Christ was perfect—and we are to strive for perfection. While this will be complete only in heaven, it should be our goal right now. This is what the Bible means when it commands us, "Like the Holy One who called you, be holy yourselves also in all your behavior; because it is written, 'You shall be holy, for I am Holy' " (1 Peter 1:15, 16). Whether we realize it or not we are growing spiritually through the conflicts, turbulence, troubles, temptations, testings, and so on that afflict all Christians slowly or rapidly. But there is coming a day when all of this will be past, and we will be completely sanctified, "We know that, when He appears, we shall be like Him, because we shall see Him just as He is" (1 John 3:2).

In the meantime, Christians, day by day, week by week, and month by month, are told to walk in the Spirit. Walking in the Spirit means being led and directed by the Holy Spirit. This comes as we progressively yield various areas of our lives to the Spirit's control. Paul said, "Walk by the Spirit, and you will not carry out the desire of the flesh" (Gal. 5:16). Now desire in itself is not wrong, it's *what* we desire or lust for that is wrong—and *when* we yield.

The Old Self-Life

When Eve had a desire to "know" (but based on self)—Satan turned healthy desire into unhealthy. And Eve disobeyed God. Flesh is the Bible's word for unperfected human nature. Leaving off the "h" and spelling it in reverse we have the word *self*. Flesh is the self-life: it is what we are when we are left to our own devices. At times our *self* behaves itself very well. It can do good things, it can be moral, and it can have extremely high ethical standards. But sooner or later your self and mine will show itself to be *selfish*.

We try to educate self, to train and discipline it. We pass laws to compel it to behave. But Paul said that the flesh has a mind of its own and that "the natural mind" is not subject to the law of God. God clearly says He has no confidence in our flesh. Paul declared, "I know that nothing good dwells in me, that is, in my flesh" (Rom. 7:18). The moment we realize this and yield to the dictates of the Holy Spirit in our lives, greater victory, greater spiritual maturity, greater love, joy, peace and other fruits will manifest themselves.

Recently, a friend of ours was converted to Christ. He had previously led a wild life. One of his old friends said to him, "I feel sorry for you. You now go to church, pray, and read the Bible all the time. You no longer go to the nightclubs, get drunk, or enjoy your beautiful women." Our friend gave a strange reply. He said, "I do get drunk every time I want to. I do go to nightclubs every time I want to. I do go with the girls when I want to." His worldly friend looked puzzled. Our friend laughed and said, "Jim, you see, the Lord took the *want* out when I was converted and He made me a new person in Christ Jesus."

St. Augustine once said, "Love God and live as you please." If we truly love God we will want to do what pleases Him. It is as the Psalmist says in Psalm 37, "Delight yourself in the Lord; And He will give you the desires of your heart" (v. 4). Delighting in the Lord alters the desires.

The Battle with the Flesh

If we as Christians try to make ourselves better or good or even acceptable to God by some human effort, we will fail. Everything we have and are and do comes through the Holy Spirit. The Holy Spirit has come to dwell in us, and God does His works in us by the Holy Spirit. What we have to do is yield ourselves to the Spirit of God so that He may empower us to put off the old and put on the new.

Paul makes all of this clear in Galatians 5:17, "For the flesh sets its desire against the Spirit, and the Spirit against the flesh; for these are in opposition to one another." This indicates what the real conflict is in the heart of every true believer. The flesh wants one thing and the Spirit wants another. The black dog and the white dog are often fighting. As long as there is not the surrender of mind and body every moment of the day, the old nature will assert itself.

Conscious of my own weakness, sometimes on rising in the morning I have said, "Lord, I'm not going to allow this or that thing to assert itself in my life today." Then the devil sends something unexpected to tempt me, or God allows me to be tested at that exact point. Many times in my life the thing I never meant to do in my mind I did in the flesh. I have wept many a bitter tear of confession and asked God the Spirit to give me strength at that point. But this lets me know that I am engaged in a spiritual warfare every day. I must never let down my guard—I must keep armed.

Many of the young people I meet are living defeated, disillusioned, and disappointed lives even after coming to Christ. They are walking after the flesh because they have not had proper teaching at this precise point. The old man, the old self, the old principle, the old force, is not yet dead or wholly renewed: it is still there. It fights every inch of the way against the new man, the new force, that God made us when we received Christ. Only as we yield and obey the new principle in Christ do we win the victory.

"Yielding" is the secret! Paul said, "I appeal to you therefore, brethren, and beg of you in view of [all] the mercies of God, to make a decisive dedication of your bodies—presenting all your members and faculties—as a living sacrifice, holy (devoted, consecrated) and well pleasing to God, which is your reasonable (rational, intelligent) service and spiritual worship" (Rom. 12:1, *Amplified*). When total surrender occurs, there is another "experience." For most Christians it is not just a second experience—but it comes many times throughout our lives.

The Works of the Flesh

Thus, we see that there is a continuing conflict going on in every one of us between the flesh on the one hand and the Spirit on the other. When Paul uses the word "flesh," he really means human nature in all its weakness, its impotence, and its helplessness. The flesh is the lower side of man's nature. The flesh is all that man is without God and without Christ. Paul lists the works of the flesh in Galatians 5:19–21. When we read this terrible list, we should also read Romans 1:17–32. In these passages the depravity of human nature is pictured for us. We see it for what it is.

Every day we read about this depravity in our newspapers. We watch it on the newscasts on our television screens daily. Everywhere, unregenerate human nature calls the signals and produces the works of the flesh. The sins of the flesh are flaunted shamelessly. They are committed blatantly and without repentance by unregenerate men. However, the Christian can sometimes temporarily yield to one or more of these terrible things. He is immediately convicted by the Holy Spirit and quickly repents and finds forgiveness.

In Galatians 5 there is a catalog of fifteen *works of the flesh* which range from sexual sins to drunkenness and include idolatry and sorcery. What strikes terror in every Christian heart is the knowledge that these sins can easily creep into our lives unless we are spiritually vigilant and strong. "Therefore let him who thinks he stands take heed lest he fall" (I Cor. 10:12). With this in mind, let us look at the list of sins Paul lists in Galatians 5, so we will be better prepared to fight against the flesh.

Some have suggested that these can be divided into three categories, or sets. The first set are sexual immorality, impurity, and sensuality (Gal. 5:19).

1. Immorality. The Greek word here is broad enough to cover all kinds of sexual wickedness and is, incidentally, the word (*porneia*) from which the word "pornography" comes. Premarital sex, extramarital sex, abnormal sex, incest, prostitution, and surely sex sins in the heart are part of what the apostle has in mind here.

2. Impurity. Here the Greek word suggests any kind of impurity, whether in thought or deed. It might even include unnatural lust as described by Paul in Romans 1:24. It surely would cover some of the modern films, pornographic literature, and "evil imaginations." William Barclay describes it as the pus of an unclean wound; a tree that has never been pruned; material that has never been sifted.

3. Sensuality. This Greek word can be thought of as wantonness or debauchery. But there may be more to it than that. It has in it the notion of reckless shamelessness, or even an open indulgence in impurity. The same word is used in 2 Peter 2:7 when the apostle speaks of the licentiousness of Sodom and Gomorrah. It can be no less than lewdness and sensuality of any kind.

The second set of the works of the flesh enumerated by Paul are these:

1. Idolatry. The Greek word for idolatry is the worship of false gods of which there are many today. By implication we think of it as including anything that comes between us and God. Money can become an idol if we worship it above our worship of God. Pleasure can become an idol, even a relationship to another person can become an idol if it takes the place of God.

2. Sorcery. The Greek word here can be translated witchcraft; the idea especially is the administering of magical potions and drugs. Thus it is related also to the use of drugs; we get our word "pharmacy" from this Greek word, *pharmakia*. Throughout Scripture, witchcraft and sorcery are condemned. This evil is spreading rapidly in Western societies at an alarming rate.

3. Enmities. The Greek word for enmities has to do with hatred. Hatred contains within it the idea of something latent, like an animal ready to spring on its prey. Hostility, antipathy, antagonism, animosity, rancor, and intense dislike are all comparable terms for what is translated here as hatred.

4. Strife. The Greek word refers to variance, contentions, strife, fighting, discord, wrangling, and quarreling. Many churches are hard hit by internal discord that divides laymen from pastors, and laymen from laymen. When members of a congregation do not speak to each other and when they fight with one another, this sin is at work and the Spirit of God is quenched. Numerous families are infected by this spirit. Many marriages, even Christian ones, are being destroyed by this sin.

5. Jealousy—a very common sin. It involves envy when someone gets an honor we wanted, or it can mar a marriage relationship when a husband or a wife is jealous of his or her partner. We read of murders being committed because of jealousy, of friends who have not spoken for years. On the other hand, there is the beautiful example of Jonathan who was *not* jealous of David (1 Sam. 20).

6. Outbursts of anger. The Greek word for wrath means unrighteous fits of rage, passionate outbursts of anger and hostile feelings. John uses the same root word in the Apocalypse about the righteous wrath of God. Man's wrath can be righteous or unrighteous, but God's wrath is always righteous for He cannot sin. There is a righteous wrath, but it is not a fit of anger. Here anger or wrath is a sin we must cast out of our lives. Someone has well said, "Righteous indignation is usually one part righteous and nine parts indignation."

7. Disputes. This Greek word for disputes or strife means selfish ambition, self-seeking, and selfishness. This violates both parts of the Ten Commandments (Exod. 20). First it is a sin against God when selfish ambition replaces the will of God for our lives. Then it violates the command to love our neighbors, for acts of self-seeking are always committed at someone else's expense.

8. Dissensions. The Greek word means seditions, dissensions, or divisions. Believers are to be of one mind. "He is the God that maketh men to be of one mind in an house" is the Prayer Book version of Psalm 68:6.[5] Unless principles are at stake or the Word of God is threatened, then discord can become sinful. We are to contend for the faith, but even when doing so we are not to be contentious. Truth often divides, but when truth is not at stake, God's people should be able to live together in love by the grace of the Holy Spirit.

9. Factions. The Greek word for factions, or heresies, has to do with sects and sectarianism. It means to choose that which is bad, or to form an opinion contrary to the revelation of God in Scripture. This is the same word found in 2 Peter 2:1 (NIV): "But there were also false prophets among the people, just as there will be false teachers among you. They will secretly introduce destructive heresies, even denying the sovereign Lord who bought them— bringing swift destruction on themselves." Thus this is a serious sin. As Alexander said, "Error is often plausibly dressed in the outer garb of truth."

10. Envyings. This Greek word means resentment at the excellence or good fortune of another, a jealous spirit. We may envy someone his beautiful voice, his great wealth, his superior position, or his athletic attainments. Or we may begrudge a girl her beauty, a person his position in public office. Envy has been the downfall of many a Christian. Normally, there can be no envy that does not involve covetousness.

11. Drunkenness. This Greek word means overindulgence in alcohol. Alcohol may be used for medicine, but it can also become a terrible drug. The way it is used in our world is probably one of the great evils of our day. It is a self-inflicted impediment that springs from "a man taking a drink, a drink taking a drink, and drink taking the man." Distilled liquors as we have them today were unknown in Bible times. This modern use of alcohol is far more dangerous than the use of wine, which was also condemned when taken to excess. Teetotalism or nonteetotalism cannot be proven from Scriptures. Whatever we do, we should do it to the glory of God (1 Cor. 10:31).

I had a wonderful Christian friend in England many years ago. He was a godly man with a great knowledge of the Scriptures and a deep and holy walk with God. Once when we had a meal with him he said, "I serve wine at my table to the glory of God. I know you don't take wine, to the glory of God, so we have provided ginger ale for you." He continued, "We are taught to respect each other's liberty and each other's conscience."

12. Carousings. In the Greek this means orgies. In Romans 13:13 and 1 Peter 4:3 it is associated with illicit sex, drunkenness, and other evils in which no Christian should indulge.

There may be someone reading this who has been guilty of one, or even all of the sins listed here. Does this mean you can never enter the kingdom of Heaven; that the door is forever closed to you? Certainly not. The Bible says that by repentance and faith anyone can be forgiven (1 John 1:9).

However, Galatians 5:21 constitutes the most serious warning to those who may think they can sin that grace may abound. The apostle sternly says, "Those who practice such things [i.e. those things just enumerated] shall not inherit the kingdom of God." Paul's whole terrible list when practiced by men violates God's will for them. God hates these things so much that He will judge those who do them. People whose lives are characterized by such deviations from the will of God will be separated from Him and lost in outer darkness. The reason I have listed all this is because millions of professing Christians are only just that—"professing." They have never possessed Christ. They live lives characterized by the flesh. Tens of thousands have never been born again. They will go into eternity lost—while thinking they are saved because they belong to the church, or were baptized, and so on.

But there is another truth we should not forget. Today people do many of these forbidden things in the name of freedom. What they fail to see is that such activities actually enslave those who become involved in them. And when liberty becomes license, liberty not only is misconstrued—those who misconstrue are themselves shackled so that they lose the liberty of which Scripture speaks. True freedom consists not in the freedom to sin, but the freedom *not* to sin.

Another truth is that those who live in the flesh can be changed only by the Spirit of God. This is why a deep spiritual awakening is so desperately needed today. You cannot legislate successfully against these problems. No matter how many laws are passed, or how many good intentions there may be, in those persons outside of Christ the old nature is in control. It may be subdued at times; it may be controlled by sheer discipline on other occasions, but there will come times when these works of the flesh will manifest themselves by boiling over in strife and eventually war.

However, the Christian has become a new creation. He can come under the control of the Holy Spirit and produce the fruit of the Spirit, which is a whole new set of principles that develop a new man and could eventually produce a new society.

Paul says, "Now those who belong to Christ Jesus have crucified the flesh with its passions and desires" (Gal. 5:24). During the lifetime of our Lord Jesus Christ, He lived as a man, He was tempted as a man, yet He kept the whole law of God and had victory over the flesh. Those of us who are bound to Him by faith are, in principle at least, finished with all that belongs to the flesh. Yet Paul recognizes that these old fleshly tendencies still lurk within us and that we must almost hourly yield to the Holy Spirit to have total and complete victory.

The Scripture does not say, "They that are Christ's *should* crucify the flesh." This took place positionally and legally when Jesus Christ hung on the cross. Galatians 2:20 reads, "I *have been* crucified with Christ" (italics mine). Romans 6:6 says, "Knowing this, that our old self *was crucified* with Him" (italics mine). It is a completed action, a settled matter. Since we believers have already been crucified even as we have already been saved, we are now called upon to work out that crucifixion in the flesh so that we do not make provision for the works of the flesh. We have been buried with Christ and now are raised from the dead unto the new life in Him.

Many people say, "I cannot live a life like this. I cannot hold out." If it were up to you and me, we could not. The apostle Paul says, "Consider yourselves to be dead to sin" (Rom. 6:11). He also said sin shall no longer reign in our mortal bodies. This means that "by faith" we accept what Jesus Christ has done for us at the cross. By faith we turn over our lives totally and completely and without reservation to the Holy Spirit. Christ sits on the throne of our hearts. No one, or anything, is going to push Him off. The Holy Spirit produces the "fruit of the Spirit." While the works of the flesh would like very much to manifest themselves—and sometimes do—they no longer reign, they are no longer in control. It is no longer a practice; it is no longer a habit; we are transformed by His grace and live the new life in Christ. But this is only possible as we are filled with the Holy Spirit. It is to this important topic that we now turn.

8

The Fullness
of the Spirit

OUR HOME IS supplied by a reservoir fed by two mountain springs. These two springs on the mountain above the house, according to the mountain people who lived here before we did, never fluctuate. Rainy season or dry, they remain the same. We draw on the water as we need it, and the springs continually flowing into the reservoir keep it filled to overflowing. That is literally what it means to "be being filled with the Spirit."

All Christians are committed to be filled with the Spirit. Anything short of a Spirit-filled life is less than God's plan for each believer.

What does the Bible mean when it speaks of the fullness of the Holy Spirit? Let's define the fullness of the Spirit. To be Spirit-filled is to be controlled or dominated by the Spirit's presence and power. In Ephesians 5:18 Paul says, "And do not get drunk with wine, for that is dissipation, but be filled with the Spirit." Here he draws a contrast between two things. A person who is filled with alcohol is controlled or dominated by alcohol. Its presence and power have overridden his normal abilities and actions.

It is interesting that we often say someone is "under the influence" of alcohol. Now that is somewhat the meaning of being. filled with the Spirit. We are "under the influence" of the Spirit. Instead of doing things only with our own strength or ability, He empowers us. Instead of doing only what we want to do, we now are guided by Him. Unfortunately millions of God's people do not enjoy the unlimited spiritual wealth at their disposal because they are not filled with the Holy Spirit.

I remember a great woman Bible teacher by the name of Ruth Paxson whom I heard speak on this theme many times. She was a guest in our home, and I still have some of the notes I made from her lectures.

As she reminded us, the lives of many reflect the practices and standards of this present world. True, they have been baptized with the Holy Spirit into the body of Christ, and they are going to heaven. But they are missing so much of what God wants them to have in this life. Consciously or unconsciously they are more interested in imitating the world system dominated by Satan than in imitating Christ. They do not really want to share the reproach of Christ outside the camp (Heb. 13:13). Their gifts are often unused, and spiritual fruit is absent from their lives. Nor do they have any great concern to evangelize the spiritually needy in their own community. Their zeal to walk in obedience to the commandments of Christ grows weak. Their devotional life is uneven, if not totally neglected, and they anticipate reading the newspaper more than reading the Word of God. If they do pray, it is a cheerless duty and a tedious task rather than a joy. As with Lot in Sodom, sin for them has lost some of its sinfulness; their sensitivity to sin has been numbed and the edge of conscience blunted. Known sins remain unconfessed.

Christians have more equipment and technology for evangelizing the world than ever before. And there are better trained personnel. But one of the great tragedies of the present hour is this: Christians so often lack the fullness of the Spirit with its true dependence on God's power for their ministry. Illustrations of the kind of spiritual power they need but lack abounded in the first century. It was said of the Christians in one city, "These men who have turned the world upside down have come here also" (Acts 17:6 RSV). And from time to time in later centuries this same Holy Spirit power was unleashed upon the world. Isolated instances of it exist right now. But what if the *full* power of the Holy Spirit were to be loosed today through all true believers? The world could again be turned upside down.

The Biblical Basis for Being Filled with the Spirit

I think it proper to say that anyone who is not Spirit-filled is a defective Christian. Paul's command to the Ephesian Christians, "Be filled with the Spirit," is binding on all of us Christians everywhere in every age. There are no exceptions. We must conclude that since we are ordered to be filled with the Spirit, we are sinning if we are not filled. And our failure to be filled with the Spirit constitutes one of the greatest sins against the Holy Spirit.

It is interesting to note that the command to "Be filled with the Spirit" actually has the idea of continuously being filled in the original Greek language which Paul used. We are not filled once for all, like a bucket. Instead, we are to be filled constantly. It might be translated, "Be filled and keep on being filled," or "Be being filled."

Ephesians 5:18 literally says, "Keep on being filled with the Spirit." Dr. Merrill C. Tenney has compared this to the situation of an old-time farmhouse kitchen. In one corner was a sink; above it was a pipe through which came a continuous stream of water from the spring outside. The water, by running constantly, kept the sink brimful of good water. In like manner the Christian is not to let himself be emptied of the Spirit that he may later become full again; rather he is constantly to accept the direction and energy of the Spirit so he is always overflowing.

The overflowing rivers and the abundant life are available blessings for all Christians. Rivers of living water fail to flow in our lives not because God denies them to us, but because we do not want them or we refuse to meet the conditions to get them.

This continuous filling by the Holy Spirit is also what Jesus was teaching in John 4, in speaking to the Samaritan woman at Jacob's well: "Everyone who drinks of this water shall thirst again; but whoever drinks of the water that I shall give him shall never thirst; but the water that I shall give him shall become in him a well of water springing up to eternal life" (John 4:13, 14). Jesus spoke of the Holy Spirit in the same way in John 7:38: "He who believes in Me, as the Scripture said, 'From his innermost being shall flow rivers of living water.'" The overflowing spring and the continual river speak of the constant supply of the Holy Spirit's blessing available to all Christians. This living water of which Jesus speaks—this continual filling by the Holy Spirit—fails to flow in our lives not because God denies it to us, but because we do not want it or we refuse to meet the conditions God sets up to get it.

In reading John 7:38 one day, I was stopped short and struck with awe by the grandeur of Jesus' words. He did not speak of drops of blessings, few and far between, as in a light shower on a spring day. He spoke of rivers of living water. Consider the Mississippi, the Amazon, the Danube, or the Yangtze Rivers: However much may be taken from them, they do not run dry but continue to flow generously. The sources from which they come keep sending water down their course. These rivers illustrate the life of the Spirit-filled Christian. The supply is never exhausted because it has its source in the Holy Spirit who is inexhaustible.

Bishop Moule once said, "Never shall I forget the gain to conscious faith and peace which came to my own soul not long after a first decisive and appropriating view of the crucified Lord as the sinner's sacrifice of peace." What was the cause of this gain? He says it was "a more intelligent and conscious hold upon the living and more gracious personality of the Spirit through whose mercy the soul had got that blessed view. It was a new contact as it were with the inner and eternal movements of redeeming goodness and power. A new discovery in divine resources."

One of the prayers of the great Welsh revival was:

> "Fill me, Holy Spirit, fill me,
> More than fulness I would know:
> I am smallest of Thy vessels,
> Yet, I much can overflow."[1]

We must make ourselves available to the Holy Spirit so that when He fills us we will become vessels of blessing to the world, whether large and beautiful in great service, or small and unnoticed by men. To me the Corinthian church was one of the saddest and most tragic churches in the New Testament. Its members had been baptized with the Spirit; they had been given many of the gifts of the Spirit; and therefore they had much to commend them. Yet Paul said they were fleshly and unspiritual. "And I, brethren, could not speak to you as to spiritual men, but as to men of flesh, as to babes in Christ. . . . for you are still fleshly" (1 Cor. 3:1, 3). This means that you and I may have one or more gifts of the Spirit and still be unspiritual, lacking in "the fullness of the Spirit." To say that having the gift of evangelism, or the gift of a pastor, or of a teacher, or the gift of tongues, or the gift of healing (or any other gift), is proof that we have the fullness of the Spirit is misleading. Furthermore, any gift we may have will never be used to its fullest potential for God unless it is brought under the control of, and empowered by, the Holy Spirit. There is nothing more tragic than a gift of God which is misused for selfish or unspiritual purposes.

So it is critical that we be filled with the Spirit. In considering this, however, we must not be confused by mere terminology. Some Christians have used terms like "the second baptism" or "the second blessing" or "a second work of grace." None of these terms are used in the Bible, but I realize that for many people they are simply semantic equivalents for the fullness of the Spirit. The name we give the experience is less important than that we actually *be* filled with the Spirit.

I prefer not to use these terms, however, since they can lead to confusion in some people's minds. Personally I believe the Bible teaches there is one baptism in the Spirit—when we come to faith in Christ. The Bible teaches there are many fillings—in fact, we are to be continuously filled by the Holy Spirit. One baptism—many fillings! I do not personally find anything in Scripture which indicates there must be some later "baptism of the Spirit" into our lives after conversion. He is already there, and we are called to yield to Him continually, but never do I condemn those who hold a different view. Many of those holding a different view are among my closest friends. Differences at this point do not constitute a basis for division of Christian fellowship.

Maybe we need to reverse the figure we use. When we are filled with the Spirit, it is not a question of there being more of Him, as though His work in us is quantitative. It is not how much of the Spirit *we* have, but how much the Spirit has of *us*. He is in us in all His fullness, whether we see this exhibited in our lives or not. When we receive Christ as Savior and Lord, you and I receive Him in full, not just in part. Then as we come to understand more and more of Christ's lordship, we surrender and yield more and more. So, seeking the fullness of the Spirit, we receive and enjoy His filling and His fullness more and more.

When we receive Christ as Savior, our spiritual capacities are extremely small. At that moment we have surrendered to Him as Savior and Lord as best we know how. It may even be proper to say we are filled with the Spirit at that time, in the sense that we are under His influence and control. However, there are still many areas of our lives which need to be yielded to His control, and we may not even be aware of them at that moment. As we grow in the grace and knowledge of Christ, our spiritual capacities enlarge. We soon discover in our Christian life that we are not yet "perfect." We often stumble and fall into sins—including sins of which we may not be conscious at the time. There are many sins of omission also—things we should be doing or attitudes we should be having, but they have not become part of us yet. Part of the work of the Holy Spirit is to convict us of these sins and bring us to true repentance. At such a time we need a new filling of the Holy Spirit, that He might control and dominate us. There also may be new tasks or challenges that God gives us, and this should always cause us to seek afresh the power and presence—the filling—of the Holy Spirit.

It is also common for a young Christian to believe that he must rely on his own wisdom and strength to fight sin in his life, or to undertake some task God has given him. Such a person may realize that his salvation is based totally on what God has done in Christ, but at the same time be unaware that he is just as dependent on God the Holy Spirit for his Christian growth. Often he will fight bravely and struggle against temptations, or zealously seek to witness for Christ, and yet see little or no real progress. Why? It is because he is doing everything in the energy of the flesh, not in the power of the Spirit. Such a person needs to understand God's provision of the Holy Spirit and be yielded to His control. He needs to be filled with the Spirit.

Sometimes in this situation the Holy Spirit may fill such a person in deeply moving and memorable ways. Other Christians who may be more mature may still have an overwhelming spiritual experience in which the Holy Spirit fills them in fresh and wonderful ways. Some people call this a "baptism of the Spirit," but I think it is more Scriptural to speak of it as "a new filling of the Holy Spirit." This experience may come at a critical point in one's life when he is facing some crucial decision or some particularly difficult problem or challenge. Or this experience may come very quietly. In fact, there can even be times in which the filling of the Holy Spirit is very real, and yet we may be almost completely unaware of it.

Both of these experiences have been true in my own life. There have been times of deep awareness of the Holy Spirit's presence. There have been other times in which I have felt weak and inadequate, and yet in retrospect I know the Holy Spirit was in control of my life.

In my own life there have been times when I have also had the sense of being filled with the Spirit, knowing that some special strength was added for some task I was being called upon to perform.

We sailed for England in 1954 for a crusade that was to last for three months. While on the ship, I experienced a definite sense of oppression. Satan seemed to have assembled a formidable array of his artillery against me. Not only was I oppressed, I was overtaken by a sense of depression, accompanied by a frightening feeling of inadequacy for the task that lay ahead. Almost night and day I prayed. I knew in a new way what Paul was telling us when he spoke about "praying without ceasing." Then one day in a prayer meeting with my wife and colleagues, a break came. As I wept before the Lord, I was filled with deep assurance that power belonged to God and He was faithful. I had been baptized by the Spirit into the body of Christ when I was saved, but I believe God gave me a special anointing on the way to England. From that moment on I was confident that God the Holy Spirit was in control for the task of the 1954 Crusade in London.

That proved true.

Experiences of this kind had happened to me before, and they have happened to me many times since. Sometimes no tears are shed. Sometimes as I have lain awake at night the quiet assurance has come that I was being filled with the Spirit for the task that lay ahead.

However there have been many more occasions when I would have to say as the apostle Paul did in 1 Corinthians 2:3: "I was with you in weakness and in fear and in much trembling." Frequently various members of my team have assured me that when I have had the least liberty in preaching, or the greatest feeling of failure, God's power has been most evident.

In other words it is still true, as Paul continued in his letter to the church at Corinth, "My message and my preaching were not in persuasive words of wisdom, but in demonstration of the Spirit and of power, that your faith should not rest on the wisdom of men, but on the power of God" (1 Cor. 2:4, 5).

But note, those who *heard* the word sensed the power, not necessarily the one who proclaimed it. Filling does not necessarily imply "feeling."

Full and Filled

Two words used in the New Testament sometimes puzzle Christians: the words are *full* and *filled*. Some people make a distinction between them. I agree that there may be some distinction, but it is only minor. For instance, to be *full* of the Spirit seems to me to refer to the "state of being" of the believer. I think that John the Baptist and the apostle Paul were full of the Spirit all the time; that is, it was a continuous state. However, for them to be "filled with the Spirit" might also refer to a particular and occasional empowering or "anointing" for special purposes and special tasks. On occasion some of the New Testament saints God used for special assignments were said to be "filled with the Spirit." They might not have been able to bear it if that surcharge of power filled them all the time. But in moments of great need they could bear it for a season.

I believe God gives us the strength of the Holy Spirit commensurate with the tasks He gives us.

We have a friend who is a retired Presbyterian clergyman. His father operated a pile driver. He once told of watching the great pile drivers driving the posts into the river bed of the Mississippi in the process of building a bridge. Each pole was lifted into place and then with a mighty pounding of the pile driver each pole was driven securely into the riverbed.

That evening the little boy, Grier Davis, was playing in his sandpile and trying to reenact what he had seen earlier. But try as he would, he could not drive the sticks into the sand as he had seen the pile driver drive the poles into the Mississippi River bottom. Then he had a bright idea. Running to his father he asked if he might have permission to borrow one of the pile drivers. With a chuckle the father explained that the pile driver was much too powerful for the small job he was attempting to accomplish, and that a hammer would be more like it.

So it is with the power of the Holy Spirit. When God calls us to any task He also supplies the power for that task.

Thus it should be the normal situation of the Christian to be filled with the Spirit because we keep on being filled. But, then, what are we to make of the repeated, specific times of filling mentioned in the Book of Acts? Dr. Merrill C. Tenney uses a city house to illustrate this:

Most homes are connected to a water main. This supplies the house with adequate water for normal life. But suppose a fire breaks out. Then firemen tap a nearby hydrant to secure a much greater flow of water to meet the emergency. To be "full" of the Spirit is like a house supplied continuously with adequate water. But to be "filled" on occasion, as the apostles were in Acts 4:31, is to be given extra energy and power for special service. "And when they had prayed, . . . they were all filled with the Holy Spirit, and began to speak the word of God with boldness" (Acts 4:31). For the special task of persisting in evangelism, even when the religious leadership violently opposed them, the apostles needed a special filling of God's power. They had been "full of the Spirit" all along. Now they needed "extra filling" to meet the extra demands on them.

Filled for a Purpose

Of course, God has a purpose in wanting us to be filled with the Spirit. We saw this in Acts 4:31, "And they were all filled with the Holy Spirit, and began to speak the word of God with boldness." In other words, the disciples were filled *for a purpose*—to proclaim the Word of God. The great question every believer must face is, "What is my motivation in wanting to be filled with the

Spirit? Do I desire this fullness merely in the interest of self-enjoyment and self-glorification, or in order that Christ might be glorified?"

Often a Christian may sincerely seek the power of the Holy Spirit, and yet—either by ignorance or design—seek it for the wrong reasons. Some look for some type of emotional experience and want the fullness of the Spirit simply to give them a new (and even spectacular) experience. Some seek certain sensations because they see other Christians who may have had a particular form of experience which they believe has come from the Holy Spirit. Perhaps out of a misguided desire to be spiritually like others, or even spiritually superior, a person seeks the Spirit's fullness. Or again, a person may seek the Spirit's fullness only because he is encountering some particular problem, and he is hoping he can get out of the difficulty by having an experience of the Spirit's power. In short, people may yearn for the Spirit's power for all kinds of reasons.

It is true that the Spirit may bring some of these happenings into our lives. On occasion He may give us a deeply emotional sense of His presence, or make us particularly happy, or help us overcome a particularly troublesome difficulty. But we must be very careful that we do not seek His fullness for selfish reasons. He has come that we might glorify Christ.

The purpose of filling is that those who are filled may glorify Christ. The Holy Spirit came for this purpose. Jesus said, "He shall glorify Me; for He shall take of Mine, and shall disclose it to you" (John 16:14). That is, the Holy Spirit does not draw attention to Himself, but to Christ. Jesus said, "When the Helper comes, whom I will send to you from the Father, that is the Spirit of truth, who proceeds from the Father, He will bear witness of Me" (John 15:26). I believe this is one of the tests of a Spirit-filled life. Is Christ becoming more and more evident in my life? Are people seeing more of Him, and less of me?

For this reason I was hesitant about writing a book like this. I am a bit suspicious of people who make a fetish of talking about Him: "The Holy Spirit ... this," and "the Holy Spirit ... that." The Holy Spirit did not come to glorify Himself; He came to glorify Christ.

One other point—a person who is filled with the Spirit may not even be conscious of it. Not one biblical character said, "I am filled with the Spirit." Others said it about them, but they did not claim it for themselves. Some of the most godly people I have known were not conscious that they were filled with the Spirit. Someone has said that the nearer to heaven we get, the more conscious of hell we feel.

We've been considering power for use, but what about its abuse? What about those who want the Spirit's power for wrong reasons? One example in the New Testament of a person wanting the power of the Spirit for selfish reasons is found in Acts 8. Simon the sorcerer "believed," was baptized, and then was amazed by the signs and great miracles performed by the apostles. He was particularly interested when he noted how the converts received the Holy Spirit. Offering Peter and his fellow workers money, he said, "Give me also this power, that any one on whom I lay my hands may receive the Holy Spirit" (Acts 8:19 rsv). Peter immediately rebuked him, saying "your heart is not right before God" (v. 21). The Holy Spirit's power is for a purpose—but that purpose is always for the glory of God, not personal advantage or advancement.

Power for a Holy Life

Ultimately we need the filling of the Holy Spirit so that we may glorify Christ. But how do we glorify Christ? We glorify Christ when we live for God—trusting, loving, and obeying Him. Jesus said, "Let your light shine before men in such a way that they may see your good works, and glorify your Father who is in heaven" (Matt. 5:16). Paul said, "Whether, then, you eat or drink or whatever you do, do all to the glory of God" (1 Cor. 10:31). What a concept—everything we do should glorify God!

And yet this brings us to the heart of the problem. Why do we need the fullness of the Holy Spirit? *Because only in the power of the Spirit can we live a life that glorifies God.* We cannot glorify God in the energy of the flesh. This was Paul's cry in Romans 7: "I do not understand my own actions. For I do not do what I want, but I do the very thing I hate. . . . I can will what is right, but I cannot do it. For I do not do the good I want, but the evil I do not want is what I do" (Rom. 7:15, 18, 19 RSV). But in the power of the Holy Spirit we can live a life that increasingly glorifies God. God the Holy Spirit gives us power for a purpose—power to help us glorify God in every dimension of our lives.

In the Christian life, power is dynamically related to a Person. This Person is the Holy Spirit Himself, indwelling the Christian and filling him with the fullness of His power. As we said earlier, He supplies His power for a purpose; it is to be used. Although His limitless resources are available to us, He will permit us to have only as much power as He knows we will use or need. Unfortunately, many Christians are disobedient and, having prayed for power, have no intention of using it, or else neglect to follow through in active obedience. I think it is a waste of time for us Christians to look for power we do not intend to use: for might in prayer, unless we pray; for strength to testify, without witnessing; for power unto holiness, without attempting to live a holy life; for grace to suffer, unless we take up the cross; for power in service, unless we serve. Someone has said, "God gives dying grace only to the dying."

Power for Service

We glorify God by living lives that honor Him, and we can only do this in the power of the Holy Spirit. But we also glorify God as we serve Him, and we can only do that in the power of the Holy Spirit also. We are filled by the Spirit to serve.

Peter was so filled with the Holy Spirit that when he preached, 3,000 people were saved in one day at Pentecost. It is interesting that the Bible is full of statistics; this is one of them. Someone must have counted the number who were converted on that day, and Luke, inspired by the Holy Spirit, wrote down the number. In Acts 4:4 he says the number of men who believed "came to be about five thousand." And the same Spirit who inspired this keeping of statistics, saw to it that they were kept accurately.

In Acts 4:8 Peter and John, who had been arrested for preaching, were brought before the religious leaders. Then Scripture says Peter, "filled with the Holy Spirit," fearlessly proclaimed the death and resurrection of Christ. This same Peter, now full of the Holy

Spirit, was so bold he was ready to face death for Christ. Yet only a few weeks earlier he had denied Him with curses. The fullness of the Holy Spirit made the difference.

Shortly afterward, Peter and his companions went to a prayer meeting. As we have already seen when they prayed "they were all filled with the Holy Spirit, and began to speak the word of God with boldness" (Acts 4:31). The filling was given to them to serve Christ by boldly proclaiming the gospel. It is significant to me that here Peter had two fillings. He was filled before he preached (v. 8), and he was filled again after he and his fellow workers prayed (v. 31).

But the filling of the Spirit for power was not limited to preaching. The apostles became so tied down with the daily ministrations to the multiplied new believers that they were unable to devote themselves fully to the ministry of the Word. So they asked for seven men to be appointed for this practical job—a job of administration.

They laid down three qualifications for the officeholders: they were to be "of good reputation, full of the Spirit and of wisdom" (Acts 6:3).

This admonition tells us something important. If all the believers were "of good reputation, full of the Spirit and of wisdom," then the instructions make no sense. Some must have lacked some vital requirement. A good reputation, being full of the Holy Spirit, and wisdom were all required.

No man should be an officer in the church today who does not possess these qualifications. Of how many church members today can it be said they are "of good reputation, full of the Spirit and of wisdom"? Yet these requirements were for a practical, not a spiritual, ministry.

Does this not show us that to carry out the most practical job to the glory of God (be it as a craftsman, an administrator, a housekeeper, or secretary) we need to be filled with God's Holy Spirit— as well as of good reputation and wisdom?

We could go on and on because the early Church was empowered for every form of service by the filling of the Holy Spirit.

I am convinced that to be filled with the Spirit is not an option, but a necessity. It is indispensable for the abundant life and for fruitful service. The Spirit-filled life is not abnormal; it is the normal Christian life. Anything less is subnormal; it is less than what God wants and provides for His children. Therefore, to be filled with the Spirit should never be thought of as an unusual or unique experience for, or known by, only a select few. It is intended for all, needed by all, and available to all. That is why the Scripture commands all of us, "Be filled with the Spirit."

9

How to Be Filled with the Holy Spirit

IN MY MINISTRY I am frequently asked, "How can I be filled with the Spirit?" We have been commanded to be filled, but how do we obey? How does the presence and power of the Holy Spirit become a reality in each of our lives? This is the heart of the matter. Everything I have said so far about the filling of the Spirit will only be an intellectual curiosity, unrelated to our lives, unless we learn in our own experience what it means to be filled with the Spirit.

It is interesting that the Bible nowhere gives us a neat, concise formula for being filled with the Spirit. I believe that may be because most believers in the first century did not need to be told how to be filled. They knew that the Spirit-filled life was the normal Christian life. It is a sad commentary on the low level of our spiritual lives today that we are so confused about the filling of the Spirit.

And yet the Bible does say a great deal about this subject, and when we look at the New Testament as a whole there can be little doubt in our minds either about the meaning of the Spirit-filled life, or how the Spirit-filled life becomes a reality in our lives. *I believe the New Testament's teaching on how to be filled with the Holy Spirit can be summarized in three terms: Understanding, Submission, and Walking by Faith.*

Understanding

The first step in being filled with the Spirit is *understanding*. That is, there are certain things we must know and *understand—*certain truths God has revealed to us in His Word, the Bible. Some of these we have already mentioned, but let us be sure we have them clearly in our minds. What are these truths?

The first truth we must understand is that God has given us His Holy Spirit, and that He dwells within us. If I have accepted Christ as my Savior, the Spirit of God dwells within me. Remember—I may not necessarily *feel* His presence, but that does not mean He is absent. It is the *fact* of His presence that we must understand. God has promised that the Spirit lives within you if you belong to Christ, and God cannot lie. *We accept this fact by faith.*

We also must understand that God *commands* us to be filled with the Spirit. That means it is His will for you to be filled—and to refuse to be filled with the Spirit is to act contrary to the will of God. It is His command, and therefore it is His will. Just to make it even clearer—God *wants* to fill us with His Spirit. That is a wonderful truth to me. God does not give us a full measure of the Spirit grudgingly or unwillingly. No, He wants us to live our lives controlled and guided by the Holy Spirit. "If you then, being evil, know how to give good gifts to your children, how much more shall your heavenly Father give the Holy Spirit to those who ask Him?" (Luke 11:13). If I fail to be filled with the Spirit, remember that it is not because of God's reluctance. The fault is entirely on my side.

This leads to a further point we must understand, and that is the presence of sin in our lives. What is it that blocks the work of the Holy Spirit in our lives? It is sin. *Before we can be filled with the Holy Spirit we must deal honestly and completely with every known sin in our lives.* This may be very painful for us, as we face up to things that we have hidden or not even realized about our lives. But there will be no filling by the Holy Spirit apart from cleansing from sin, and the first step in cleansing from sin is awareness of its presence.

Most of us have had the experience at one time or another of having pipes clogged in our homes so that the water came through only in a trickle, or perhaps was stopped entirely. Where I live in North Carolina we rarely have extremely cold weather, but once in a while I have seen the temperature go below zero. Even though the pipes are buried quite deep coming from the spring into our house in a natural flow, I have seen them completely frozen. On one occasion we had to dig up the hard frozen ground and use blowtorches to melt the ice at an elbow in the pipe. So it is with sin in our lives. Sin is like the ice in our pipes—our spiritual lives have been "frozen" by a hostile world. There is only one solution, and that is repentance to clear the blockage and restore the flow of the Holy Spirit.

We are all familiar with "hardening of the arteries" as being one of the dangerous diseases to which a large percentage of the population is subject. The arteries become clogged with substances that still baffle medical experts. They still do not know how to unclog these arteries so that the blood can have free flow. Frequently bypass surgery is used, but medical opinion is divided even over this method in some instances. Vast amounts of money are being spent on medical research in many countries of the world trying to discover a chemical that will unclog arteries and save millions from death every year.

In the same way, our lives need that chemical provided by the blood of Christ to unclog the pipes, or arteries, of our lives so that the vital sap of the vine may flow. Sin is the great clogger, and the blood of Christ is the great cleanser when applied by repentance and faith.

Sometimes new believers are startled to find they are still sinners, and they not only continue to be tempted but they can still yield to temptation. Actually this should be no surprise, because the old sin nature is still within us. Before a person comes to Christ there is only one force at work in him—the old carnal nature. But when we accept Christ into our lives the Holy Spirit comes to dwell within us. Now there are two natures at work in our lives— the old sinful nature that wants us to live for self, and the new spiritual nature that wants us to live for God. The question is— which of these two natures will rule over our actions? This is why being filled with the Holy Spirit is so important. Unless the Spirit controls our lives, we will be dominated by our old sinful nature.

The Spirit's work will be blocked, however, as long as we allow sin to remain.

So we must deal completely with sin in our lives if we are to know the infilling of the Holy Spirit. This is not easy for several reasons. For one thing, it may be extremely painful for us to face the reality of sin in our lives. Pride is often at the root of our sins, and our pride is often deeply wounded when we honestly admit before God and before men that we are not as good as we had thought we were.

Dealing with sin in our lives is also hard because (as we shall see) we must not only know our sin, but we must repent of it. And some of us may be harboring sin and tolerating it, unwilling to give it up. Like the rich young ruler in Mark 10, we want what Jesus has for us, but we want to cling to our sin even more.

There is a further reason it is difficult for us to deal with sin in our lives, and it is simply this: sin blinds us spiritually, and one of the things about which we are blinded often is the awesome depth of sin. We do not see how much it has invaded every area of our lives, and just how much it has infected everything we say and think and do. It is all too easy to confess the sins which we see in our lives, and yet fail to see the many other sins possibly hindering even more directly our walk with the Lord.

That is why the Bible is so vital in this matter. We must not be content with a casual examination of our lives, thinking that only the sins which seem to give us the most trouble are worthy of being confessed. Instead, as we prayerfully study the Word of God, the Holy Spirit—who is, remember, the author of Scripture—will convict us of other areas of sin which need confessing to God. We must confess not only what we think is sin, but what the Holy Spirit labels as sin when we really listen to His voice from the Word of God. "All Scripture is inspired by God and profitable for teaching, for reproof, for correction, for training in righteousness" (2 Tim. 3:16).

Confession should be as broad as sin. The Song of Solomon warns us about "the little foxes, that spoil the vines" (2:15 KJV). This is a picture of the way "little" sins can destroy our fruitfulness for the Lord. There may be pride, jealousy, or bitterness in our lives. There may be backbiting, impatience, unkindness, or an uncontrolled temper—any one of which can make life miserable for those around us. Unclean thoughts may need to be brought to God for cleansing. Gluttony or laziness may need to be faced. Or the Holy Spirit may speak to us about our use of time, our use of money, or our lifestyle, or our use (or abuse) of some gift He has given us. Perhaps our treatment of someone near to us has become cold and indifferent. In other words, every sin that we can identify we should bring to God for confession. Sin takes all sorts of forms, and the Holy Spirit must guide us as we prayerfully examine our lives.

A young man came to me recently and said that he had lost the Holy Spirit. I replied that he had not lost the Holy Spirit, but he might well have grieved the Spirit through some particular sin. He replied that he could not think of a single thing in his life that stood between him and God. I asked him, "What about your relationship with your parents?" In response he said, "Well, it's not the best." I dug deeper and asked him, "Do you honor your father?" He agreed that he had sinned in this area. I said, "Why don't you go and have a straight, frank talk with him, and confess your sin, if you have been wrong?" He did that, and a few days later he came to me with a broad smile and said, "Fellowship restored!"

There is one other point we need to make about confession of our sins. We must not only be honest about the various sins in our lives, but we must get down to the deepest sin of all—our failure to let Christ rule our lives. *The most basic question any Christian can ask is this: Who is ruling my life, self or Christ?*

Sin will always be a continuing problem—our lives will always be marked by defeat and discouragement—as long as we try to keep "self" at the center of our lives. It is amazing how many Christians never really face this issue of Christ's Lordship, and yet the New Testament is full of statements about Christ's demand for our full commitment. "If anyone wishes to come after Me, let him deny himself, and take up his cross daily, and follow Me" (Luke 9:23). How easy it is for us to set up our own goals, operate by our own motives, and seek our own desires, without ever asking God for His will above all else. He calls us to renounce our plans and practices, and seek His way. He asks us to step off the throne of our lives, and let Him rule in every area of every thing we are and do. "And He died for all, that they who live should no longer live for themselves, but for Him who died and rose again on their behalf" (2 Cor. 5:15). Have you seen how completely—and tragically—sin has dominated your life, and are you willing to yield to Christ's authority and rule in everything?

We also need to understand that the Holy Spirit is in us, and God wants our lives to be controlled by Him. But we must understand our sin in all its dimensions. Most of all we need to face the crucial question of who is controlling our lives—we or Christ? Only when we understand these matters can we move to the second step.

Submission

The second step in being filled by the Holy Spirit is what we might term *submission*. What do I mean by this? By submission I mean that we renounce our own way and seek above all else to submit to Christ as Lord and be ruled by Him in every area of our lives.

The importance of this will be seen from what we said above about the way sin blocks the control of the Spirit in our lives. The essence of sin is self-will—placing ourselves at the center of our lives instead of Christ. The way to be filled—controlled and dominated—by the Spirit is to place Christ at the center of our lives, instead of self. This only happens as we submit to Him—as we allow Him to become Lord of our lives.

How does submission become a reality in our lives? There are, I believe, two steps.

First, there is the step of confession and repentance. We have just seen that one of the things we must understand is the depth of our sin. But we must move beyond understanding. Sin must be confessed to God and we must repent of it. There are many people who know they are sinners, and they can tell you what particular sins are a problem to them. They may even feel sorry for their sins and wish things were different. But there is never any change. Why? Because they have never confessed their sins to God and repented of them.

There is actually a difference between confession and repentance, although I believe the Bible sees them as being intimately related, like two sides of the same coin. Confession is acknowledgment of sin. It is admitting before God that I know I am a sinner, because I have committed certain sins which are known to me. The wonderful thing is that God has promised to forgive us when we turn to Him in humble confession. One of the great promises of the Bible is 1 John 1:9: "If we confess our sins, He is faithful and righteous to forgive us our sins and to cleanse us from all unrighteousness."

To repent means to *renounce* sin. In the Greek (the language in which the New Testament was originally written) the word "repent" meant a complete and total change of mind. To repent is not only to feel sorry for my sin, or even just to confess it to God. To repent of my sin is to turn from it, and to turn to Christ and His will.

If I have been guilty of evil thoughts, I renounce them when I repent of them and determine by God's grace to fill my mind with things that honor Him. If I have mistreated someone and acted in an unloving way toward him, I determine to do whatever is necessary to replace my mistreatment with loving acts toward that person. If my lifestyle is not pleasing to God, I will change it to bring it more in line with God's will. Repentance is a conscious turning from my sins. "Remember therefore from where you have fallen, and repent" (Rev. 2:5).

If the first step in our submission is confession and repentance of every known sin in our lives, *the second step is yielding ourselves to God and His will.* Confession and repentance might be described as the negative side of submission; this involves getting rid of everything which hinders God's control over our lives. Yielding to God might be described as the positive side; this involves placing ourselves totally and completely (as best we know how) into the hands of God in complete submission to His will for our lives.

This step of yielding ourselves to God is clearly presented in the sixth chapter of Romans. In that passage Paul talks vividly about the way sin has ruled our lives in the past. But now we belong to

Christ—we are no longer living for our old master, sin—we are now living for Christ, our new Master. Therefore we should not yield to sin, but yield ourselves to God. "Neither yield ye your members as instruments of unrighteousness unto sin: but yield yourselves unto God, as those that are alive from the dead" (Rom. 6:13 KJV). Paul then goes on to tell us that we have been set free from our slavery to sin—we no longer belong to sin. We have changed masters. Just as a slave in the first century might be sold and come under the ownership of a new master, so we have been purchased with the blood of Christ, and we belong now to God. "Having been freed from sin, you became slaves of righteousness" (Rom. 6:18).

In the original Greek language the words which are translated "yield yourselves to God" in the King James Version have a beautiful meaning. The thought has been translated in various ways by other versions: "Put yourselves in God's hands" (Phillips); "offer yourselves to God" (NIV); "present yourselves to God" (New American Standard Version). However, the fullest meaning of the word "yield" is "to place yourself at the disposal of someone." In other words, when we yield ourselves to Christ, we do not simply sit back and hope that God will somehow work through us. No, instead we place ourselves at His disposal—we say, in effect, "Lord, I am Yours, to be used in whatever way You want to use me. I am at Your disposal, and You may do with me whatever You will. I seek Your will for my life, not my own will." "Put yourselves at the disposal of God" (Rom. 6:13 NEB).

The same term is used in Romans 12:1: "I urge you therefore, brethren, by the mercies of God, to present your bodies a living and holy sacrifice, acceptable to God." This includes every area of our lives. It includes our abilities, our gifts, our possessions, and our families—our minds, wills, and emotions. Nothing is excluded. We can hold nothing back. In principle He must control and dominate us in the whole and the part. This verse reminds us of the sacrifices in the Old Testament, which the worshiper presented wholly to God. He could keep back no part of it, and it was all consumed on the altar. In the same way our surrender—our submission and yielding—must be total. It is a surrender without any conditions attached.

More and more I am coming to see that this *surrender* is a definite and conscious act on our part in obedience to the Word of God. It should, in fact, occur at the time of our conversion when we repent and receive Christ not only as our Savior but as our Lord. But for many people it may well be a crisis event which comes after conversion.

Perhaps we have not understood fully what it means to follow Christ as Lord, but later we begin to see that Jesus Christ calls us not simply to believe in Him but to follow Him without reserve as His disciples. If we find ourselves fuzzy and confused about Christ's Lordship, we should take action immediately. Our intention should be a complete and final act of submission in principle, even though in months ahead the Holy Spirit may well show us other areas of our lives that need to be surrendered. This is, in fact, one of the signs of our yieldedness—as we place ourselves at God's disposal, He leads us into new areas of commitment.

The Holy Spirit may test us many times to see if we really mean business. He may even call on us to surrender something in principle that He really does not want us to surrender in fact, but which He wants us to be willing to surrender. We must be open to everything He wants to do in and through our lives.

Perhaps several illustrations will help us understand more clearly this matter of yielding ourselves to God's will. In Romans 6, Paul (as we have seen) uses the illustration of a slave who has a new master. Professor William Barclay reminds us about the real meaning of Paul's analogy:

"When we think of a servant, in our sense of the word, we think of a man who gives a certain agreed part of his time to his master, and who receives a certain agreed wage for doing so. Within that agreed time he is at the disposal and in the command of his master. But, when that time ends, he is free to do exactly as he likes. . . . But, in Paul's time, the status of the slave was quite different. Quite literally he had no time which belonged to himself. He had no moment when he was free. Every single moment of his time belonged to his master. He was the absolutely exclusive possession of his master, and there was not one single moment of his life when he could do as he liked. In Paul's time a slave could never do what he liked; it was impossible for him to serve two masters, because he was the exclusive possession of one master. That is the picture that is in Paul's mind."[1]

Now the parallel between the slave of Paul's time and the Christian is not exact (as Paul himself says) because there is a sense in which the Christian is the freest person in the world since he knows the spiritual freedom Christ brings. But on the other hand, you and I are called to belong to God, and to be His people. We are called to be at His disposal, ready and eager to do His will. Paul told Titus that Christ "gave himself for us to redeem us from all wickedness and to purify for himself a people that are his very own, eager to do what is good" (Titus 2:14 NIV).

Perhaps another illustration will help me make my point. The principle of yielding to Christ is like the commitment a bride and groom make when they are linked together in marriage. A new situation is created that becomes an enduring reality. In principle it is a complete and final act once they have repeated the vows and consummated the marriage. They are married, in fact and in principle, but—and this is a crucial thing—in practice husband and wife discover that their lives have to be constantly surrendered to each other in line with the new fact of their mutual commitment to each other in marriage.

Two people are not less married because there are defects in their lives and problems in the everyday details of living. Instead, they each grow, learning more of what it means to love each other and adjust to each other as a result of that love. Likewise in our spiritual pilgrimage we see sins which mar our relationship with God, but beneath it is a commitment which seeks to move beyond to a higher life, based on wholehearted surrender to God.

Have you ever submitted your life to God? Have you ever confessed your sin to Him, and repented of your sin as best you know how? Are there particular sins that are obstacles to your full commitment? Are there other sins, which you have not even begun to admit? Most of all, have you ever really told God—as fully and as simply as you know how—that you want His will in your life, whatever it may be?

There are people who suggest we should pray for God to fill us with His Holy Spirit. While this may be a valid prayer, I personally see little or no example of this in the New Testament. Instead, I believe we should pray that God will take possession of our lives totally and completely. We should pray that we will be emptied of self—self-love, self-will, self-ambition—and be placed completely at His disposal.

If you have never taken the step of submission to God and His will, I urge you to get on your knees before you read another page of this book, and give your life without reserve to your Master and Lord. "Therefore, shake off your complacency and repent. See, I stand knocking at the door. If anyone listens to my voice and opens the door, I will go into his house and dine with him, and he with me" (Rev. 3:19, 20 *Phillips*).

Faith

We now come to the last step in the infilling of the Holy Spirit, which I like to call "Walking in Faith." We must first *understand* certain things—then we must *submit* and yield ourselves to God—and then we must learn the secret of *walking in faith*.

The main point is this: When we are yielded to God and His will, we are filled with the Holy Spirit. The Holy Spirit controls and dominates us. Now we are to *act* on that truth and *walk* or live with full assurance that God has already filled us, and we are under His control.

The Apostle Paul puts it this way: "Likewise reckon ye also yourselves to be dead indeed unto sin, but alive unto God through Jesus Christ our Lord" (Rom. 6:11 KJV). The word in Greek which we translate "reckon ye" was sometimes used in accounting or mathematics. After a business transaction, for example, the amount of money would be computed and entered in the books. The entry in the accounting books demonstrated that the transaction had already taken place and payment had been made. Now when we yield ourselves to Christ and follow Him as Lord of our lives, we know that something has happened. The Holy Spirit has taken over our lives, to guide and empower us. We are now to walk in faith, reckoning ourselves to be dead to sin and alive to God.

We *are* filled with the Holy Spirit; now we *are to live* in light of this truth. This is not pretending; it is acting on God's promise. Dr. John Stott puts it this way:

"Now 'reckoning' is not make-believe. It is not screwing up our faith to believe something we do not believe. We are not to pretend that our old nature has died when we know perfectly well that it has not. . . . We are simply called to 'reckon' this—not to pretend it, but to realize it. It is a fact. And we have to lay hold of it. We have to let our minds play upon these truths. We have to meditate upon them until we grasp them firmly."

Dr. Stott then continues: "Can a married woman live as though she were still a single girl? Well, yes, I suppose she can. It is not impossible. But let her feel that ring on the fourth finger of her left hand, the symbol of her new life, the symbol of her identification with her husband, let her remember who she is, and let her live accordingly. . . . Our minds are so to grasp the fact and the significance of our death and resurrection with Christ, that a return to the old life is unthinkable. A born-again Christian should no more think of going back to the old life than an adult to his childhood, a married man to his bachelorhood, or a discharged prisoner to his prison cell."[2]

If you have fulfilled the Scriptural requirements for being filled with the Holy Spirit—especially the repentance and submission we have considered—then you and I can privately say to ourselves, "By faith I know I am filled with the Holy Spirit." I've never known a person whom I thought was truly filled with the Holy Spirit who went out and bragged about it, or sought to draw attention to himself. If we are filled with the Holy Spirit others will soon notice it, because the filled person produces the fruit of the Spirit. But we may not even be aware of this. In fact, some of God's greatest saints have indicated that the closer they came to Christ the more sinful they felt. My friend and associate, Roy Gustafson, once said, "The Holy Spirit didn't come to make us Holy-Spirit-conscious, but Christ-conscious." Thus, when we say to ourselves that we are filled with the Spirit it means that every known sin and hindrance is out of the way and then we claim by faith that we are filled.

There are, I believe, several things we should remember at this point.

First, we must remember that the filling of the Spirit is not a matter of feeling, but of faith. We may feel strongly the closeness of God when we are filled, or we may not. Instead of trusting in our feelings, we must trust God's promises. We must reckon ourselves to be filled by His Spirit. James McConkey put it this way:

"Nothing is more hurtful than to be constantly inspecting our own inner lives to see if God is fulfilling His promise in our experience. It is like the child constantly digging up the seed to see if it has sprouted. The question of the experience of fullness of the Spirit belongs to the Lord."[3]

Also, we must remember that the filling of the Spirit does not mean we are perfect and without sin. It means we are controlled by the Spirit, but sin is still a reality, lurking around the corner ready to lunge at the first opportunity. We may be blameless in our desire to serve Christ, but that does not make us without fault. A Scottish preacher of another generation explained it this way:

"I have lying on the table beside me a letter, which will illustrate the point at issue. I received it when I was away in New Zealand on a mission tour, in 1891. It was from my eldest daughter, then a child of five years of age. It reads: 'Dear father, I wrote all this myself. I send you a kiss from Elsie.' The fact of the matter is, that it is not writing at all, but an attempt at printing in large capitals, and not one of the letters is properly formed; there is not as much as one straight stroke on the page. . . . Now, this letter which I prize so dearly is certainly not a 'faultless' production; it is as full of faults as it is full of letters, but most assuredly it is 'blameless.' I did not blame my child for her crooked strokes, and answer with a scold, for I judged her work by its motive. I knew it was the best she could do, and that she had put all the love of her little heart into it. She wanted to do something to please me, and she succeeded. By the grace of the indwelling Christ . . . this is what our daily life, our daily life-work may be, viz., 'blameless.'"

This brings me to the last truth about the filling of the Holy Spirit: *the filling of the Holy Spirit should not be a once-for-all event, but a continuous reality every day of our lives.* It is a process. We must surrender ourselves to Him daily, and every day we must choose to remain surrendered. In every situation involving conflict between self and God's will, we must make our decisions on the basis of our constant submission to Christ.

As we have seen, the Greek verb used by Paul in his command in Ephesians 5:18, "Be filled with the Spirit," carries with it the idea that we should keep on being filled with the Spirit. We are already the temple of God, indwelt by the Holy Spirit, but He wants to fill us. However, He can fill only those who wish to be emptied of self and yielded to Him. Therefore, this active surrender must continue day by day, concerning little things as well as big ones. If we sin we need to repent so that He can fill us again. And if on occasion we face exceptional pressure, we need to pray for His additional help.

And so the four steps we have outlined above are not only a beginning, but a process. Each day we should seek to understand more from God's Word. We should pray that God will help us see our sin each day. Each day we should confess and repent. And each day we should submit our wills to His will. We should so walk in faith that He is continually filling us as we submit to Him. Each day we should walk in obedience to His Word.

Personally I find it helpful to begin each day by silently committing that day into God's hands. I thank Him that I belong to Him, and I thank Him that He knows what the day holds for me. I ask Him to take my life that day and use it for His glory. I ask Him to cleanse me from anything which would hinder His work in my life. And then I step out in faith, knowing that His Holy Spirit is filling me continually as I trust in Him and obey His Word. Sometimes during the day I may not be aware of His presence; sometimes I am. But at the end of the day, I can look back and thank Him, because I see His hand at work. He promised to be with me that day—and He has been!

This can be your experience also as you daily yield to the Lordship of Jesus Christ in your life. May you yield each day to Him. And may you be able to look back at the end of each day and know that His Holy Spirit has been your guide and your strength as you have yielded to Him.

10

Sins against the Holy Spirit

ONE OF THE most solemn themes in all Scripture concerns sins against the Third Person of the Trinity, the Holy Spirit. Believers and unbelievers alike can and do sin against Him. What is the nature of these sins, and how can we guard ourselves against committing them?

Blaspheming the Holy Spirit

Of all the sins men commit against the Holy Spirit none is worse than that of blaspheming Him. The reason for this is clear: It is the one sin for which there is no forgiveness. All other sins against the Holy Spirit are committed by *believers*. We can repent of them, be forgiven, and make a new start.

Not so with blaspheming the Spirit. This sin is committed by *unbelievers* and is often called "the unpardonable sin." It was committed by the enemies of Jesus when they accused Him of casting out devils by the power of Satan after Jesus had clearly stated that they were cast out by the power of the "Spirit of God." He then continued: "Therefore I say to you, any sin and blasphemy shall be forgiven men, but blasphemy against the Spirit shall not be forgiven. And whoever shall speak a word against the Son of Man, it shall be forgiven him; but whoever shall speak against the Holy Spirit, it shall not be forgiven him, either in this age, or in the age to come" (Matt. 12:31, 32).

When my father was a young man, he attended a revival meeting in North Carolina and became convinced through a sermon on this subject that he had committed the unpardonable sin.

And he lived with this awful thought for many years. He agonized over it, was frightened by it, and thought of himself as a doomed man who could never repent of his sin. In time he discovered that his sin was not one which excluded him from the mercy and grace of God. He came to know that the Holy Spirit would not be convicting and wrestling with him and drawing him to Christ if he had really committed this unpardonable sin.

Perhaps I can venture a definition of what I understand the unpardonable sin to be. It seems to me, negatively, that no one has committed this sin who continues to be under the disturbing, convicting, and drawing power of the Holy Spirit. So long as the Spirit strives with a person he has not committed the unpardonable sin. But when a person has so resisted the Holy Spirit that He strives with him no more, then there is eternal danger. In other words, the unpardonable sin involves the total and irrevocable rejection of Jesus Christ.

I believe this is what Stephen was talking about in the sermon he preached just prior to his martyrdom. In that message he said, "You . . . who are stiff-necked . . . are always resisting the Holy Spirit" (Acts 7:51).

The context makes it clear that Stephen was saying, first of all, that just as their fathers had refused to take seriously the proclamations of the prophets and messengers of God, or to believe them, so his listeners were guilty of like sins. In the Old Testament we read that some opposed, maligned, persecuted, and ridiculed the prophets. Since the prophets were inspired by the Holy Spirit, these people were in fact resisting the Spirit. So Stephen says that when the people to whom he was speaking refused to hear Christ's apostles and chosen ones, who were speaking through the Holy Spirit, they were in effect resisting the Holy Spirit.

Now the fatal infection of sin in the hearts of unregenerate people will always cause them to resist the Holy Spirit. The flesh and the reprobate mind always fight Him. When people do this, they will not receive the Word of God in its power unless the Holy Spirit gains victory over them.

But Stephen was saying something more, too. He was telling them and us that just as God the Spirit strove in vain with people in the Old Testament and they were doomed, so his listeners would be doomed if they did not heed the work of the Spirit in their hearts. Resisting the Spirit is a sin committed only by unbelievers. But it is a sin that, when carried on long enough, leads to eternal doom. Only certain judgment remains for those who so resist the Spirit.

The only way any sinner can be forgiven for resisting the Holy Spirit is to cease resisting and to embrace Jesus Christ, to whom the Spirit bears witness. That person has hope only if he repents immediately and allows the Spirit to work in his heart.

I think pastors, teachers, evangelists, and all Christian workers should handle this subject very carefully. For the most part Christian workers should be extremely hesitant to draw their own conclusions dogmatically as to when someone has committed the unpardonable sin. Let the Holy Spirit and God the Father make that decision. We should always urge men everywhere to repent and turn to Jesus since we do not know when the Spirit has stopped dealing with them. And let us pray that those about whom we are most uncertain may yet respond to the good news that Jesus saves.

Are you perhaps one of those who worries about having committed the unpardonable sin? If so, you should face squarely what the Bible says on this subject, not what you may have heard from others. The unpardonable sin is rejecting the truth about Christ. It is rejecting, completely and finally, the witness of the Holy Spirit, which declares that Jesus Christ is the Son of God who alone can save us from our sins. Have you rejected Christ in your own life, and said in your heart that what the Bible teaches about Him is a lie? Then I tell you as solemnly and as sincerely as I know how that you are in a very dangerous position. I urge you without delay to accept the truth about Christ, and come to Him in humble confession and repentance and faith. It would be tragic for you to persist in your unbelief, and eventually go into eternity without hope and without God.

On the other hand you may be a believer, but you have committed some sin which you have thought might keep you from being saved. No matter what it is, remember that God loves you, and He wants to forgive you of that sin. Right now you need to confess that sin to Him and seek His forgiveness. You need to be freed from the burden of guilt and doubt that has oppressed you. Christ died to free you from it. If you have come to Christ, you know on the basis of God's Word that this sin—whatever it is—is not the unpardonable sin. It will not send you to hell, because you are saved by faith in the shed blood of Christ. But you need to put it out of your life by casting it on Christ. Remember the words of the Psalmist, "As far as the east is from the west, so far has He removed our transgressions from us" (Ps. 103:12).

Grieving the Spirit

We now come to two sins against the Holy Spirit which can be committed by *Christians.* One is to grieve the Holy Spirit, and the other is to quench the Spirit. These are inclusive terms, for almost any wrong action we take can be included under one of these two headings. Let us look first at grieving the Spirit.

Paul warns his readers that they are not to "grieve the Holy Spirit of God, by whom you were sealed for the day of redemption" (Eph. 4:30). It is important and consoling to hear Paul say that we are "sealed for the day of redemption." This means we are and will remain Christians. So he is not speaking of judgment in the sense that what we do here will separate us from the love of God and cause us to go to hell. He is speaking rather of things we do that are inconsistent with the nature of the Holy Spirit and thus hurt His heart and wound Him in His own selfhood. We can bring pain to the Spirit by what we do.

"Grieve" is a "love" word. The Holy Spirit loves us just as Christ did, "Now I urge you, brethren, by our Lord Jesus Christ and by the love of the Spirit, to strive together with me in your prayers to God for me" (Rom. 15:30). We may hurt or anger one who has no affection for us, but we can grieve only a person who loves us.

I once heard a father tell his son, "Unless you are good, I won't love you any more." This was unfortunate. He had every right to tell the boy to be good, but he had no reason to tell him that he would withdraw his love. A father should always love his son—whether he is good or bad. But when he is bad, his father's love for him is mixed with pain and even sorrow and anguish.

How do Christians grieve the Holy Spirit? In Ephesians 4:20–32 Paul says that whatever is unlike Christ in conduct, speech, or disposition grieves the Spirit of grace. In one of her books, Ruth Paxson suggests that we can know what hurts the Spirit when we consider our conduct in light of the words Scripture uses to depict the Spirit. The Holy Spirit is the Spirit of:

1. *Truth* (John 14:17); so anything false, deceitful, or hypocritical grieves Him.

2. *Faith* (2 Cor. 4:13); so doubt, distrust, anxiety, worry, grieve Him.

3. *Grace* (Heb. 10:29); so whatever in us is hard, bitter, malicious, ungracious, unforgiving, or unloving grieves Him.

4. *Holiness* (Rom. 1:4); so anything unclean, defiling or degrading grieves Him.

What happens when we grieve the Holy Spirit? Ordinarily He delights to take the things of Christ and reveal them to us. He also imparts to us joy, peace, and gladness of heart. But when we grieve Him this ministry is suspended.

I come from that region of the United States where the textile industry is prominent. Some years ago I walked through a very large factory where hundreds of looms were spinning cloth made of very fine linen threads. The manager of the mill said, "This machinery is so delicate that if a single thread out of the whole thirty thousand which are weaving at this moment should break, all of these looms would stop instantly." To demonstrate it he stepped to one of the machines and broke a single thread. Instantly every loom stopped until the thread had been fixed; then they went on automatically.

This mechanical wonder provides a rough analogy of "that which is spiritual." When I commit one sin, one disobedient act, one departure from the clearly seen pathway of the will and the fear of God, then the ministry of the Spirit in my life is impaired. While the ministry of the Spirit in my life is withdrawn it is not stopped. Unlike the machinery, it is impaired. As soon as the broken thread has been repaired the full ministry of the Spirit commences again as He illuminates my mind, satisfies my heart needs, and makes the ministry of Christ effective to me.

There is one glorious and gracious aspect to this, however. To grieve the Holy Spirit is not to lose Him in my life. He does not cease to seal me; He does not remove Himself from me. Indeed a believer cannot grieve Him so that He goes away totally. I have been singularly blessed by the hymns of William Cowper, who was an associate of John Newton. But these lines have always troubled me:

> Return, O holy Dove! return,
> Sweet messenger of rest!
> I hate the sins that made Thee mourn,
> And drove Thee from my breast.[1]

I have the uneasy impression that these words suggest more than just causing the Spirit within me to stop His wonderful work. They imply that I lose Him. If that is what Cowper meant, I think he was mistaken.

It is possible that the sense of the Holy Spirit's presence may be taken away or withdrawn from men. Psalm 51 makes this clear when David cried, "Do not take Thy Holy Spirit from me" (v. 11). But remember that the Holy Spirit has sealed every believer for the day of redemption, that is, the redemption of our bodies (Eph. 1:13; 4:30; Rom. 8:23). You and I may backslide, but this is quite different from falling from grace, or having the Holy Spirit totally withdrawn from us.

If the Spirit were to withdraw Himself from a believer He has sealed, would He not be denying the whole scheme of salvation? But when He is grieved, He does bring about an absence of joy and power in our lives until we can renounce and confess the sin. Though we may appear happy, we are inwardly wretched when we are out of communion with the Holy Spirit. This is not because the Spirit has abandoned us, but because He deliberately makes us wretched until we return to Christ in brokenness, contrition, and confession. Psalm 32—which many think was written by David after his sin with Bathsheba—is an excellent example of this: "When I kept silent about my sin, my body wasted away through my groaning all day long. For day and night Thy hand was heavy upon me; My vitality was drained away as with the fever-heat of summer. I acknowledged my sin to Thee, and my iniquity I did not hide; I said, 'I will confess my transgressions to the Lord'; and Thou didst forgive the guilt of my sin. . . . Be glad in the Lord and rejoice you righteous ones, and shout for joy all you who are upright in heart" (Ps. 32:3–5, 11).

I believe that once we have been baptized into the body of Christ and indwelt by the Holy Spirit we will never be abandoned by the Spirit again. We are sealed forever. And He is the earnest, the pledge, of what is to come. I realize that many of my brethren in the faith hold a different view, but as far as I have light at this moment, I believe we are kept by the Holy Spirit.

On the one hand the Holy Spirit who indwells us secures us for God. He does this on the basis of Christ's blood in which we have trusted and by which we know we have been redeemed. On the other hand, He gives us continuous enjoyment in the knowledge that we belong to God; that enjoyment is interrupted only when some work of the flesh grieves the One who has sealed us. As translated by Weymouth, James 4:5 says He "yearns jealously over us." I seriously doubt if, this side of heaven, we will ever know how great is the power of the force we could have utilized in this life: the power of the Holy Spirit, which we tap through prayer.

When we yield ourselves totally every moment of every day to Jesus Christ as Lord, the wonder-working power of the Holy Spirit in our lives and witness will be overwhelming. It is at this point of surrender that the secret of purity, peace, and power lies. I believe it also carries with it what George Cutting used to call Safety, Certainty, and Enjoyment. It also conveys the thought of outward achievement and inward rest.

Yes, as the Spirit of love the Holy Spirit is grieved when we sin, because He loves us.

Quenching the Spirit

To blaspheme the Spirit is a sin committed by unbelievers. Grieving and quenching the Spirit are sins committed by believers. Now we must consider what is meant by quenching the Spirit.

Paul's terse admonition is this: "Do not quench the Spirit"
(1 Thess. 5:19). The word *grieve* suggests the sense of being hurt,
of being made sorrowful. This has to do with the way we bruise
the heart of the Spirit in our individual lives. The word *quench*
means "to put out, to put a damper on." It is pertinent to the
Scripture's reference to the Holy Spirit as a fire. When we quench
the Spirit, we put the fire out. This does not mean we expel Him,
but that we extinguish the love and power of the Spirit as He seeks
to carry out His divine purpose through us. We may quench Him
in a number of ways, but the figure of fire suggests two aspects by
way of warning.

A fire goes out when the fuel supply is withdrawn. When we do
not stir up our souls, when we do not use the means of grace, when
we fail to pray, witness, or read the Word of God, the fire of the
Holy Spirit is banked. These things are channels through which
God gives us the fuel that keeps the fire burning. And the Holy
Spirit wants us to use those gifts to maintain His burning in our
lives.

The second way to put out a fire is to extinguish it, by throw-
ing water on it or smothering it with a blanket or a shovelful of
dirt. In a similar way, willful sin quenches the Spirit. When we
criticize, act unkindly, belittle the work of others by careless or
unappreciative words, we smother the fire and put it out. This
happens many times when there is a fresh, new, or different movement of the Spirit of God—perhaps not using the old traditional
methods in proclamation or service. For example, when some
Christians sometimes seek to block what God may be doing in a
new way.

I want to be very clear at one point: No Christian *must* sin. Yet,
conversely, he has not been rendered *incapable* of sinning. I believe
a Christian *can* sin, but he does not *have to*. It is possible to keep
the fire burning; it is possible to avoid grieving the Spirit. God
never would have told us to reject evil acts if in point of fact we
could not help but do them. Thank God we need not sin, even
though we can sin!

I do not know their source, but the following words about the
Holy Spirit have been a help to me: "Resist not His incoming;
grieve not His indwelling; quench not His outgoing. Open to Him

as the Incomer; please Him as the Indweller; obey Him as the Outgoer in His testimony of the things concerning Christ, whether through yourself or others."

Have you in any sense grieved the Spirit, or quenched the Spirit in your life? These are serious matters, and they call for our careful attention. If this has been the case, realize that now is the time to confess these to God, and repent of them. And then walk each day in the fullness of the Spirit, sensitive to His leading and power in your life.

11

Gifts of the Spirit

WHEN OUR CHILDREN were growing up, Christmas morning would find the Christmas tree surrounded by gifts. They had been selected lovingly according to each child's enjoyment and need. Each would be opened with anticipation and excitement—accepted with expressions of love and appreciation—enjoyed and used (depending on age) all day. Alas, however, (again depending on age) by evening jealousy and squabbling had begun.

Is this not somewhat true of spiritual gifts (with the exception that spiritual gifts were given for service, not for personal enjoyment)? Still, the spiritually immature wind up eyeing with a bit of jealousy gifts which they have not received. Sometimes there is a touch of smugness and pride on the part of the receiver. But the spirit in which the gift was given cannot be judged by the attitudes of the receivers.

The New Testament lists "the gifts of the Spirit" in three passages—Romans 12:6–8; 1 Corinthians 12:8–10; and Ephesians 4:11. (There is a fourth listing in 1 Peter 4:10, 11, although it seems to duplicate material included in the previous lists.)

Gifts and the Body

The Bible teaches that every redeemed person is given at least one gift by the Holy Spirit: "Now there are varieties of gifts, . . . But to each one is given the manifestation of the Spirit for the common good" (1 Cor. 12:4, 7). God holds us responsible for the way we use our gifts.

The apostle Paul likens the Church to our physical bodies, where each member has a unique function yet all parts work together. Paul said, "For the body is not one member, but many. If the foot should say, 'Because I am not a hand, I am not a part of the body,' it is not for this reason any the less a part of the body. . . . But now God has placed the members, each one of them, in the body, just as He desired." Paul continued by saying that "there are many members, but one body. And the eye cannot say to the hand, 'I have no need of you'; or again the head to the feet, 'I have no need of you'" (1 Cor. 12:14–21). He added that even those members of the body that seem the most feeble or the least needed are necessary parts of the perfect body. They are all essential for the body's proper functioning.

As with the human body, so the body of Christ is a complete organism made by God. Yet each member of the body is unique. There can never be another "you" or "me." In a sense, your gift or mine is unique. God often gives similar gifts to different people, but there is a uniqueness about this that makes each of us distinct from any other person who has ever lived. And if any one of us is missing, the body is incomplete, lacking some part.

The Meaning of Charisma

The New Testament uses the Greek word *charisma* (plural, *charismata*) to speak of the various gifts God has given by the Holy Spirit to Christians. Actually, the word "charisma" has come into our English language to describe someone who has a certain indefinable quality which attracts people to his personality. We speak of certain well-known people as having charisma. A biblical illustration might be Apollos (Acts 18:24–28). This New Testament evangelist and Bible teacher seemed to have charisma, in its modern English sense. The apostle Paul lacked it. However, both men had definite spiritual gifts—*charismata*—that God had supernaturally given them. In the worldly sense charisma is an intangible influence that no one can put his finger on. But in the biblical use of the word *charisma*, it means "a gift of holy grace." Thus the word *charisma* in the Bible has a different meaning from the one the world thinks of when it says a man has "charisma."

The word *charismata* is the plural of *charisma* and, except for one passage in 1 Peter, is found only in the writings of the apostle Paul. If we define it precisely, it means "manifestations of grace," and is translated, "gifts." This word was used to denote the various spiritual gifts given to individuals for the benefit of the Church, and these gifts are the subject of this chapter. In Ephesians 4 Paul uses two other words translated "gifts," *dorea* and *doma*. They are similar to *charismata* and indeed to a fourth word for "gifts," *pneumatika*, which, precisely defined, means "things belonging to the Spirit." These various Greek terms lie behind our single English translation, "gifts," and mean about the same thing.

The Origin of Spiritual Gifts

Before dealing with the gifts of the Spirit more specifically I must emphasize one point. These gifts come to us from the Holy Spirit. He chooses who gets which gifts, and He dispenses them at His good pleasure. While we are held accountable for the use of any gifts He gives us, we have no responsibility for gifts we have not been given. Nor are we to covet what someone else has or be envious of that person. We may wish to have certain gifts and even ask for them, but if it is not the will of the Holy Spirit, we will not get what we ask for. And if we are dissatisfied because the Holy Spirit does not give us the gifts we want, we sin. In my case I believe God has given me the gift of evangelism, but I did not ask for it.

If I had the gift of evangelism and failed to use it, it would be a sin for me. If, on the other hand, someone else does not have the gift of evangelism, and yet is disgruntled because he does not have it, he also is sinning. There are many things I cannot do very well, but that is because there are some gifts I do not have, nor should I be discontented. The gifts you and I have are the ones God has seen fit to give us, and we should seek to discover and use them for His glory.

One other point should be stressed. We have talked about the fruit of the Spirit (and will have three chapters devoted to the fruit), and we have shown that every one of the fruits of the Spirit should be characteristic of every single Christian. But the gifts of the Spirit are different. Every believer should have the same fruit as every other believer, but not every believer will have the same gifts as every other believer. No, the Holy Spirit distributes the gifts in such a way that every believer has at least one gift which is uniquely his. You may have been given a certain gift by God, but it would be a mistake for you to say everyone else should have that same gift.

Spiritual Gifts and Talents

In studying the three passages where the gifts are listed, we find a total of about twenty. In addition, the Old Testament mentions a number of gifts not listed in the New Testament. Many of these seem quite similar to natural abilities or talents people may have, although others are clearly spiritual in character.

Certainly, most of us know of people who have a special gift of "music" which is not listed among these twenty. Moreover, many people wonder what the difference is between a spiritual gift and a natural talent. One may have the talent of making beautiful handicrafts; another may have a talent for music. Actually, most people have talents of one kind or another, and these too come from the Creator.

It appears that God can take a talent and transform it by the power of the Holy Spirit and use it as a spiritual gift. In fact, the difference between a spiritual gift and a natural talent is frequently a cause for speculation by many people. I am not sure we can always draw a sharp line between spiritual gifts and natural abilities—both of which, remember, come ultimately from God. Nor do I believe it is always necessary to make a sharp distinction. On most occasions, however, in the context we are discussing, the gifts I have in mind are supernatural ones the Spirit gives a person for the good of the Church.

A gift might also be called a "tool" or an instrument that is to be used, rather than a piece of jewelry for decoration, or a box of candy for personal enjoyment. We could think of the different types of tools a carpenter uses, or the different types of tools a surgeon needs. These "tools" have been given to people for use in the functioning of the Body of Christ.

There's an interesting passage in Exodus 31 about Bezalel. The Bible says, "And I have filled him with the Spirit of God in wisdom, in understanding, in knowledge, and in all kinds of craftsmanship, to make artistic designs for work in gold, in silver, and in bronze, and in the cutting of stones for settings, and in the carving of wood, that he may work in all kinds of craftsmanship" (vv. 3–5). This indicates that many of the skills and talents that people have are gifts of God.

This unique ability of Bezalel, given by the Spirit, included not only manual skill but also the intellectual wisdom and understanding essential to all art. Artistic talent of every kind is a divine gift. "Every good thing bestowed and every perfect gift is from above, coming down from the Father of lights, with whom there is no variation, or shifting shadow" (James 1:17). God has given to mankind aesthetic faculties which, like all the human faculties, were corrupted by man's rebellion against God in the Garden of Eden— but they are still there!

Purpose of Gifts

Paul says that the purpose of these spiritual gifts is, "for the equipping of the saints for the work of service, to the building up of the body of Christ" (Eph. 4:12). In other words, God has given each of us a task to do, and supernatural gifts to equip us for it. If we fail to perform this task we face censure at the "judgment seat of Christ."

Scripture teaches that every believer will someday have to stand before the judgment seat of Christ to give an account of how faithfully he used his gifts, as well as his personal life before God and man. This is called the "bema" or the judgment seat of Christ: "For we must all appear before the judgment seat of Christ, that each one may be recompensed for his deeds in the body, according to what he has done, whether good or bad" (2 Cor. 5:10). This will not be a judgment for the unbelieving world. That is called the Great White Throne judgment. This will be a special judgment for Christians. Our sins have been atoned for by Christ on the cross, but after salvation every work must come into judgment. The result is reward or loss (1 Cor. 3:11–15) "but he himself [the believer] shall be saved."

In 1 Corinthians 12:7, the apostle Paul says the gifts are given "for the common good" so we are not to use them selfishly. Instead, we are to use them to help each other. As Paul says in Philippians 2:3, 4, "Do nothing from selfishness or empty conceit, but with humility of mind let each of you regard one another as more important than himself; do not merely look out for your own personal interests, but also for the interests of others."

God has also designed the gifts to help "unite" the body of Christ. Just before listing the gifts in Ephesians 4:3–7, the apostle Paul urges us to be "diligent to preserve the unity of the Spirit in the bond of peace. There is one body and one Spirit, just as also you were called in one hope of your calling; one Lord, one faith, one baptism, one God and Father of all who is over all and through all and in all. But to each one of us grace [a special gift] was given according to the measure of Christ's gift." Notice how Paul emphasizes unity by repeating the word "one."

Thus the gifts of the Spirit should never divide the body of Christ; they should unify it.

How to Recognize Your Gift

I am often asked, "How can I discover what gift I have?" And "How can I utilize my gift to the best advantage?" I would make the following suggestions:

First, realize that God has given you at least one spiritual gift, and He wants you to know what it is and to use it for His glory. Paul wrote to young Timothy and said, ". . . kindle afresh the gift of God which is in you" (2 Tim. 1:6). Just as the first step in being filled with the Spirit is understanding that God has given us the Spirit, so the first step in finding our spiritual gifts is understanding God's provision.

Second, I believe the discovery of our spiritual gifts should be a matter of careful and thoughtful prayer on our part. We should pray that God will guide us to know our spiritual gifts. Also we should be sure we are willing to make use of our spiritual gifts in a way that is honoring to God. For example, if God showed you that you had the gift of teaching others, would you be willing to put that gift to use in a Sunday school class? If we find we are reluctant to know God's gifts because we are afraid of what He might call us to do with them, this needs to be faced and confessed before God.

Along with this is a third step, which involves an intelligent understanding of what the Bible says about spiritual gifts. It is my prayer that this book will be a reliable guide, but there is no substitute for firsthand study of the Bible's teaching on the gifts of the Spirit.

A fourth step in finding out your spiritual gifts involves a knowledge of yourself and your abilities. There may be certain experiences in your personal background which would tend to lead you one way or another. We may find we like to do certain things, and we may discover we are good at them. There are few short-cuts here; we simply have to discover specific ways in which our gifts begin to emerge. Often it is good to try a variety of situations—for example, in various ministries of the church. Other people can help us. For example, we may not be aware of an ability we have to be a good listener and counselor to people. But as time goes along we find more and more people coming to us and sharing their personal problems with us; we also may find other Christians telling us they think we have certain gifts along this line.

The process of discovering our spiritual gifts may be a lengthy one, and we may even find gifts emerging as the years go by and we confront new opportunities and challenges. However, we cannot let that discourage us. God wants to use us, and we will never be used by Him in the fullest way until we know our gifts and have committed them to Him. Actually, I believe a person who is Spirit-filled—constantly submitting to the Lordship of Christ—will come to discover his gifts with some degree of ease. He wants God to guide in his life, and that is the kind of person God stands ready to bless by showing him the gifts the Holy Spirit has bestowed on him.

Humbly and gratefully accept the gift God appears to have given you, and use it as fully as possible. We should accept ourselves as we are and use the gifts we have. Our gift may call us to service in some prominent position, with its own difficulty and danger. But it may also mean we are to serve in some humble sphere. I rather like David Howard's comment: "God has not called a spiritual elite to carry out the work of the ministry, bypassing the ordinary believer in the church. Rather, '*to each* is given the manifestation of the Spirit for the common good' (1 Cor. 12:7 [RSV])."[1]

This does not do away with the office of elder or bishop, or the deacon either, for that matter. It simply means that the laity as well as elders and deacons have a role to play and obligations to discharge in the congregation.

What we have said so far lays the groundwork for discussing each gift Paul lists. When it comes to the gifts of the Spirit mentioned by the apostle Paul, we see that he does not group gifts by category and no grouping I'm familiar with is wholly satisfactory. In the rest of this chapter we will limit ourselves to those five gifts listed in Ephesians 4:11 (apostle, prophet, evangelist, pastor, and teacher); several of these are also mentioned in 1 Corinthians 12:28. In a separate chapter we will deal with other gifts mentioned in 1 Corinthians 12 and Romans 12. A further chapter will deal with the sign gifts.

Apostle

The Greek word for this gift means "one sent with a commission." John R. W. Stott says, "The word 'apostle' is probably used in *three senses* in the New Testament. . . . [*Firstly,*] in the general sense that all of us are sent into the world by Christ and thus share in the apostolic mission of the church (Jn. 17:18; 20:21), all of us are in the broadest term 'apostles'. . . . [*Secondly,*] the word is used at least twice to describe 'apostles of the churches' (2 Cor. 8:23; Phil. 2:25), messengers sent on particular errands from one church to another. In this sense the word might be applied to missionaries and other Christians sent on special missions. . . . [*Thirdly,*] the gift of apostleship which is thus given precedence must refer, therefore, to that small and special group of men who were 'apostles of Christ', consisting of the Twelve (Lk. 6:12, 13), together with Paul (e.g. Gal. 1:1), . . . They were unique in being eyewitnesses of the historic Jesus, especially of the risen Lord. . . . In this primary sense, therefore, in which they appear in the lists, they have no successors, in the very nature of the case, although there are no doubt 'apostles' today in the secondary sense of 'missionaries'."[2] (italics mine)

Dr. Merrill C. Tenney has suggested that a present-day missionary may have this gift in its secondary meaning if he is a church planter. He would then need (1) to be sent with a message, (2) to be responsible to establish a church, and (3) to exercise authority in setting policies and enforcing them. I have a friend in the Caribbean who has spent a lifetime going from one community to another establishing churches. During his life he has established more than fifty. There are hundreds, and perhaps thousands, of men and women of God throughout the world today who are doing just that—even though the church may meet in a storefront building or a home.

Prophet

The English word *prophecy* derives from the Greek word meaning "public expounder." In apostolic times the gift of prophecy had two parts. One concerned the communication of words from God to men through the prophet. This was a supernatural gift. And in order for men to discern between false and true prophets, the Spirit gave the gift of "discerning the spirits" to other believers. The very fact that a prophet spoke by revelation virtually assured the existence of false prophets, too, as we note from both Old and New Testaments. New Testament Christians were not to despise prophesying but they were told to test all things.

According to 1 Corinthians 14:3, the second part of the prophetic office was the edification, instruction, consolation, and exhortation of the believers in local congregations. The prophet, who was usually an itinerant, took precedence over the local minister. But as time went on the gift of prophecy was exercised by local ministers who preached the Word of God for the edification of their parish members.

The gift of prophecy in the first sense, that of foretelling or predictive prophecy, no longer exists to the extent it did in first century Christianity.

I am aware of the evidence for rare instances in which Christians believe they have been given foreknowledge about future events. Hans Egede (1686–1758), the pioneer missionary to Greenland, was said to have prophesied the coming of a vessel with food at a time when starvation was close at hand. And the vessel came as he predicted. But instances of this sort are rare, not ordinary and frequent. I would not wish to rule out such occurrences as impossible to a sovereign God, though they are not binding on believers as scriptural prophecy. Also, I would think of them as distinct from what is the normal or ordinary function of the gift of prophecy today, which is the ability to understand and to engage in the exposition of the Word of God.

God no longer directly reveals "new truth"; there is now a back cover to the Bible. The canon of Scripture is closed. I understand the gift of prophecy to be used "in the extended sense of presenting God's people truths received, not by direct revelation, but from careful study of the completed and infallible Word of God."[3]

It is the work of the Holy Spirit to illumine the minds of those who are called to the prophetic office so they understand the Word of God and apply it with a depth impossible to those who do not have the gift of prophecy. It may sound like new truth freshly revealed—but to be biblical it must be based on the Word of God. There is a difference between doctrine and direction. There is nothing new in doctrine, but God does give new directions, which many times are mistaken as prophecies.

When prophecy is mentioned in connection with speaking in tongues another dimension appears. As I understand it from some of my brethren, individuals in the congregation might prophesy in tongues and then be interpreted by someone who has that latter gift. I am willing to grant that possibility, with the understanding that it does not involve *new* revelation but something the Holy Spirit would do that would be dynamically related to the written Word of God. The gift of prophecy deserves a stronger emphasis, perhaps, than that of either pastor or evangelist. Apparently, the New Testament prophets instructed, exhorted, rebuked, and warned of judgment.

I listened to a tape sometime ago that was reputed to be a new prophecy by an outstanding charismatic leader. However, upon listening to the tape I found that almost everything he said was biblically based. It was nothing new—only his emphasis was new. He gave biblical truth in a dramatic way, applying it to our own world.

In my own preaching I have done all these things. And I have encountered some evangelists whom I thought were prophets/evangelists/teachers/pastors; they had all these gifts and the gifts overlapped. The Old Testament prophets foretold the future, especially the future as it related to judgment to fall on cities and nations, or to the coming of Messiah. The New Testament prophets had ministries more like that of the evangelists. They proclaimed the Word of God and called upon people to repent of their sins; they disturbed people in their sins. The apostle Paul devotes a large portion of 1 Corinthians 14 to the subject of prophecy. The people of Corinth were so taken with the sign gifts that Paul chose to emphasize the importance of prophecy.

One word of caution, however. The Scriptures plainly teach that we are to exercise the gift of discernment—because many false prophets will appear. As a matter of fact, both in the writings of Jesus and the apostles, there is warning after warning that false prophets would appear, especially as we approach the end of the age. Many of them will be wolves in sheep's clothing. They will often fool God's own people. Thus the Christian must have those who can distinguish between false and true prophets. Paul was concerned about the Corinthians because they seemed to have little discernment, and they welcomed anyone as a true prophet of Christ. "For if someone comes to you and preaches a Jesus other than the Jesus we preached, or if you receive a different spirit from the one you received, or a different gospel from the one you accepted, you put up with it easily enough. . . . such men are false apostles, deceitful workmen, masquerading as apostles of Christ" (2 Cor. 11:4, 13 NIV).

There is a sense in which every Christian should be discerning, ascertaining truth from falsehood. This is so because every Christian should be rooted in the Bible, and he should know what the Bible teaches. However, the Bible also indicates some Christians have the gift of discernment in special measure.

What about people who claim to foretell the future? I have often been asked this question. The requirement (or test) of the true prophet (the forthteller) in the Scriptures was that he be 100 percent accurate. Not 50 percent. Not 75 percent. Not even 99 percent. But 100 percent accurate.

Evangelist

The term "evangelist" comes from a Greek word meaning "one who announces good news."

In his excellent book, *Good News Is for Sharing,* Leighton Ford points out something that comes as a surprise to some Bible students. The word translated "evangelist" occurs only three times in the New Testament: (1) Luke called Philip an evangelist (Acts 21:8); (2) Paul said God gave evangelists to the churches (Eph. 4:11); (3) he also urged Timothy to "do the work of an evangelist" (2 Tim. 4:5). The gift of evangelism, then, is simply a special ability in communicating the gospel.

The evangelist's message almost necessarily centers around the "content" of the gospel. The evangelist primarily is a "messenger"; he is a deliverer of "the good news." Incidentally, the evangelist in his proclamation may teach and do the work of a pastor, but his primary message centers in the death, burial, and resurrection of Christ, His coming again, and the need for all men everywhere to repent and believe.

The evangelist is the special proclaimer of the good news that God was in Christ reconciling the world to Himself. The Church through history has missed great blessings because some denominations have not as clearly recognized the gift of the evangelist as they have that of the teacher or pastor. Indeed, sometimes evangelists have been ignored or opposed by churches, as in the case of John Wesley, whose mission was rejected by his own church. Despite this, in almost every generation God has raised up evangelists, who often have had to pursue their calling outside the structured church.

Caricatures of evangelists abound because false evangelists in the Elmer Gantry image have libeled the hundreds of true ones throughout the world. But then the same can be said of some pastors, or teachers, who turn out to be false. A well-known pastor, teacher, or evangelist is often a special target of Satan. The higher the visibility, the easier the target. That's the reason those well known for their gifts need to be surrounded by prayer constantly on the part of God's people.

True evangelism speaks to the intellect and may or may not produce emotion, but its main job is to speak to the will. At times the gifts of teaching and evangelism are given to the same person. Some of the most effective evangelists I have known were essentially teachers who informed the minds of people even as they pricked their consciences by their use of the Word of God. I have known many teachers and expository preachers who claimed they were not evangelists—but indeed they did have the gift of evangelism! For example, though the late Dr. Donald Grey Barnhouse was a pastor/teacher, I have met many people who received Christ through his ministry.

Unfortunately, some evangelists spend too much time thinking and even planning about how to achieve visible results. This is an easy trap to fall into. Evangelists rightly desire to see results, but the gift itself is not a guarantee that these will be immediate.

The Reverend James R. Graham, Sr., pioneer missionary to China, proclaimed the gospel for three years without seeing results. When asked if he ever became discouraged, he replied, "No. 'The battle is the Lord's, and He will deliver it into our hands.'"

Nowhere do the Scriptures tell us to seek results, nor do the Scriptures rebuke evangelists if the results are meager. Men and women do make decisions wherever the gospel is proclaimed; whether publicly or privately, some say yes, some say no, and some procrastinate. No one ever hears the gospel proclaimed without making some kind of decision!

We should never forget that Noah was a preacher of righteousness. Yet after an evangelistic and prophetic ministry of 120 years only those in his immediate family believed and entered the ark (Heb. 11:7). On the other hand, some who obviously had the gift of evangelism have modestly subdued their gift because they are afraid of being accused of nonintellectualism, emotionalism, commercialism, or being too concerned with statistics. These are subtleties of Satan to keep the man with the gift of evangelism from being used.

For example, I remember there was a time in my own ministry when we quit keeping statistics (due to criticism). We found almost immediately that the public press exaggerated what was happening, and often used the wrong terminology. For example, we were in one city and the newspaper the next day reported, "1,000 saved at Billy Graham Crusade." Two things were wrong with that headline. First, only God knows whether they were saved or not—that is the reason we call them inquirers and not decisions. Second, it was not 1,000, but less than 500 (over half of those who came forward were trained counselors). Thus, we went back to giving accurate statistics.

Evangelism is not limited to professional evangelists, that is, those whose lives are wholly spent in this calling. The gift of evangelism is also given to many lay people. Philip is the only person in the Bible who was called an evangelist, and he was a deacon! In some sense every Christian who is not called to the vocation of evangelism is still called upon to do the *work* of an evangelist.

People often misunderstand the methods of evangelism. One can use hundreds of different methods, but it is the message that counts. Let us take note, however, of what evangelists cannot do. They cannot bring conviction of sin, righteousness, or judgment; that is the Spirit's work. They cannot convert anyone; that is the Spirit's work. The evangelist can invite men to receive Christ, and exhort them. But the effectual work is done by the Spirit as He works on the minds, hearts, and wills of the unsaved. We are to take care of the possible and trust God for the impossible.

Yet there is more. If the evangelist is to carry on a truly effective ministry to the glory of the Lord, the message must be backed by a Spirit-filled, fruit-producing life. Jesus promised, "Follow Me, and I will make you become fishers of men" (Mark 1:17). He provides the strength, through the Spirit. I urge all Christians to do the work of an evangelist—whether they go into full-time evangelism or not! I believe they have no option. It is a command from our Lord Jesus Christ, and the general injunction of Scripture. "Go therefore and make disciples of all the nations, baptizing them in the name of the Father and the Son and the Holy Spirit, teaching them to observe all that I commanded you; and lo, I am with you always, even to the end of the age" (Matt. 28:19, 20).

Pastor

The Bible does not often use the word *pastor*. In the Old Testament it occasionally translates the Hebrew word for shepherd. The New Testament uses the word *pastor* only once with the root idea of "shepherd" (Eph. 4:11). Here it is closely linked with the Old Testament translation of the word for shepherd. It is also closely linked with the word for teacher. Forms of the underlying Greek word also appear in two other places.

Among many Christians the word *pastor* is one of the most commonly preferred designations for ordained clergy. Its use is consistent with the ministry of our Lord who applies the term "shepherd" to Himself. So those called to the pastoral ministry by the Holy Spirit are undershepherds of the sheep.

Jesus Christ is called "the good shepherd" (John 10:11), and "the great Shepherd of the sheep" (Heb. 13:20). Peter talks about the "Chief Shepherd" who will someday appear (1 Peter 5:4). If Jesus is the chief shepherd, then there must be assistant shepherds; these include ministers of the gospel and unordained saints in the congregation who have gifts of counseling, guiding, warning, and guarding the flock. A number of people have acted as spiritual shepherds in my own life although they were never formally ordained to the ministry.

Many youth counselors, Sunday school teachers, and leaders of home Bible studies and Christian nurture groups actually perform functions that are part of the pastoral gift. Three of Paul's letters, 1 and 2 Timothy and Titus, were called pastoral epistles. They tell the shepherds how to watch over the flock. In our crusades, we use a "shepherd plan": Each person who comes forward as an inquirer talks to a trained counselor (or shepherd). This person may be a layman or an ordained pastor. We ask the counselor (or shepherd) to follow up with letters, phone calls, and visits until the inquirer is either in a warm Christian atmosphere, has made other Christian contacts, or is in a nurture group or prayer group. If he is in forced solitude (in prison), the shepherd teaches him to study the Bible on his own.

I believe that thousands of Christians throughout the world who will never become pastors of churches do have the gift of a pastor that can be used to assist the clergy in their work. Those who have the gift should use it as fully as possible, remembering that failure to do so is to grieve the Holy Spirit. Many pastors of churches are overworked and could use a little help. Each of us might well ask his pastor what to do to help him.

Teacher

The Greek word in Ephesians 4:11 for the gift of teacher means "instructor." When the message of the gospel has resulted in conversions, the new Christians must then be taught. In the Great Commission (Matt. 28:18–20), the command to disciple is followed immediately by the injunction, "teaching them to observe all that I commanded you."

One of the great needs in the Church at the present hour is for more teachers of the Bible. Yet this, too, is in the sovereign hands of God. Teaching is simply a Spirit-given ability to build into the lives of Christians a knowledge of God's Word and its application to their thinking and conduct. Teaching has for its goal the conformity of Christians to the likeness of Jesus. It can and should be done both simply, compassionately, and searchingly. Many years ago I had two doctrine professors. Both had earned doctors' degrees and were scholars in their own right. Both had one thing in common. When they taught their classes, they did it with such great brokenness and compassion that often tears would come to their eyes. I have long ago forgotten a great deal of what they taught, but I still remember those "tears."

Along this line, I am told that Paul's Greek phrasing of the list of gifts in Ephesians 4 suggests such a close connection between the gift of pastor and teacher that his words could almost be translated "pastor-teacher" as if it were one gift. This reinforces the idea that the spiritual teacher must have a compassionate sensitivity to the needs of the taught.

Some of the best teachers of the Word to whom I have listened have not had much formal education. By contrast, some of the poorer teachers have had Ph.D. degrees in various biblically related disciplines, but they lacked the teaching gift with which to communicate their knowledge. It is unfortunate that some seminaries fall into the secular world's qualifications for teachers—and some of the best Bible teachers do not have earned degrees. Therefore they are not qualified to teach in a modern seminary. I believe to the extent that this is practiced it could be dangerous to the future of the Church. That does not mean God does not use our intellectual abilities when they are committed to Him, but spiritual teaching, like all spiritual gifts, is a supernatural ability the Holy Spirit gives, not a university degree. In recent years I have changed my emphasis somewhat: in my proclamation of the gospel I have emphasized the cost of discipleship and the need for learning. God has providentially brought into being thousands of Bible classes as a result of our emphasis in the preparation and follow-up of our Crusades. Likewise, God has raised up hundreds of evangelical Bible schools and seminaries throughout the world. But the Church still lacks enough teachers. Yet I believe that the Spirit has given the gift of teaching to hundreds and perhaps thousands of people who either do not know they have the gift, or are not using it!

The gift of teaching may be used in all kinds of contexts—from a theological seminary and Bible school to a Sunday school class or home Bible study. The important thing for a person who has this gift is to use it whenever and wherever God leads.

One of the first verses of Scripture that Dawson Trotman, founder of the Navigators, made me memorize was, "The things that thou hast heard of me among many witnesses, the same commit thou to faithful men, who shall be able to teach others also" (2 Tim. 2:2 KJV). This is a little like a mathematical formula for spreading the gospel and enlarging the Church. Paul taught Timothy; Timothy shared what he knew with faithful men; these faithful men would then teach others also. And so the process goes on and on. If every believer followed this pattern, the Church could reach the entire world with the gospel in one generation! Mass crusades, in which I believe and to which I have committed my life, will never finish the Great Commission; but a one-by-one ministry will.

Apostle—prophet—evangelist—pastor—teacher: five of the gifts of the Holy Spirit. But perhaps you are saying, "I'm not a pastor or an evangelist. These are someone else's gifts, not mine. What do they have to do with me?" They have much to do with you!

First, it may be God *has* given you one of these gifts. God may be calling you to be a pastor, or an evangelist, or a teacher of the Bible. Perhaps you are a young person whom God is calling to the mission field. You may be older, and God wants to use you to teach a Sunday school class or a home Bible study group.

Second, the Bible commands us to support those whom God has called as leaders in the Church. For example, you should pray regularly for your pastor, for missionaries, and for others who are involved in God's work. "Pray on my behalf" the apostle Paul said (Eph. 6:19). Let them know you are supporting their work and are interested in what God is doing through them.

Third, learn from those God has placed in positions of Christian leadership. "Remember those who led you . . . imitate their faith. . . . Obey your leaders" (Heb. 13:7, 17). Give thanks to God for the gifts He has given to these leaders "for the equipping of the saints for the work of service, to the building up of the body of Christ" (Eph. 4:12).

12

Further Gifts of the Spirit

IN THE LAST chapter we studied the gifts Paul lists in Ephesians 4. Next we will consider others that he mentions in 1 Corinthians 12 (which are somewhat duplicated in Romans 12) where we find the primary list of gifts, the ones probably best known to most of us. Because the sign gifts (such as tongues) have caused so much controversy, we will deal with them in a separate chapter.

We must note first that Paul says, "Now there are varieties of gifts, but the same Spirit" (v. 4). Whatever I say about the gifts is based on a crucial presupposition: these gifts are supernatural gifts from the Spirit. The Christian himself cannot manufacture or produce them in any way. This does not mean, of course, that we should understand the gifts apart from the written Word of God. We are to study the Word and apply it.

The Spirit grants some people special wisdom, knowledge, faith, and the like, but the granting of these special gifts does not mean other Christians are barren. Rather, such spiritual gifts are often heightened forms of a rudimentary ability God gives all Christians. The gift of wisdom illustrates this. We all have some spiritual wisdom, but a person with this *gift* has wisdom in a very special degree. On the other hand, I believe the gift of healing or miracles is one a believer has or does not have. And God gives such a gift to very few, a policy He appears to have followed throughout the history of the Church. At any rate, we must now consider the first two spiritual gifts Paul mentions in 1 Corinthians 12.

We can possess three kinds of wisdom. The first comes to us naturally. The second comes from learning, so it is something we can be taught. But the highest kind of wisdom comes directly from God and is associated with the particular work of the Holy Spirit. Though He is the fountainhead of all truth from whatever source, yet He gives believers wisdom in a unique way—through the Scriptures. In addition, He gives a special gift or capacity for wisdom to some.

Dr. Merrill C. Tenney of Wheaton College defines this gift as "the ability to make correct decisions on the basis of one's knowledge."

This then leads us to a second gift, the gift of knowledge, which concerns acquaintance with spiritual information. Yet we all know believers with striking information about God and doctrine, but who do not know how to apply this to practical situations. I have a friend whose head is crammed full of biblical knowledge, yet the tragic mistakes he has made in judgment have almost destroyed his ministry. For this reason, the gifts of wisdom and knowledge must work together, that is, they illustrate the need for those with varying gifts to cooperate.

Jesus discusses a case where a believer may need both gifts. He says, "And when they bring you to trial and deliver you up, do not be anxious beforehand what you are to say; but say whatever is given you in that hour, for it is not you who speak, but the Holy Spirit" (Mark 13:11 RSV). Time after time Jesus' disciples had to defend themselves before mobs, governors, princes, and kings; the apostle Paul may have made his defense before Caesar himself. That knowledge which is the gift of the Spirit is based on long hours of disciplined study in which God teaches us. But the capacity to apply what we learn to actual situations goes beyond study and comes directly from the Holy Spirit. Wisdom is the gift from the Spirit which shows us how to use knowledge. Paul defended himself by using both. In doing this he illustrated Peter's advice about "always being ready to make a defense to every one who asks you to give an account for the hope that is in you, yet with gentleness and reverence" (1 Peter 3:15).

It is interesting that Peter also said we are to "grow in the grace and knowledge of our Lord and Savior Jesus Christ" (2 Peter 3:18). Through our communion with God we gain a higher knowledge and a higher wisdom than the world has. And believers given these in a peculiar degree can consider that they have the gift of knowledge or wisdom.

All of us face pressures, dilemmas, and problems for which we have no answer humanly speaking. A board of twenty-six capable men and women, both black and white, handles the personnel and financial affairs of our evangelistic association. From the very beginning of our ministry we have tried to be scrupulous in the way our business affairs are handled. Time after time in our board meetings when we reached an impasse about priorities, or when we were faced with critical financial needs, or had to face an unjust attack from some quarter, we would get on our knees to ask God for wisdom. He gave us answers immediately again and again. Every fellowship of believers needs at least one person with the gift of wisdom to aid in practical decisions. Such a person would often be the one, after we had prayed, who came up with the direction for the right decision we should make.

Faith

Faith comes from a Greek word meaning faithfulness or steadfastness: "To another faith by the same Spirit" (1 Cor. 12:9). In this passage the apostle Paul assumes the existence of saving faith. The Scripture says, "By grace you have been saved through faith" (Eph. 2:8). We are also told that "we walk by faith, not by sight" (2 Cor. 5:7). However, faith in 1 Corinthians 12 is a very special gift the Holy Spirit gives at His good pleasure.

We must distinguish between the grace of faith and the gift of faith. The grace of faith means that we can believe God will do whatever He has promised to do in His Word. All Christians have the grace of faith. Therefore, if we do not have faith in what the Bible promises, we sin. But many things come into our lives concerning which there are no specific promises from the Word. Therefore, when we pray, we add, "if it be Thy will." But sometimes the Holy Spirit gives us the gift of faith to believe for things about which the Bible is silent. If we do not have this special gift of faith, it is not sin.

We see a classic example of the gift of faith in the life of George Muller of Bristol, England, who cared for thousands of orphans over a period of many years. Muller refused to ask anyone for a single penny, but he prayed the money in. This is the gift of faith described by Jesus when He said, "If you have faith as a mustard seed, you shall say to this mountain, 'Move from here to there,' and it shall move; and nothing shall be impossible to you" (Matt. 17:20).

At times in my own ministry it has seemed to me that I was a man of little faith, and yet there have been a number of occasions when the Holy Spirit has given me the special gift of faith and forced me into seemingly impossible situations where there was no specific promise from God in the Word.

For example, in our 1957 New York Crusade, Madison Square Garden had been packed out night after night for six weeks and thousands had made their commitment to Christ. However, though we were scheduled to close at the Yankee Stadium on July 20, a burden grew in the hearts of a few of us that the Crusade should continue. Some felt that returning to the Garden after the Yankee Stadium would be anticlimactic; people would no longer be interested, especially with vacation time at hand.

I became so terribly burdened that I found it impossible to sleep at night. I knew that the ultimate decision would be up to me and my longtime colleague, Cliff Barrows, before God. Finally, one night while on my knees before God I said, "Lord, I do not know what is right, but by faith I am going to tell the committee tomorrow we shall go on." I called Cliff on the phone and he indicated God seemed to be saying the same thing to him.

Based on that decision we continued on for ten more weeks, ending with an open-air rally in Times Square where 75,000 people jammed the streets. The service was carried live on television and radio to the nation on prime evening time. Now, if that decision had not been made on the basis of the gift of faith from the Holy Spirit, hundreds of people who now know Christ might not have known Him.

I firmly believe there are times in all our lives when we make decisions on the basis of the will of God, and we are given faith by the Spirit to do what God wants us to do, regardless of the consequences.

Discernment of Spirits

The word *discernment* in 1 Corinthians 12:10 comes from a Greek word embodying several ideas: to see, consider, examine, understand, hear, judge closely. The New American Standard Bible calls the capacity for this gift, "the distinguishing of spirits."

As I stated in the last chapter, the Bible points out that many false prophets and deceivers will emerge inside and outside the Church through the ages. However, at the end of the age they will intensify their activities. Paul said, "Even Satan disguises himself as an angel of light. Therefore it is not surprising if his servants also disguise themselves as servants of righteousness" (2 Cor. 11:14, 15). I am convinced that hundreds of religious leaders throughout the world today are servants not of God, but of the Antichrist. They are wolves in sheep's clothing; they are tares instead of wheat.

Spiritism, the occult, the worship of Satan, and the activities of demons have increased rapidly throughout the Western world. False teachings (Paul calls them "doctrines of demons" in 1 Timothy 4:1) have gone hand in hand with their rise.

The great question is: How can we know the false from the true? This is why believers need the gift of discernment, or at least respect for the opinions of those who have it. The apostle John said, "Beloved, do not believe every spirit, but test the spirits to see whether they are from God; because many false prophets have gone out into the world" (1 John 4:1). In other words, believers are to test the various spirits and doctrines that abound today. Most of all we are to test them against the standard of the Word of God, the Bible. However, God gives to some individuals extraordinary abilities to discern the truth. In 1 Corinthians 12:10 we read, "to another [is given] the distinguishing of spirits."

A man named Joe Evans had this gift, I believe. I always called him "Uncle" Joe. He was probably the closest friend of Dr. V. Raymond Edman, the late president of Wheaton College. Many times the three of us (and sometimes members of my team) knelt down for long and glorious periods of prayer when we were faced with challenges, opportunities, or problems. At certain periods in my ministry I have been tempted to accept offers to move from evangelism to some other field. Many times, offers came through "an angel of light." I needed discernment. Since I did not always have it myself, one person to whom I went was "Uncle" Joe so I could profit from his special gift of discernment. I sought his advice and prayer. It is important to realize that a person with the gift of discernment can often tell the difference between what is of God and what is not. Such a person can often point out false teachings or false teachers—he has an almost uncanny ability to perceive hypocrisy, shallowness, deceit, or phoniness.

Certainly, this gift enabled Peter to see through the hypocrisy of Ananias and Sapphira. He also saw through Simon of Samaria who claimed to be converted and baptized in the Spirit but who turned out to be a counterfeit (Acts 8:9ff). Paul warned that "in later times some will fall away from the faith, paying attention to deceitful spirits and doctrines of demons" (1 Tim. 4:1).

Scripture teaches us everywhere that anything religious should be evaluated very carefully; that even the churches to which we go must be examined to see if they are sound in the faith.

Helps

The gift of "helps," mentioned in 1 Corinthians 12:28, gains its name from the Greek word having the idea of supporting, or assisting.

We have an example of the use of helps when the apostles decided to appoint deacons to take over the business affairs of the church (Acts 6). Their duties consisted primarily in waiting on tables and in the distribution of funds to the poor. The use of this gift makes it possible for thousands of lay people to engage in helping to promote the kingdom of God in such ways as counseling, prayer, handling the business affairs of the church and parachurch organizations, and witnessing. But, also, "helps" embodies the idea of social service, such as assisting the oppressed who suffer from social injustice and caring for orphans and widows. It could mean preparing a meal for a sick neighbor, writing a letter of encouragement or sharing what we have with someone in need. Helps is the gift of showing mercy. It also carries with it the idea of helping in some of the ordinary activities of Christian service so that others, endowed with other gifts, can be released to utilize them more freely. "If anyone serves, he should do it with the strength God provides, so that in all things God may be praised through Jesus Christ" (I Peter 4:11 NIV).

During my early crusades I had a compulsion to be involved in virtually all aspects of our evangelism ministry. Obviously, this meant demands so heavy upon me that I was physically exhausted most of the time. I remember how Dawson Trotman, whom I had asked to head our counseling, came to me one night. "Billy," he said, "you are wearing yourself out." He added, "Why can't we go at this as a team? Let Cliff Barrows lead the singing, you do the preaching, and trust me and those I have trained to do the counseling." I agreed to give it a try. This was one of the most momentous and profitable decisions of my life. For the first time I began to realize that God can and does use others to take charge of certain phases of the work of evangelism just as effectively as he could use me or Cliff Barrows or some of the other leaders on our team. This is an illustration of how God can use all the gifts to help one another, but that the gift of "helps" is special.

My later study of Scripture showed me that even our Lord gathered a team of people around Him and then sent them out on one occasion to minister two by two. Mark was the helper for Paul and Barnabas (Acts 12:25). Paul traveled continually with a team of workers, without whom he could never have carried on his ministry effectively. At the end of his letters Paul usually mentioned some of those faithful helpers. In Romans the list contains more than a score of names, many of them women. Writing to the Philippians, Paul mentions Epaphroditus who "ministered to my wants" (Phil. 2:25 KJV).

While I was writing this chapter, my wife Ruth and I, along with Grady and Wilma Wilson, were the guests of Mr. and Mrs. Bill Mead of Dallas, Texas. Every morning we had a Bible study. One morning Grady Wilson suggested that we break into our regular Bible study schedule and go instead to the Book of Philemon. I thought this was rather strange, but we went along with him. As we studied Philemon I prayed, "Thank you, Lord, for giving me a perfect illustration of one who had the gift of helps." The example was Onesimus, the slave. Paul wrote to his master Philemon and said, Onesimus was "useful . . . to me" (Philem. 11).

Do you have the particular gift of "helps"? You could be a businessman faithfully serving on a board of a parachurch organization or missionary society. Or you could be involved in a Bible society or be a trustee or deacon of a church. One could be a busy housewife and mother. Another could be a student.

A relative of mine named Uncle Bo used to take every Saturday afternoon to clean the little church in the heart of Charlotte where he was a member. He mowed the grass and cut the hedges. Few people ever noticed the helps he gave so cheerfully. This was about all he could do. He couldn't preach; he couldn't teach; he had a difficult time praying in public; but he had the gift of helps. And God used him.

The Gift of Governments

This gift gains its name from the Greek word carrying the idea of steering, piloting, or directing. Some versions call it the gift of administrations (1 Cor. 12:28). Certain people have been given the gift of leadership that is recognized by the Church.

The Scriptures teach that churches must have government; they require leadership, whether professional or nonprofessional. Christ spent more than half His time with just twelve men, developing them into leaders who would carry on His work after He ascended to heaven. Wherever the apostles went they appointed leaders over the churches they founded. The Scripture says that Paul and Barnabas "appointed elders for them in every church" (Acts 14:23). In 1 Timothy 3:1–7 Paul gives qualifications for "bishops" (KJV). The word for "bishop" is thought by many to be equivalent to "pastor," carrying the idea of overseer, superintendent, or governor.

While some churches and assemblies attempt to conduct the work of the Lord without an appointed leadership, I believe this is virtually impossible. Some Christian groups do not have an appointed ordained leader. Yet services are conducted decently and in order, and the other ministries of the group are carried out. There are those who exercise leadership, even if the official titles are not given to them. If we do not recognize this gift it leads to confusion, and it appears to me to be unbiblical since it hinders the work of the Holy Spirit who gives men the gift of government. The writer of the Book of Hebrews went so far as to say, "Obey your leaders, and submit to them" (Heb. 13:17). Certainly he was talking about those who had authority in the Church.

The qualifications of a leader are listed several times in the New Testament. He must not be dictatorial, egotistical, or dogmatic; he is to be anything but that. Rather he is to be humble, gracious, courteous, kind, and filled with love; yet at times he must be very firm. For this reason the gift of knowledge combined with wisdom is necessary. Further, the leadership idea outlined in the New Testament is decisively in opposition to the notion of great pomp and pageantry. Rather, it emphasizes the graces of humility and service.

The Lord Jesus Christ is the most perfect example of a governor, or a leader. "For even the Son of Man did not come to be served, but to serve, and to give His life a ransom for many" (Mark 10:45). He humbled Himself to become a servant (Phil. 2:7); He washed the disciples' feet and then said, "A servant is not greater than his master" (John 13:16 RSV). Jesus, by example, tells us that every true leader should be a helper, a servant, or even a bondslave. We are exhorted to, "through love serve one another" (Gal. 5:13). This is a command, not a suggestion, and applies with special force to leaders.

The End of the Matter

God did not ordain that the Church should drift aimlessly in the seas of uncertainty without compass, captain, or crew. By His Spirit He has provided for the operation of the Church in history through the gifts of His Spirit, and we are told to "earnestly desire the greater gifts" (1 Cor. 12:31). Whether the Holy Spirit gives us one or several, it is important for us to do two things: First we should recognize the gift or gifts God has given us. Second, we should nurture those gifts and do everything, humanly speaking, to improve them as we use them. One who has the gift of prophecy should be better able to fill this role with the passage of every year of his life. And the person with the gift of wisdom should be wiser at the end than he was at the beginning.

Some day all of us will give account of the way we have used the gifts God has given. The person to whom much has been given will find much required of him. Let's use our gifts as fully as possible and wait with expectation for our Lord's "Well done, good and faithful servant" (Matt. 25:21 RSV) at the judgment of the saints.

13

The Sign Gifts

I THINK A WORD of explanation and caution will be helpful here in connection with the so-called sign gifts listed in 1 Corinthians 12:9, 10. By "sign gifts" I mean those gifts of the Holy Spirit which are often obvious outward indications or signs of the working of God. The sign gifts include *healings, miracles,* and *tongues.* They seem to rate the most attention in the Church today, exciting the imagination and producing outward manifestations that attract multitudes.

One Christian leader said that if he heard a clergyman down the street was preaching the gospel, he would just turn on his T.V. and go back to watching his favorite program. But if he was told that someone down the street was performing miracles, he would drop everything to see what was happening. Why is this? Simply because we seem to be fascinated by the spectacular and the unusual. This kind of curiosity is not necessarily good or helpful, but it is, nevertheless, very common.

It is interesting to note that in the Bible's four discussions of the gifts of the Spirit (Rom. 12:6–8; 1 Cor. 12:8–10; Eph. 4:11; and 1 Peter 4:10, 11), these sign gifts are listed together only in the first letter to Corinth, a church that was abusing at least one of these gifts. Christians should remember that the Holy Spirit did not intend gifts to be misused so that they become divisive, or disrupt our fellowship. When this occurs the greatest of all manifestations of the Spirit, love, is diminished.

Healing

The Holy Spirit gives the gift of healing (literally, the gift of cures). Many cases of healing appear in the Old Testament, and certainly the New Testament is full of instances when Jesus and His disciples healed the sick. Throughout the history of the Christian Church countless instances of physical healing have been recorded.

The ministry of physical healings through spiritual means is sometimes associated with faith healers. Many of these claim to have the gift of healing or at least some special power. Tens of thousands of people flock to these healers. And thousands more are urged to write certain radio and television preachers who claim to have this gift of healing. Indeed, mass attention has been focused in recent years on the Christian faith and physical healing.

Yet sickness and infirmity are a part of life: no one can escape them at last. All people, including the most famous faith healers, get sick, and all eventually die. Kathryn Kuhlman, the famous faith healer, died early in 1976. For years she had suffered from a heart condition, and late in 1975 underwent open heart surgery from which she never recovered. People were healed under her ministry. She was not. Sickness brought death to her at last.

However, we must distinguish the operation of what the Bible calls the gift of healing from a second method of healing. Some place their emphasis on the faith of the one who needs healing— telling him it will happen if only he believes. By this they mean more than those who believe that forgiveness, cleansing, and acceptance with God spring from the atoning work of Jesus on the cross. They think that any Christian who becomes ill can claim healing by faith. Note that this has nothing to do with the gift of healing as such. Such teachers may believe, for example, that physical healing for disease is in the atonement of Jesus Christ. To them the death of Christ on the cross not only results in the offer of forgiveness for our sins, but also physical healing for the body. Both, they believe, come to us by faith.

This kind of healing has to do with *faith* rather than just the gift of healing itself.

In support of this position it is pointed out that the Old Testament foretold the coming of the Messiah and said of Him, "And by His scourging we are healed" (Isa. 53:5). Personally I do not believe the Scripture makes it clear to us that Christ's work on the cross included physical healing. The passage found in Isaiah 53:5 is quoted once in the New Testament in 1 Peter 2:24: "And He Himself bore our sins in His body on the cross, that we might die to sin and live to righteousness; for by His wounds you were healed." It seems clear from this that the "healing" of the Savior is primarily spiritual in nature, not physical.

Some Christians, regardless of whether they believe God heals through the spiritual gift or through the exercise of faith alone, believe it is unnecessary to consult a physician when they are ill, except possibly as a last resort. Several avenues are open to them: They can believe God for healing, in which case it does not involve the gift of healing but rather the gift of faith. Or they may go to someone whom they believe has the gift of healing. The gift of healing means that a person so gifted can do exactly what Jesus did; by that power which is his as a gift from the Holy Spirit he can make the sick well immediately and permanently: a broken arm is mended instantly, a cancer disappears, the process of pneumonia stops and the lungs become well.

Healing from illnesses must be considered from a broader perspective, I feel. James teaches that all good gifts come from above. I believe that healing can and may come from God through the gift of healing and the gift of faith, but it also comes from Him through the use of medical means. Paul told Timothy to take some medicinal wine for his stomach problems (1 Tim. 5:23). We must keep in mind that Luke was a physician and accompanied Paul on many of his trips, and probably gave him medical help.

I know the Lord has used physicians and medicine to cure illnesses I have suffered. Furthermore, we must be open to the idea that it may not be the will of God for us to be cured of all our infirmities, something true of the apostle Paul (see 2 Cor. 12:7–10). I think Christians should therefore use God-given wisdom to determine whether they should seek the use of natural means or rely solely on prayer or those with the genuine gift of healing.

If medication is not available, or if doctors have pronounced a case incurable, and God lays it on our hearts to look to Him in simple faith for the impossible, then we must follow His leading. But this leading must come from God, not the urging of fellow Christians.

However, if medication and doctors are available, to ignore them in favor of asking God to heal seems to me to border on presumption.

I had a friend who was struck with a deadly disease. The doctors knew there was no hope. He knew there was no hope. So he sent for one he knew to have the gift of healing. After prayer and spiritual counseling, the healer laid her hands on my friend. Immediately he felt what seemed to be an electric shock, and he was healed instantly. When he was checked by the doctors, all evidence of the disease had disappeared.

Overjoyed, he became totally taken up with the sign-gifts: healing, miracles, speaking in tongues and their interpretation. The person and work of Christ were all but ignored. The fruit of the Spirit was not in evidence. Three years later the disease recurred with a vengeance. This time God did not choose to heal him. He died slowly, bitterly disillusioned, as if all glory plus the Lord Himself were not awaiting him.

Prudence differs from presumption, and we ought not tempt God. If a sick Christian resorts to faith for healing, he should be certain God has given him that faith. Lacking it, he ought to seek the help of physicians. And in my judgment it is normal for a Christian to use the medical help God provides. Medicine and physicians (such as Luke) are of God, too.

Sometime ago I conversed with a psychiatrist of impeccable qualifications. In the conversation he underscored a well-known fact: People suffer from both organic and functional diseases. Under the latter category the medical books list many diseases which have no organic basis but are psychosomatic. Yet they do produce outward physical ailments which cannot be cured by ordinary medical treatment; they can be cured, however, when the mind is treated. When the mind is made well, the physical manifestations stemming from this functional situation disappear. The Romans had a famous saying: *mens sana in corpore sano*, a sound mind in a sound body. A diseased mind can produce disease in the body. A healthy mind will keep the body from functional diseases that derive from disease of the mind.

Having said all this, I do know that God heals under certain circumstances in accordance with His will. My own sister-in-law is an outstanding example. She was dying of tuberculosis. The X-rays showed the seriousness of her condition, but she asked her surgeon father for permission to discontinue medical treatment because she believed God was going to heal her. It was granted, and some godly men and women anointed her with oil and prayed the prayer of faith. Then a new series of X-rays was taken, and to the astonishment of the physicians at the sanatorium she no longer showed any signs of active tuberculosis. Immediately she began to gain weight, and thirty-five years later she is an active Bible teacher, a healthy person. Obviously, she was healed. But note that the healing came, not through someone who had the gift of healing, but through faith.

It is interesting to note that Jesus did not always heal people the same way. On some occasions He simply spoke the word and the healing took place. At other times He used what might be considered *means*. Jesus took the hand of Simon Peter's mother-in-law, and she was healed instantly (Matt. 8:15). When Jesus raised Lazarus from the dead, He cried out with a loud voice, "Lazarus, come out" (John 11:43 RSV). But Jesus healed the man born blind in quite a different way: He mixed clay and spittle, spread it on the eyes of the blind man, and commanded him to wash it off in the pool of Siloam (John 9:1ff). In the case of the centurion's servant, the sick man was not even near Jesus when he was healed (Matt. 8:5ff). And the woman with the issue of blood was healed simply by touching the garment of the Lord (Matt. 9:18ff).

The laying on of hands or the anointing with oil has both spiritual and psychological significance. The sick and those who anoint them must not suppose that the healing is due to the laying on of hands, the anointing with oil, their own personal faith, or even their prayers. The healing is from God and is of God. "The *Lord* will raise him up" (James 5:15, italics mine).

But God does not always choose to heal us. As I have said, I can find no evidence in Scripture that it is the will of God to heal all people of all illnesses. If the Holy Spirit gives a sick person or someone who is praying for a sick person the gift of faith that the person will be healed, then we can be sure the person will be healed. But God does not always give the gift of faith. This means that sick people and their loved ones should certainly pray for the one who is ill, but in the absence of the gift of faith they must pray, "If it be Thy will." I believe that true faith involves a complete surrender of our life to the will of God, whatever it is, even when God does not choose to heal us. This means we are willing to be healed, or willing to remain afflicted, or willing to die—willing for whatever God wants!

We have the classic example of Job who was afflicted with boils from head to foot. Satan was responsible for this, but it is interesting to note that Satan had to get God's permission before he could even touch Job's possessions, much less Job.

Yet the Book of Job is the result of the situation. What would believers have done down through the centuries without this tremendous account?

Then there is the example of Amy Carmichael of India who spent over fifty years ministering to children. The last twenty years of her life were spent in bed in almost constant pain due to an injury from a severe accident. Yet it was during these years that she did all her writing—poems, devotional books, and accounts of the ministry of the Dohnavur Fellowship. These books continue to minister to thousands throughout the world though she has long since gone to be with the Lord. Had she not been confined to her bed, she would never have had the time to write.

I have attended a number of healing meetings. Some sickened me because of the emotional hysteria present. I have also attended healing meetings where the services were conducted decently and in order. At those, I have witnessed the quiet moving of the Spirit of God in a way that could offend no one. In meetings like that the Spirit used God's servants with special gifts to do His will.

Every sickness, every infirmity, and every wrong thing in our lives can be traced back to original sin. But this does not mean that those of us who experience these difficulties do so because we have been guilty of overt transgressions. Certainly in some cases we do suffer from illnesses that are the direct or indirect result of some evil we have committed. But not always.

One day Jesus encountered a man who was blind from birth. And it was His disciples, not the Pharisees or the Sadduccees who asked this question, "Who sinned, this man or his parents, that he should be born blind?" (John 9:2). Even Jesus' disciples could not conceive of blindness that was not a direct result of sin. Jesus told them, "It was neither that this man sinned, nor his parents; but it was in order that the works of God might be displayed in him" (v. 3).

When we see someone with an infirmity or illness, we should be careful not to assume he is suffering because of his sin. Many illnesses are not the result of the person's sin. Accidents or inherited defects can cause sickness. Neither the sin of a retarded baby or its parents caused its misfortune, though all illness arises from original sin. God never meant for us to get sick and die, but man's rebellion against God in the Garden of Eden changed all that. We must remember, too, that the devil spitefully tries to use every sickness to hinder our fellowship with God, to cause us to have a neurotic sense of guilt, or even to charge God with injustice, lack of love for us, or harshness.

At the same time we have the promise of God that some day all the effects of sin on this creation will be destroyed, including sickness. "And He shall wipe away every tear from their eyes; and there shall no longer be any death; there shall no longer be any mourning, or crying, or pain; the first things have passed away" (Rev. 21:4).

Many Christians do suffer physical, mental, and even spiritual illnesses from time to time. Chronic physical impediments, minds disposed to periods of depression, or weak spirits subject to doubt all cause acute suffering. God's help is available for those impediments, and His sympathy and understanding abound. We can expect the Holy Spirit to be present and to work in our lives. "The Spirit also helpeth our infirmities" (Rom. 8:26 KJV), and through Hebrews 4:16 God promises us help: "Let us therefore draw near with confidence to the throne of grace, that we may receive mercy and may find grace to help in time of need."

In circumstances like these the Holy Spirit takes over. He is called "the divine Paraclete." The Greek word *parakletos* occurs five times in the New Testament. Four times it is translated "helper" (John 14:16, 26; 15:26; 16:7) and once "advocate" (1 John 2:1). It means "one who walks by our side as our counselor, helper, defender, and guide."

The Holy Spirit *does* help us in the midst of our sicknesses, infirmities, and weaknesses. Sometimes these very sicknesses indicate that we are Spirit-filled. Three times the apostle Paul asked God to remove the "thorn" that gave him great difficulty, but God answered, "No." He also said, "My grace is sufficient for you, for power is perfected in weakness" (2 Cor. 12:9). Paul responded quickly, "Most gladly, therefore, I will rather boast about my weaknesses, that the power of Christ may dwell in me" (2 Cor. 12:9). He went even further: "I am well content with weaknesses, with insults, with distresses, with persecutions, with difficulties, for Christ's sake; for when I am weak, then I am strong" (2 Cor. 12:10). Paul, even while being filled with the Holy Spirit, bore a sickness in his body that God allowed him to suffer for His glory.

So if God allows a sickness and refuses healing, we should accept it with gratitude. And we should ask Him to teach us all He wants us to learn through the experience, including how to glorify Him in it.

Paul's experience teaches us a lesson concerning healing in relation to the atonement of our Lord. Matthew says that "He took our infirmities and bore our diseases" (Matt. 8:17 RSV). This is absolutely true. By His death on Calvary we are assured that we shall be delivered from every infirmity and every disease. But God permits some of us to be afflicted with infirmities and diseases now. So we know that deliverance from them was never meant for all God's people, and for all diseases at all times, including today.

There are a growing number of churches that hold occasional healing services. When I inquired about these healing services, it was explained that few of the healings had to do with physical illness—rather they deal with relationships, memories, attitudes, guilt feelings. As a result, marriages have been healed; parents reconciled with children; employers with employees.

To summarize, there is no doubt in my mind that there is a gift of healing—that people are healed in answer to the prayer of faith—

and that there are other healings, such as healings of relationships. There is also need for a word of caution. There are many frauds and charlatans in the fields of medicine and faith healing. Again, one must have spiritual discernment.

Miracles

The gift of performing miracles takes its key term, "miracles," from a Greek word meaning "powers" (2 Cor. 12:12). A miracle is an event beyond the power of any known physical law to produce; it is a spiritual occurrence produced by the power of God, a marvel, a wonder. In most versions of the Old Testament the word "miracle" is usually translated "a wonder" or "a mighty work." Versions of the New Testament usually refer to miracles as "signs" (John 2:11) or "signs and wonders" (John 4:48; Acts 5:12; 15:12).

Clearly, the wonders performed by Jesus Christ and the apostles authenticated their claim of authority and gave certitude to their message. And we must remember that people did ask Jesus and the apostles this question, "How do we know that you are what you say you are, and that your words are true?" That was not an improper question. And at strategic moments God again and again manifested Himself to men by miracles so they had outward, confirming evidence that the words they heard from God's servants were true.

One notable case that illustrates this principle has to do with Elijah on Mount Carmel. He was engaged in a terrible battle in which the people of Israel had to decide between God and Baal. Elijah challenged the priests of Baal to set up an altar and lay an animal sacrifice on it. He told the people of Israel they should look for a confirming sign to convince them whether the true God was Baal or the Lord. The priests of Baal cried out in desperation to their god, but nothing happened. Then Elijah poured barrels of water over the animal sacrifice on his altar, and God sent fire from heaven that consumed the sacrifice in spite of the water. This was a miracle!

Paul argues that men could know he was an apostle when he said, "The signs of a true apostle were performed among you with all perseverance, by signs and wonders and miracles" (2 Cor. 12:12).

The Holy Spirit gave the gift of performing miracles to the early apostles as an evidence that they were Christ's messengers for a special task: that of ushering in a new era in mankind's history.

However, it has always interested me that many of the great men of both the Old and New Testaments performed no miracles. John the Baptist illustrates this: "And many came to Him; and they were saying, 'While John performed no sign, yet everything John said about this man was true.' And many believed in Him there" (John 10:41, 42). So though John performed no miracles, he exalted the Lord Jesus Christ, whom many then received. Remember that Jesus said of John, "Truly, I say to you, among those born of women there has not arisen anyone greater than John the Baptist" (Matt. 11:11).

Why do we not see the spectacular miracles today that we read about in the Bible? Are few such miracles occurring because our faith is small—or could it be that God does not will the spectacular right now? Could it be that signs and wonders were gifts particularly appropriate to the special circumstances of the early Church? I think so. And today when the gospel is proclaimed on the frontiers of the Christian faith that approximate the first century situation, miracles still sometimes accompany the advance of the gospel. As indicated by both the prophets Hosea and Joel, as we approach the end of the age we may expect miracles to increase.

Yet Jesus, referring to His miracles, told the disciples they would perform "greater works than these" (John 14:12). What could be greater than the works He did: healing the sick, restoring sight to the blind, raising the dead, casting out demons? It has been said, "Jesus did not come to preach the gospel but in order that there might be a gospel to preach."

Because of His death and resurrection we now have a gospel that can provide forgiveness of sins and the transformation of lives. A transformed life is the greatest of all miracles. Every time a person is "born again" by repentance of sin and faith in Jesus Christ, the miracle of regeneration is performed.

This is not to reject the further truth that in some places in the world the Holy Spirit has sovereignly appointed certain people to be workers of miracles. I have just stated that as we approach the end of the age I believe we will see a dramatic recurrence of signs and wonders which will demonstrate the power of God to a skeptical world. Just as the powers of Satan are being unleashed with greater intensity, so I believe God will allow signs and wonders to be performed.

Tongues

A leading minister in the Church of Scotland lay in the Intensive Care Unit of a Glasgow infirmary. He knew that his life hung in the balance—at any minute he might be seeing his Lord face to face. And so, he began talking to Him. As he did, he found himself praying in a language he had never heard before. After confiding this to a friend, he never mentioned it again. He recovered to serve His Lord for several more years.

A frantic young wife and mother, for whom everything had gone wrong one day, sat up in her bed that night literally "fussing at God."

"Have you ever heard of praying in tongues?" she paused to ask my wife when she was recounting the incident. Ruth nodded. "Well, I never had. I'd never heard of it. I'd never asked for it. I didn't even know what was happening. And suddenly it was as if I were orbiting the earth in a spaceship and as I passed over each continent I thought of the Christians there, mentioning the missionaries I knew by name. In this way I circled the entire globe. Then I glanced at the clock, thinking I had been praying at least thirty minutes. To my amazement it was dawn. And I was refreshed. The burden was lifted. The frustration, the anger, the complaining—it was all gone. And I felt as if I'd had a good night's sleep."

A Sunday school class was studying the person and work of the Holy Spirit in a neighborhood where speaking in tongues had become a divisive issue among believers. After one particularly exciting meeting the college Sunday school teacher was asked to speak on the Holy Spirit. One by one the students shared their experience with this phenomenon. The teacher, recalling the class some months later, mentioned three people who stood out in his memory. One, whose testimony had the ring of truth to it, for a few months after his experience became totally preoccupied with tongues, speaking of little else, and doing his best to see that other believers had the same experience. Eventually, however, he leveled off, realizing that the Holy Spirit has been given to enable us to glorify the Lord Jesus in differing ways. Today he is a uniquely gifted minister of the gospel.

A second class member, who also claimed to speak in tongues, was expelled from his college a few weeks later for open, repeated, and unrepentant immorality.

A third who stands out in the teacher's memory was a recently converted street-fighter from one of our large cities. After the class, he had taken the teacher to one side and confided that he had been in the same meeting where he had recognized the language spoken. When the teacher asked him what language it was, he replied, "The language I used to hear when I assisted my grandmother who was a spirit medium." The teacher told me he thought these cases illustrated three sources for what are called tongues: (1) the Holy Spirit; (2) psychological influence; (3) satanic influence.

While I do not pose as an expert on the subject of tongues, my opinions have come from my study of the Bible and from my experience and conversations with many people. Of one thing I'm certain: neither the Holy Spirit nor any of His gifts were given to divide believers. This does not mean that we ought not have our own opinions about what the Bible teaches on tongues. Or that we should not have local congregations in which prominence is given to tongues as well as those in which tongues are not prominent. But I am certain about one thing: when the gift of tongues is abused and becomes divisive, then something has gone wrong. Sin has come into the body of Christ.

Historical Background

For almost a century speaking in tongues has been given an important role among many Christians and certain churches. For them tongues-speaking is related to the life of the Christian subsequent to conversion.

It is true, however, that thousands of so-called "charismatic" believers have never spoken in tongues. Yet they are accepted as true believers in the Lord Jesus. Thus, among many churches which consider themselves charismatic, speaking in tongues is not regarded as an essential sign of having been born again. They agree that regenerated believers have been baptized into the body of Christ by the Spirit, of which water baptism is an outward sign. At the time of regeneration the Spirit took up His abode in their hearts. But for them the baptism in the Spirit is something that occurs after regeneration.

More recently the neo-Pentecostal or charismatic movement has come into being. Many of these people hold their memberships in mainline denominations and some of them are Roman Catholics. They agree with Pentecostal churches in their emphasis on healing and often accept speaking in tongues as a sign of baptism with the Holy Spirit, an experience occurring subsequent to regeneration. But the old-time Pentecostal churches are bothered because they do not always see a change in lifestyle among the neo-Pentecostals, something they cherish as being intrinsic to the Spirit-anointed life.

No one can escape the fact that the neo-Pentecostal emphasis has brought Protestants and Roman Catholics closer together in some parts of the world, not on the basis of having worked out their theological disagreements on matters like justification by faith, the sacrifice of the Mass, or the infallibility of the Pope, but on the basis of speaking in tongues and baptism with the Holy Spirit. However, I have met many Roman Catholics, like Protestants, who call themselves charismatic but have never spoken in tongues. For them it has been a new discovery of a personal relationship with Christ.

The Biblical Data on Tongues

Speaking in tongues (or "glossolalia," a term formed from the equivalent Greek words) is mentioned in *only two* New Testament books: The Acts of the Apostles and Paul's First Letter to the Corinthians (though it is mentioned in Mark 16:17, which most scholars believe is not in the original manuscripts). The word seems to be used in two different ways. One way is found in connection with the events at Pentecost, when the promised coming of the Holy Spirit occurred. A careful study of that passage in Acts 2 indicates that the "tongues" were known languages which were understood by foreign visitors in Jerusalem. Thus the little band of Christians was given a supernatural ability to speak in other languages.

What happened at Pentecost? The second chapter of Acts tells us that four things took place which signaled the advent of the new age. First, a sound from heaven like that of a violent wind filled the house. Second, something that looked like tongues of fire sat on each one of the people in the upper room. Third, all of them were filled with the Holy Spirit. Fourth, all of them spoke in tongues as the Spirit gave them the ability to do so. These tongues were languages known to the people from all over the Roman Empire who had come to Jerusalem for Pentecost. Some believe that the miracle took place in the ears of the hearers. Others believe that the apostles were given a supernatural gift of speaking in a foreign language that they did not know. Whatever position we take, a "miracle" took place!

The same basic word for "filled" appears in Acts 4:8 where Peter, "filled with the Holy Spirit" (speaking in tongues is not mentioned), preached his short sermon to the high priest and the rulers of the Jews. The same root word is used in connection with John the Baptist in Luke 1:15 where the Scripture says that "he will be filled with the Holy Spirit, while yet in his mother's womb." However, we have no record that John ever spoke in tongues. In Paul's conversion experience we are told that Ananias came to him "that you may regain your sight, and be filled with the Holy Spirit" (Acts 9:17). His sight then returned, he was baptized, and "immediately he began to proclaim Jesus in the synagogues, saying, 'He is the Son of God'" (Acts 9:20). Again, speaking in tongues is not mentioned.

Acts 19 recounts the story of Paul at Ephesus. He found some believers there who had heard nothing about the Spirit's coming. We are then told that "when Paul had laid his hands upon them, the Holy Spirit came on them, and they began speaking with tongues and prophesying" (Acts 19:6). Here the Scripture does not say they were filled with the Spirit. At any rate they spoke with tongues and prophesied, though there were no tongues of fire nor rushing mighty wind as at Pentecost. Moreover, the account in Acts 19 does not say whether the tongues spoken were languages the people there understood nor does it say interpreters were present. At least we can assume they spoke in tongues used somewhere in the world.

When I go to a foreign country, I speak in English. This is an unknown tongue to the majority of my listeners. For example, in northeast India I spoke to many thousands at each meeting; seventeen separate interpreters were used to translate my message into seventeen different dialects so that the people could understand my "unknown tongue." In my judgment this is analogous to what happened at Pentecost, except there it was a divine miracle. Either a given speaker spoke in a language certain listeners knew, or the Holy Spirit interpreted what was being said to each listener in his own language, the miracle then being in his capacity to understand.

"Unknown" Tongues in 1 Corinthians

In 1 Corinthians speaking in tongues appears to be something quite different from the occurrences in the Acts of the Apostles, although the same Greek word is used in Acts and 1 Corinthians to speak of "tongues."

At Pentecost the disciples spoke in tongues known to the people visiting Jerusalem. The Spirit-empowered speakers did not know these languages, but their listeners did. However, in 1 Corinthians the listeners did not hear a language they knew, so interpreters were required. The question is whether or not the tongues in 1 Corinthians were known languages. Some Bible students suggest they were, while others say they were simply some form of ecstatic utterance unrelated to any known human language. Personally, I lean toward the latter position. Actually, however, it probably makes little difference in our understanding of the passage, although some point out that if the Corinthian gift of tongues was a known language, then it is unrelated to much of what is labeled as "tongues" today. The fact that "interpretation" is seen as a spiritual gift makes me believe that the gift of tongues mentioned in 1 Corinthians was not a known language which might be understood by someone who naturally spoke that language.

First Corinthians 13 has its own puzzle. Paul mentions tongues of men and of angels. Now it should be apparent that angelic tongues are not known to any of us, yet the implication is there that some might speak in such tongues. However, in Corinthians Paul speaks of tongues as a gift that comes from the Holy Spirit, so He might give someone the ability to speak an angelic tongue. Of course, Paul makes it quite plain that not everyone is given this particular gift. It is for these reasons that I have difficulty linking the filling of the Holy Spirit to a second baptism and to a necessary accompanying sign, speaking in tongues. I cannot see solid Scriptural proof for the position that tongues as a sign is given to all who are baptized with the Spirit while tongues as a gift is given only to some.

Furthermore, I sometimes think the modern usage of the term "charismatic" may be incorrect. In 1 Corinthians, the Greek word for gifts God gives believers is *charismata*. No one can get such a gift by himself. According to Paul, the gifts, as we shall see in a moment, come from the sovereign operation of the Spirit of God "distributing to each one individually just as He wills" (1 Cor. 12:11). Paul says, "For by one Spirit we [for that is what the Greek says] were all baptized into one body" (1 Cor. 12:13). But in addition to this the Spirit distributes gifts to the various members of the body. Thus, every believer gets some gift. And *every* believer is therefore a charismatic!

Moreover, Paul does not indicate that any one gift belongs to every believer. He says only that each receives "some" gift. He does tell the Corinthians to "covet" (which Cruden's Concordance defines as "to earnestly desire") the best gifts, however. And in I Corinthians 13 he insists that any gift unaccompanied by love is worthless.

Observations on the Gift of Tongues

Concerning the gift of tongues as mentioned in 1 Corinthians 12:30 and the lengthy discourse on the subject in 1 Corinthians 14, the following points must be noted:

First, there is a definite gift of tongues apparently different from the one expressed at Pentecost because no interpretation was required there. And other signs accompanied it: the tongues as of fire and the violent rushing wind. These are nowhere mentioned in connection with the gifts of the Spirit in 1 Corinthians.

Although there is honest disagreement among Christians about the validity of tongues today, I personally cannot find any biblical justification for saying the gift of tongues was meant exclusively for New Testament times. At the same time, it easily becomes a misunderstood and even divisive issue; the fact that Paul found it necessary to deal with it at such length in 1 Corinthians 12–14 is testimony to this. (While stressing it was the least of the gifts, Paul also devoted the most space to discussing it of any of the gifts.) Therefore, when it does occur today it must be surrounded very carefully with the biblical safeguards Paul sets forth.

Also, while the gift of tongues may occur today as a valid spiritual gift, this does not mean every manifestation of tongues is according to the will of God and should be approved uncritically by us.

Second, it should be stressed, as is clearly indicated in 1 Corinthians 12–14, that tongues is a gift of the Holy Spirit, not a fruit of the Spirit. As we shall see, the fruit of the Spirit outlined in Galatians 5:22, 23 should mark every Christian who is walking in the Spirit. On the other hand, gifts are distributed among believers by the sovereign will of God. Therefore, it is a gift that some may have but not others. I simply cannot find any biblical reason for saying that tongues is a gift God desires to give to all believers. Some may be given the gift, while many others will not be given it. It would be wrong for someone who has not been given the gift of tongues to feel he is somehow a "second-rate" Christian, or earnestly covet this gift if God has not seen fit to give it to him. It would be equally wrong for someone who has this gift to try to compel others to have it, or to teach that everyone must experience it.

Third, the gift of tongues mentioned in 1 Corinthians 12–14 is clearly one of the less important gifts of the Spirit—in fact, it appears to be the least important. The reason for this is that it often does not give any spiritual benefit to other believers. The other gifts clearly are exercised to build up and strengthen the body of Christ, however. While tongues may do this in a public worship service (if there is an interpreter present), the other gifts are more directly involved in the mutual strengthening of believers.

This is why the gift of tongues should not be thought of as the high point of Christian maturity. In fact, millions of spiritually mature Christians have never spoken in tongues, and many who have spoken in tongues are not spiritually mature.

Fourth, the gift of tongues is not necessarily a sign of the baptism of the believer by the Holy Spirit into the body of Christ. That is especially true in 1 Corinthians, because these people had already been incorporated once-for-all into the body of Christ. Nowhere in the Bible do I find it said that the gift of tongues is a necessary evidence of being baptized with the Holy Spirit into Christ's body, the Church. Even in Acts where speaking in tongues is mentioned there is no indication it was necessary evidence that one had been baptized with the Holy Spirit.

In like manner the gift of tongues is not necessarily to be equated with being filled with the Spirit. We may be Spirit-filled and never speak in tongues. The filling of the Spirit may result in many different experiences in our lives, of which tongues on occasion may be only one evidence. Some of the most Spirit-filled Christians I have ever known had never experienced the gift of tongues, but they were no less filled with the Spirit.

Fifth, both the Bible and experience warn us that the gift of tongues may easily be abused and in fact may be dangerous. For example, the gift of tongues has often led to spiritual pride. Perhaps someone experiences the gift of tongues and immediately believes he is better or more spiritual than other believers who have not been given this gift. Such an attitude is directly contrary to the proper attitude of a Spirit-filled believer.

Other dangers should be mentioned. For example (as has been indicated), tongues may easily lead to divisiveness. Often this happens because of pride or because a person with the gift of tongues tries to force it on others. On the other hand, it is possible for some people to be proud because they don't speak in tongues, and that is equally wrong!

One of the greatest dangers in this matter of tongues is imbalance. That is, sometimes a person who has experienced this gift will become almost completely absorbed or preoccupied with tongues. The other gifts of the Spirit are forgotten (except, perhaps, the other sign gifts which are also spectacular or impressive), and there is often little interest in holy living and the fruit of the Spirit. Some who insist on making it their central focus to call others to seek this gift, fail to show any interest in evangelism, an emphasis the Spirit wants to give. I am thinking, for instance, of a small group of tongues-speaking people who rarely win other souls to Christ. They wait until someone else does the soul-winning, and then approach the new convert in an effort to persuade him that he must speak in tongues to grow in the Lord.

Still another danger is that some would see an experience of speaking in tongues as a short-cut to spiritual power and maturity. A member of my staff was in seminary with a young man who was going to various meetings constantly hoping to get the gift of tongues. When asked why he wanted this gift, he said it was because he felt a deep lack of power and fellowship with God, and he thought this would give him both spiritual power and a sense of God's presence. When asked if he prayed with any frequency, or read his Bible regularly, or spent much time in fellowship with other believers, he admitted he did not do any of these. God had given him the means of spiritual growth—prayer, the Bible, fellowship—but he was unwilling to be disciplined enough to make use of them. For him, tongues would be a short-cut to spiritual maturity. It was probably no accident that he dropped out of seminary shortly after this and gave up his plans to become a minister.

One final danger might be mentioned, and that is the possibility that the gift may sometimes be counterfeited. This may be due to deliberate deception, or possibly because the "gift" sometimes has its sources not in God but in our psychological make-up. It also may be the result of demonic activity.

Perhaps it should be noted that the ancient Greek oracle of Delphi spoke what might be called "tongues," as did the priests and priestesses at the great temple above Corinth. Dr. Akbar Abdul-Haqq tells me it is not an uncommon phenomenon in India among non-Christian religions today.

Also, there are certain well-substantiated instances of demon-possessed people given the ability to speak in certain known languages with which they were totally unfamiliar when in their right minds. The Bible records how Pharaoh's magicians were able to duplicate God's miracles up to a certain point.

No wonder John says, "Do not believe every spirit, but test the spirits to see whether they are from God" (I John 4:1). We have already gone into this in the discussion of the gift of discernment in chapter 12.

Even Christians have counterfeited this gift. One girl who attended a charismatic meeting wanted desperately to receive the gift of tongues as had so many of her friends. So, having been raised in another country, she prayed in that native language, pretending it was the operation of a spiritual gift. The others thought she had received the gift of tongues. As a result, in this little circle where speaking in tongues was so important, she was finally accepted!

No experience—no matter how much it may mean to us, or how impressive it may seem to be—must take the place of God's Word in our lives. Our experiences must always be judged in light of the Bible; we must not judge the Bible by our experiences. God the Holy Spirit has given us the Bible, and no gift which is truly from the Holy Spirit will contradict the Bible.

Sixth, what about the private, devotional use of tongues as a means of praising God and experiencing His fellowship? A number of friends have told me that after they had prayed for a long period of time, they suddenly found themselves speaking in an unknown language. For the most part they have kept it private and have not said everyone else must have the same experience. They have not said that all Christians must speak in tongues as a sign of spiritual maturity. Everyone knew that Corrie ten Boom had spoken in tongues, but she never talked about it and never discussed it. She often rebuked those who did talk about it excessively.

Actually, the Bible has little to say about this. The private use of tongues is implied by Paul when he remarks that "I speak in tongues more than you all; however, in the church I desire to speak five words with my mind, that I may instruct others also, rather than ten thousand words in a tongue" (1 Cor. 14:18, 19). Some have suggested that Paul's command to "pray at all times in the Spirit" (Eph. 6:18) involves praying in tongues, but the emphasis on specific prayer requests (in which the mind is clearly at work concentrating on the subjects of the prayer) in this passage would indicate this is not what is implied by Paul.

In conclusion, I must say I cannot help but be impressed by the wide differences of opinion about tongues on the part of the people who would call themselves charismatic. Many feel it is utterly wrong to say that tongues are essential to being baptized or filled with the Holy Spirit. A large group of evangelicals do not even regard tongues as a relevant gift of the Spirit today, just as the office of the apostolate is no longer a relevant gift.

I know of one Bible conference ministry which has been greatly used of God, but it would not knowingly invite to its platform anyone, however gifted and acceptable he might be in evangelical circles, who professed to speak in tongues. Others may disagree with this policy, but the leaders of this ministry are sincere in their convictions and should be respected for their views.

On the other hand, many evangelicals who do not themselves profess to speak in tongues now adopt an entirely neutral stance. They have seen the charismatic movement penetrate deeply into all the denominations with great blessing and renewal. So they are prepared to recognize that all the supernatural gifts of 1 Corinthians 12 are relevant today and therefore to be accepted as gifts of the Spirit.

In fairness to some of my charismatic friends I must add that even though I disagree with them on the issue of the "baptism with the Spirit" as accompanied by the sign of tongues, yet I do know and teach the need for believers to be filled with the Spirit. Setting aside the issue of tongues as the necessary sign, we may be talking about a phase of the same experience. In my judgment the Bible says that any believer can enjoy the filling of the Holy Spirit and know His power even though he or she has not had any sign such as speaking in tongues. On the occasion of a particular infilling, tongues may be a sign God gives some, but I do not find that it is a sign for all. I do think it is important, though, for each of us to hold our opinion without rancor and without breaking our bonds of fellowship in Jesus Christ. We worship the same Lord, and for this we are grateful.

In 1 Corinthians 14 Paul certainly says that prophesying is greater than speaking in tongues. At the same time he says, "Do not forbid to speak in tongues" (1 Cor. 14:39). Paul apparently spoke in many different tongues, but he did not emphasize this unduly. We must be careful not to put the Holy Spirit into a position where He must work our way. The Holy Spirit is sovereign; He gives His gifts as He wills! Peter Wagner says: "It must be remembered that the body of Christ is universal, with many local manifestations. Spiritual gifts are given to the body universal, and therefore certain ones may or may not be found in any particular local part of the body. This explains why, for example, a local church or even an entire denomination may not have been given the gift of tongues, while other parts of the body might have it."[1]

To summarize. *First*, there is a real, as contrasted with a counterfeit, gift of tongues. Many of those who have been given this gift have been transformed spiritually—some temporarily and some permanently!

Second, God uses tongues at certain times, in certain places, especially on the frontiers of the Christian mission, to further the kingdom of God and to edify believers.

Third, many are convinced that we may be living in what Scripture calls "the latter days." Both Joel and Hosea prophesy that in those days great manifestations of the Spirit and many of the sign gifts will reappear. We may be living in such a period of history. Certainly we cannot blind ourselves to the fact that many of the sign gifts which vindicate the authenticity of the gospel are reappearing at this hour.

Many years ago in a class discussion at the Florida Bible Institute a teacher said something on the subject of tongues that has stayed with me. He advised his students to "seek not; forbid not."

Indeed, tongues is a gift of the Spirit. Today there are Presbyterians, Baptists, Anglicans, Lutherans, and Methodists, as well as Pentecostals, who speak or have spoken in tongues—or who have not, and do not expect to.

But if tongues is the gift of the Holy Spirit, it cannot be divisive in itself. When those who speak in tongues misuse it so that it becomes divisive, it indicates a lack of love. And those who forbid it do the Church a disservice because they appear to contradict the teaching of the apostle Paul. Those believers who do speak in tongues and those who do not should love each other and work for the greater glory of God in the evangelization of the world, remembering one thing: those who do speak in tongues and those who do not *will* live with each other in the New Jerusalem.

Is this a gift God has seen fit to give you? Don't let it be a source of pride or preoccupation. Become grounded in the whole Word of God. And above all, learn what it means to love others, including believers who may not agree with your emphasis.

Is this a gift you do not have? Don't let it preoccupy you either, and don't let it be a source of division between you and other believers if at all possible. There may be other believers who have a different emphasis from you, but they are still your brothers and sisters in Christ.

Above all, we are called to "walk by the Spirit, and you will not carry out the desire of the flesh" (Gal. 5:16).

The sign gifts—healings, miracles, and tongues—probably attracted as much attention in the first century as they do today. They also sometimes caused confusion and abuses just as they do today. Nevertheless, God the Holy Spirit gave them to some within the Church, to be used for His glory. They must never be exploited for selfish reasons, nor must they ever become sources of either division or pride. We are not to become preoccupied or obsessed with them, and most of all whenever gifts of this nature are given, they must be used strictly in accordance with the principles God has set forth in the Bible. This should also contribute to the unity of the Spirit. And if God chooses to give these gifts to some today, we should always pray that they will be used "for the common good" (1 Cor. 12:7) and the furtherance of the kingdom of God.

14

The Fruit
of the Spirit

A HANDFUL OF men had been waiting at a dock on the
Thames since five o'clock that bitter cold winter morning. Along
with scores of others, they had been selected to unload a docked
freighter. This was done by balancing a wheelbarrow on planks that
stretched from the dock to a barge and from the barge to the
freighter. Among the working men, unknown to them, was a clergyman. Deeply concerned for the men of that area, he had decided
that the only way he could communicate with them was to live
and work among them. Dressed like them, he denied himself even
a cup of hot tea before leaving his room, and went without an
overcoat. He knew the men who would be standing in line for jobs
along the docks that day would not have had the comfort of a cup
of tea, and would, for the most part, be inadequately clothed.

In the days before he landed a job, he learned what it was to be
treated as a stranger. He learned what it was to stand all day in
the cold and the fog, only to be told there were no jobs available.
These men would have to go back to inadequate lodgings and face
hungry families without so much as a piece of bread for them.

But this day he had been fortunate and was hired. On his twelfth
trip, as he was crossing the plank with his loaded wheelbarrow, it
began to jiggle so that he lost his footing and fell into the Thames,
amid roars of laughter on all sides.

Fighting to control his temper, he managed finally to struggle to his feet, grinning as he did so. One of the workmen (the culprit who had jiggled the plank) had shouted, "Man overboard," and stood there laughing. As he watched the unrecognized clergyman struggling good-naturedly in the mud, some better impulse seemed to move him to drop some empty boxes into the slush and jump down to help the man out. His would-be rescuer's first remark justified the clergyman's attitude which the Holy Spirit had prompted.

"You took that all right," his former tormenter said as he helped the clergyman to clamber onto the boxes. He did not have the accent of a cockney, for he was not the usual docker.

"You haven't been long at this game," the clergyman remarked.

"Neither have you," replied his tormenter-turned-rescuer. The clergyman agreed, then invited the man to accompany him to his rooming house.

As they talked, the clergyman learned to his amazement that the man had once been a highly successful physician, but due to heavy drink he had lost a thriving practice and his lovely wife and family. The outcome of the story was that the clergyman was able to lead this man to Christ and eventually see him reunited with his family.

Perhaps this is what the fruit of the Spirit is all about. If life were always kind to us, if people were always pleasant and courteous, if we never had headaches, never knew what it was to be tired or under terrific pressure, the fruit of the Spirit might go unnoticed.

But life is not always like that. It is in the midst of difficulties and hardships that we especially need the fruit of the Spirit, and it is in such times that God may especially work through us to touch other people for Christ. As we bear the fruit of the Spirit in our lives, others will see in us "the family likeness of his Son" (Rom. 8:29, Phillips) and be attracted to the Savior.

It is no accident that the Scriptures call the Third Person of the Trinity the *Holy* Spirit. One of the main functions of the Holy Spirit is to impart the holiness of God to us. He does this as He develops within us a Christlike character—a character marked by the fruit of the Spirit. God's purpose is that we would "become mature, attaining the full measure of perfection found in Christ" (Eph. 4:13, NIV).

Fruit: God's Expectation

God the Holy Spirit uses the word *fruit* frequently in Scripture to denote what He expects of His people in the way of character. We have noted in the chapters on the gifts of the Holy Spirit that believers are given various gifts. I may have a gift someone else does not have, while another person may have been given gifts I do not have. However, when we come to the Bible's teaching on the fruit of the Spirit, we find there is a basic difference between the *gifts* of the Spirit and the *fruit* of the Spirit.

Unlike the gifts of the Spirit, *the fruit of the Spirit is not divided among believers.* Instead, *all* Christians should be marked by *all* the fruit of the Spirit. The fruit of the Spirit is God's expectation in our lives. This is clearly seen in many passages of Scripture. In Matthew 13 Jesus told the familiar parable of the seed and the sower. He likens the work of anyone who declares the Word of God—a pastor, teacher, evangelist or any other Christian—to a man sowing seed. Some seed falls by the wayside and is eaten by the birds; some falls on rocky ground and withers in the sun; still other seed begins to grow but is choked by thorns. The fourth group of seeds falls into good soil, takes root, and brings forth fruit abundantly. So you and I are to bear fruit, as the Word of God begins to work in our lives in the power of the Spirit.

It is interesting that the Bible talks of the *fruit* of the Spirit rather than *fruits.* A tree may bear many apples, but all come from the same tree. In the same way, the Holy Spirit is the source of all fruit in our lives.

Put in simplest terms, the Bible tells us we need the Spirit to bring fruit into our lives because we cannot produce godliness apart from the Spirit. In our own selves we are filled with all kinds of self-centered and self-seeking desires which are opposed to God's will for our lives. In other words, two things need to happen in our lives. *First,* the sin in our lives needs to be thrust out. *Second,* the Holy Spirit needs to come in and fill our lives, producing the fruit of the Spirit. "*Put to death,* therefore, whatever belongs to your earthly nature: . . . as God's chosen people, holy and dearly loved, *clothe yourselves* with compassion, kindness, humility, gentleness and patience" (Col. 3:5, 12 NIV, italics mine).

Let me use an illustration. Many people have a fence around their home with a gate for entering and leaving. Remember, a gate can be used for two purposes: it can be opened to let people in, or it can be shut to keep people out.

Spiritually our lives are like this gate. Inside our lives are all sorts of things that are wrong and unpleasing to God. We need to let these things out, and allow the Holy Spirit to come in and control the very center of our lives. But we do not have the power even to open the gate. Only the Holy Spirit can do that, and when He does—as we yield to Him and look to Him for His fullness—He not only comes in but He helps us thrust out the evil things in our lives. He controls the gate, and as He purges the heart of its wickedness He can bring in new attitudes, new motivations, new devotion and love. He also strengthens the door with bars that keep out evil. So the works of the flesh depart and the fruit of the Spirit comes in. The Scripture says that the Holy Spirit wants us to have fruit—and then more fruit, and even much fruit.

In his book, *The Fruit of the Spirit,* Manford George Gutzke compares the fruit of the Spirit to light: "All the colors of the rainbow are in every beam of sunlight. They all are there at any one time. They may not always come into vision, but they are all present. It is not necessary to think of them as being so many separate colors. Just as these colors of the rainbow are present in light, so these traits of personal conduct are in the working of the Holy Spirit."[1]

How the Fruit Grows

How does the Holy Spirit work in our lives to produce the fruit of the Spirit? There are two passages of Scripture especially helpful in answering this question.

The first passage is Psalm 1, which compares the godly man to a tree planted by a river: "But his delight is in the law of the Lord, and in His law he meditates day and night. And he will be like a tree firmly planted by streams of water, which yields its fruit in its season, and its leaf does not wither; and in whatever he does, he prospers" (Ps. 1:2,3). Here the bearing of spiritual fruit is clearly related to the place the Word of God has in our lives. (Notice, it does not just say read, but meditate.) As we read and meditate on the Bible, the Holy Spirit—who, we remember, inspired the Bible—convicts us of sin which needs to be purged and directs us to God's standard for our lives. Apart from the Word of God there will be no lasting spiritual growth or fruit-bearing in our lives.

The second passage is found in John 15, where Jesus compares our relationship to Him to the branches of a vine. "Abide in Me, and I in you. As the branch cannot bear fruit of itself, unless it abides in the vine, so neither can you, unless you abide in Me. I am the vine, you are the branches; he who abides in Me, and I in him, he bears much fruit; for apart from Me you can do nothing" (John 15:4,5).

There are many wonderful truths in this passage, but there are several points we should especially notice. First, this is a command to every believer: "Abide in Me." By that is meant we are to have the closest, most intimate relationship with Christ, with nothing coming between us. This is one reason why the disciplines of prayer, Bible study, and fellowship with other believers are so important.

Also, this tells us that we can *only* bear spiritual fruit if we abide in Christ: "Apart from me you can do nothing." It may be possible for us to make use of the *gifts* of the Spirit even when we are out of fellowship with the Lord. But we cannot display the *fruit* of the Spirit all the time when our fellowship with Christ has been interrupted by sin. We can see, then, how crucial it is to be filled with the Spirit, and we are being filled as we abide in Christ, the vine. The secret of abiding is obedience. As we, through obedient living, abide in Christ, the life of Christ (like the life-giving sap in a vine) flows into us, producing fruit to the glory of the Father and the nourishment and blessing of others.

I believe there is something about this relationship which we cannot fully understand. If we were to ask a branch on a grapevine, "How do you grow such luscious fruit?" the branch would probably reply, "I don't know. I don't grow any of it; I just bear it. Cut me off from this vine and I will wither away and become useless." Without the vine the branch can do nothing. So it is with our lives. As long as I strain and work to produce the fruit of the Spirit from within myself, I will end up fruitless and frustrated.

But as I abide in Christ—as I maintain a close, obedient, dependent relationship with Him—God the Holy Spirit works in my life, creating in me the fruit of the Spirit. That does not mean we instantly become mature, bearing all the fruit of the Spirit fully and immediately. The fruit on a fruit tree takes time to mature, and pruning may be necessary before fruit is produced in quantity. So it may be with us.

My wife and I enjoy the beautiful trees surrounding our house in North Carolina. In the autumn most leaves drop off and are blown away, but thousands of the old dead leaves cling to the branches even in March and April. However, when the sap in the trees begins to flow, the new leaves form—and life and power pulsate and surge through every living branch. Then all of the old dry leaves fall off, unnoticed. What an analogy for the Christian! "Old things have passed away; behold, new things have come" (2 Cor. 5:17).

Furthermore, each summer we cut down some of the trees that obstruct the view or keep out the sunlight. And some have been badly damaged during the winter storms. Similarly, we have trees in our lives to which the axe must be laid—trees which either lie rotting on the ground or produce only ugly sights. Jesus said, "Every plant which My heavenly Father did not plant shall be rooted up" (Matt. 15:13). We have a few fruit trees on our property. We take special care of those with the best fruit—pruning, feeding, and spraying at proper times. A good tree brings forth good fruit and should be kept. But whether a tree is worth keeping or cutting down depends on the distinction Jesus made. He said, "You will know them by their fruits" (Matt. 7:20 RSV).

Then there are a few grapevines. Some years we pick only a small crop of substandard grapes for personal use. But we do not cut the vines down. Rather, we prune them carefully. Then the next year the vines bring forth more and better fruit. Similarly, as the pruning process goes on in our lives under the guidance of the Holy Spirit, the vines, speaking spiritually, are useful for the production of more spiritual fruit.

Remember, the picture in John 15 is of the Lord Jesus as the vine, we as the branches, and God as the husbandman, or gardener.

Verse three says, "You are already clean because of the word which I have spoken to you," or as J. B. Phillips translates it, "Now, you have already been pruned by my words." There is no better way for the child of God to be pruned than through studying and applying the Bible to his own heart and situation. Somehow God can correct us, tell us where we have fallen short and gone astray, without once discouraging us.

In the Acts of the Apostles we read of Apollos whose earnestness, love, and great gift of oratory appealed to the hearts of Priscilla and Aquila. However, he was immature and unprepared to lead others into the deeper Christian life. He had progressed barely beyond the baptism of John. But this godly couple, instead of laughing at his ignorance or decrying his lack of understanding of true biblical orthodoxy, took him into their home and in love expounded the way of the Lord more perfectly to him (Acts 18:26). Then he began to use his great gifts for the glory of God and the winning of souls. He left an indelible impression on the early Church and helped promote the kingdom of God in the first century.

Are you abiding in Christ? This is the primary condition God sets down for us before we can really bear the fruit of the Spirit. Is there any unconfessed sin in your life which is keeping you from a close walk with Christ? Is there any lack of discipline? Is there any broken relationship with another person which needs healing? Whatever the cause may be, bring it to Christ in confession and repentance. And then learn what it means each day to "Abide in Me."

15

The Fruit of the Spirit: Love, Joy, Peace

OF ALL THE passages in the Bible which sketch the character of Christ and the fruit which the Spirit brings to our lives, none is more compact and challenging than Galatians 5:22, 23. "But the fruit of the Spirit is love, joy, peace, patience, kindness, goodness, faithfulness, gentleness, self-control." In the next three chapters we will examine in detail the meaning of each of these. For purposes of study, we can divide these nine words into three "clusters" of fruit. Love, joy, and peace make up the first cluster. They especially speak of our Godward relationship. The second "cluster"—patience, kindness, and goodness—especially are seen in our manward relationship, i.e. our relationship with other people. The third "cluster" of faithfulness, gentleness, and self-control are especially seen in our inward relationship—the attitudes and actions of the inner self.

At the same time, of course, these three "clusters" are all related to each other, and *all* should characterize our lives. And all *will* characterize our lives when we abide in Christ and allow the Holy Spirit to do His work in us.

The Fruit of the Spirit: Love

There should be no more distinctive mark of the Christian than love. "By this all men will know that you are My disciples, if you have love for one another" (John 13:35). "We know that we have passed out of death into life, because we love the brethren" (1 John 3:14). "Owe nothing to anyone except to love one another; for he who loves his neighbor has fulfilled the law" (Rom. 13:8).

No matter how else we may bear our testimony for the Lord Jesus Christ, the absence of love nullifies it all. Love is greater than anything we can say, or anything we can possess, or anything we can give. "If I speak with the tongues of men and of angels, but do not have love, I have become a noisy gong or a clanging cymbal. And if I have the gift of prophecy, and know all mysteries and all knowledge; and if I have all faith, so as to remove mountains, but do not have love, I am nothing. And if I give all my possessions to feed the poor, and if I deliver my body to be burned, but do not have love, it profits me nothing" (1 Cor. 13:1–3).

The greatest chapter on love in the Bible is 1 Corinthians 13. Its description of love should be written in letters of gold on every Christian heart. If any chapter of the Bible should be memorized besides John 3, it is 1 Corinthians 13. When we reflect on the meaning of love, we see that it is to the heart what the summer is to the farmer's year. It brings to harvest all the loveliest flowers of the soul. Indeed, it is the loveliest flower in the garden of God's grace. If love does not characterize our lives, they are empty. Peter said, "Above all, keep fervent in your love for one another, because love covers a multitude of sins" (1 Peter 4:8).

In his little book, *The Four Loves*, C. S. Lewis discusses the different Greek words translated "love" in English. When Scripture describes God's love for us and the love God wants us to have, it often uses the Greek word *agape* (pronounced ah-*gah*-pay). *Agape* love is found everywhere in the New Testament. When Jesus said, "Love your enemies," Matthew in his Gospel used the word *agape*. When Jesus said we were to love one another, John used the word *agape*. When Jesus said, "Thou shalt love thy neighbor," Mark used the word *agape*. When the Scripture says, "God is love," it uses the word *agape*. The New Bible Dictionary defines *agape* love in Greek as "that highest and noblest form of love which sees something infinitely precious in its object."[1]

God's greatest demonstration of *agape* love was at the cross where He sent His Son Jesus Christ to die for our sins. Since we are to love as God does, believers should have *agape* love. But we do not have it naturally, nor can we develop it, for the works of the flesh cannot produce it; it must be supernaturally given to us by the Holy Spirit. He does this as we yield ourselves to the will of God.

We should be clear about one thing concerning *agape* love. All too often today love is seen only as an emotion or feeling. Certainly there is emotion involved in love, whether it is love for others or love for God. But love is more than an emotion. Love is not a feeling—love is doing. True love is love which *acts*. That is the way God loves us: "For God so loved the world, that He *gave* His only begotten Son" (John 3:16, italics mine). "Little children, let us not love with word or with tongue, but in deed and truth" (1 John 3:18).

Love is, therefore, an act of the will—and that is why our wills must first be yielded to Christ before we will begin to bear the fruit of love. Bishop Stephen Neill has defined love as "a steady direction of the will toward another's lasting good."[2] He points out that much human love is really selfish in nature, while *agape* love involves self-giving. As Neill says:

"The first love [human love] says, 'I wish to make my own something that another has, and which it is in his power to give me.'

"The second love [God's love] says, 'I wish to give to this other, because I love him.'

"The first love wishes to make itself richer by receiving a gift which some other can give.

"The second love wishes to make another richer by giving all that it has.

"The first love is a matter of feeling and desire. This love comes and goes as it will; we cannot call it into being by any effort of our own.

"The second love is much more a matter of the will, since to give or not to give is largely within our power."[3]

We are to love as the Good Samaritan loved (Luke 10:25–38), which is nothing less than love finding its best demonstration in action. This is a love which reaches out to all—wives, husbands, children, neighbors, and even people we have never met on the other side of the world. It will include those who are easy to love, because they are like us, and those who are hard to love because they are so different. It will even extend to people who have harmed us or brought sorrow to us.

A young wife and mother whose husband had become unfaithful and left her to live with another woman was bitter and full of resentment. However, as she began to think about the love of Christ for us she found a new love growing in her for others— including the woman who had taken her husband. At Christmas time she sent the other woman one red rose with a note: "Because of Christ's love for me and through me, I can love you!" This is *agape* love, the fruit of the Spirit.

The command to love is not an option; we are to love whether we feel like it or not. Indeed, we may say that love for others is the first sign that we have been born again and that the Holy Spirit is at work in our lives.

Certainly above all, love should be the outstanding mark among believers in every local congregation. Dr. Sherwood Wirt has written: "I have learned there is no point in talking about strong churches and weak churches, big churches and little churches, warm churches and cold churches. Such categories are unrealistic and beside the point. There is only a loving church or an unloving church."[4]

It can be so easy at times to say we love people, and be completely honest and sincere in our expression. But so often we don't see the lonely person in the crowd, or the sick or destitute man or woman whose only hope of escape may be the love we can give through Christ. The love God would have us show reaches down to each person.

A friend of ours is a well-known singing star. I have noticed that when he enters a room full of people he does not look around to find the people he knows. He looks for the little guy, unknown, uneasy, out of place, and he walks right over, hand out, his rugged face alight with a kindly smile as he introduces himself, "Hello, I'm. . . ."

As a young boy growing up in Boston a dear friend of mine of many years, Allan Emery, had an experience which made a deep impression upon him. His father received a call saying a well-known Christian had been found at a certain place drunk on the sidewalk. Immediately his father sent his chauffered limousine to pick the man up, while his mother prepared the best guest room. My friend watched wide-eyed, as the beautiful coverlets were turned down on the exquisite old four-poster bed, revealing the monogrammed sheets.

"But, mother," he protested, "he's drunk. He might even get sick."

"I know," his mother replied kindly, "but this man has slipped and fallen. When he comes to, he will be so ashamed. He will need all the loving encouragement we can give him."

It was a lesson the son never forgot.

Jesus looked at the multitudes of people and was moved with compassion for each of them. He loved as no human is able to love. His love engulfed the whole world, the whole human race, from time's beginning to end. His love knew no bounds, no limit, and no one was excluded. From the lowliest beggar to the greatest monarch, from the deepest sinner to the purest saint—His love embraced them *all*. Nothing but the Spirit of God working in our lives can produce such fruit, and it will be evident in our public as well as private lives.

The Fruit of the Spirit: Joy

Returning from his young son's grave in China, my father-in-law wrote to his mother in Virginia, "There are tears in our eyes, but joy in our hearts." The joy which the Spirit brings to our lives lifts us above circumstances. Joy can be ours, even in the midst of the most trying situations.

The Greek word for joy is used repeatedly in the New Testament to denote joy from a spiritual source such as "the joy of the Holy Spirit" (1 Thess. 1:6). The Old Testament likewise uses phrases like "the joy of the Lord" (Neh. 8:10) to point to God as the source.

Just before Calvary our Lord met with His disciples in the Upper Room. He told them He had spoken as He did "that My joy may be in you, and that your joy may be made full" (John 15:11). Bishop Stephen Neill has remarked: "It was because they were a joyful people that the early Christians were able to conquer the world."[5]

Today's world is joyless, full of shadows, disillusionment, and fear. Freedom is rapidly disappearing from the face of the earth. Along with the loss of freedom, a great many of the superficial joys and pleasures of life are also disappearing, but this need not alarm us. The Scriptures teach that our spiritual joy is not dependent on circumstances. The world's system fails to tap the *source* of joy. God, by His Spirit, directs His joy to our bleak, problem-riddled lives, making it possible for us to be filled with joy regardless of our circumstances.

America's Declaration of Independence speaks of "the pursuit of happiness," but nowhere in the Bible are we told to pursue this. Happiness is elusive, and we don't find it by seeking it. It comes when outward conditions are favorable, but joy goes much deeper. Joy is also different from pleasures. Pleasures are momentary, but joy is deep and abiding despite the worst circumstances of life.

Not only are we given the source of joy which is the person of Christ, but we are assured that it is constantly available to the Christian, no matter what the circumstances.

I once visited Dohnavur in South India where Amy Carmichael had lived for fifty years, caring for hundreds of girls originally dedicated to temple service. As I said earlier, she was bedridden for the last twenty years of her life, during which time she wrote many books that have blessed millions. Joy filled her sick room so that everyone who visited her came away praising God. In her book *Gold by Moonlight* she said, "Where the things of God are concerned, acceptance always means the happy choice of mind and heart of that which He appoints, because (for the present) it is His good and acceptable and perfect will."[6]

Even after her death, when I visited the room where she had served the Lord for twenty years, writing from her bed, I was asked by her former nurse to lead in prayer. I began, but was so overwhelmed by a sense of God's presence I broke down (a thing I seldom ever do). So I indicated to my companion that he should continue. The same thing happened to him. As I left that room, I sensed the joy of the Lord in my own heart. Many times I have visited sick people to encourage them. Some suffered from terminal illnesses. Strangely enough, I have come away blessed in my own soul by their contagious joy.

Deep joy crowned the apostle Paul's final testimony as he wrote his last letter to young Timothy from death row. Despite the suffering he had endured, the horror of prison, and the frequent threat of death, the joy of the Lord filled his heart.

Charles Allen puts it this way, "Just as all the water in the world cannot quench the fire of the Holy Spirit, neither can all the troubles and tragedies of the world overwhelm the joy which the Spirit brings into the human heart."[7]

It has been said that "Joy is the flag that flies above the palace when the King is in residence."

The Fruit of the Spirit: Peace

Peace carries with it the idea of unity, completeness, rest, ease, and security. In the Old Testament the word was *shalom*. Many times when I meet Jewish friends I greet them with *"Shalom."* And often, when I greet my Arab friends I use a similar term that they use for peace, *salam.*

Recently as I watched the televised report of passengers disembarking from a hijacked plane, I saw terror, horror, and fear on their faces. But one woman had a little child in her arms, calmly sleeping through it all. Peace in the midst of turmoil.

Isaiah said, "Thou wilt keep him in perfect peace, whose mind is stayed on thee: because he trusteth in thee" (Isa. 26:3 KJV). This is the picture of any Christian who stands alone on the battlefield, by faith garrisoned round about with God's holy weapons, and in command of the situation. Such a man is not troubled about the future, for he knows who holds the key to the future. He does not tremble on the rock, for he knows who made the rock. He does not doubt, for he knows the One who erases all doubt.

When you and I yield to worry, we deny our Guide the right to lead us in confidence and peace. Only the Holy Spirit can give us peace in the midst of the storms of restlessness and despair. We should not grieve our Guide by indulging in worry or paying undue attention to self.

There are different kinds of peace, such as the peace of a graveyard, or that of tranquilizers. But for the Christian, peace is not simply the absence of conflict, or any other artificial state the world has to offer. Rather it is the deep, abiding peace only Jesus Christ brings to the heart. He describes it in John 14:27: "Peace I leave with you; My peace I give to you; not as the world gives, do I give to you." This is the peace that can come only from the Holy Spirit.

The peace *of* God that can reign in our hearts is always preceded by peace *with* God, which must be the starting point. When this is so, the peace of God can follow. From this standpoint, Christ's work of salvation has two stages: First He was able to end the war between sinful man and the righteous God. God indeed was angry with man because of his sin. But Jesus by His blood made peace. The war ended; peace came. God was satisfied. The debt was cancelled, and the books were balanced. With his accounts settled, man was set free, if willing to repent and turn in faith to Christ for salvation. God is now able to look on him with favor.

But Jesus Christ not only freed us from bondage and war. He also made possible a further stage—we can have the peace *of* God in our hearts here and now. For us, peace with God is not simply an armistice; it is a war ended forever; and now the redeemed hearts of former enemies of the cross are garrisoned with a peace that transcends all human knowledge and outsoars any wings of flight we can possibly imagine.

Concerning the peace of God, Spurgeon said: "I looked at Christ, and the dove of peace flew into my heart; I looked at the dove of peace, and it flew away." So we should not look at the fruit itself, but at the source of all peace, because Christ through the Holy Spirit wisely cultivates our lives to allow us to bring forth peace. The greatest psychiatric therapy in the world is appropriating what Jesus promised, "I will give you rest"—or peace (Matt. 11:28). King David became living proof of the spiritual therapy for the soul which the Holy Spirit dispenses when he said, "He maketh me to lie down" (Ps. 23:2 KJV). This is peaceful resting. But David continues, "He restoreth my soul." This is peaceful renewing. Though men continue to seek peace, they will not find it until they come to the simple realization that "Christ is peace."

A woman full of despair and frustration wrote me that her case was hopeless because God could not possibly forget all her gross sins. In reply I said that although she felt forsaken by God and others, He had not forsaken her, but had allowed distress and despair to flood her heart so she might realize her need for God's forgiveness and peace. She wrote later that she jumped up and down with delight when she realized she could have God's peace. Jesus said that not our peace but His peace makes the difference: "My peace I give to you; not as the world gives" (John 14:27).

In Romans Paul gives us these wonderful words, "May the God of hope fill you with all joy and peace in believing, so that by the power of the Holy Spirit you may abound in hope" (15:13 RSV). How can joy and peace be any better described? Indeed the fruit of the Spirit is peace—do you have it in your heart?

16

The Fruit of the Spirit: Patience, Kindness, Goodness

THE FIRST CLUSTER of the fruit of the Spirit has a primary Godward relationship with outward results others can see. Thus, we speak of the love of God, the joy of the Lord, and the peace of God. The second cluster—patience, kindness, and goodness—has to do with the kind of Christians we are in our outward relationships. If we are short-tempered, unkind, and rude, we lack the second cluster of the fruit of the Spirit. But when the Spirit controls us, He works to transform us so that the buds of patience, kindness, and goodness begin to blossom and then to be fruitful.

The Fruit of the Spirit: Patience

The English word *patience* (or *long-suffering* in the King James Version) comes from a Greek word that speaks of a person's steadfastness under provocation. Inherent in the word is the thought of patiently enduring ill-treatment without anger or thought of retaliation or revenge. Thus, this part of the fruit of the Spirit is seen in our relationship to our neighbors. It is patience personified—love's patience. If we are irritable, vengeful, resentful, and malicious to our neighbors, we are short-suffering, not long-suffering. And when that condition exists, the Holy Spirit is not in control.

Patience is the transcendent radiance of a loving and tender heart which, in its dealings with those around it, looks kindly and graciously upon them. Patience graciously, compassionately and with understanding judges the faults of others without unjust criticism. Patience also includes perseverance—the ability to bear up under weariness, strain, and persecution when doing the work of the Lord.

Patience is part of true Christlikeness, something we so often admire in others without demanding it of ourselves. Paul teaches us that we can be "strengthened with all might, according to his glorious power, unto all patience and longsuffering with joyfulness" (Col. 1:11 KJV). Patience in our lives springs from God's power based upon our willingness to learn it. Whenever we are selfish, or when anger or ill will begins to build, or when impatience or frustration overtakes us, we must recognize that we are the source of our problems, not God. We must refuse, renounce, and repudiate the situation immediately. It comes from the old sinful nature.

Patience and Testing

Patience is closely related to testings or trials in the Bible, and that is only logical. We may be patient in ordinary life, but how do we react when trials come? It is then that we especially need the fruit of the Spirit—patience. This is one reason why the Bible tells us that trials can be good for us, because they allow us to be strengthened, and especially they allow patience to be developed by the Spirit. "Consider it all joy, my brethren, when you encounter various trials, knowing that the testing of your faith produces endurance" (James 1:2, 3).

If this is true, we should welcome trials and testings when they come, because they force us to draw more and more upon the source of all strength, producing more of the patience which is the fruit of the Spirit. It is the regular exercise of patience and longsuffering in the small day-to-day frustrations and irritations which prepares us to endure when the great battles come.

Inner erosion of the heart leaves us vulnerable to the cunning, and often disguised, attacks of Satan. But the heart that has learned to call *instantly* in prayer on the Holy Spirit at the first sign of temptation has no reason to fear any such erosion. In a short time prayer will become so automatic and spontaneous that we will have uttered the prayer almost before we are aware of the need. The Bible says we are to be "patient in tribulation; continuing instant in prayer" (Rom. 12:12 KJV). For me, the best time to pray is the *very moment* a tense situation or an unspiritual attitude overtakes me. God the Holy Spirit is always there, ready to help me gain victory in the spiritual battles I face—big or small. However, in order for prayer to become an involuntary, or subconscious reaction to my problem, I must voluntarily and consciously practice it day after day until it becomes an integral part of my being.

A dear friend and trusted counselor once told me that sometimes the greatest test comes to us when we ask God the question, "Why?"

As Charles Hembree has pointed out, "In the full face of affliction it is hard to see any sense to things that befall us and we want to question the fairness of a faithful God. However, these moments can be the most meaningful of our lives."[1]

One of God's great servants, Paul Little, was killed in an automobile accident in 1975. I immediately asked God, "Why?" Paul was one of God's outstanding young strategists and Bible teachers. He was a theological professor, a leader of Inter-Varsity Christian Fellowship, and a former member of our team. I am sure his wife, Marie, must have asked in the agony of her heart, "Why?" And yet, a few months later when she came to our team retreat, she manifested a marvelous spirit as she shared her victory with the wives of our team members. Instead of our comforting her, she was comforting us.

We may suffer affliction or discipline, yet the Psalmist said, "Weeping may last for the night, but a shout of joy comes in the morning" (Ps. 30:5). No Spirit-filled Christian will fail to evince long-suffering and patience if he has faithfully endured "the fellowship of His sufferings" (Phil. 3:10).

In order for the fruit to appear in our lives God allows us to face chastening, discipline, affliction, and persecution. Had Joseph not been sold into slavery by his brothers who hated him, and been wrongly accused by Potiphar who put him in prison, he would not have developed the fruit of patience and long-suffering that was to become the hallmark of his life. Even after he had told Pharaoh's cupbearer he would be restored to the king's court and asked him to tell Pharaoh of his unjust imprisonment, he had to wait two more years for release from prison.

As we wait upon the Lord, God may sometimes seem slow in coming to help us, but He never comes too late. Paul wrote, "For momentary, light affliction is producing for us an eternal weight of glory far beyond all comparison" (2 Cor. 4:17). Jesus told His disciples, "By your perseverance you will win your souls" (Luke 21:19). It is this long-suffering and patience that the Holy Spirit uses to bless others.

We must guard against one thing, however, when we speak about long-suffering. Sometimes we use it as an excuse for failing to take specific action when it is called for. Sometimes we enjoy a kind of neurotic self-flagellation because we don't want to face the truth, and we mistakenly call it long-suffering. But Jesus vigorously "drove out all who sold and bought in the temple, and he over-turned the tables of the money-changers and the seats of those who sold pigeons" (Matt. 21:12 RSV). Moreover He furiously castigated the scribes and the Pharisees (Matt. 21:13ff). It is the Spirit-filled Christian who knows when to have "righteous indignation" and when to be patient, and who knows when long-suffering becomes an excuse for inaction or a crutch to hide a defect of character.

The Fruit of the Spirit: Kindness

Kindness, or *gentleness*, is the *second segment* of the fruit that grows outward. This term comes from a Greek word referring to the kindness that pervades and penetrates the whole nature. Gentleness washes away all that is harsh and austere. Indeed, gentleness is love enduring.

Jesus was a gentle person. When He came into the world, there were few institutions of mercy. There were few hospitals or mental institutions, few places of refuge for the poor, few homes for orphans, few havens for the forsaken. In comparison to today, it was a cruel world. Christ changed that. Wherever true Christianity has gone His followers have performed acts of gentleness and kindness.

The word gentleness occurs only a few times in our English Bible. It is spoken of in connection with the three persons of the Trinity. In Psalm 18:35, it is the gentleness of God; in 2 Corinthians 10:1, the gentleness of Christ; and in Galatians 5:23, the gentleness of the Holy Spirit.

Charles Allen points out: "In one's disdain of sin, one can be harsh and unkind toward a sinner. . . . Some people seem to have such a passion for righteousness that they have no room left for compassion for those who have failed."[2]

How easy it is to be impatient or harsh toward those who may have failed in life! When the hippie movement began in America, many people reacted to it with a critical and unloving attitude toward the hippies themselves. The Bible teaches us otherwise. Jesus would have responded to them with loving "kindness" or "gentleness." The only people with whom He dealt harshly were the hypocritical religious leaders, but to everyone else He manifested a wonderful gentleness. Many sinners on the verge of repentance have been disillusioned by a pharisaical and coldly rigid Christianity that hangs on to a legalistic religious code minus the quality of compassion. But Jesus dealt tenderly, gently, and kindly with everyone. Even small children sensed His gentleness and approached Him eagerly and without fear.

Paul told his young friend Timothy, "The servant of the Lord must not strive; but be gentle unto all men" (2 Tim. 2:24 KJV). James said, "The wisdom that is from above is first pure, then peaceable, gentle, and easy to be entreated" (James 3:17 KJV).

Some claim that gentleness is a sign of weakness, but they are wrong! Abraham Lincoln was well-known for his gentleness and humility, but it can never be said that he was weak. On the contrary, it was the combination of his great strength of character and his gentle and compassionate spirit that made him the great person he was.

In *Fruits of the Spirit*, Hembree says, "In our age of guided missiles and misguided men there is desperate need for us to learn how to share gentleness. It seems strange that in an age when we can reach the moon, bounce signals off far planets, and receive pictures from whirling satellites we have great difficulty communicating tenderness to those about us."[3]

The logical place to turn for guidance and instruction in such things of the Spirit is the minister in the pulpit, and the compelling need of this generation is to be exposed to great preaching. But however eloquent, however well prepared, and however gifted any preacher may be, if his ministry lacks tenderness and gentleness, he will be unable to lead many people to Jesus Christ. The gentle heart is the broken heart—the heart that weeps over the sins of the bad as well as the sacrifices of the good.

The Fruit of the Spirit: Goodness

The *third element* in this trio is *goodness.* This is derived from a Greek word referring to that quality found in the person who is ruled by and aims at what is good, that which represents the highest moral and ethical values. Paul writes, "For the fruit of the light consists in all goodness and righteousness and truth" (Eph. 5:9). He also says, "To this end also we pray for you always that our God may count you worthy of your calling, and fulfill every desire for goodness and the work of faith with power; in order that the name of our Lord Jesus may be glorified in you" (2 Thess. 1:11, 12). Again Paul says in commending the church in Rome, "And concerning you, my brethren, I myself also am convinced that you yourselves are full of goodness, filled with all knowledge, and able also to admonish one another" (Rom. 15:14).

As I said in an earlier chapter, on the grounds that surround our home we have a number of fresh water springs. One spring sends forth a never ending supply of pure water, and from it we get the water for our house. The comment of the man who tested it was, "It's the purest water I've ever found." A good heart, like a good spring, perpetually pours out goodness.

The word "good" in the language of Scripture literally means "to be like God," because He alone is the One who is perfectly good. It is one thing, however, to have high ethical standards but quite another for the Holy Spirit to produce the goodness that has its depths in the Godhead. The meaning here is more than just "doing good." Goodness goes far deeper. Goodness is love in action. It carries with it not only the idea of righteousness imputed, but righteousness demonstrated in everyday living by the Holy

Spirit. It is doing good out of a good heart, to please God, without expecting medals and rewards. Christ wants this kind of goodness to be the way of life for every Christian. Man can find no substitute for goodness, and no spiritual touch-up artist can imitate it.

Thoreau wrote, "If a man does not keep pace with his companions, perhaps it is because he hears a different drummer. Let him step to the music which he hears, however measured or far away."[4] As Christians we have no alternative but to march to the drumbeat of the Holy Spirit, following the measured steps of goodness, which pleases God.

We can do good deeds, and by practicing principles of goodness can witness to those around us that we have something "different" in our lives—perhaps something they themselves would like to possess. We may even be able to show others how to practice the principles of goodness in their own lives. But the Bible says, "Your goodness is as a morning cloud, and as the early dew it goeth away" (Hosea 6:4 KJV). True goodness is a "fruit of the Spirit," and our efforts to achieve it in our own strength alone can never succeed.

We should be careful that any goodness the world may see in us is the genuine fruit of the Spirit and not a counterfeit substitute, lest we unwittingly lead someone astray.

We must be constantly aware that Satan can take any human effort and twist it to serve his own purposes, but he cannot touch the spirit that is covered by the blood of Christ and rooted deep in the Holy Spirit. Only the Spirit can produce the goodness that can stand up under any test.

Goodness is never alone so far as the outward facets of the fruit of the Spirit are concerned, but it is always accompanied by patience and kindness. These three go together and all were beautifully manifested in the life of the One who is the perfect prototype of what you and I ought to be. By the power of the Holy Spirit these traits of character become part of our lives that we might remind others of Him.

17

The Fruit of the Spirit:
Faithfulness, Gentleness, Self-Control

AUTHENTIC CHRISTIAN LIVING has its own order of priority in our lives: God first, others second, self third. It is proper, therefore, when speaking about the third cluster of the fruit of the Spirit to focus our attention upon the *inward man.* The Spirit works *in* us that He might work through us. "Being" is far more important than "doing." But when we are what we should be inside, we will bring forth fruit, more fruit, and much fruit. This is the ultimate purpose the apostle Paul had in mind when he wrote, "It is God who is at work in you, both to will and to work for His good pleasure" (Phil. 2:13). He also says, "He who began a good work in you will perfect it until the day of Christ Jesus" (Phil. 1:6).

The third cluster of the spiritual fruit has to do with the inward man. It includes faithfulness, gentleness, and self-control.

The Fruit of the Spirit: Faithfulness

The reference to faithfulness (or "faith" in the KJV) is not to faith exercised by the Christian, but rather to *faithfulness* or *fidelity,* produced by the Holy Spirit in a yielded Christian life.

The same word occurs in Titus 2:10 where it is translated "fidelity" in the King James Version. This trait of character is highly commended in Scripture. Fidelity in little things is one of the surest tests of character, as our Lord indicated in the parable of the talents: "You were faithful with a few things, I will put you in charge of many things" (Matt. 25:21). Morality is not so much a matter of magnitude, but of quality. Right is right, and wrong is wrong, in small things as well as in big things.

Peter contrasts those who walk faithfully with God over against those who become entangled again with the pollution of the world. He writes, "For it had been better for them not to have known the way of righteousness, than, after they have known it, to turn from the holy commandment delivered unto them. But it is happened unto them according to the true proverb, The dog is turned to his own vomit again; and the sow that was washed to her wallowing in the mire" (2 Peter 2:21, 22 KJV).

The Third Epistle of John contains only fourteen verses. Diotrephes and Demetrius are the two main characters. The faithful follower was Demetrius who is described as receiving a "good testimony from everyone, and from the truth itself" (v. 12). He is commended because in word and in truth, in practice and in precept, he followed the Lord faithfully.

A familiar expression in industry is "turn around time," the time that elapses between the receipt of an order and the day it is delivered. Many Christians will some day regret the self-imposed time lag that came between the point when God first showed them His plan for them, and the point when they took action. The ancient Israelites could have completed their journey from Egypt to Canaan in a few months. Instead, the journey took forty years and a whole generation died because of their unfaithfulness.

Lack of faithfulness is actually a sign of spiritual immaturity. One sign of emotional immaturity is the refusal to accept responsibility. A young person may want all the privileges of adulthood, but refuse to accept the responsibilities. The same thing is true spiritually. God has given us certain responsibilities as mature Christians. When we are disobedient and refuse to accept these responsibilities, we are unfaithful. On the other hand, when we are faithful, it means we have accepted the responsibilities God has given us. This is a sign of spiritual maturity, and it is one of the important fruits the Spirit brings to our lives.

Surely most of us grow at a slower rate than we should because we refuse to allow the Holy Spirit to control all areas of our lives.

Rather, our faithful obedience to allow God the Holy Spirit to remove any vile habit or developing infection should be immediate. We can become impatient when we discover it takes so long to become like Him, but we should be patient and faithful, for becoming like Him is worth waiting for. However, even if we could become totally mature Christians I am not sure that we would be conscious of it. Who of us can claim total perfection in this life? But we know that when we stand with Him in eternity, we will be glorified with Him. And the Holy Spirit will begin to perform the deeper work of God's plan in our lives any time we are willing to faithfully say "yes" to His will!

The Scriptures are replete with stories of men like Abraham (Heb. 11:8–10), who were faithful in their walk before God. The entire eleventh chapter of Hebrews should be studied as it recounts the men and women whom God calls faithful.

It is dangerous to tempt God, as did "unfaithful" men in the day of Amos. To them God declared, "Behold, days are coming . . . when I will send a famine on the land, not a famine for bread, or a thirst for water, but rather for hearing the words of the Lord" (Amos 8:11).

Rather we should heed the advice of James: "Blessed is a man who perseveres under trial; for once he has been approved, he will receive the crown of life, which the Lord has promised to those who love him" (1:12). James later says, "One who looks intently at the perfect law, the law of liberty, and abides by it, not having become a forgetful hearer but an effectual doer, this man shall be blessed in what he does" (1:25).

Over and over we are admonished to be *faithful*. As we saw earlier we read in the Bible about a number of judgments at the end of this age. One of these is called the judgment seat of Christ. Someday all Christians will stand before Jesus Christ to give an account of the works we have done since our conversion. We will be judged, not on the basis of how successful we were in the eyes of the world, but on how faithful we were in the place God put us. The apostle Paul indicates this in 1 Corinthians 3:9–16: faithfulness will be the basis on which God renders judgment.

Sometimes the greatest test of our faithfulness is how much time we spend reading the Scriptures, praying, and living in accord with the principles of righteousness when we have been blessed with prosperity. A devout Christian surprised me recently by saying, "It's hard to be a faithful Christian in modern-day America." It is so easy to forget and to forsake our God in the midst of prosperity and especially when materialism is rampant. This is the reason Jesus told us that it is hard for rich men to enter the kingdom of God. Rich men can be saved—but the Bible talks about "the deceitfulness of riches" (Matt. 13:22). The burdens and cares of this world often interfere with our faithful walk before the Lord. In the midst of material prosperity we should beware lest we fall into the same pitfall as the Laodiceans, who incurred God's wrath and displeasure because they felt they had need of nothing since they were materially rich (Rev. 3:17). "But those who want to get rich fall into temptation and a snare and many foolish and harmful desires which plunge men into ruin and destruction. For the love of money is a root of all sorts of evil, and some by longing for it have wandered away from the faith, and pierced themselves with many a pang" (1 Tim. 6:9, 10).

If we could carve an epitaph on the tombstone of the apostle Paul, it might read: "Faithful unto death." As he awaited execution Paul could say without hesitation, "I have fought a good fight, I have finished my course, I have kept the faith: Henceforth there is laid up for me a crown of righteousness, which the Lord, the righteous judge, shall give me at that day" (2 Tim. 4:7, 8 KJV). Whatever the failures of Paul and however short he fell of perfection, he knew that he had been faithful to the Lord to the end.

This wonderful segment of the cluster of the fruit of the Spirit—faithfulness—constitutes faithfulness to our testimony, faithfulness to our commitments and calling, and faithfulness to the commands of Christ. And the ultimate reward for faithfulness is given in Revelation 2:10: "Be faithful until death, and I will give you the crown of life."

The Fruit of the Spirit: Gentleness

The word gentleness here (or in the KJV, meekness) comes from a Greek word meaning "mild; mildness in dealing with others." Jesus said, "Blessed are the gentle, for they shall inherit the earth" (Matt. 5:5). Nowhere in Scripture does this word carry with it the idea of being spiritless and timid. In biblical times gentleness or meekness meant far more than it does in modern day English. It carried the idea of being tamed, like a wild horse that has been brought under control. Until tamed by the Holy Spirit Peter was a rough and ready character. Then all of his energy was used for the glory of God. Moses was called the meekest of men, but prior to God's special call to him he was an unbroken, high-spirited man who needed forty years in the desert before he was fully brought under God's control. A river under control can be used to generate power. A fire under control can heat a home. Meekness is power, strength, spirit, and wildness under control.

In another sense, gentleness can be likened to modesty in that it is the opposite of a flamboyant and self-indulgent spirit. Rather, it displays a sensitive regard for others and is careful never to be unfeeling for the rights of others.

Gentleness enjoys a quiet strength that confounds those who think of it as weakness. This is seen in the response of Jesus following his arrest—throughout His trial, torture, and crucifixion he endured the emotional and physical pain inflicted mercilessly by his captors and taunting spectators. "He was oppressed and He was afflicted, yet He did not open His mouth; Like a lamb that is led to slaughter, and like a sheep that is silent before its shearers, so He did not open His mouth" (Isa. 53:7). Meekness is referred to as love under discipline. Charles Allen states, "God never expects us to be less than we really are. . . . Self-belittlement is an insult to the God who made us. Meekness comes another way. . . . Pride comes from looking only at ourselves, meekness comes through looking at God."[1]

All Christian growth, including meekness, takes place in the heavy atmosphere of hostility. This kind of spiritual poise and inward quiet strength as a growing work of the Holy Spirit does not come on a playground, but on a spiritual battleground.

In still another definition of meekness, David Hubbard says that meekness is making ourselves consistently available to those who count on us; we are at peace with our power, so we do not use it arrogantly or hurtfully. When speaking of meekness, DeWitt Talmadge said, "As the heavens prophetically are taken by violence, so the earth is taken by meekness, and God as proprietor wants no tenants more or grants larger leases than to the meek of heart and spirit."

In his appraisal of Andrew Murray, the great Keswick speaker, Dr. V. R. Edman states in his book, *They Found the Secret*, "Such indeed is the abiding life that draws its sustenance and strength from the Vine. By the refreshing and reviving flow of the Holy Spirit through that life there is prayer that prevails, preaching that is powerful, love that is contagious, joy that overflows, and peace that passes understanding. It is the adoration that is stillness to know God for one's self. It is the obedience that does the Saviour's bidding in the light of the Word. It is the fruitfulness that arises spontaneously from abiding in the Vine."[2]

Another illustration that has helped me to understand gentleness is the iceberg. I have seen some of them from shipboard when crossing the Atlantic. However high an iceberg may be above the water line, the greater part of it is submerged. Icebergs are particularly formidable and destructive when they drift along the sea lanes.

But the greatest threat to icebergs comes from something beneficent, the sun. The sun's rays bring warmth to life, and death to icebergs. As gentleness is a powerful force, so the sun proves to be more powerful than the mightiest iceberg. God's gentleness, or meekness, in us permits the rays of the sun of God's Holy Spirit to work on our icebound hearts, transforming them into instruments for good and for God. Spiritually, the gentle, Spirit-filled Christian is a prism through whom the rays of the sun's spectrum are gathered to minister to the icebergs of our carnality.

How do you and I apply gentleness to ourselves? Jesus set before us His own example by calling upon us to be "gentle and humble in heart" (Matt. 11:29).

First, we do not rise up defensively when our feelings are ruffled, as did Peter when he slashed the ear of the soldier at the arrest of Jesus in the garden, only earning His Lord's rebuke (Matt. 26:51, 52).

Second, we do not crave to have the preeminence, as Diotrephes did (3 John 9). Rather, we desire that in all things Jesus Christ might have the preeminence (Col. 1:18).

Third, we do not seek to be recognized and highly regarded, or to be considered the voice of authority, as Jannes and Jambres did (2 Tim. 3:8). These magicians of Egypt rejected the Lord's authority through Moses, and opposed him just before the Exodus. "Do not think of yourself more highly than you ought, but rather think of yourself with sober judgment, . . . Be devoted to one another in brotherly love. Honor one another above yourselves" (Rom. 12:3, 10 NIV).

The enthronement of Jesus Christ in our lives makes it possible for meekness to become one of our virtues. Gentleness may be the most tangible sign of greatness displayed in us. You and I may never be respected as voices of authority; we may never gain the plaudits of the world; we may never rule or swing the baton of power. But one day the meek will inherit the earth (Matt. 5:5), for no one can take away our rightful share of God's divine and delightful bequest to us.

The Fruit of the Spirit: Self-control

Self-control (temperance in the KJV) is the third fruit in this cluster. It comes from a Greek word meaning strong, having mastery, able to control one's thoughts and actions.

John Wesley's mother once wrote him while he was a student at Oxford that "anything which increases the authority of the body over the mind is an evil thing." This definition has helped me understand "self-control."

Intemperance has brought about the fall of kings and tycoons. History illustrates this. Someone has said: "There are men who can command armies, but cannot command themselves. There are men who by their burning words can sway vast multitudes who cannot keep silence under provocation or wrong. The highest mark of nobility is self-control. It is more kingly than regal crown and purple robe."

Elsewhere it has been said:

"Not in the clamor of the crowded street,
Not in the shouts and plaudits of the throng,
But in ourselves, are triumph and defeat."[3]

Past history and current public examples illustrate how the excesses of uncontrolled appetite and fleshly indulgence wreak damage in our hearts.

The sin of intemperance, lack of self-control, springs from two causes: first, physical appetite; second, mental habit.

When we think of temperance we usually think of alcohol. This is not unexpected because of the great efforts of temperance leaders who for years sought to eradicate this poison that affects so many people in the world. But somehow we silently countenance gluttony, which the Bible condemns as clearly as drunkenness. We also tend to overlook unkindness, gossip, pride, and jealousy. It is possible to be intemperate in all these areas, too. The Scripture says, "Those who live according to their sinful nature have their minds set on what that nature desires; but those who live in accordance with the Spirit have their minds set on what the Spirit desires" (Rom. 8:5 NIV). Temperance, self-control, as a fruit of the Spirit is the normal Christian life taking its exercise.

Temperance in our use of food is moderation. Temperance with respect to alcohol is soberness. Temperance in sexual matters is abstinence for those who are not married. Even for those of us who are married there may be times for temperance, when we abstain by mutual consent from legitimate sexual activity so we can give ourselves more fully to the study of God's Word, prayer, and good works (see 1 Cor. 7:5).

Temperance in regard to temper is self-control. Recently I was with a man who parked in a prohibited zone at the airport. An attendant kindly asked him if he would move the car as he was in a no-parking zone. Angrily he replied, "If you don't have police credentials, shut your mouth." This Christian was so nervous and tense from shouldering so many responsibilities that he had almost totally lost control of his temper. He was intemperate. It was just as much a sin as if he had become drunk.

Temperance in matters of dress is appropriate modesty. Temperance in defeat is hopefulness. Temperance in relation to sinful pleasure is nothing short of complete abstinence.

Solomon wrote, "He who is slow to anger is better than the mighty, and he who rules his spirit, than he who captures a city" (Prov. 16:32). The Living Bible paraphrases the latter part of that verse to read, "It is better to have self-control than to control an army." The writer of Proverbs said, "A man without self-control is as defenseless as a city with broken-down walls" (25:28 LB).

Paul taught the importance of self-control. Any athlete who would win a race must train himself to become the complete master of his body, he told his readers. He emphasized that the goal was not merely a corruptible, but an incorruptible crown: "Everyone who competes in the games exercises self-control in all things. They then do it to receive a perishable wreath, but we an imperishable. . . . but I buffet my body and make it my slave, lest possibly, after I have preached to others, I myself should be disqualified" (1 Cor. 9:25, 27).

In Peter's list of Christian virtues, he says, "Add . . . to knowledge temperance; and to temperance patience" (2 Peter 1:5, 6 KJV). All these go together. And it is quite clear that when we allow our passions to rule us, the outcome at last is far more undesirable than can be imagined during the moment of pleasurable fulfillment.

Who is to say where temperance stops and intemperance begins? Some Christians have an elastic conscience when it comes to their own foibles—and an ironbound conscience when it comes to the foibles of others. Maybe that's why it is so easy for some Christians to condemn a person who takes an occasional sip of wine but never rebuke themselves for the sin of habitual overeating. Compulsive overeating is one of the most widely accepted and practiced sins of modern Western Christians. It is easy to condemn an adulterer, but how can the one who condemns do so when he is guilty of some other form of intemperance? Should each of us not have clean hands and a pure heart in all of life? Is one form of slavery more wrong in principle than another? Are we not just as tightly bound if the chains are made of ropes as of steel?

The appetite that controls one person may differ from the appetite that controls another. But if one person submits to a craving for possessions, is he so different from others who crave sex, gambling, gold, food, alcohol, or drugs?

The need for temperance in *every* aspect of life has never been greater than it is today. At a time when violence, selfishness, apathy, and undisciplined living threaten to destroy this planet, it is imperative that Christians set an example. The world needs this example—something, steadfast it can hold on to, an anchor in a raging sea.

For centuries Christians have proclaimed Christ as the anchor. If we who have the Holy Spirit living and working within us falter and fail, what hope is there for the rest of the world?

Space for Fruit-growing

We have now considered these nine wonderful facets that comprise the fruit of the Spirit: love, joy, peace, patience, kindness, goodness, faithfulness, gentleness, and self-control. It is my prayer that they will characterize your life and mine.

The Holy Spirit is already in every Christian heart, and He intends to produce the fruit of the Spirit in us. However, there must be a displacement. A boat does not sink when it is in the water, but it does sink when the water comes into the boat. We do not fail to enjoy the fruit of the Spirit because we live in a sea of corruption; we fail to do so because the sea of corruption is in us.

The internal combustion engine's worst enemy is the deadly carbon that builds up in the cylinder chamber. It reduces the power and causes the motor to lose efficiency. Oil will improve the engine's performance, but it will not remove the carbon so that the motor can run more efficiently. Mechanical surgery must be performed to remove the carbon so that the oil can do its best work and the motor perform as it was designed to do. Similarly, we must eliminate the works of the flesh from our inner lives so that deadly carbon and grit do not impair the effectiveness of our spiritual performance. One oil company advertised, "More power for smoother performance." Spiritually this is possible only as we yield our lives to the control of the Holy Spirit. We must let the searchlight of God's Word scan us to detect the abiding sins and fruitless qualities which impair our personal growth and fruitfulness.

The story is told of a man who glanced at the obituary column in his local newspaper. To his surprise he saw his own name, indicating that he had just died. At first he laughed about it. But soon the telephone began to ring. Stunned friends and acquaintances called to inquire and to offer their sympathy. Finally, in irritation, he called the newspaper editor and angrily reported that even though he had been reported dead in the obituary column he was very much alive. The editor was apologetic and embarrassed. Then in a flash of inspiration he said, "Do not worry, sir,

I will make it all right, for tomorrow I will put your name in the births column."

This may sound like merely a humorous incident, but it is actually a spiritual parable. Not until we have allowed our old selves to be crucified with Christ can our new selves emerge to display the marvelous fruit characteristic of the life of Jesus Christ.

And only the Holy Spirit can make possible the out-living of the in-living Christ. The kind of persons God wants us to be can never be produced through human effort. But when the Holy Spirit fills us, He brings forth His fruit in people who manifest a growing likeness to Christ, the prototype of what we will someday be.

18

The Need
of the Hour

THE 1850s IN America brought a marked decline in religion in the United States. The discovery of gold in California, as well as a number of other developments, had turned people's minds and hearts away from religion and toward material things. The political turmoil over slavery and the threatened disintegration of the nation also preoccupied public attention. A severe financial panic in the late 1850s led to even greater concern about material things.

In September of 1857 a quiet businessman named Jeremiah Lanphier decided to invite other businessmen to join him in a noonday prayer meeting once a week, seeking for the renewing work of the Holy Spirit. He distributed hundreds of handbills advertising the meeting, but the first day only half a dozen showed up, meeting in the rear of a church on Fulton Street. Two weeks later there were forty, and within six months some ten thousand were gathered daily for prayer in New York City alone. Awakening swept the country, and within two years an estimated one million people had professed faith in Christ.

The effects of the awakening were profound, both in individual lives and in society. Tragically, the awakening was too late to avoid the Civil War which threatened the very life of the nation. But untold good came from the awakening, including many movements for evangelism and social betterment.

The Need for Spiritual Revival

The world today is again in desperate need of a spiritual awakening. It is the only hope for the survival of the human race. In the midst of the vast problems which face our world Christians are strangely silent and powerless, almost overwhelmed by the tides of secularism. And yet Christians are called to be "the salt of the earth" (Matt. 5:13), keeping a decaying world from further corruption. Christians are to be "the light of the world" (Matt. 5:14), illuminating the darkness caused by sin and giving guidance to a world that has lost its way. We are called to be "children of God above reproach in the midst of a crooked and perverse generation, among whom you appear as lights in the world" (Phil. 2:15).

Why are we not "salt" and "light" as we should be? Why are we not doing much more to bring the kingdom of God to the hearts and lives of humanity?

There certainly are many instances of Christians who have been touched by God, and are in turn touching the lives of others for Christ. But for every instance of that, there are many more Christians who are living defeated, joyless lives. These people have no sense of victory over sin or effectiveness in witnessing. They have little impact on those around them for the sake of the Gospel.

If, then, the greatest need of our world is to feel the effects of a spiritual awakening, the greatest need within the Christian Church throughout the world today is to experience the touch of the Holy Spirit, bringing true "revival" and "renewal" to the lives of countless Christians.

Many centuries ago God gave Ezekiel, the prophet, a remarkable vision in which he saw national Israel scattered among the nations. Israel's bones were described as many and dry. All hope for the future seemed to be gone. According to the word of the prophet, Israel might as well be buried as far as the secular world was concerned. However, Ezekiel was staggered when God asked this question: "Can these bones live?" (Ezek. 37:3). To this the prophet replied, "Thou knowest." Then the man of God was commanded to speak the word of God and the bones stood up, a great host of men who were clothed with flesh. But they still seemed strangely impotent. They lacked spirit or breath. Then the Spirit of God gave them breath and they became a mighty army.

Again we face a dark time in the history of God's people. In spite of some encouraging signs, the forces of evil seem to be gathering for a colossal assault on the work of God in the world. Satan has unleashed his power in a way perhaps unparalleled in the history of the Christian Church. If ever there was a time we needed renewal, it is now. Only God can thwart the plans of Satan and his legions, because only God is all-powerful. Only His Holy Spirit can bring true spiritual awakening which will stem the tide of evil and reverse the trend. In the darkest hour God can still revive His people, and by the Holy Spirit breathe new vigor and power into the body of Christ.

Our world needs to be touched by Christians who are Spirit-filled, Spirit-led, and Spirit-empowered. Are you that kind of Christian? Or is there in your own life the need for a new touch of the Spirit? Do you stand in need of genuine spiritual renewal within your own life? If so, know that God the Holy Spirit wants to bring that renewal to you right now.

The Time Is Now

The time for spiritual revival is *now*. We must not delay. Dr. Samuel Johnson wore a watch on which was engraved the words from John 9:4, "The Night Cometh." We Christians ought to carry written in our hearts the solemn truth of how short is our opportunity to witness for Christ and live for Him. We do not know—any of us—how much time we have left on this earth. Death may cut our lives short. Christ could come again at any moment.

I once read about a sundial on which was inscribed the cryptic message, "It is later than you think." Travelers would often pause to meditate on the meaning of that phrase. We Christians have a sundial—the Word of God. From Genesis to Revelation it bears its warning, "It is later than you think." Writing to the Christians of his day Paul said, "It is already the hour for you to awaken from sleep; for now salvation is nearer to us than when we believed. The night is almost gone, and the day is at hand. Let us therefore lay aside the deeds of darkness and put on the armor of light" (Rom. 13:11, 12).

Billy Bray, a godly clergyman of another generation, sat by the bedside of a dying Christian who had been very shy about his testimony for Christ during his life. The dying man said, "If I had the power I'd shout glory to God." Billy Bray answered, "It's a pity you didn't shout glory when you had the power." I wonder how many of us will look back over a lifetime of wasted opportunities and ineffective witness and weep because we did not allow God to use us as He wanted. "Night is coming, when no man can work" (John 9:4).

If ever we are to study the Scriptures, if ever we are to spend time in prayer, if ever we are to win souls for Christ, if ever we are to invest our finances for His kingdom—it must be *now.* "Since all these things are to be destroyed in this way, what sort of people ought you to be in holy conduct and godliness, looking for and hastening the coming of the day of God, on account of which the heavens will be destroyed by burning, and the elements will melt with intense heat! But according to His promise we are looking for new heavens and a new earth, in which righteousness dwells. Therefore, beloved, since you look for these things, be diligent to be found by Him in peace, spotless and blameless" (2 Peter 3:11–14).

The Effects of an Awakening

What would happen if revival were to break into our lives and our churches today? I believe there are at least *eight characteristics* of such an outpouring of the Holy Spirit.

1. There will be a new vision of the majesty of God. We must understand that the Lord is not only tender and merciful and full of compassion, but He is also the God of justice, holiness, and wrath. Many Christians have a caricature of God. They do not see God in all of His wholeness. We glibly quote John 3:16, but we forget to quote the following verse, "he who does not believe has been judged already" (v. 18). Compassion is not complete in itself, but must be accompanied by inflexible justice and wrath against sin and a desire for holiness. What stirs God most is not physical suffering but sin. All too often we are more afraid of physical pain than of moral wrong. The cross is the standing evidence of the fact that holiness is a principle for which God would die. God cannot clear the guilty until atonement is made. Mercy is what we need and that is what we receive at the foot of the cross.

2. There will be a new vision of the sinfulness of sin. Isaiah saw the Lord upon a throne high and lifted up, His train filling the temple, and he saw the seraphim bowing in reverence as they cried, "Holy, Holy, Holy, is the Lord of hosts, the whole earth is full of His glory" (Isa. 6:3). Then it was that Isaiah realized his own unworthiness and his utter dependence upon God. When Simon Peter, on the Sea of Galilee, realized that it was the very Lord with him in the boat, he said, "Depart from me, for I am a sinful man, O Lord!" (Luke 5:8). The consciousness that Jesus was God Himself brought to Peter's mind his own human sinfulness. In the presence of God, Job said, "I abhor myself" (Job 42:6 ASV).

When a man is tempted, James tells us, his own passions carry him away and serve as a bait (James 1:14, 15). And whatever his lust may be it conceives and becomes the parent of sin, and sin when fully matured gives birth to death. We need to see sin as it really is. The greatest vision of sin that a person can ever receive is to look at the cross. If Jesus Christ had to die for sin, then sin indeed must be dark and terrible in the sight of God.

3. There will be an emphasis on the necessity of repentance, faith, and the new birth. Jesus came preaching repentance and saying that unless a man is born from above he cannot see the kingdom of God. He said that sinners love darkness and will not come to the light for fear their deeds will be exposed and condemned. Those whose hearts have been changed are new creatures. They come to the light out of love for truth and for God. If anyone is in Christ Jesus, he is a new creature, for the old things have passed away and everything has become new.

4. There will be the joy of salvation. The prayer expressed in the Psalm was for a requickening "That Thy people may rejoice in Thee" (Ps. 85:6). David's desire was for a restoration of the joy of salvation. The express purpose of Jesus for the disciples was "that your joy may be made full" (John 15:11). When Philip went down to Samaria and led a great spiritual awakening, Scripture says, "There was much rejoicing in that city" (Acts 8:8). Jesus also tells us that there is joy in heaven, joy in the presence of the angels of God over one sinner who repents (Luke 15:7). So a true revitalization of the Church would bring about the salvation of tens of thousands of sinners, and this in turn would bring joy in heaven as well as joy here on earth.

If there were no heaven and no hell I would still want to be a Christian because of what it does for our homes and our own families in this life.

5. *There will be a new realization of our responsibility for world evangelization.* John the Baptist pointed his hearers to "the Lamb of God" and his two disciples followed Jesus from then on (John 1:36, 37). Andrew first found his own brother Peter and told him that they had found the Christ. When Philip had begun to follow Christ he went after Nathanael (John 1:40–45). The apostles were to be witnesses anywhere and everywhere, even unto the uttermost part of the earth (Acts 1: 8). And when persecution scattered the church which was at Jerusalem, they went everywhere preaching Christ and the glorious gospel (Acts 8:4). One of the first and best evidences of being a true believer is the concern which we feel for others.

6. *There will be a deep social concern.* In Matthew 22:37–39, Jesus said, "You shall love the Lord your God with all your heart, and with all your soul, and with all your mind. . . . You shall love your neighbor as yourself." Our faith is not only vertical, it is horizontal. We will become interested in the hurts of those around us and those far away. But I would have to say that to a world which really wants to be saved from the consequences of its own sin and folly a revived Christianity can have only one message, "Repent." Too many people today want a brotherly world in which they can remain unbrotherly; a decent world in which they can live indecently. Too many individuals want economic security without spiritual security. But the revitalization that we long for must be biblical. If it is Christian, it will be Bible-centered. If this is true, then its leaders must have the courage of Amos to condemn those who "buy the helpless for money and the needy for a pair of sandals" (Amos 8:6).

We must lift high the moral, ethical, and social teachings of Jesus, agreeing that He offers the only standard for personal and national character. The Sermon on the Mount is for today and every day. We cannot build a new civilization on the chaotic foundation of hatred and bitterness.

7. *There will be increased evidence of both the gifts and the fruit of the Spirit.* Renewal is brought by the Holy Spirit, and when He

comes in all His power upon the Church there will be clear evidences of the gifts and the fruit of the Spirit. Believers will learn what it means to minister to one another and build each other up through the gifts the Holy Spirit has given. They will be given a new measure of love for each other and for a lost and dying world. No longer will the world say that the Church is powerless and silent. No longer will our lives seem ordinary and indistinguishable from the rest of the world. Our lives will be marked by the gifts only the Holy Spirit can give. Our lives will be marked by the fruit only He can bring.

8. *There will be renewed dependence upon the Holy Spirit.* There are already evidences that this is taking place in many parts of the world. No spiritual revitalization can come without Him. The Holy Spirit is the one who reproves, convicts, strives, instructs, invites, quickens, regenerates, renews, strengthens, and uses. He must not be grieved, resisted, tempted, quenched, insulted, or blasphemed. He gives liberty to the Christian, direction to the worker, discernment to the teacher, power to the Word, and fruit to faithful service. He reveals the things of Christ. He teaches us how to use the sword of the Spirit which is the Word of God. He guides us into all truth. He directs in the way of godliness. He teaches us how to answer the enemies of our Lord. He gives access to the Father. He helps us in our prayer life.

There are things which money cannot buy; which no music can bring; which no social position can claim; which no personal influence can assure; and which no eloquence can command. No clergyman however brilliant, no evangelist no matter how eloquent or compelling, can bring about the revival we need. Only the Holy Spirit can do this. Zechariah said, "Not by might nor by power, but by My Spirit, says the Lord of hosts" (Zech. 4:6).

Steps to Awakening

If spiritual revival is the great need for many Christians today, how does it come? What are the steps to revival in our own lives and the lives of others? I believe there are three steps which the Bible sets forth.

The first step is admitting our spiritual poverty. All too often we are like the Laodicean Christians who were blinded to their own spiritual needs, "You say, 'I am rich, and have become wealthy, and have need of nothing,' and you do not know that you are wretched and miserable and poor and blind and naked" (Rev. 3:17).

Is there sin in our lives which is blocking the work of the Holy Spirit in and through us? We must not be too quick to answer "no." We must examine ourselves in the light of God's Word, and pray that the Holy Spirit will reveal to us every sin which hinders us. It may be something we are doing that is wrong—a habit, a relationship, an evil motive or thought. It may be something we are neglecting—a responsibility we are shirking or an act of love we have failed to perform. Whatever it is, it must be faced honestly and humbly before God.

The second step in spiritual renewal is confession and repentance. We can know we have sinned, and still do nothing about it. But we need to bring our sin to God in confession and repentance, not only acknowledging our sins before Him but actually turning from sin and seeking to be obedient to Him. One of the great promises of the Bible is 1 John 1:9, "If we confess our sins, He is faithful and righteous to forgive us our sins and to cleanse us from all unrighteousness." The prophet Isaiah said, "Seek the Lord while He may be found; call upon Him while He is near. Let the wicked forsake his way, and the unrighteous man his thoughts; and let him return to the Lord" (Isa. 55:6, 7).

It is no accident that some of the great awakenings in history have begun in prayer. A prayer meeting under a haystack in a rainstorm in 1806 led to the first large-scale American missionary efforts. In 1830 some 30,000 people were converted in Rochester, New York, under the ministry of Charles Finney; later Finney said the reason was the faithful praying of one man who never attended the meetings but gave himself to prayer. In 1872 the American evangelist Dwight L. Moody began a campaign in London, England, which was used of God to touch countless lives. Later Moody discovered that a humble bedridden girl had been praying. The list could go on and on.

Are you praying for revival, both in your own life and in the lives of others? Are you confessing sin to Him and seeking His blessing on your life?

The third step is a renewed commitment on our part to seek and do the will of God. We can be convicted of sin—we can pray and confess our sin—we can repent—but the real test is our willingness to obey. It is no accident that true revival is always accompanied by a new hunger for righteousness. A life touched by the Holy Spirit will tolerate sin no longer.

What is it that is hindering spiritual revival in your life today? Ultimately, of course, it is sin. Sometimes it hurts deeply to face the truth about our own lack of spiritual zeal and dedication. But God wants to touch us and make us useful servants for Himself. "Let us also lay aside every encumbrance, and the sin which so easily entangles us, and let us run with endurance the race that is set before us, fixing our eyes on Jesus, the author and perfecter of faith" (Heb. 12:1, 2). James A. Stewart has observed, "A church that needs to be revived is a church that is living below the norm of the New Testament pattern. . . . It is a tragic fact that the vast majority of Christians today are living a sub-normal Christian life. . . . the Church will never become normal until she sees revival."[1]

Are you living a "subnormal" Christian life—a life that is ineffective, lukewarm, and lacking in love for Christ and for others? Let God the Holy Spirit bring you in humility to God, confessing sin and seeking His face. Let Him touch you as you yield yourself to Him. The greatest need in the world today is for fully committed Christians.

Over 100 years ago, two young men were talking in Ireland. One said, "The world has yet to see what God will do with a man fully consecrated to Him." The other man meditated on that thought for weeks. It so gripped him that one day he exclaimed, "By the Holy Spirit in me I'll be that man." Historians now say that he touched two continents for Christ. His name was Dwight L. Moody.

This can happen again, as we open our lives to the recreating power of the Holy Spirit. No person can seek sincerely the cleansing and blessing of the Holy Spirit, and remain the same afterward. No nation can experience the touch of awakening in its midst, and remain the same afterward.

As we have seen in this book, Pentecost was the day of power of the Holy Spirit. It was the day the Christian Church was born.

We do not expect that Pentecost will be repeated any more than that Jesus will die on the cross again. But we do expect pentecostal blessings when the conditions for God's moving are met, and especially as we approach "the latter days." We as Christians are to prepare the way. We are to be ready for the Spirit to fill and use us.

NOTES

Chapter 1

1. Matthew Henry, *Commentary on the Whole Bible*, Vol. 1 (Old Tappan, N. J.: Fleming H. Revell Co.), p. 2.

Chapter 2

1. W. A. Criswell, *The Holy Spirit in Today's World* (Grand Rapids: Zondervan Publishing House, 1966), p. 87.
2. J. D. Douglas, ed., *Let the Earth Hear His Voice* (Minneapolis: World Wide Pub., 1975), p. 277.
3. John R. W. Stott, *Your Mind Matters* (Downers Grove, IL: Inter-Varsity Press, 1973), pp. 5, 7.
4. Ibid, p. 10.

Chapter 3

1. Al Bryant, *1,000 New Illustrations* (Grand Rapids: Zondervan Publishing House, 1960), p. 30.
2. B. H. Carroll, *Inspiration of the Bible* (New York, Chicago, London, Edinburgh: Fleming H. Revell Co., 1930), p. 54ff.
3. John R. W. Stott, *The Authority of the Bible* (Downers Grove, IL: Inter-Varsity Press, 1974), pp. 30, 40.
4. John Calvin (Trans. Ford Lewis Battles) ed. John McNeill, *Institutes of the Christian Religion* (Philadelphia: Westminster Press, 1960) Book One, Chapter 7, Sections 4 & 5, pp. 79, 80.
5. J. D. Douglas, ed., *Let the Earth Hear His Voice* (Minneapolis: World Wide Pub., 1975), p. 259.
6. Henry H. Halley, *Halley's Bible Handbook* (Grand Rapids: Zondervan Publishing House, 1962), p. 5.
7. J. B. Phillips, *Letters to Young Churches* (New York: The Macmillan Company, 1955), p. xii.

Chapter 4

1. *The Open Bible* (Nashville: Thomas Nelson, 1975), p. 988.
2. J. Gresham Machen, *The Christian Faith in the Modern World* (Grand Rapids: Wm. B. Eerdmans Co., 1947), p. 63.

Chapter 5

1. John R. W. Stott, *Baptism and Fullness* (London: Inter-Varsity Press, 1975), p. 28f.
2. David Howard, *By the Power of the Holy Spirit* (Downers Grove, IL: Inter-Varsity Press, 1973), p. 34f.
3. Ibid.

Chapter 6

1. A. T. Robertson, *Word Pictures in the New Testament*, Vol. 1 (Nashville: Broadman Press, 1930), p. 239.
2. Matthew Henry, *Commentary on the Whole Bible*, Vol. 6 (Old Tappan, N.J.: Fleming H. Revell Co.), p. 688f.
3. Ibid.
4. C. S. Lewis, *Letters to Malcolm: Chiefly on Prayer* (London and Glasgow: Collins Fontana Books, 1966), p. 22f.
5. John Wesley, *A Compend of Wesley's Theology*, eds. Burtner and Chiles (Nashville: Abingdon Press, 1954), p. 95.

Chapter 7

1. Horatius Bonar, *God's Way of Holiness* (Chicago: Moody Press, 1970), p. 93.
2. C. I. Scofield, ed., *The New Scofield Reference Bible* (New York, Oxford University Press, 1967), p. 1276.
3. Ibid, p. 1219.
4. Bonar, *God's Way of Holiness*, p. 91.

Chapter 8

1. *Keswick Week* (London: Marshall Brothers, 1907), p. 105.

Chapter 9

1. William Barclay, *The Daily Study Bible: The Letter to the Romans* (Philadelphia: Westminster Press, 1957), p. 90.
2. John R. W. Stott, *Men Made New* (London: Inter-Varsity Fellowship, 1966), pp. 49–51.

3. James H. McConkey, *The Threefold Secret of the Holy Spirit* (Chicago: Moody Press, 1897), p. 65.
4. John MacNeil, *The Spirit-filled Life* (Chicago: Moody Press, n.d.), pp. 58–59.

Chapter 10

1. "Oh For a Closer Walk," in *Christian Praise* (London: Tyndale Press, 1963), p. 337.

Chapter 11

1. David Howard, *By the Power of the Holy Spirit* (Downers Grove, IL: Inter-Varsity Press, 1973), p. 101.
2. John R. W. Stott, *Baptism and Fullness*, p. 99ff.
3. Merrill C. Tenney, ed. *The Zondervan Pictorial Encyclopedia of the Bible*, Vol. 4 (Grand Rapids: Zondervan Publishing House, 1977), p. 903.

Chapter 13

1. Peter Wagner, *Frontiers in Missionary Strategy* (Chicago: Moody Press, 1971), p. 71.

Chapter 14

1. Manford George Gutzke, *The Fruit of the Spirit* (Atlanta: The Bible For You, n.d.), pp. 10, 11.

Chapter 15

1. J. D. Douglas, ed., *The New Bible Dictionary* (London: The Inter-Varsity Fellowship, 1965), p. 753.
2. Stephen Neill, *The Christian Character* (New York: Association Press, 1955), p. 22.
3. Ibid., p. 21.
4. Sherwood Wirt, *Afterglow* (Grand Rapids: Zondervan Publishing House, 1975), p. 82.

5. Neill, *The Christian Character*, p. 29.
6. Amy Carmichael, *Gold by Moonlight* (Fort Washington, PA: Christian Literature Crusade, n.d.), p. 31.
7. Charles Allen, *The Miracle of the Holy Spirit* (Old Tappan, N.J.: Fleming H. Revell Co., 1974), p. 56.

Chapter 16

1. Charles Hembree, *Fruits of the Spirit* (Grand Rapids: Baker Book House, 1969), pp. 57, 58.
2. Charles Allen, *The Miracle of the Holy Spirit* (Old Tappan, NJ.: Fleming H. Revell Co., 1974), p. 60.
3. Hembree, *Fruits of the Spirit*, p. 74.
4. Henry David Thoreau, *Walden* (Boston: Houghton, Mifflin & Co., 1906), p. 358ff.

Chapter 17

1. Charles Allen, *The Miracle of the Holy Spirit* (Old Tappan, N.J.: Fleming H. Revell Co., 1974), p. 63.
2. V. Raymond Edman, *They Found the Secret* (Grand Rapids: Zondervan Publishing House, 1960), p. 98.
3. Henry Wadsworth Longfellow, *The Poets*, quoted from Bartlett's *Familiar Quotations* (Boston: Little, Brown, and Co., 1968), p. 624b.